Christianity and Social Work

Readings on the Integration of Christian Faith and Social Work Practice

SECOND EDITION

Beryl Hugen and T. Laine Scales
Editors

The editors and publisher gratefully acknowledge permission to reprint or adapt material from the following works:

"Ethical Integration of Faith and Social Work Practice: Evangelism," by David A. Sherwood, *Social Work and Christianity*, vol. 29 (1), pp 1-12, © 2001, Reprinted with permission of North American Association of Christians in Social Work.

Table 1 from *Changing for Good,* by James Prochaska, John Norcross and Carlo C. Diclemente, © 1998, Reprinted with permission of Harper Collins Publishers, Inc.

"Spiritual and Religious Dimensions of Mental Illness Recovery Narratives," by Roger D. Fallot, *New Directions for Mental Health Services*, vol. 80, pp 35-44, © 1998, Jossey Bass Publishers, Reprinted with permission of John Wiley and Sons, Inc.

Excerpts from *Sacred Stories of Ordinary Families: Living the Faith Everyday,* by Diana R. Garland, © 2003, Excerpts used with permission of Jossey Bass Publishers.

North American Association of Christians in Social Work
P.O. Box 121
Botsford, CT 06404-0121

ISBN 0-9623634-9-9

CONTENTS

Spiritual Dimensions in Social Work Practice

The Changing Environment and Social Work Practice

PREFACE

The first edition of this book developed from the experience of teaching social work on the undergraduate level at Christian colleges and finding that almost all social work textbooks were produced for the secular market. Most texts were at best neutral, with others often antagonistic to Christian concerns. There was clearly a need for a text that would not only offer a Christian perspective on the social work profession as a whole, but also on specific topics within the profession. In discussions with colleagues, they also saw a similar need.

After some research and discussion it seemed that the best approach was to produce a collection of articles dealing with a variety of topics and issues related to the practice of social work. Effort was given to recruit Christian social workers from a wide variety of colleges and universities and practice settings who could address topics in which they were most competent.

The development of the second edition has followed a somewhat similar pattern. We began by surveying NACSW members and Christian college teachers inquiring which chapters in the first edition they felt were most informative and useful and should be included in a second edition. In addition, we asked what new topics or issues would be important to address in this second edition. From this feedback, we again sought to recruit contributors.

The contributors represent a variety of academic and social work practice settings, along with a broad range of theological and social work perspectives. Several contributors in this edition are not social workers, but offer a unique perspective to the contemporary debate regarding the role of Christian faith in human service delivery. The contributors were not given a strict outline to follow, but rather were supplied with the basic purposes of the book and general stylistic guidelines. As editors, we have attempted to allow the authors' ideas to stand with as few editorial changes as possible. This collection has been written so that it may be used by itself in the classroom, supplemented by lecture material, or used as a supplement to standard texts.

The reader may agree with some of the contributors' ideas and disagree with others. It is our hope that the reader, whether agreeing or disagreeing, will be stimulated to integrate his or her Christian worldview with the professional social work perspective on helping. We sincerely hope that readers will catch a glimpse of the potential contributions that being a Christian in social work can make to the competent and holistic practice of professional social work and, not incidentally, to the furtherance of the gospel of Jesus Christ and the growth of His Kingdom.

Acknowledgements

Special thanks are due the contributors. We have had the entirely enjoyable task of working with a group that without exception not only produced substantive manuscripts, but shared a clear commitment to the integration of Christian faith and social work practice.

We thank our respective institutions, Calvin College and Baylor University for their support. Special thanks go to Rick Chamiec-Case, Executive Director of NACSW, for his support and encouragement, and to Bob Alderink from Publishing Services at Calvin College for his work on the layout.

We also wish to acknowledge the influence of Alan Keith-Lucas on the initial thinking and development of this project. Both his life and writings continue to provide encouragement and motivation for many social workers in the continuing effort to integrate their Christian faith and social work practice.

CHAPTER 1

INTRODUCTION

Beryl Hugen and T. Laine Scales

One of the developments in social work in the second half of the 20th century has been a marked decline in the recognition of the Christian religion in the teaching and practice of professional social work. The secularization of the social work profession, the notion of religion in both an ideological and institutional sense having little or no part in forming or informing the world of social work, has been very extensive (Hugen, 1994). For many in the social work profession, this question of the relationship of Christian faith and social work is inconsequential, irrelevant, and for some, an inappropriate topic for professional investigation. Even presently, when spirituality is being recognized by the profession as a legitimate area of inquiry, Christianity, as one spiritual voice, is recognized only hesitantly.

This is unfortunate for a number of reasons. First, social work once used the language of Christianity as a basis for its existence. Historically, such language was widely and eloquently used by both social work educators and practitioners. Second, spirituality, and to a large degree Christian spirituality, is very much part of our society and continues to play a significant role in providing moral rationale and reasoning to our political, social, and charitable institutions. As a result, many social workers want to know what role Christian faith plays in a helping profession—specifically, the professional existence and activities of social work. The purpose of this book is to help respond to this question.

Looking at history, and particularly the history of social welfare, it would be hard for anyone to deny that the Christian church is one of the true originators of charity. Out of ancient Israel's concern for justice and mercy toward the sick, the poor, the orphaned, the widowed — from Micah and Hosea, Jeremiah and Isaiah — grew the compassion of Jesus and the devotion of Paul. Both the justice and love of God set forth and exemplified in the Judeo-Christian tradition have given motivation and direction to much of western culture's charities. Historically the whole shape and operation of organized welfare is inexplicable apart from this religious conviction and commitment. Jewish, Catholic, and Protestant thought have continuously shaped the ideological basis of social work practice. One writer has suggested that these religious traditions, along with the secular philosophy of humanism, are the four foundational roots out of which has emerged the value base of the social work profession (Kohs, 1966). Many social workers find the assumptions, beliefs, and values of the Christian faith helpful in providing a frame of reference for understanding and responding to both individual and societal problems.

Many social workers who are Christians do not hold to the idea that there is such a thing as Christian social work—only Christians in social work (we belong to this group). They believe that one's Christian perspective comes into play in social work practice when one is deciding *what* to do, *when* to do it, *how* to do it, and *why* one should do it. They clearly identify with those who seek to follow Christ in a servant role focusing upon the alleviation of pain and suffering and the establishment of justice and peace in the world. It is for this significant group of social workers - from students, whose motivations to enter the profession are informed by their Christian faith, to seasoned professionals, whose desire is to further develop Christian approaches to helping - that this book is written.

A Christian Worldview and Social Work

It is increasingly being recognized that social work, despite its preoccupation in the last half century with 'science' and with developing objective and empirically validated practice techniques, is also a normative profession (Siporin, 1982, 1983). Normative means that the social work profession is also concerned with how persons and societies ought to behave "on principle," and that the purposes and goals of the social work profession are anchored in particular values. A normative principle is an objective rule that when properly applied distinguishes between what is right and wrong. Such rules may be applied to the behavior of individuals, whether client or professional, to social institutions, as well as social and political change processes. So when the social work profession advocates for a more just redistribution of resources that are deemed valuable to society, a value basis or normative principle for such a redistribution proposal is needed. For example, to advocate for a national health care plan because one believes that for persons in the United States adequate health care is a basic human right, requires a value or normative principle as to what is the basis for such a right. Human behavior, both individual and collective, is also socially defined as good or bad, normal or deviant. Whether one chooses as a social worker to enforce such normative standards or advocate for their change, the essential "morality" of these norms or standards requires justification.

Social work has always been guided by such normative principles, although the basis of these principles rarely has been clearly explicated. For Christians, the normative principles used to make moral decisions have always been based upon the principles set forth in the Bible. An important professional task for Christian social workers, therefore, is to relate or test the values of the profession with principles derived from a biblical perspective. Articulating these Christian principles — helping the reader develop a Christian worldview related to social work — is one of the focuses of this book, and is addressed in section one, chapters 2 through 7.

In chapter 2, David Sherwood lays out a framework for a Christian worldview for social work practice. Beryl Hugen, in chapter 3, addresses how one's Christian faith and one's professional work are related through the Christian concept of calling. In chapters 4 and 5, Katherine Amato-von Hemert and Mary Anne Poe, both identify central biblical principles and theologies (at times in tension) related to the understandings of human nature and of God's action in the world and the problem of poverty. Sarah Kreutziger, in chapter 6, offers a historical look at how Christian principles gave shape to the policy and practice of an early twentieth century Christian settlement house program. In the seventh and last chapter in this section, Lawrence Ressler speaks to some of the current tensions and conflicts involved in working out a Christian worldview within the social work profession.

Spiritual Dimensions in Social Work Practice

Today there is a small but growing movement within the social work profession that affirms that spirituality and religious beliefs are integral to the nature of the person and have a vital influence on human behavior. These spiritual and religious dimensions are being increasingly recognized as important features of social work practice, at all phases of the social work helping process and in all areas of practice. This perspective embraces a holistic conception of the person, with this view more recently being elaborated as the bio-psycho-social-spiritual perspective. This perspective reintroduces spiritual issues as a legitimate focus for social work practice and provides for a more complete understanding of client strengths, challenges, and resources. As a result, there is now a need for the development of theoretical frameworks and practice models, including assessment tools and intervention strategies that flow from this perspective.

Social work research also has shown that although many social workers see religious and spiritual issues as important parameters in practice and important in their own lives as well as in the lives of their clients, many are hesitant to initiate discussion of spiritual issues with clients (Canda & Furman, 1999; Derezotes & Evans, 1995; Joseph, 1988). Much of this hesitation is due to the lack of knowledge and skill in this area. Greater sensitivity to the concerns of the religious client has also been shown to be related to the social worker's own spiritual awareness — the ability to integrate the personal, spiritual and religious self with the professional self. Again, there has been a reluctance to incorporate such knowledge into social work education, considering such discussions an intrusion into a private sphere.

This movement within the profession to embrace a bio-psycho-social-spiritual focus in practice, along with the promotion of a professional learning environment that is more supportive of personal religious and spiritual experiences, has resulted in the development of models for incorporating spirituality in a wide variety of practice areas. Christian social workers now have the opportunity to truly minister to the whole person. Several chapters in section two address these spiritual dimensions focusing on a broad range of practice areas.

Diana Garland, in chapter 8, presents a model for understanding faith as a dimension of family life. In chapter 9, Hope Straughan reviews and critiques several theoretical perspectives on individual spiritual development. David Hodge and Crystal Holtrop present a variety of spiritual assessment tools useful in different social work practice settings in chapter 10. In chapter 11, Jason Pittman and Scott Taylor offer a comprehensive model for incorporating Christian spirituality in substance abuse practice. Chapters 12, 13, and 14 each address the role of spirituality in practice with a specific vulnerable population. Roger Fallot outlines in chapter 12 a model for practice with persons experiencing severe mental illness. Cheryl Brandsen proposes a model for addressing spirituality in end of life care with the elderly in chapter 13. The role of spirituality and religion in child welfare, specifically foster care, is presented in chapter 14 by Gary Anderson and Jill Mikula. In the concluding chapter (15) in this section, David Sherwood offers a Christian perspective on ethical decision making in social work practice.

The Changing Environment for Social Work Practice

Social work as a profession has undergone a variety of changes in the twentieth century. Many of these reflect both significant material and technological changes in our society, along with a shift in our ideas about relationships between people and their social environments, particularly government. The early twentieth century was fertile ground for the development and expansion of broad governmental responsibility for social welfare. The idea of the welfare state and of the centrality of government and public service seemed both inevitable and probably necessary.

But the latter part of the twentieth century was much less hospitable to the concept of the welfare state. A perceived lack of results from publicly funded and delivered human services along with a focus on renewing civil society propels today's government leaders to call for community and faith-based organizations to take increasing responsibility for the social and economic needs of communities and persons in poverty. A central question is whether government can better meet the country's critical social needs by working in partnership with the faith community, focusing particularly on congregations and faith-based community development organizations.

Several legislative and legal changes have helped facilitate this increased involvement of faith-based organizations in the delivery of social services. The Section 104 "Charitable Choice" provision of the 1996 welfare reform legislation enabled religious organizations to receive government funding for the delivery of social services, without requiring changes in governance, employment practices, or religious characteristics (Center for Public Justice, 1999). President Bush's development of the Office of Community and Faith-Based Initiatives along with several recent legislation initiatives has given further support to this movement. Social workers who are able to understand and relate to both the public (governmental) and faith-based service communities are today in an important and advantageous position to influence the development of policies and programs that help meet important social needs in their communities (Aker & Scales, in press 2003). Section three includes several chapters focused on this changing environment of social work practice.

The increased involvement of faith-based organizations in human service delivery also brings new challenges, as the purposes and mission of some of these faith-based organizations include an evangelistic outreach. Previously, such faith-based organizations have been seen as "pervasively sectarian"—too religious to receive public financial support. How do social workers in these faith-based organizations balance the mandate for professional service delivery with an evangelistic mission? Two chapters in this section address the role of evangelism in professional social work practice, each from a different perspective.

In chapter 16, Amy Sherman outlines a model for developing congregational social ministries, along with identifying a variety of exemplar programs. Heidi Unruh and Ron Sider, in chapter 17, offer a holistic community ministry model that includes evangelistic (proselytizing) efforts while considering professional social work values. David Sherwood posits a more limited and cautious perspective for the role of evangelism in social work practice in chapter 18. The larger political context (legislative and legal) to this changing ideology regarding the role of faith in human service programming is addressed by Doug Koopman in chapter 19. Finally, in chapter 20, Rick Chamiec-Case offers a model for how congregations can be more inclusive of persons with mental retardation.

Getting the Most Out of This Resource

This collection is intended for a variety of audiences, including social work practitioners, educators, and students at the undergraduate and graduate levels. The book is organized so that it can be used as training or reference materials for practitioners, or as a textbook or supplemental text in a social work class.

As we planned this edition, we contacted instructors and asked them how they were using the first edition. We found that many social work instructors are using selected portions of the book as supplemental reading in a variety of classes across the curriculum. Instructors may require students to purchase the book at the beginning of their coursework and assign a few chapters each semester, with written assignments and class exercises to help students digest the material. For example, in an introductory social work course, students might read Chapters 2 and 3 on worldviews and on calling and then write about their own worldviews or reflect upon their own sense of vocation. Chapter 7 introduces students to the professional context of social work and the tensions they may encounter. Instructors may ask students to browse professional literature or web resources to identify notations on Christian religion in professional literature. Another idea is to assign and discuss in class Chapters 4, 5, and 6, to provide a historical foundation that emphasizes the role of Christian charity before the profession was established as well as early twentieth century Christian settlements and charity organizations; a role that is often minimized in introductory social work texts.

In a human behavior class, Chapters 8 and 9 provide alternative views to classic theories of behavior and introduce additional theorists who consider spirituality as a dimension of human behavior, such as James Fowler. Students may read these chapters vis a vis the work of classical theorists such as Freud, Erickson, Kohlberg, or Carter and McGoldrick and reflect on how consideration of the spiritual dimension of persons broadens our view of human behavior.

There are a variety of articles useful for practice courses. Chapter 15 provides a framework for ethical decision making that students could try out by applying the model to case studies or vignettes. Chapter 10 provides a variety of tools of spiritual assessment that students could practice in a laboratory setting, interviewing one another. Chapters 12, 13, and 14 provide specific information about practice with particular populations at risk; students may research these populations and bring to class specific examples of how Christians may apply common practice principles.

In macro-practice, organizational behavior, or policy courses, Chapters 16-20 introduce readers to congregations and faith based organizations. These articles provide a context for current policy debates surrounding initiatives that encourage partnerships between congregations and government agencies. Chapters 17 and 18 could be used as a framework for a role play or structured debate on the role of evangelism in social services. Chapters 16 and 19 may be assigned with a variety of web resources that provide the latest information on this changing policy and practice landscape. Chapter 20 features several case vignettes that can serve as classroom tools to stimulate discussion.

Humility and Competence

One of the primary goals of this book is to apply a Christian perspective to the realities of contemporary social work practice. It is important to remember that in offering a Christian understanding and response to social problems that it does not mean that Christians in social work have all the answers. The Bible may provide guidance, but does not always provide clear and specific direction for the sometimes confusing moral and ethical situations social workers encounter in practice. As Christian social workers, we know that we live and practice in a broken world, and that our only real comfort is that we are not our own, but we belong, body and soul, in life and in death, to our faithful Savior Jesus Christ.

It is also easy to assert the evident Christian goodness of helping people. And it can be easier still to assume that a Christian perspective on the profession and practice of social work furthers that good. But goodness of motivation may be and frequently is unrelated to outcome. There is always the possibility that our Christian perspectives are no more than self-serving rationales (promoting judgmentalism, discrimination and selective helping motives) rather than the product of a thoughtful analysis. With this book, therefore, we have attempted to offer a Christian perspective for social work practice that is within the parameters of contemporary models of professional social work research and scholarship. We believe that all knowledge is God's knowledge, and clearly the social work profession can also inform the Christian community.

References

Aker, R., & Scales, T.L., (In press 2003). "Charitable choice, social workers and rural congregations: Partnering to build community assets", in Scales, T.L. and Streeter, C. (Eds.), *Asset Building to Sustain Rural Communities*. Pacific Grove, CA, Brooks/ Cole.

Canda, E.R., & Furman, L.D. (1997). *Spiritual diversity in social work practice: The heart of helping*. New York: The Free Press.

Center for Public Justice. (1999). A guide to charitable choice: An overview of section 104.

Derezotes, D.S. & Evans, K.E. (1995). Spirituality and religiosity in practice: In-depth interviews of social work practitioners. *Social Thought, 18*(1), 39-54.

Hugen, B. (1994).The secularization of social work. *Social Work and Christianity*, 21(4), 83-101.

Joseph, M.V. (1988). Religion and social work practice. *Social Casework, 60*(7), 443-452.

Kohs, S.C. (1966). *The Roots of Social Work*. Association Press.

Siporin, M. (1982). Moral philosophy in social work today. *Social Service Review, 56*, 516-38.

Siporin, M. (1983). Morality and immorality in working with clients. *Social Thought, 15, (3/4)*, 42-52.

CHAPTER 2

THE RELATIONSHIP BETWEEN BELIEFS AND VALUES IN SOCIAL WORK PRACTICE: WORLDVIEWS MAKE A DIFFERENCE

David A. Sherwood

In some circles (including some Christian ones) it is fashionable to say that what we believe is not all that important. What we do is what really counts. I strongly disagree. The relationship between what we think and what we do is complex and it is certainly not a simple straight line, but it is profound. Social work values, practice theories, assessments, intervention decisions, and action strategies are all shaped by our worldview assumptions and our beliefs.

I believe that a Christian worldview will provide an interpretive framework which will solidly support and inform commonly held social work values such as the inherent value of every person regardless of personal characteristics, self-determination and personally responsible freedom of choice, and responsibility for the common good, including help for the poor and oppressed. And it will challenge other values and theories such as might makes right, exploitation of the weak by the strong, and extreme moral relativism. At the same time, other worldviews, including materialism, empiricism, and postmodern subjectivism will lead to quite contrasting conclusions regarding these values.

Worldviews Help Us Interpret Reality

What is a "Worldview?"

Worldviews give faith-based answers to a set of ultimate and grounding questions. Everyone operates on the basis of some worldview or faith-based understanding of the universe and persons— examined, or unexamined, implicit or explicit, simplistic or sophisticated. One way or another, we develop functional assumptions that help us to sort through and make some sort of sense out of our experience. And every person's worldview will always have a faith-based component (even belief in an exclusively material universe takes faith). This does not mean worldviews are necessarily irrational, unconcerned with "facts," or impervious to critique and change (though they unfortunately might be). It matters greatly how conscious, reflective, considered, or informed our worldviews are. The most objectivity we can achieve is to be critically aware of our worldview and how it affects our interpretations of "the facts." It is far better to be aware, intentional, and informed regarding our worldview than to naively think we are (or anyone else is) objective or neutral or to be self-righteously led by our biases which we may think are simply self-evident truth.

These worldviews affect our approach to social work practice, how we understand and help people. What is the nature of persons—biochemical machines, evolutionary products, immortal souls, all of the above? What constitutes valid knowledge—scientific empiricism only, "intuitive" discernment, spiritual guidance (if so, what kind)? What kinds of social work theories and practice methods are legitimate? What are appropriate values and goals—what is healthy, functional, optimal, the good?

Worldviews and the Hermeneutical Spiral: A Beginning Place

I like to use the concept of the *"hermeneutical spiral"* (the term is not original with me, cf. Osborne, 1991, Wood, 1998). We always come to the world, including social work practice, with our faith(worldview assumptions)—wherever we got it, however good or bad it is, and however embryonic it may be. This worldview faith strongly affects what we perceive (or even look for). But the world (God's creation, in the Christian worldview) is not a totally passive or subjective thing. So, we run the risk of coming away from any encounter with the world having our faith and our categories somewhat altered, perhaps even corrected a bit. Then we use that altered faith in our next encounter with the world.

So, for me, the starting place for integration of my beliefs and social work practice is always at the level of basic faith, worldview assumptions. What are the implications of my core beliefs? And what are the implications of the idea, theory, interpretation, or practice that I am examining? To use a currently fashionable phrase, how do they "interrogate" each other? What kind of assumptions about the nature of the world lie behind Freudian theory? Behavioral theory? The scientific method? The strengths perspective? The social work belief that all persons have intrinsic value (a radical notion not particularly supported by modernism or postmodernism in their materialist, subjectivist versions)?

To put it another way, we all form stories that answer life's biggest questions. As I become a Christian, I connect my personal story to a much bigger story that frames my answers to these big questions. For Christians, the biblical story of God's nature and action in human history, culminating in Jesus Christ, is the "meta-narrative" that frames our personal stories and within which the meaning of our stories is rooted. Middleton and Walsh (1995, p. 11) summarize the basic worldview questions this way (with my illustrative additions):

1. **Where are we?** ***What is the nature of the reality in which we find ourselves?*** Is the nature of the universe meaningful or absurd? Created or accidental? Materialistic only, or also spiritual?

2. **Who are we?** ***What is the nature and task of human beings?*** What does it mean to be a person? What is human life? What is its source and value? Is there such a thing as freedom or responsibility?

3. **What's wrong?** ***How do we understand and account for evil and brokenness?*** And how do we account for our sense of morality, love, and justice? Is evil only stuff I happen not to prefer? Or are some things really good and other things really wrong? Is love only lust or well-disguised self-centeredness? Does justice have a claim on us and what we call "ours"?

4. **What's the remedy?** ***How do we find a path through our brokenness to wholeness?*** What kinds of things will help? Do we need a Savior or just a positive (or cynical) attitude? Will chemicals or incarceration do the trick?

Interpreting the Facts

"Facts" have no meaning apart from an interpretive framework. "Facts" are harder to come by than we often think, but even when we have some "facts" in our possession, they have no power to tell us what they mean or what we should do.

That human beings die is a fact. That I am going to die would seem to be a reliable prediction based on what I can see. In fact, the capacity to put those observations and projections together is one of the ways we have come to describe or define human consciousness. But what do these "facts" mean and what effect should they have on my life? One worldview might tell me that life emerged randomly in a meaningless universe and is of no particular value beyond the subjective feelings I may experience from moment to moment. Another worldview might tell me that somehow biological survival of life forms is of value and that I only have value to the extent that I contribute to that biological parade (with the corollary that survival proves fitness). Another worldview might tell me that life is a gift from a loving and just Creator and that it transcends biological existence, that death is not the end of the story. Different worldviews lend different meanings to the same "facts."

The major initial contribution of a Christian worldview to an understanding of social work values and ethical practice is not one of unique, contrasting, or conflicting values. Rather, a Christian worldview gives a coherent, solid foundation for the basic values that social workers claim and often take for granted (Holmes, 1984; Sherwood, 1993, 2000). Subsequently, a Christian worldview will shape how those basic values are understood and how they interact with one another. For example, justice will be understood in the light of God's manifest concern for the poor and oppressed, so justice can never be defined only as a procedurally "fair" protection of individual liberty and the right to acquire, hold, and transfer property (Lebacqz, 1986; Mott, 1982; Wolterstorff, 1983).

The Interaction of Feeling, Thinking, and Behavior

Persons are complex living ecological systems—to use a helpful conceptual model common in social work—systems of systems, if you will. Systems within our bodies and outside us as well interact in dynamic relationships with each other. For example, it is impossible to meaningfully separate our thinking, feeling, and behavior from each other and from the systems we experience outside ourselves, yet we quite properly think of ourselves as separate individuals. The lines of influence run in all directions. What we believe affects what we experience, including how we define our feelings. For example, does an experience I might have of being alone, in and of itself, *make* me feel lonely, or rejected, or exhilarated by freedom, for that matter? Someone trips me, but was it accidental or intentional? I have had sex with only one woman (my wife Carol) in over sixty years of life. How does this "make" me feel? Are my feelings not also a result of what I tell myself about the meaning of my experience? But it works the other way too.

All this makes us persons harder to predict. And it certainly makes it harder to assign neat, direct, and one-way lines of causality. The biblical worldview picture is that God has granted us (at great cost) the dignity and terror of contributing to causality ourselves through our own purposes, choices, and actions. We have often used this freedom to hurt others and ourselves, but this also means that we are not mechanistically determined and that significant change is always possible. And change can come from many directions—thinking, emotions, behavior, experience. We are especially (compared to other creatures) both gifted and cursed by our ability to think about ourselves and the world. We can form purposes and act in the direction of those purposes. Our beliefs about the nature of the world, other persons, and ourselves interact in a fundamental way with how we perceive reality, how we define our own identity, and how we act.

If this is true in our personal lives, it is equally true as we try to understand and help our clients in social work practice. And it is no less true for clients themselves. What we believe about the nature of the world, the nature of persons, and the nature of the human situation is at least as important as the sheer facts of the circumstances we experience.

Worldviews Help Construct Our Understanding of Values

Cut Flowers: Can Values Be Sustained Without Faith?

One significant manifestation of the notion that beliefs aren't all that important is the fallacy of our age which assumes that fundamental moral values can be justified and sustained apart from their ideological (ultimately theological) foundation. Take, for example, the fundamental Christian and social work belief that all human beings have intrinsic dignity and value.

Elton Trueblood, the Quaker philosopher, once described ours as a "cut-flower" generation. He was suggesting that, as it is possible to cut a rose from the bush, put it in a vase, and admire its fresh loveliness and fragrance for a short while, it is possible to maintain the dignity and value of every human life while denying the existence or significance of God as the source of that value. But the cut rose is already dead, regardless of the deceptive beauty which lingers for awhile. Even uncut, "The grass withers, and the flower falls, but the Word of the Lord endures forever" (I Peter 1:24-25).

Many in our generation, including many social workers, are trying to hold onto values—such as the irreducible dignity and worth of the individual—while denying the only basis on which such a value can ultimately stand. We should be glad they try to hold onto the value, but we should understand how shaky such a foundation is. A secular generation can live off its moral capital only so long before the impertinent questions (Why should we?) can no longer be ignored.

Doesn't Everybody "Just Know" That Persons Have Dignity and Value?

But doesn't everybody "just know" that human beings have intrinsic value? You don't have to believe in God, do you? In fact, according to some, so-called believers in God have been among the worst offenders against the value and dignity of all persons (sadly true, in some cases). After all, a lot of folks, from secular humanists to rocket scientists to New Age witches to rock stars, have declared themselves as defenders of the value of the individual. Isn't the worth of the person just natural, or at least rational and logically required? The plain answer is, "No, it's *not* just natural or rational or something everyone just knows."

I received a striking wake-up call in regard to this particular truth a number of years ago when I was a freshman at Indiana University. I think the story is worth telling here. I can't help dating myself—it was in the spring of 1960, the time the Civil Rights movement was clearly emerging. We were hearing of lunch room sit-ins and Freedom Riders on buses. Through an older friend of mine from my home town I wound up spending the evening at the Student Commons talking with my friend and someone he had met, a graduate student from Iran named Ali. I was quite impressed. My friend Maurice told me Ali's father was some sort of advisor to the Shah (the ruling despot at that point in Iran's history).

The conversation turned to the events happening in the South, to the ideas of racial integration, brotherhood, and social justice. Ali was frankly puzzled and amused that Maurice and I, and at least some other Americans, seemed to think civil rights were worth pursuing. But given that, he found it particularly hard to understand what he thought was the wishy-washy way the thing was being handled. "I don't know why you want to do it," he said, "but if it's so important, why don't you just do it? If I were President of the United States and I wanted integration, I would do it in a week!" "How?" we asked. "Simple. I would just put a soldier with a machine gun on every street corner and say 'Integrate.' If they didn't, I would shoot them."

Naive freshman that I was, I just couldn't believe he was really saying that. Surely he was putting us on. You couldn't just do that to people. At least not if you were moral! The conversation-debate-argument went on to explore what he really did believe about the innate dignity and value of the individual human life and social responsibility. You don't just kill inconvenient people, do you? I would say things like, "Surely you believe that society has a moral responsibility to care for the widows and orphans, the elderly, the disabled, the emotionally disturbed." Incredibly (to me at the time), Ali's basic response was not to give an inch but to question *my* beliefs and values instead. "Society has no such moral responsibility," he said. "On the contrary. You keep talking about reason and morality. I'll tell you what is immoral. The rational person would say that the truly *immoral* thing is to take resources away from the strong and productive to give to the weak and useless. Useless members of society such as the disabled and mentally retarded should be eliminated, not maintained." He would prefer that the methods be "humane," but he really did mean eliminated.

It finally sunk into my freshman mind that what we were disagreeing about was not facts or logic, but the belief systems we were using to interpret or assign meaning to the facts. Ali was a thoroughly secular man; he had left Islam behind. If I were to accept his assumptions about the nature of the universe (e.g. that there is no God, that the material universe is the extent of reality, that self-preservation is the only given motive and goal), then his logic was flawless and honest. As far as he was concerned, the only thing of importance left to discuss would be the most effective means to gain and keep power and the most expedient way to use it.

In this encounter I was shaken loose from my naive assumption that "everybody knows" the individual person has innate dignity and value. I understood more clearly that unless you believed in the Creator, the notion that all persons are equal is, indeed, *not* self-evident. The Nazi policies of eugenics and the "final solution" to the "Jewish problem" make a kind of grimly honest (almost inevitable) sense if you believe in the materialist worldview.

The "Is-Ought" Dilemma

Not long afterward I was to encounter this truth much more cogently expressed in the writings of C. S. Lewis. In *The Abolition of Man* (1947) he points out that both the religious and the secular walk by faith if they try to move from descriptive observations of fact to any sort of value statement or ethical imperative. He says "From propositions about fact alone no *practical* conclusion can ever be drawn. 'This will preserve society' [let's assume this is a factually true statement] cannot lead to 'Do this' [a moral and practical injunction] except by the mediation of 'Society ought to be preserved' [a value statement]" (p. 43). "Society ought to be preserved" is a moral imperative that no amount of facts alone can prove or disprove. Even the idea of "knowing facts" involves basic assumptions (or faith) about the nature of the universe and human beings. The secular person (social worker?) tries to cloak faith by substituting words like natural, necessary, progressive, scientific, rational, or functional for "good," but the question always remains—For what end? and Why? And the answer to this question always smuggles in values from somewhere else besides the facts.

Even the resort to instincts such as self-preservation can tell us nothing about what we (or others)*ought* to do. Lewis (1947, p. 49) says:

> We grasp at useless words: we call it the "basic," or "fundamental," or "primal," or "deepest" instinct. It is of no avail.

> Either these words conceal a value judgment passed *upon* the instinct and therefore not derivable *from* it, or else they merely record its felt intensity, the frequency of its operation, and its wide distribution. If the former, the whole attempt to base value upon instinct has been abandoned: if the latter, these observations about the quantitative aspects of a psychological event lead to no practical conclusion. It is the old dilemma. Either the premise is already concealed an imperative or the conclusion remains merely in the indicative.

This is called the "Is-Ought" dilemma. Facts, even when attainable, never have any practical or moral implications until they are interpreted through the grid of some sort of value assumptions. "Is" does not lead to "Ought" in any way that has moral bindingness, obligation, or authority until its relationship to relevant values is understood. And you can't get the values directly from the "Is." We always comes down to the question—what is the source and authority of the "Ought" that is claimed or implied?

The social work Code of Ethics refers to values such as the inherent value of every person, the importance of social justice, and the obligation to fight against oppression. It is a fair question to ask where those values come from and what gives them moral authority and obligation.

A Shaky Consensus: "Sexual Abuse" or "Intergenerational Sexual Experience?"

For an example of the "Is-Ought" dilemma, is child sexual abuse a fact or a myth? Or what is the nature of the abuse? Child sexual abuse is an example of an area where there may seem to be more of a consensus in values than there actually is. In any event, it illustrates how it is impossible to get values from facts alone. Some intervening concept of "the good" always has to come into play.

Fact: Some adults have sexual relations with children. But so what? What is the practical or moral significance of this fact? Is this something we should be happy or angry about? Is this good or bad? Sometimes good and sometimes bad? Should we be encouraging or discouraging the practice? Even if we could uncover facts about the consequences of the experience on children, we would still need a value framework to help us discern the meaning or practical implications of those facts. And to have moral obligation beyond our own subjective preferences or biases, this value framework must have some grounding outside ourselves. What constitutes negative consequences? And even if we could agree certain consequences were indeed negative, the question would remain as to what exactly was the cause.

In the last few years there has been a tremendous outpouring of attention to issues of child sexual abuse and its effects on adult survivors. I must say that this is long overdue and much needed. And even among completely secular social workers, psychologists, and other therapists there currently appears to be a high degree of consensus about the moral wrong of adult sexual activity with children and the enormity of its negative consequences on the child at the time and in later life. As a Christian I am encouraged, especially when I recall the self-described "radical Freudian" professor I had in my master's in social work program who described in glowingly approving terms high levels of sexual intimacy between children and each other and children and adults as "freeing and liberating" (that was the early 1970s).

However, if I look more closely at the worldview faith underlying much of the discussion of sexual abuse and its effects, the result is not quite so comforting to me as a Christian. The moral problem tends not to be defined in terms of a well-rounded biblical view of sexuality and God's creative design and purpose or an understanding of the problem of sin. Rather, it tends to be based on a more rationalistic and individualistic model of power and a model of justice that pins its faith on reason. Sexual abuse grows out of an inequity in power which a person rationally "ought not" exploit. Why not, one might ask.

But what if we take away the coercive element and get rid of the repressive "body-negative" ideas about sexual feelings? What if much or all of the negative effects of non-coercive sexual activity between adults and children is the result of the misguided and distorted social attitudes which are passed on to children and adults? Defenders of "non-exploitive" sexual activity between adults and children can (and do) argue that any negative consequences are purely a result of sex-negative social learning and attitudes. Representatives of a hypothetical group such as P.A.L. (Pedophiles Are Lovers!) would argue that what needs to be changed is not the intergenerational sexual behavior, but the sexually repressive social values and behavior which teach children the negative responses. These values are seen as the oppressive culprits. Then, the argument might go, should we not bend our efforts to eradicating these repressive sexual values and attitudes rather than condemning potentially innocent acts of sexual pleasure? Indeed, why not, if the only problem is exploitation of power?

You should also note that this argument in favor of intergenerational sexual behavior is not exclusively scientific, objective, or based only on "facts." It has to make faith assumptions about the nature of persons, the nature of sexuality, the nature of health, and the nature of values. By the same token, my condemnation of adult sexual activity with children is based on faith assumptions about the nature of persons, sexuality, health, and values informed by my Christian worldview. It is never just "facts" alone that determine our perceptions, conclusions, and behavior.

Right now, it happens to be a "fact" that a fairly large consensus exists, even among secular social scientists and mental health professionals, that adult sexual activity with children is "bad" and that it leads quite regularly to negative consequences. Right now you could almost say this is something "everyone knows." But it would be a serious mistake to become complacent about this or to conclude that worldview beliefs and faith are not so important after all.

First, not everyone agrees. Although I invented the hypothetical group P.A.L. (Pedophiles Are Lovers), it represents real people and groups that do exist. The tip of this iceberg may be appearing in the professional literature where it is becoming more acceptable and common to see the "facts" reinterpreted. In preparing bibliography for a course on sexual issues in helping, I ran across a very interesting little shift in terminology in some of the professional literature. One article was entitled "Counterpoints: Intergenerational sexual experience or child sexual abuse" (Malz, 1989). A companion article was titled "Intergenerational sexual contact: A continuum model of participants and experiences" (Nelson, 1989). Words do make a difference.

Second, we shouldn't take too much comfort from the apparent agreement. It is sometimes built on a fragile foundation that could easily come apart. The fact that Christians find themselves in wholehearted agreement with many secular helping professionals, for example, that sexual activity between adults (usually male) and children (usually female) is exploitive and wrong may represent a temporary congruence on issues and strategy, much more so than fundamental agreement on the nature of persons and sexuality.

But back to the "Is-Ought" dilemma. The fact that some adults have sexual contact with children, by itself, tells us *nothing* about what, if anything, should be done about it. The facts can never answer those questions. The only way those questions can ever be answered is if we interpret the facts in terms of our faith, whatever that faith is. What is the nature of the world? What is the nature of persons? What is the meaning of sex? What constitutes health? What is the nature of justice? And most important—why should I care anyway?

Worldviews Help Define the Nature and Value of Persons

So—Worldviews Have Consequences

Your basic faith about the nature of the universe has consequences (and everyone, as we have seen, has some sort of faith). Faith is consequential to you personally and the content of the faith is consequential. If it isn't *true* that Christ has been raised, my faith is worthless (I Corinthians 15:14). And if it's *true* that Christ has been raised, but I put my faith in Baal or the free market or the earth goddess (big these days) or Karl Marx (not so big these days) or human reason, then *that* has consequences, to me and to others. What are we going to *trust*, bottom-line?

In I Corinthians 15, the apostle Paul said something about the importance of what we believe about the nature of the world, the *content* of our faith. He said, "Now if Christ is proclaimed as raised from the dead, how can some of you say there is no resurrection of the dead? If there is no resurrection of the dead, then Christ has not been raised; and if Christ has not been raised, then our proclamation has been in vain and your faith is also in vain . . . If Christ has not been raised, your faith is futile and you are still in your sins . . . If for this life only we have hoped in Christ, we are of all people most to be pitied" (12-14, 17, 19).

I've been a student, a professional social worker, and a teacher of social work long enough to see some major changes in "what everyone knows," in what is assumed or taken for granted. "What everyone knows" is in fact part of the underlying operational *faith* of a culture or subculture—whether it's Americans or teenagers or those who go to college or social workers—or Southern Baptists, for that matter.

When I went to college, logical positivism was king, a version of what C. S. Lewis called "naturalism," a kind of philosophical materialism. It said that the physical world is all there is. Everything is fully explainable by materialistic determinism. Only what can be physically measured or "operationalized" is real (or at least relevantly meaningful). In psychology it was epitomized in B. F. Skinner's behaviorism.

I remember as a somewhat bewildered freshman at Indiana University attending a lecture by a famous visiting philosophy professor (a logical positivist) from Cambridge University (whose name I have forgotten) entitled "The Impossibility of any Future Metaphysic" (his takeoff on Kant's title "Prolegomena to any Future Metaphysic"). I can't say I understood it all at the time, but his main point was that modern people must permanently put away such meaningless and potentially dangerous ideas as spirituality, the supernatural, and any notion of values beyond subjective preferences. We now know, he said, that such language is meaningless (since not empirical) except, perhaps, to express our own subjective feelings.

In a graduate school course in counseling, I had an earnest young behaviorist professor who had, as a good behaviorist, trained (conditioned) himself to avoid all value statements that implied good or bad or anything beyond personal preference. When faced with a situation where someone else might be tempted to make a value statement, whether regarding spaghetti, rock and roll, or adultery, he had an ideologically correct response. He would, with a straight face, say "I find that positively reinforcing" or, "I find that negatively reinforcing." (I don't know what his wife thought about this kind of response). Notice, he was saying "I" (who knows about you or anyone else) "find" (observe a response in myself at this moment; who knows about five minutes from now) "that" (a particular measurable stimulus) is "positively reinforcing" (it elicits this particular behavior now and might be predicted to do it again).

Above all, the idea was to be totally scientific, objective, and *value-free*. After all, values were perceived to be purely relative, personal preferences, or (worse) prejudices induced by social learning. And "everyone knew" that the only thing real was physical, measurable, and scientific. If we could only get the "facts" we would know what to do.

But this was, and is, a fundamental fallacy, the "Is-Ought" fallacy we discussed earlier. Even if facts are obtainable, they have no moral power or direction in themselves. If we say they mean something it is because we are interpreting them in the context of some values which are a part of our basic faith about the nature of the world.

Shifting Worldviews: The Emperor Has No Clothes

In the meantime we have seen some rather amazing shifts in "what everyone knows." I am old enough to have vivid memories of the 1960s and the "greening of America" when "everybody knew" that people under 30 were better than people over 30 and that human beings are so innately good all we had to do was to scrape off the social conventions and rules and then peace, love, and total sharing would rule the world. An astounding number of people truly believed that—for a short time.

In the '70s and early '80s "everybody knew" that personal autonomy and affluence are what it is all about. Power and looking out for Number One became the articles of faith, even for helping professionals like social workers. Maximum autonomy was the obvious highest good. Maturity and health were defined in terms of not needing anyone else (and not having any obligation to anyone else either). Fritz Perls' "Gestalt Prayer" even got placed on romantic greeting cards:

I do my thing, and you do your thing.
I am not in this world to live up to your expectations.
And you are not in this world to live up to mine.
You are you and I am I,
And if by chance we find each other, it's beautiful.
If not, it can't be helped.
If you care too much, you are enmeshed, undifferentiated, or at the very least co-dependent.

And here we are after the turning of a new millennium and, at least for awhile, it looks as though values are in. Time magazine has had cover stories on ethics. We have had occasion to feel betrayed and outraged at the exposure of unethical behavior on the part of corporate executives, accountants, and stock brokers. Even more amazing, philosophy professors and social workers are not embarrassed to talk about values and even character again. "Family Values" are avowed by the Republicans and Democrats. The books and articles are rolling off the presses.

But we should not be lulled into a false sense of security with this recovery of values and ethics, even if much of it sounds quite Christian to us. The philosophical paradigm has shifted to the opposite extreme, from the modern faith in the rational and empirical to the postmodern faith in the radically subjective and relative, the impossibility of getting beyond our ideological and cultural horizons. Our culture now despairs of any knowledge beyond the personal narratives we make up for ourselves out of the flotsam of our experience and fragments of disintegrating culture (Middleton & Walsh, 1995). Postmodernism says each person pieces together a personal story through which we make sense out of our lives, but there is no larger story (meta-narrative) which is really true in any meaningful sense and which can bind our personal stories together.

It is remarkable, as we have seen, how rapidly some of these assumptions can shift. The seeming consensus may be only skin-deep. More importantly, unless these values are grounded on something deeper than the currently fashionable paradigm (such as a Christian worldview), we can count on the fact that they will shift, or at least give way when they are seriously challenged. It's amazing how easy it is to see that the emperor has no clothes when a different way of looking is introduced to the scene. Remember both enlightenment empiricism and postmodern subjectivity agree that values have no transcendent source.

What Is a "Person?"

Controversies regarding abortion and euthanasia illustrate the profound consequences of our worldview faith, especially for worldviews which deny that values have any ultimate source. Even more fundamental than the question of when life begins and ends is the question what is a person? What constitutes being a person? What value, if any, is there in being a person? Are persons owed any particular rights, respect, or care? If so, why?

If your worldview says that persons are simply the result of matter plus time plus chance, it would seem that persons have no intrinsic value at all, no matter how they are defined. From a purely materialist point of view, it may be interesting (to us) that the phenomena of human consciousness and agency have emerged which allow us in some measure to transcend simple biological, physical, and social determinism. These qualities might include the ability to be self-aware, to remember and to anticipate, to experience pleasure and pain, to develop caring relationships with others, to have purposes, to develop plans and take deliberate actions with consequences, and to have (at least the illusion of) choice. We may choose to define personhood as incorporating some of these characteristics. And we may even find it positively reinforcing (or not) to be persons. But then what? In this materialist worldview there are no inherent guidelines or limits regarding what we do to persons.

Do such persons have a right to life? Only to the extent it pleases us (whoever has the power) to say so. And what in the world could "right" mean in this context? But what if we do choose to say that persons have a right to life. What degree or quality of our defining characteristics do they have to have before they qualify? How self-conscious and reflective? How capable of choice and action?

It is common for people to argue today that babies aren't persons before they are born (or at least most of the time before they are born) and thus that there is no moral reason for not eliminating defective ones, or even just unwanted or inconvenient ones. And there are already those who argue that babies should not even be declared potential persons until they have lived long enough after birth to be tested and observed to determine their potential for normal growth and development, thus diminishing moral qualms about eliminating "wrongful births." After all, what is magic about the birth process? Why not wait for a few hours, days, or weeks after birth to see if this "fetal material" is going to measure up to our standards of personhood? And at any point in life if our personhood fails to develop adequately or gets lost or seriously diminished through accident, illness, mental illness, or age, what then? Was my college acquaintance Ali right? Is it immoral to take resources from the productive and use them to support the unproductive? Do these "fetal products" or no-longer-persons need to be terminated?

A Solid Foundation

If I balk at these suggestions, it is because I have a worldview that gives a different perspective to the idea of what constitutes a person. I may agree, for example, that agency—the capacity to be self-aware, reflective, remember and anticipate, plan, choose, and responsibly act—is a central part of what it means to be a person. But I also believe that this is a gift from our creator God which in some way images God. I believe that our reflection, choice, and action have a divinely given purpose. This purpose is summarized in the ideas of finding and choosing God through grace and faith, of growing up into the image of Jesus Christ, of knowing and enjoying God forever. All of this says that persons have a special value beyond their utility to me (or anyone else) and that they are to be treated with the care and respect befitting their status as gifts from God. Even when something goes wrong.

Having a Christian worldview and knowing what the Bible says about God, the world, and the nature of persons doesn't always give us easy answers to all of our questions, however. And having faith in the resurrection of Jesus Christ doesn't guarantee that we will always be loving or just. But it does give us a foundation of stone to build our house on, a context to try to understand what we encounter that will not shift with every ideological or cultural season. I can assert the dignity and worth of every person based on a solid foundation, not just an irrational preference of my own or a culturally-induced bias that I might happen to have. What "everybody knows" is shifting sand. Even if it happens to be currently stated in the NASW Code of Ethics for social workers.

Some Basic Components of a Christian Worldview

Space does not permit me to develop a detailed discussion of the components of a Christian worldview here, but I would at least like to try to summarize in the most basic and simple terms what I perceive to be quite middle-of-the-road, historically orthodox, and biblical answers to the fundamental worldview questions I posed at the beginning (cf. Middleton & Walsh, 1995). This suggests the Christian worldview that has informed me and has been (I would hope) quite evident in what has been said. This little summary is not the end of reflection and application, but only the beginning.

1. ***Where are we?*** We are in a universe which was created by an eternal, omnipotent, just, loving, and gracious God. Consequently the universe has built-in meaning, purpose, direction, and values. The fundamental values of love and justice have an ultimate source in the nature of God which gives them meaning, authority, and content. The universe is both natural and supernatural.

2. ***Who are we?*** We are persons created "in the image God" and therefore with intrinsic meaning and value, regardless of our personal characteristics or achievements. Persons are both physical and spiritual. Persons have been given the gift of "agency"– in a meaningful sense we have been given both freedom and responsibility. Persons created in the image of God are not just autonomous individuals but are relational– created to be in loving and just community with one another. Persons are objects of God's grace.

3. ***What's wrong?*** Oppression and injustice are evil, wrong, an affront to the nature and desire of God. Persons are finite and fallen–we are both limited in our capacities and distorted from our ideal purpose because of our selfishness and choice of evil. Our choice of selfishness and evil alienates us from God and from one another and sets up distortion in our perceptions, beliefs, and behavior, but we are not completely blind morally. Our self-centeredness makes us prone to seek solutions to our problems based on ourselves and our own abilities and accomplishments. We can't solve our problems by ourselves, either by denial or our own accomplishments.

4. ***What's the remedy?*** Stop trying to do it our way and accept the loving grace and provisions for healing that God has provided for us. God calls us to a high moral standard but knows that it is not in our reach to fulfill this standard completely. God's creative purpose is to bring good even out of evil, to redeem, heal, and grow us up–not by law but by grace. "For by grace you have been saved through faith, and this is not your own doing; it is the gift of God–not the result of works, so that no one may boast. For we are what he has made us, created in Christ Jesus for good works, which God prepared beforehand to be our way of life." (Ephesians 2:8-10)

Why Should I Care? Choosing a Christian Worldview

Moral Obligation and Faith: Materialism Undermines Moral Obligation

To abandon a theological basis of values, built into the universe by God, is ultimately to abandon the basis for any "oughts" in the sense of being morally bound other than for purely subjective or cultural reasons. Normative morality that is just descriptive and cultural ("This is what most people in our society tend to do"), subjective ("This is what I happen to prefer and do," or "It would be convenient for me if you would do this"), or utilitarian ("This is what works to achieve certain consequences") has no power of moral *obligation*. Why should I care? On materialist or subjective grounds I "should" do this or that if I happen to feel like it or if I think it will help me get what I want. But this is using the word "should" in a far different and far more amoral sense than we ordinarily mean by it. It is a far different thing than saying I am *morally obligated or bound* to do it.

Many will argue that reason alone is enough to support moral obligation. This is the argument used by Frederic Reamer in his excellent book on social work ethics, *Ethical Dilemmas in Social Services* (1990), based on Gewirth (*Reason and Morality*, 1978). If, for example, I understand that freedom is logically required for human personal action, then this theory says I am logically obligated to support freedom for other persons as I desire it for myself. But I have never been able to buy the argument that reason alone creates any meaningful moral obligation for altruistic behavior. Why *should* I be logical, especially if being logical doesn't appear to work for my personal advantage? Any idea of moral obligation beyond the subjective and personally utilitarian seems to lead inevitably and necessarily to God in some form or to nowhere.

The "Method of Comparative Difficulties"

Although it is logically possible (and quite necessary if you believe in a materialist or postmodernist universe) to believe that values are only subjective preferences or cultural inventions, I have never been able to completely believe that is all our sense of values such as love and justice amounts to. There are, in all honesty, many obstacles in the way of belief in God as the transcendent source of values. But can we believe, when push comes to shove, that all values are either meaningless or totally subjective? Elton Trueblood calls this the "Method of Comparative Difficulties" (1963, p. 73; 1957, p. 13).

It may often be hard to believe in God, but I find it even harder to believe in the alternatives, especially when it comes to values. It's easy enough to say that this or that value is only subjective or culturally relative, but when we get pushed into a corner, most of us find ourselves saying (or at least *feeling*), "No, *that* (say, the Holocaust) is really wrong and it's not just my opinion." (Cf. C. S. Lewis, "Right and Wrong As a Clue to the Meaning of the Universe," *Mere Christianity*, 1948)

Dostoevsky expressed the idea that if there is no God, all things are permissible. C. S. Lewis (1947, pp. 77-78) said that "When all that says 'it is good' has been debunked, what says 'I want' remains. It cannot be exploded or 'seen through' because it never had any pretensions." Lust remains after values have been explained away. Values that withstand the explaining away process are the only ones that will do us any good. Lewis concludes *The Abolition of Man* (1947, p. 91):

> You cannot go on "explaining away" forever: you will find that you have explained explanation itself away. You cannot go on "seeing through" things forever. The whole point of seeing through something is to see something through it. It is good that the window should be transparent, because the street or garden beyond it is opaque. How if you saw through the garden too? It is no use trying to "see through" first principles. If you see through everything, then everything is transparent. But a wholly transparent world is an invisible world. To "see through" all things is the same as not to see.

Looking for Christian Implications

A Christian worldview is not going to give us simple answers to all of our questions. It is not as though there is a simple translation of Christian values and principles into practice implications, or that there is a unitary "Christian" version of every human activity from French cooking to volleyball to politics. Even though we may agree on fundamental values and principles, such as love and justice, as fallen and finite human beings, the more specific we get in terms of translating love and justice into particular attempts to solve concrete problems the more we are likely to honestly and conscientiously disagree with one another in our interpretation of what the problem is or what, in fact, might actually do more good than harm in attempting to deal with it (Sherwood, 1999).

I assume, for example, that if we are Christians and we have read the Bible we have been impressed with our obligation to work for social justice and to help the poor. But what are the causes of poverty and what can we do to help the poor that will do more good than harm? Not simple and not obvious. May I be so bold as to say that there is **no** simple, single "Christian" answer to those questions? We are going to be working to deal with poverty (and conscientiously disagreeing about how to do it) until Jesus returns. And I will submit that there is *no* policy or program to help the poor, individually or collectively, privately or publicly that will not *advance some* of the legitimate values that we have at the *risk or cost of some* of our other legitimate values.

So, everything we do will be a compromise of sorts and will need to be adapted a much as possible to the unique situation. But what we do needs to be an imperfect solution shaped both by our Christian faith and by our professional social work values, knowledge, and skills.

A Christian perspective is not always totally unique or different in every respect from what another perspective might offer, but it always informs and critiques these perspectives. An example from social work is the NASW Code of Ethics. Even some Christian social workers may be laboring under the impression that it is from the Devil, or something of the sort. Far from it. Anyone who has this impression should take a closer look at the Code of Ethics. There is no principle in the Code that a Christian cannot strongly affirm. In fact, I would argue that a Christian worldview is quite compatible with the social work Code of Ethics, and in fact is the soil out of which much of the Code has sprung (Sherwood, 2000, 2002).

As we have discussed before, one of the core social work values in the Code is the inherent dignity and value of every person. Now, what in modernism or postmodernism gives such a value ground to stand on and to claim obligation over us? Not much. When push comes to shove, the inherent dignity and value of every person is pretty hard to sustain under assumptions of relativism, subjectivism, material determinism, and survival of the fittest.

At the same time that a Christian worldview upholds this core social work value, it also informs and critiques it. For example, a Christian perspective might say that individual freedom is not the only or necessarily always the highest value when legitimate values come into tension with each other in a given situation. The good of others and the community (deriving from both love and justice) has a powerful moral claim in every situation. Yet individual freedom tends to be granted privileged status in most social work ethical thinking. So, not all social workers, Christian or otherwise, will necessarily agree on how to prioritize legitimate values when they come into conflict with one another, which they inevitably do in complex cases. One of the admirable virtues of the current Code of Ethics is its clear recognition in the preamble and throughout that legitimate values ***do*** come into tension with one another in actual practice situations, that professional judgment will ***always*** be required to prioritize them, and that conscientious and competent professionals will ***not always*** be in agreement.

Furthermore (given the hermeneutical spiral), it must be remembered that other perspectives may inform and critique our Christian perspectives. Many contemporary Christians seem to need to be reminded, for example, that individual peace and prosperity do not necessarily rank high in the list of biblical virtues compared to sacrifice for the common good (Sherwood, 1999).

Seeing Through a Mirror Dimly: Real Values But Only a Limited, Distorted View

So, I believe in God as the ultimate source and authenticator of values. I believe that real values exist beyond myself. And I believe these values put us under real moral obligation. To believe otherwise, it seems to me, ultimately makes values and moral obligation empty shells, subjective and utilitarian, with no real life or content. It may be true that this is all values are, but I find it very hard to believe. Belief in a valueless world, or one with only "human" (that is to say, purely subjective) values, takes more faith for me than belief in God.

But (and this is very important) this understanding of values as having ultimate truth and deriving from God is a very far cry from believing that I fully comprehend these values and the specific moral obligations they put me under in the face of a particular moral dilemma when these values come into tension with one another and priorities have to be made. Much humility is required here, an appropriate balance. At any given moment, my (or your) understanding of these values and what our moral obligations are is very limited and distorted. In fact our understandings are in many ways subjective, culturally relative, and bounded by the interpretive "language" available to us. And any particular place where I can stand to view a complex reality at best only yields a partial view of the whole. Remember the story of the blind men and the elephant ("It's like a snake," "It's like a wall," "It's like a tree").

We can see, but only dimly. God has given us light but we will only be able to see completely when we meet God face to face (I Corinthians 13:8-13). In the meantime we are on a journey. We are pilgrims, but we are not wandering alone and without guidance. We see through a mirror dimly, but there is something to see. There is a garden beyond the window.

> Love never ends. But as for prophecies, they will come to an end; as for tongues, they will cease; as for knowledge, it will come to an end. For we know only in part, and we prophesy only in part; but when the complete comes, the partial will come to an end. When I was a child, I spoke like a child, I thought like a child, I reasoned like a child; when I became an adult, I put an end to childish ways. For now we see in a mirror, dimly, but then we will see face to face. Now I know only in part; then I will know fully, even as I have been fully known. And now faith, hope, love abide, these three; and the greatest of these is love. (I Corinthians 13:8-13)

Now we have received not the spirit of the world, but the Spirit that is from God, so that we may understand the gifts bestowed on us by God. And we speak of these things in words not taught by human wisdom but taught by the Spirit, interpreting spiritual things to those who are spiritual. Those who are unspiritual do not receive the gifts of God's Spirit, for they are foolishness to them, and they are not able to understand them because they are spiritually discerned. Those who are spiritual discern all things, but they are themselves subject to no one else's scrutiny. "For who has known the mind of the Lord so as to instruct him?" But we have the mind of Christ. (I Corinthians 2:12-16)

Now the Lord is the Spirit, and where the Spirit of the Lord is, there is freedom. And all of us, with unveiled faces, seeing the glory of the Lord as though reflected in a mirror, are being transformed into the same image from one degree of glory to another; for this comes from the Lord, the Spirit. (II Corinthians 3:17-18)

References

Gewirth, A. (1978). *Reason and morality*. Chicago: University of Chicago Press.

Homes, A. (1984). *Ethics: Approaching moral decisions*. Downers Grove, IL: InterVarsity Press.

Lebacqz, K. (1986). *Six theories of justice: Perspectives from philosophical and theological ethics*. Minneapolis, MN: Augsburg Publishing House.

Lewis, C. S. (1947). *The abolition of man*. New York: Macmillan Publishing Company.

Lewis, C. S. (1948). *Mere Christianity*. New York: Macmillan Publishing Company.

Malz, W. (1989). Counterpoints: Intergenerational sexual experience or child sexual abuse. *Journal of Sex Education and Therapy, 15*, 13-15.

Middleton, J. R. & Walsh, B. J. (1995). *Truth is stranger than it used to be: Biblical faith in a post-modern age*. Downers Grove, IL: InterVarsity Press.

Mott, S. (1982). *Biblical ethics and social change*. New York: Oxford University Press.

Nelson, J. A. (1989). Intergenerational sexual contact: A continuum model of participants and experiences. *Journal of Sex Education and Therapy*, 15, 3-12.

Osborne, G. R. (1991). *The hermeneutical spiral: A comprehensive introduction to biblical interpretation*. Downers Grove, IL: InterVarsity Press.

Reamer, F. (1990). *Ethical dilemmas in social service*. 2nd Ed. New York: Columbia University Press.

Sherwood, D. A. (1993). Doing the right thing: Ethical practice in contemporary society. *Social Work & Christianity, 20*(2), 140-159.

Sherwood, D. A. (1999). Integrating Christian faith and social work: Reflections of a social work educator. *Social Work & Christianity, 26*(1), 1-8.

Sherwood, D. A. (2000). Pluralism, tolerance, and respect for diversity: Engaging our deepest differences within the bond of civility. *Social Work & Christianity, 27*(1), 1-7.

Sherwood, D. A. (2002). Ethical integration of faith and social work practice: Evangelism. *Social Work & Christianity, 29*(1), 1-12.

Trueblood, D. E. (1963). *General philosophy*. New York: Harper and Row.

Trueblood, D. E. (1957). *Philosophy of religion*. New York: Harper and Row.

Wolterstorff, N. (1983). *When justice and peace embrace*. Grand Rapids, MI: Eerdmans Publishing Company.

Wood, W. J. (1998). *Epistemology: Becoming intellectually virtuous*. Downers Grove, IL: InterVarsity Press.

CHAPTER 3

CALLING: A SPIRITUALITY MODEL FOR SOCIAL WORK PRACTICE

Beryl Hugen

In making a career choice, many Christian students find the social work profession a good fit with their religious faith. Or at least at first glance it appears so. For example, as part of the application process for the social work program I teach in, students are asked to explain why they have chosen social work as a major. What motivates them to enter this field of study? Some answer the question by relating past experiences with social work services or role models who were social workers, but almost all describe a moderate or fairly strong religious impulse to serve people and society.

Many specifically relate their faith to their choice of social work—stating something like this: In being loved by God, they in turn wish to share some of this love with those who are poor or hurting or are in need of help of some kind. Some of these students believe that to be a Christian in social work they must work in an agency under religious auspices, whereas others plan to work in programs that do not have a specific religious base or affiliation, but are part of the larger community of governmental social welfare responses to those in need. Despite these differences, almost all are interested in finding ways to integrate their faith and their newly chosen field of study.

But it doesn't take long in their social work studies for these students to begin to recognize the complex tensions between their religious faith, agency auspices, and the secular values of the social work profession. This discovery is not surprising; social work is, after all, a secular profession. At times, students find the profession very critical of religion, even suspicious of anyone who claims to have religious motives for helping others.

This feeling is understandable, for in the last forty to fifty years, the social work profession has simply ignored religious insights and accepted the principle of separating the sacred and secular. Religion came to be seen as having no particular insight to offer or relevance for everyday professional practice. Because of this attitude, the recent professional literature does not offer much help to students in thinking through the relationship of religious faith and professional practice. It is ironic that social work, which claims as its unique focus the "whole person" in the whole environment, has for so long neglected the religious dimension of life.

Not only do students continue to come to the profession with religious motivations, but the roots of social work are largely grounded in religious faith (Devine, 1939). Social work originated and came of age under the inspiration of the Judeo-Christian traditions and the philanthropic and service motivation of religious people. As Leiby (1985) indicates, the Christian biblical command to love God and to love one's neighbor as oneself was directly translated into a sense of moral responsibility for social service. As the social work profession secularized in the 20th century, these earlier religious rationales and models for service were replaced by doctrines of natural rights, utilitarianism, and humanistic ideology.

Dealing with human need apart from religious motives and methods is actually a very recent development in the history of charity and philanthropy. The notion of a secular profession focused on responding to human suffering would have struck many of our professional ancestors as quite inconsistent and confusing. Many of them were religiously motivated and expressed their faith by means of social work as a vocation, a calling from God to serve their brothers and sisters who were in need. With their perception of social work as a calling, a vocation, they formalized a link between their religious faith and social work practice.

What is meant by viewing social work as a calling? Several recent articles have addressed this "old fashioned" concept of calling or vocation, sensing its power and value for current social work practice (Gustafson,1982; Reamer, 1992). However, these writers essentially have attempted to take the religious concept of calling and use it in a secular fashion. They have done so in order to provide a moral purpose for the profession—to counteract what they perceive to be the focus on self-interest inherent in the social work profession which has become increasingly professionalized, specialized and bureaucratic.

My intent in this chapter is to explain, or more accurately to reintroduce, the religious model of calling as used by Christian social workers, past and present, in linking Christian faith and professional social work practice. Both its attractiveness and shortcomings as a model will be addressed. My purpose is not only to help social workers and the profession understand or correct misunderstandings related to this model, but also help social workers better understand the broader issues related to the spirituality of social work practice, in that other religious models and spiritual traditions address many of the same integration of faith and practice questions. Also, reintroducing the model of calling will lead us to see the significance of how the perspectives and writings of our religiously motivated social work ancestors—of which there are many—can contribute to the profession's current discussions regarding spirituality and social work practice.

Religion, Faith, and Spirituality

Before discussing the model of calling, it is helpful to define what is meant by the terms spirituality, religion, belief and faith. The profession has long struggled with this definitional dilemma. The dilemma has focused on how to reintroduce religious or spiritual concerns into a profession which has expanded beyond specific sectarian settings and ideologies to now include diverse sources of knowledge, values and skills, and how to respond to the needs of a much more spiritually diverse clientele. Addressing this dilemma, Siporin (1985) and Brower (1984) advocated for an understanding of spirituality that includes a wide diversity of religious and non-religious expressions, with such an inclusive understanding of spirituality encouraging social workers to reflect upon their clients both within and outside of particular institutional religious settings and ideologies.

From this beginning, Canda (1988a, 1988b) further developed a concept of spirituality for social work that incorporates insights from diverse religious and philosophical perspectives. He identifies three content components to spirituality—values, beliefs and practice issues—"all serving the central dynamic of a person's search for a sense of meaning and purpose, developed in the context of interdependent relationships between self, other people, the nonhuman world, and the ground of being itself" (Canda, 1988a, p. 43).

In the same vein, the work of James Fowler, known more for his model of faith development, is particularly instructive. Fowler (1981) states that to understand the "human quest for relation to transcendence," the key phenomenon to examine is not religion or belief but faith (p. 14). According to Fowler, who draws upon the ideas of religionist Wilfred Smith, *religions* are "cumulative traditions," which represent the expressions of faith of people in the past (p. 9). Included in a cumulative tradition are such elements as "texts of scripture, oral traditions, music, creeds, theologies," and so forth. *Belief* refers to "the holding of certain ideas" or "assent to a set of propositions" (p. 13). *Faith* differs from both religion and belief. Fowler describes faith as a commitment, "an alignment of the will...in accordance with a vision of transcendent value and power, one's ultimate concern" (p. 14). One commits oneself to that which is known or acknowledged and lives loyally, with life and character being shaped by that commitment. Defined in this way, faith is believed to be a universal feature of human living, recognizably similar everywhere, and in all major religious traditions.

What does faith consist of then? Fowler describes three components of what he calls the contents of faith. The first he terms *centers of value*, the "causes, concerns, or persons that consciously or unconsciously have the greatest worth to us." These are what we worship, things that "give our lives meaning" (p. 277). The second component of faith is described as our *images of power*, "the power with which we align ourselves to sustain us in the midst of life's contingencies" (p. 277): these powers need not necessarily be supernatural or transcendent. Finally, faith is comprised of "the *master stories* that we tell ourselves and by which we interpret and respond to the events that impinge upon our lives." Essentially, our master stories reveal what we believe to be the fundamental truths, "the central premises of [our] sense of life's meaning" (p. 277).

In discussing spirituality and faith, Fowler and Canda both emphasize its pervasive, all encompassing nature in an individual's life. Faith or spirituality is not a separate dimension of life or compartmentalized specialty, but rather an orientation of the total person. Accordingly, the three components of faith—centers of value, images of power, and master stories (Fowler, 1981)—and spirituality—values, beliefs, and practices (Canda, 1988)—exert "structuring power" in our lives, shaping our characters and actions in the world, including our work. Faith and spirituality are defined here as the essence of religion. Faith and spirituality take on a Christian religious meaning when the centers of value, images of power, and master stories of one's faith, the central dynamic of one's search for a sense of meaning and purpose, are grounded in the creeds, texts of scripture, and theology of the Christian tradition. I will attempt to present the Christian religious concept of calling within these more inclusive frameworks of spirituality and faith.

Calling in Action

Perhaps the best way to develop an understanding of the religious concept of calling is to start with an illustration. Robert Coles, in his book *The Call to Service* (1993), tells of a six year old black girl who initiated school desegregation in the South in the early 1960s. Tessie, a first grader, each day facing an angry and threatening mob, was escorted by federal marshals to school. The mob almost always greeted her with a litany of obscenities. Tessie's maternal grandmother, Martha, was the family member who usually got Tessie up and off to school each morning.

Coles reports that one day Tessie was reluctant to go to school—claiming to feeling tired, having slipped and fallen while playing in a nearby back yard, and having a difficult time with a current substitute teacher. Tessie suggested to her grandmother that she might stay home that day. Her grandmother replied that that would be fine if Tessie truly wasn't well, but if she was more discouraged than sick, that was quite another matter. She goes on to say:

> It's no picnic, child—I know that, Tessie—going to that school. Lord Almighty, if I could just go with you, and stop there in front of that building, and call all those people to my side, and read to them from the Bible, and tell them, remind them that He's up there, Jesus, watching over all of us—it don't matter who you are and what your skin color is. But I stay here, and you go—and your momma and your daddy, they have to leave the house so early in the morning that it's only Saturdays and Sundays that they see you before the sun hits the middle of its traveling for the day. So I'm not the one to tell you that you should go, because here I am, and I'll be watching television and eating or cleaning things up while you're walking by those folks. But I'll tell you, you're doing them a great favor; you're doing them a service, a big service.
>
> You see, my child, you have to help the good Lord with His world! He puts us here—and He calls us to help Him out. You belong in that McDonogh School, and there will be a day when everyone knows that, even those poor folks—Lord, I pray for them!—those poor, poor folks who are out there shouting their heads off at you. You're one of the Lord's people; He's put His Hand on you. He's given a call to you, a call to service—in His name! There's all those people out there on the street. (p. 3-4)

Later Coles questions Tessie whether she understood what her grandmother meant by "how you should be of service to those people out there on the street." She replied:

> If you just keep your eyes on what you're supposed to be doing, then you'll get there—to where you want to go. The marshals say, 'Don't look at them; just walk with your head up high, and you're looking straight ahead.' My granny says that there's God, He's looking too, and I should remember that it's a help to Him to do this, what I'm doing; and if you serve Him, then that's important. So I keep trying. (p. 4-5)

The heart of what Tessie had learned was that for her, service meant serving, and not only on behalf of those she knew and liked or wanted to like. Service meant an alliance with the Lord Himself for the benefit of people who were obviously unfriendly. Service was not an avocation or something done to fulfill a psychological need, not even an action that would earn her any great reward. She had connected a moment in her life with a larger ideal, and in so doing had learned to regard herself as a servant, as a person called to serve. It was a rationale for a life, a pronouncement with enormous moral and emotional significance for Tessie and her grandmother. This call was nurtured by the larger black community, her pastor, family, and the biblical values of love and justice—the stories of exile and return, of suffering and redemption—the view of the powerful as suspect and the lowly as destined to sit close to God, in His Kingdom.

Coles himself recounts how ill-prepared professionally he was to understand this family and their sense of calling:

> I don't believe I could have understood Tessie and her family's capacity to live as they did, do as they did for so long, against such great odds, had I not begun to hear what *they* were saying and meaning, what *they* intended others to know about their reasons and values—as opposed to the motivations and reactions and "mechanisms of defense" *I* attributed to them. Not that there wasn't much to be learned by a psychoanalytic approach. Tessie and her companions, like human beings everywhere (including those who study or treat other human beings), most certainly did demonstrate fearfulness and anxiety; she also tried to subdue those developments by not acknowledging them, for instance, or by belittling their significance. Mostly, though, she clung hard to a way of thinking in which she was *not* a victim, *not* in need of "help" but someone picked by fate to live out the Christian tradition in her life. "I'm trying to think of the way Jesus would want me to think," she told me one evening. When I asked how she thought Jesus wanted her to think, she replied, "I guess of others, and not myself, I'm here to help the others." (p. 26)

Calling: The Meaning of Work

For some Christians, like Tessie and her grandmother, connecting one's work to the divine intentions for human life gives another dimension to the meaning and purpose of one's work and life. Certainly adequate pay, financial stability, social status and a sense of personal fulfillment remain significant criteria in choosing a career, but they are not the central motivation. The central motivation is the means by which one's Christian religious tradition has tied one's work and faith together, this concept of vocation, or calling.

Martin Luther originally formulated the notion of vocation or calling largely in reaction to the prevailing attitude toward work in medieval society. Medieval thinkers devalued work. They believed that in and of itself, work had little or no spiritual significance. They held, like the Greeks earlier, to the idea that the highest form of life, the form in which humans can realize their noblest potential, is the contemplative life of the mind. By thinking, we liken ourselves to God. Work was thus a hindrance to an individual's relation to God, which could be cultivated only in the leisure of contemplation. Because peasant serfs did most of the work in medieval society, and because the earthly character of their occupations prevented them from participating directly in the religious life, they received grace through the church by means of the sacraments.

Not only the life of productive work, but also the practical or active life, consisting of doing good to one's neighbor, was viewed by many medievals as an impediment to the true goals of the religious life. The activity given precedence was always the contemplative life. An early church father, St. Augustine (1950) wrote: "the obligations of charity make us undertake virtuous activity, but if no one lays this burden upon us, we should give ourselves over in leisure to study and contemplation" (p. 19). The need for the active or charitable life was temporary, whereas contemplation of God was eternal.

Luther's concept of vocation or calling fits neatly within the compass of this thought since he draws a basic theological distinction between the kingdom of heaven and the kingdom of earth. To the kingdom of heaven belongs our relationship to God, which is to be based on faith; to the kingdom of earth belongs our relationship to our neighbor, which is to be based on love. A vocation, properly speaking, is the call to love my neighbor that comes to me through the duties attached to my social place or *station* within the earthly kingdom. A station in this life may be a matter of paid employment, but it need not be. Luther's idea of station is wide enough to include being a wife or a husband, a mother or a father, a judge or politician, as well as a baker, truck driver, farmer or social worker. Thus, the call to love one's neighbor goes out to all in general. All of these callings represent specific and concrete ways of serving my neighbor, as I am commanded to do by God Himself.

What do we accomplish when we discharge the duties of our stations in life, when we heed the call of God to serve our neighbor in our daily tasks? Luther believed the order of stations in the kingdom of earth has been instituted by God Himself as His way of seeing to it that the needs of humanity are met on a day-by-day basis. Through the human pursuit of vocations across the array of earthly stations, the hungry are fed, the naked are clothed, the sick are healed, the ignorant are enlightened, and the weak are protected. That is, by working we actually participate in God's providence for the human race. Through our work, people are brought under His providential care. Far from being of little or no account, work is charged with religious significance. As we pray each morning for our daily bread, people are already busy at work in the bakeries.

Luther conceived of work as a way of serving others. He never recommended it as either the road to self-fulfillment or a tool for self-aggrandizement. We, of course, find it natural to assess the attractiveness of a particular job on the basis of what it can do for us. But Luther saw quite clearly that work will always involve a degree of self-sacrifice for the sake of others, just as Christ sacrificed himself for the sake of others.

During the time of Luther, and for many centuries preceding him, people thought of human society to be stable, static, and as incapable of change, as the order of nature itself. Shortly after Luther's time, however, European civilization underwent a dramatic transformation under the combined influence of a rapidly expanding market economy, accelerated urbanization, technological innovation, and vast political reorganization. In the face of these astounding changes on all fronts of social life, people soon saw that the structure of human society is itself in part a product of human activity, changeable and affected by sin. Once people recognized this fact, it became clear, in turn, that to the degree human activity is motivated by sinful desires and worldly ambitions, the society thus produced is also likely to be structurally unsound and in need of reform. For example, an economy based upon greed and a government based on the arbitrary use of power stand in just as much need of repentance as the individuals who are a part of them. For this reason, other reformers insisted that not only the human heart, but also human society must be reformed in accordance with the Word of God. The emergent vision of the Christian life at the dawn of modern social work practice, then, required not only that people obey God in their callings, but that the callings themselves be aligned with the will of God.

Calling Within Social Work

Although historically there have been many models of spirituality in social work, the calling model perhaps has been the most prominent, or at least the most extensively referred to in the social work literature. In fact, in the very early years, it was the dominant model. This dominance is certainly related to the fact that Protestantism was the dominant religious form at the time. Many early social workers in their writings refer to the relationship of their spirituality and social work within this calling model. Their response is not surprising, since many of them grew up in devoted religious families, many had theological training, and still others were very active as lay people in their churches. All found in their spiritual experiences something which gave impetus, meaning, and value to their work of service.

The following examples illustrate the prominence of the calling model and how it has been articulated and practiced by a variety of different leaders within the profession.

Edward Devine, a leader in the Charity Organization Society and the first director of one of the first schools of social work, records in his book *When Social Work Was Young* (1939) the early experiences in social work education and summarizes these experiences as follows:

> The real start towards the professional education of social workers as such was made in 1898, when the Society launched its summer school of philanthropy with thirty students enrolled. For several years this summer school gathered from all parts of the country a substantial number of promising candidates, and a brilliant corps of instructors, who for one day, or sometimes for an entire week, expounded and discussed the fundamentals of the slowly emerging profession. Jane Addams, Mary Richmond, Zilpha Smith, Mrs. Glendower Evans, Graham Taylor, Jeffrey Brackett, John M. Glenn, Mary Willcox Brown, before and also after she became Mrs. John M. Glenn, James B. Reynolds, Mary Simkhovitch—a full roster of the lecturers in the school would be like a list of the notables in the National Conference of Social Work. Certainly no religious gathering could have a deeper consecration to that ideal of learning how to do justly, and to love mercy, and to walk humbly, which Micah described as being all that is required of us. (p. 125-6)

He ends the book by stating that in his opinion the spirit of social work finds its power, value, and purpose from the biblical Sermon on the Mount.

Richard Cabot (1927) addressed the model of calling more specifically in an article entitled "The Inter-Relation of Social Work and the Spiritual Life." He writes:

> religion is the consciousness of a world purpose to which we are allied...when I speak of the purpose being a personality, I speak of the person of God of whom we are children... I think it makes absolutely all the difference in social work to know this fact of our alliance with forces greater than ourselves. If a person wants to find himself and be somebody he has got to find his particular place in the universal plan. In social work, we are trying to help people find themselves, find their places

> and enjoy them. The chief end of man is to glorify God and to enjoy Him forever. (p. 212)

Cabot also articulated several spiritual powers applicable to social work practice that come to those who hold this faith: courage, humility and the ability to stand by people. He goes on to explain that the goal of social work is to:

> ...maintain and to improve the channels of understanding both within each person and between persons, and through these channels to favor the entrance of God's powers for the benefit of the individuals....
> Unblocking channels is what social workers do. The sort of unblocking that I have in mind is that between capital and labor, between races, or between the members of a family who think they hate each other....
> Spiritual diagnosis, I suppose, means nothing more than the glimpse of the central purpose of the person, unique and related to the total parts of the world. Spiritual treatment, I suppose, is the attempt to open channels, the channels I have been speaking of, so as to favor the working of the world purpose. In this way social workers participate in the providence of God. (p. 215-16)

Perhaps the most prominent example of the power and dominance of the calling model is illustrated in Owen R. Lovejoy's presidential address to the National Conference of Social Work in 1920, entitled "The Faith of a Social Worker." In the speech he attempts to draw upon the foundations of faith of the members in order to aid in their approach to discussions during the Conference and to help create a real basis for unity. He begins by first disclaiming any intention of committing the Conference to any specific creed of social service. His desire, rather, is to discover "some of the those underlying principles which bind people together."

He states that all social workers have a philosophy of life, a faith, a "basic enthusiasm," and those who act on this faith can choose to:

> regard this as a sacred ministry and claim their commission as the ancient prophet claimed his when he said: "The Lord hath anointed me to preach good tidings to the meek, to bind up the broken hearted, to proclaim liberty to the captives, the opening of prison to them that are bound, to give a garland for ashes, the oil of joy for mourning, the garment of praise for the spirit of heaviness." Certainly this is not a slight task to which we are called, but the expression of a joyful faith carried with cheer-

> fulness to those in the world most in need of it...a field of service based on the conviction that men are warranted in working for something corresponding to a divine order "on earth as it is in heaven. (p. 209)

He warns those "who look upon the visible institutions connected with their religion as the essential embodiment of faith," recognizing such a sectarian position frequently leads to imposing one's own values on others and proselytizing—similar issues we face today. He ends the address stating that the secret of their usefulness as social workers is found in the following litany.

> God is a Father,
> Man is a brother,
> Life is a mission and not a career;
> Dominion is service,
> Its scepter is gladness,
> The least is the greatest,
> Saving is dying,
> Giving is living,
> Life is eternal and love is its crown. (p. 211)

It is difficult to imagine an address on such a topic being given today. Such was the significance of spirituality and the calling model in the social work profession at that time.

The calling model's chief apologist, however, was Ernest Johnson, a prolific writer and interpreter of Protestant religion and the social work profession. His writings detail the principles which he hoped would govern efforts to bring Protestantism to bear through the social work profession in meeting human needs. Recognizing that Protestantism had a majority position and influence in the culture, he strongly advocated, with some exceptions, for a pattern of social work based on the calling model. The result was to minimize the operation and control of agencies and social welfare enterprises by churches or religious groups and maximize Protestant participation in non-sectarian agencies.

Later in life he recognized that Protestantism, particularly when its pre-eminent position was beginning to wane, would never obtain complete cultural dominance or create an approximation to the ideal of a Christian society—the Corpus Christianum. The result, he lamented, would be only a partial transformation of the culture—and regrettably, a partial accommodation on the part of Protestantism to the culture. But despite this limitation, he still believed the Protestant pattern or model of influencing social work enterprises and social movements "indirectly" (through the means of one's calling or vocation) was essentially sound. Johnson (1946) states:

> It [the calling model] affords the most effective channel through which our churches, in the midst of a religiously heterogeneous population, can bring to bear their testimony through community endeavor and make their impact on a secular culture. This means, however, a recovery of the sense of lay Christian vocation, which has been so largely lost. The major Protestant contribution to social work can be made, I believe, through the consciously Christian activities of persons engaged in non-sectarian enterprises and movements. In the existing situation in America a revival of a sectarian, possessive attitude toward social work would be definitely reactionary....
>
> In a word, then, we need to devise our social strategy in the light of our Protestant history, with its emphasis on freedom, and in the light of our cultural situation, which puts a premium on vocational work as Christian testimony. We can make our best contribution without seeking to enhance Protestant prestige, seeking rather to influence contemporary life and to meet human need through the activities of those whose lives have been kindled at our altars and nourished in our fellowship. (p. 2-4)

As Johnson relates, the calling model has not always functioned as intended. Already in 1893, one leader of the new social work profession, responding to the widening gap between religion and the emerging influence of scientific models in social work, characterized social work as "a revolutionary turning of thought in our society from a religious service to God to a secular service to humanity" (Huntington, 1893). Along this line of thought, Protestant theologian Reinhold Niebuhr (1932) grappled with the practical consequences of the calling model for social work. With three-fourths of social workers then functioning under secular auspices, many had become "inclined to disregard religion." This development he regarded as a significant loss for social work—"destroying or remaining oblivious to powerful resources and losing the insights religion provided in keeping wholesome attitudes toward individuals" and "preserving the sanity and health in the social worker's own outlook upon life" (p. 9). He believed social workers needed, therefore, a renewed sense of vocation or calling. In addition, this loss of calling partially contributes to what church historian Martin Marty (1980) later referred to as "godless social service," or the migration (privatization) of faith or spirituality from social work.

Conclusion

Because of our distance from the thoughts and assumptions of our predecessors in social work and perhaps from the language of spirituality itself, efforts regarding such historical reflections as these may seem awkward and archaic. The goal is not, however, to recreate the past, but rather to identify the models of spirituality that guided our social work ancestors and then to find ways to translate and apply the spirit of these models to our present situation.

This model of calling offers significant insight into current discussions relating spirituality and professional social work practice. Within this calling model, religious faith is not the private possession of an individual, but is grounded in tradition and divine revelation, permeating the whole of life, connecting public and private spheres, and linking the individual with the community. The model also places professional techniques and methods in the context of larger goals and values that give life meaning and purpose for both clients and practitioners.

Historically, religiously motivated persons and groups found their faith propelling them into actions of concern for others, especially the poor and the vulnerable in society. These social workers have affirmed in a variety of ways their shared belief that the faith dimension of life leads to a transcendence of individualism, and to a commitment to others—to social work practice motivated by a calling to a life of service.

The model presented is helpful to social workers from the Christian faith tradition, but also to others who seek to acquire a better understanding of the meaning and effects of spirituality in their own and their clients' lives. A social worker's own cultivation of spirituality is a crucial preparation for the competent application of knowledge and skills in practice. The model is particularly helpful in taking into account the distinctive values, sources of power and master stories of one particular religious and cultural tradition, Christianity—represented by many persons like Tessie and her grandmother whom social workers daily encounter in practice, as well as by many social workers themselves.

Although the model does not resolve the tensions and conflicts which exist between the Christian spiritual tradition and the current largely secular profession, it does provide a beginning framework for integrating Christian spirituality and social work at both the personal and professional levels. The profession's roots are significantly tied to this particular model of spiritual/professional integration, and many social workers as well as clients continue to define their lives, personally and professionally, in the context of this Christian-based spiritual call to service. The Christian values of love, justice, and kindness; its stories related to the poor, the vulnerable, and those of liberation from oppression; and its emphasis on self-sacrifice, are the "passion of the old time social workers" that many find attractive and wish to bring back—albeit in a form more adaptable to a more diverse clientele and changed environment (Constable, 1983; Gustafson, 1982; Reamer, 1992; Siporin, 1982, 1985; Specht & Courtney, 1994).

References

Augustine, St. (1950). *City of God*. XIX, 19, New York: Modern Library.

Brower, I. (1984). *The 4th ear of the spiritual-sensitive social worker*. Ph.D. diss., Union for Experimenting Colleges and Universities.

Cabot, R. C. (1927). The inter-relation of social work and the spiritual life. *The Family*, 8(7), 211-217.

Canda, E. R. (1988a). Conceptualizing spirituality for social work: Insights from diverse perspectives. *Social Thought*, Winter, 30-46.

Canda, E. R. (1988b). Spirituality, religious diversity and social work practice. *Social Casework*, April, 238-247.

Coles, R. (1993). *The call of service*. New York: Houghton Mifflin Company.

Constable, R. (1983). Religion, values and social work practice. *Social Thought*, 9, 29-41.

Devine, E. T. (1939). *When social work was young*. New York: Macmillan Company.

Fowler, J. W. (1981). *Stages of faith*. San Francisco: Harper and Row.

Gustafson, J. M. (1982). Professions as "callings." *Social Service Review*, December, 105-515.

Huntington, J. (1893). Philanthropy and morality. In Addams, J. (Ed.), *Philanthropy and social progress*, New York: Crowell.

Johnson, E. F. (1946). The pattern and philosophy of protestant social work. *Church Conference of Social Work*, Buffalo, New York.

Leiby, J. (1985). Moral foundations of social welfare and social work: A historical view. *Social Work*, 30(4), 323-330.

Lovejoy, O. R. (1920). The faith of a social worker. *The Survey*, May, 208-211.

Marty, M. E. (1980). Social service: Godly and godless. *Social Service Review*, 54, 463-481.

Niebuhr, R. (1932). *The contribution of religion to social work*. New York: Columbia University Press.

Reamer, F. G. (1992). Social work and the public good: Calling or career? In Reid, N. P. & P. R. Popple (Eds.), *The moral purposes of social work*, (11-33), Chicago: Nelson-Hall.

Specht, H. & Courtney, M. (1994). *Unfaithful angels*. New York: The Free Press.

Siporin, M. (1982). Moral philosophy in social work today. *Social Service Review*, December, 516-538.

Siporin, M. (1985). Current social work perspectives on clinical practice. *Clinical Social Work Journal*, 13, 198-217.

CHAPTER 4

BATTLE BETWEEN SIN AND LOVE IN SOCIAL WORK HISTORY

Katherine Amato-von Hemert
Editorial Assistance, Anisa Cottrell

Is it heresy to discuss "sin" and "love" in the context of social work? Many social workers believe it is. This chapter, however, argues that it is impossible to understand the history of social work without understanding the pivotal roles that attitudes toward sin and love played in the founding institutions, actors and actions of American social work. Religiously-trained leaders dominated the pioneer decades of social work (Leiby, 1984). American social work is indebted to two social movements which straddled the launch of the twentieth century: the Charity Organization Society (COS) movement and the Social Settlement movement. Religious ideas influenced both threads of historical social work. The COS writings regarding human nature tend to emphasize the role of sin and the need to cultivate morally uplifting habits to combat it. Late nineteenth and early twentieth century Protestantism struggled with the influence of Calvinist Puritanism. Among the most liberal of these Puritans were the Unitarians, who counted among their members social leaders Josephine Shaw Lowell and Joseph Tuckerman. Social Settlement movement writings tended to emphasize the role of love in human relations and focus on the goal of creating an ideal community. Early twentieth century Protestant social gospel theology influenced many Settlement leaders, such as Graham Taylor and Robert Woods. The social work techniques that emerged from both movements are, in revised form, still apparent in contemporary social work. The COS legacy includes the individual-focused work of casework and clinical practice. The Settlement tradition spawned community organizing and group work. Social work technologies from both traditions grew from particular theologies.

The differences and conflicts between the Christian theologies of these two foundational social work movements will be discussed. The Puritan-based theology and the social gospel-based theologies are examined. These beliefs are explicitly and implicitly revealed in the documents written by social activists of the late nineteenth century and early twentieth century. In the 1930's, Protestant social critic and theologian Reinhold Niebuhr critiqued social work. His insights synthesize the schism between the love-based and sin-based competing visions of social work. Listen to the voices of those early social workers who sought to cure personal and social "ills." References to sin, love and justice are unmistakable in them.

Why are these issues relevant to social workers now? They are important because these same divergent understandings of human nature and of God's action in the world operate in the language that modern day social workers use to discuss social problems and to justify practice and policy decisions. By elucidating the theological concepts of "sin" and "love" as held by some of the diverse mothers and fathers of our profession, we can understand better how these same concepts affect our work as social workers today.

Sin

The idea of sin is relevant to the dispute between the Charity Organization Society movement and the Social Settlement movement because one of the hallmark differences between these groups' perspectives arose from their divergent beliefs about sin.

Charity Organization Society Perspective on Sin

The concept of "sin" has been defined in many ways. Sin can be conceptualized as individual, willful acts that are contrary to the will of God. It can also be viewed as a general state of alienation from God. This later perspective focuses less on human action and more on the human state of being. Many of the more liberal COS movement leaders were influenced by a form of Puritan theology which rejected the Calvinist doctrine of predestination.[1] This doctrine of predestination maintained that all people are sinful and thereby bring Divine wrath upon themselves. Some people are saved, not through their own merit but through God's love and mercy. In this way of thinking, everyone "deserves" damnation and salvation occurs through God's mercy. Adamantly against the idea that one can attain salvation through works, "works righteous", adherents of this doctrine believed that a person's eternal fate was sealed with Adam's fall. Viewing sinfulness as an ingrained and intractable personality trait logically results from these beliefs. Many charity leaders, however, felt that people could improve their situation, both on earth and in life after death. Their belief, called "Arminianism," originated during the Protestant Reformation as a reaction to the Calvinist doctrines of original sin and predestination. By embracing Arminianism, COS leaders affirmed the belief that people, regardless of their environment, could improve their situation, build their character, and work toward salvation through reforming their life.

The sin-related issue for these COS leaders included three significant features — attitudes toward character, attitudes toward salvation and particular images of poverty. Charity Organization leadership believed that people were born morally neutral; they were intrinsically neither good nor bad. They were born with the capacity to shape their own character and thus had a moral obligation to self-improvement. These Puritans trained their attention on habits and disposition. They believed bad habits enslaved the sinner to his/her vices, while good habits protected him/her against temptations. "Once a sinner had started down the path of bad habits, it was nearly impossible for him to return to the path of rectitude." This moral philosophy maintained an implicit tendency "to classify people as 'good' or 'bad'" (Howe, 1988, p. 111). At the same time, consistent with earlier forms of Puritanism, these leaders "judged men on the basis of their disposition rather than their deeds, their character rather than their individual acts. Character was hard to develop and not easy to change" (Howe, 1988, p. 111). Thus, the issue of salvation was of paramount importance. Unlike predestinarian theology, Arminianism contended that individuals had the freedom to work out their own salvation (Howe, 1988, p. 68). The conscience was autonomous and therefore needed to be trained to regulate the passions. Self-mastery was the aim of these training efforts.

Sin consisted in a breakdown of internal harmony, an abdication by the higher faculties of their dominion over the lower. No longer was sinfulness considered inherent in the human condition; instead, it was an abnormal state of disorder, 'the abuse of a noble nature.' Sin represented a failure to regulate impulses that were not in themselves evil (Howe, 1988, p. 60-61). Individuals were charged with the responsibility to foster good habits to protect against sinfulness and to exonerate themselves for sinful actions.

The prevalent attitudes toward poverty of this time were derived from widespread beliefs about the human person and about salvation. Most nineteenth century Americans believed that poverty was the result of sinfulness or laziness. Poverty was viewed as either an act of God's punishment, or as a result of the individual's disposition or habits. The goal of charity was to teach the poor morally uplifting habits which would cause them to love and seek virtue. Tuckerman maintained, "the best resources for improving the condition of the poor are *within themselves*, they often need enlightenment respecting these resources more than alms." Regardless of whether poverty was punishment for sinfulness or the result of the individual's propensities, "the conditions of poverty could lead to sin" so Christians were obligated to help the poor improve their economic condition (Howe, 1988, p. 240).[2]

"Charity was intended to reform and uplift the poor, not merely to mitigate their sufferings" (Howe, 1988, p. 239). Indiscriminate almsgiving was considered dangerous because alms were believed to "encourage indolence and wastefulness." Rationally disciplined educational approaches were "intended to be judicious and discriminating, designed to get to the root of problems" (Howe, 1988, p. 240). These perspectives on the individual, sin and poverty resulted in a moralistic charity.

The COS theology of sin provides additional insight into the expectations and hopes of the charity programs designed to serve the poor. Giving to the poor person "a friend, not alms" makes sense when it is understood in the context of the belief that individuals needed to foster good habits to stave off sinfulness and to learn the love of virtue. Good habits could be taught within the relationship nurtured between a "friendly visitor" and an impoverished person. The assumption that poverty in some way resulted from sin leads reasonably to the conclusion that the development of virtue would eradicate poverty. This reading of the COS is not especially novel. What is of greater importance is consideration of its long term implications — the COS legacy.

Mary Richmond articulated the theory of social casework within the context of this COS theology.[3] Social casework placed particular importance on service to the individual, on social investigation and on the caseworker-client relationship.[4] All of these techniques assumed that sin plays a pivotal role in human nature. The priority attention given to the individual derived from the COS leaders' Arminian beliefs. Cultivating self-improvement was necessary because salvation resulted from individual effort. Social investigation was the practice of interviewing neighbors, family members and employers of potential service recipients in order to generate a detailed profile of need. This derived both from the rationalism of the theology as well as from the expectation that individuals in need may not necessarily be truthful about the specifics of their situation. One of the staunchest arguments on behalf of organizing the charity societies into COS's was the belief that fraud was rampant and duplication of requests for assistance could be reduced by greater communication among charity organizations.

Finally, the healing relationship between caseworker and client derived from the expectation that moral uplift is best achieved at close quarters. Accountability played an important role in this relationship and was therefore as much an opportunity for the caseworker to monitor and point out client's "bad habits" as well as for the client to learn good ones. These techniques, influenced by an understanding of the individual as a sinful being, have been passed down to contemporary social work (with modifications of course). Social casework's emphasis on service to the individual now holds a dominant position in current clinical social work practice. Its assumptions regarding human nature warrant closer attention; they may illuminate the current debates in the profession between those who seek to assist individuals psychotherapeutically versus those who engage in social reform. This line of inquiry may lead to additional insights when applied to the Social Settlement theology as well. Social Settlement leaders rejected many of these assumptions and created alternative institutions aimed to address social conditions of poverty. As in the case of the COS leaders, Settlement leaders had theological reasons for doing so. Contrary to the COS leaders, these Settlement advocates were more compelled by a theology focused on love rather than on one based on sin. This does not mean, however, that the Settlement leaders held no opinion on sin. The Social Settlement perspective on sin is just more difficult to tease out from within the overall love-focused sensibility.

Social Settlement Movement Perspective on Sin

The social gospel movement was an American religious phenomenon prominent during the early decades of the twentieth century. It aimed to move society toward a vision of justice; toward the incarnation of the "kingdom of God" on earth. Its adherents focused more on societal reform and less on individual salvation. Social work practice which was influenced by social gospel theology acknowledged the existence of sin but viewed it as embedded within social relations which were subject to political, social and/or economic reform. A person who might have been seen by the COS leaders as "sinful" or in need of character reform was seen through the lens of the social gospel as a person at the mercy of an unjust, sinful society. The social environment caused people to receive fewer choices or to make unwise decisions. It is difficult to find explicit references to sin among Social Settlement writings and social gospel writings regarding social work. This theology's concern centered on issues of love; God's love for humanity, and our consequent love for one another. The individual was understood to be primarily defined by the social group (family, neighborhood, church or synagogue, industrial organization, etc.).

The most explicit shift in theological focus can be seen in the writings of the Anglican couple, Henrietta and Samuel Barnett. Prior to founding England's Toynbee Hall, the Barnetts were active in organized charity efforts. They became disenchanted and critical of the literal, evangelical appeals associated with the Charity Organization Societies. In 1882 Henrietta criticized the COS's "materialist" reification of sin and hell and charged that, "religion has been degraded by these teachers until it is difficult to gain the people's ears to hear it" (Barnett, 1895a, p. 91). Within two years, her critique of the COS orientation included stronger appeals to the role love must play in charity and from then on, discussion of love received greater emphasis than attention to sin in all her writings. Her concern shifted to those charity workers who "fear the devil more than they love God; or, in other words, they fear to do harm more than they love to do good" and she claimed "personally, I doubt if anything but love for God will mean social reform" (Barnett, 1895b, p. 213, 219).

Graham Taylor, the founder of the Chicago Commons, a 100 year old social settlement house, is representative of the Social Settlement pioneers. In his first book, *Religion in Social Action* (1913), Taylor referred to sin fewer than one dozen times. If sin was an important dimension of Taylor's understanding of human character, his chapter, "Personality: A Social Product and Force," would refer to it. It does not. This omission is suggestive. In commenting upon the changes in Christian thought of the time, he noted that "the individual and the race are coming to be more inseparable in our consciousness of both sin and salvation" (Taylor, 1913, p. 97). Sin was viewed not as a feature of an individual's character or destiny but as a consequence of environmental influences. Salvation's goal "is more closely brought to bear upon turning the self from sin" (Taylor, 1913, p. 91) in order to retain focus upon the promise of the Kingdom on earth. Sin was seen primarily as evil events spawned by evil circumstance.[5] This emphasis on the social leads to the assertion that "more and more men need to be convicted of and turned away from their social, industrial, and political sins, in order to be made conscious of and penitent for their personal sins" (Taylor, 1913, p. 100).

Walter Rauschenbusch, "the acknowledged professorial leader" of the social gospel movement (Marty, 1986, p. 288), spoke of those whom social workers serve as peoples who "have gone astray like lost sheep" (Rauschenbusch, 1912, p. 30). These are not people with sinful natures, they are people who have merely stepped off the path of righteousness. He spoke of the sacrifice and suffering intrinsic to social work's service to humanity with reference to the crucifixion of Jesus, claiming, "without the shedding of blood in some form there has never been cessation of sin" (Rauschenbusch, 1912, p. 27). Above all, Rauschenbusch focused on the redemptive task and nature of social work. A measure of the close linkage between social work and social religion at the beginning of this century comes from this text which to late twentieth century ears is quite shocking: "Social workers are in the direct line of apostolic succession. Like the Son of Man they seek and save the lost" (Rauschenbusch, 1912, p. 12). This pattern is consistent throughout the social gospel social work literature. The primary focus is on the social nature of individual life and whatever minimal references to sin that exist are located within this type of context. The concept of "social sin," as reflected in Taylor's statement above, fleetingly appears occasionally, though it is not fully developed. Conceptualizing sin was less important to the development of the Social Settlement movement. Social Settlement leaders emphasized love; something that the COS leaders did to a much lesser degree.

Love

It is also helpful to explore the contrasting perspectives on love found in writings from Charity Organization Society leaders with those found among Social Settlement movement leaders. COS leaders tended to view love as a remedy for evil while Social Settlement leaders discussed love in terms of both its personal expression and social necessity.

Charity Organization Society Perspective on Love

In 1890, Charles Stewart Loch reflected on the first twenty years of England's Charity Organization Society movement. He claimed, the "new movement," was vigorously dedicated to serve the best interests of the State, the stability of which was threatened by the existence of pauperism. "The new charity does not seek material ends, but to create a better social and individual life" (Loch, 1892, p. 6). Of the three forces at work in the new movement—a stronger sense of citizenship, a renewed commitment to remind the rich of their community obligations and a deepening religious consciousness—discussion of the need for a change in religious consciousness took precedence. Loch argued,

> Yet [religious communities'] efforts to improve the general conditions of the life of the poor were often but *feeble and transient*. Their charity was *not allied to any wider conception of citizenship*. It was too often, perhaps, the hopeless push and protest of the saint against the evils of a hopeless world, where he had no abiding place; and then, *if zeal grew cold, it found a sufficient expression in a charity from which love had evaporated, and which was no better than the payment of a toll on the high road of life* (Loch, 1892, p. 7-8, emphasis added).

Loch criticized the instability of emotionally motivated charity. Charity motivated by mere sentiment, he claimed, is isolated from the larger concerns of "citizenship," undependable because "transient," and when its religious passion "grows cold," it is merely the scattering of coins among bystanders. The COS intent, therefore, was to improve upon such efforts by creating scientifically based systems of moral support which express commitment to a higher order of love. This love is a disciplined one. It demands development of virtuous habits. "The social life implies discipline. This may spring from habits grown almost instinctively and handed down from the past like heirlooms. . . .Or the discipline may be newly imposed in order to brace the individual, or the family, or the nation, to a new endeavor" (Loch, 1904, p. 190).

The love that motivated the COS enterprise assumed that moral defect among the poor had to be uplifted. Reverend D.O. Kellogg, an advocate of "scientific charity" and organizing charity societies, addressed this issue in the *Journal of the American Social Science Association* in 1880.

> Defective classes are not a social evil; but pauperism is, and it is a sign of moral weakness. The weak and depressed, and *all the victims of unsocial habits, need to be awakened to a proper love of approbation from their fellow men, to have their hearts kindled* to a sympathetic glow by neighborliness and respect; to be quickened to hope by examples among their associates of courage, versatility and self-reliance; to see a world of pleasure and honor opened to them in the companionship of the refined and the pure-souled. *To these add suitable industrial training; but without the other this will be of small avail.* (Kellogg, 1880, p.89, emphasis added)

"Industrial training" without moral regeneration was considered ineffective. Love's primary implications are personal rather than social. The "victims of unsocial habits" needed to learn or re-learn *love of virtue*. Kellogg was not interested in the charity worker's expression of love, or in charity as such, as an expression of love. Love may have motivated charitable action but it was primarily a redemptive ideal. As such, it entailed certain demands. These lead Kellogg to envision a relationship between love and science.

In Kellogg's view, the practice of charity must be scientific, not only to achieve greater effectiveness but because it is required by "the law of love" which is its originating impulse.

> Charity has its laws which can only be detected by a study of past experience. It is, therefore, a science—the science of social therapeutics. Again, as art is the application of science, *it follows that there can be no true art of charity until its laws are*

> *formulated.* Until this is done, benevolence is not much else but quackery, however amiable its motive. Indeed *the true impulse of love cannot rest until it has found its science;* for it cannot stop short of effective methods and sound principles. (Kellogg, 1880, p. 86, emphasis added)

Love in this perspective, motivated not the particular practice of a single or collective group of charity workers—love was an ideal which required articulation and organization. It was concerned with issues that can be discovered and formulated as law.

Social Settlement Movement Perspective on Love

A review of settlement leaders' writings reveals liberal use of a theologically influenced language of love.[6] Graham Taylor and Jane Addams are illustrative.[7] Taylor's first book, *Religion in Social Action* (1913), (for which Addams wrote the Introduction), reflects the influence of the social gospel thinkers of the time. Taylor spoke publicly and in print of his "social work" in explicitly theological terms throughout his career. In a 1908 review of the Social Settlement movement Cole stated, "Professor Graham Taylor defines a settlement as a 'Group of Christian people who choose to live where they seem most needed, for the purpose of being all they can to the people with whom they identify themselves, and for all whose interests they will do what they can'" (Cole, 1908, p. 3). After citing a second definition[8] which did not use religious language, Cole concluded that:

> In both of these definitions, brief as they are, the underlying spirit and purpose [of the Social Settlement movement] are emphasized. The spirit is one which may be shared by many who do not call themselves Christians. *It is a spirit of adventurous friendship which the Gospel of Christ has made familiar to the world. From this has arisen the purpose which may be described in a word as service through sharing.* Whatever the social worker may have in character, attainment, or experience, he draws upon in meeting the needs of the less fortunate" with whom he has contact (Cole, 1908, p. 3, emphasis added).

In the late 1930's Taylor spoke of a settlement house colleague as a "shepherdess of sheep without a fold, serving the one flock of the one Shepherd" who when she took "up the arms of *love* and *persuasion,* of *service* and *sacrifice*, she was moved by her *reverence for the sanctity and worth* of every human life, which *her religion told her was created in the image of God and capable of being restored to that image by grace* divine"

(Taylor, 1937, p. x, emphasis added). The language of love, grace and sanctity of human life is the context in which the term "service" must be understood. This language is the most consistent thread found among Taylor's major works (Taylor, 1931; Taylor, 1936; Wade, 1964).

Jane Addams, the reformer most often associated with the Social Settlement movement, told the stories of Hull House's visitors to ever larger audiences as her platform became an international one. Even though religious language is less prominent in her work, Addams made clear her motivation and aim with reference to the words of "the Hebrew prophet [who] made three requirements from those who would join the great forward moving procession led by Jehovah. 'To love mercy' and at the same time 'to do justly'..." (Addams, 1967, p. 69-70). The difficulty of this is great. Addams' solution was to advocate the prophet's third requirement, 'to walk humbly with God,' which may mean to walk for many dreary miles beside the lowliest of His creatures, not even in that peace of mind which the company of the humble is popularly supposed to afford, but rather with the pangs and throes to which the poor human understanding is subjected whenever it attempts to comprehend the meaning of life (Addams, 1967, p. 70).

Creating a place that enabled the poor to mingle with the affluent so that individuals may share their common burdens was one of Addams' primary aims. Interestingly, her writings reveal virtual total silence on the question of individualistic sin or evil. (This is not uncommon among Settlement leaders as demonstrated previously). For Social Settlement leaders, love entailed a socially structured way of being. It was not an antidote to evil.

Sin, Love, and Justice

Eminent social critic and theologian Reinhold Niebuhr's work on sin, love and justice as they relate to social work offers a way to bridge the schism between historic social work's emphasis on individual (sin-based) approaches and social (love-based) approaches. In 1928-29 Niebuhr gave a series of six lectures to social workers at the Columbia University School of Social Work. The book that anthologizes these pieces, *The Contribution of Religion to Social Work* (1932), bridges the sin-based theology which motivated the Puritan-oriented social reformers and the love-based social gospel oriented activists. In his lectures, Niebuhr challenged social work to rise above sentimentality, claiming, "social work, in its acceptance of philanthropy as a substitute for real social justice, and for all its scientific pretensions, does not rise very much higher than most sentimental religious generosity" (Niebuhr, 1932, p. 82).

For Niebuhr, the tension between love and sin is complicated and illuminated by his overarching emphasis on social justice. Instead of focusing on either sin or love in an exclusive and individualistic way, Niebuhr urged social work to adopt a more balanced view of human nature and to use its unique position in the community to further the aims of social reform.

> The fact that *social workers so frequently fail to think beyond the present social and economic system, and confine their activities to the task of making human relations more sufferable within terms of an unjust social order, places them in the same category as the religious philanthropists* whose lack of imagination in this respect we have previously deplored. *A great deal of social effort, which prides itself upon its scientific achievements and regards religious philanthropy with ill-concealed contempt, is really very unscientific in its acceptance of given social conditions* (p. 80, emphasis added).

Niebuhr chastised social work for its piecemeal approach to socially embedded injustice. He believed this approach inevitably resulted from a misguided sentiment of love. Niebuhr charged that social work, "...builds a few houses for the poor, but does not recognize that an adequate housing scheme for the poor can never be initiated within the limits of private enterprise. Every modern society must come, even if slowly, to the recognition that only a state, armed with the right of eminent domain and able to borrow money at low interest rates, can secure ground and build such houses for the poor as they can afford to buy or rent" (*Contribution*, p. 80-81). Therefore he urged upon social work a realist approach to human nature which would issue in advocacy for social justice.

The question of justice is what launched Niebuhr's theology of love. Niebuhr considered love both in personal and social terms, though discussion of love's social implications predominate. Niebuhr's perspective on love is not Romantic. Indeed, his concern for the dangers or potential problems that arise from love dominates his treatment of the concept. This is perhaps the single most important contribution Niebuhr offered social work thought. For Niebuhr, several particular dangers inhere with the conventional philosophies of love. Of primary relevance to social work is the danger of sentimentality. Niebuhr's cautionary remarks to social work in *Contribution* derive from his years of experience ministering in a Detroit parish and working in numerous left-wing political struggles. He worked with social workers both in Detroit as well as after he wrote *Contribution*, when he was professor of social ethics in New York City (Brown, 1992; Phillips, 1957).

Niebuhr underscores four major dangers regarding love. First, romanticized love can quickly degenerate into sentimentality as referred to previously. This theme figures prominently in Niebuhr's critique of liberalism. An additional feature of this critique is that liberalism discredits the transcendent nature of love. Diminishing the province of love as known through relationship with God, eclipses the realistic sin/love paradox. Love expressed in human relational terms alone disguises the realities of sin because of its "blindness," and because it unduly inflates human capacity. A third danger of a sentimentalized conception of love is that it seduces people into self-righteousness and pride. Niebuhr illustrates this feature of love through extended commentary on the hypocrisies of philanthropy, wherein the selfish can convince themselves of their unselfishness by "giving of their superfluity." Finally, the Christian love ideal is always in danger of betraying its ethical imperative by sinking into social conservatism. In this case, the inherent perfectionism of idealized love restricts critical analysis of political and economic conditions because it potentially tarnishes the ability to express positive emotional responses.[9] It therefore maintains existing unjust economic and power distributions. All of these snares are embedded in the conflictual relation between love and justice, and he believed, commanded additional attention by the social work profession. These ideas were pivotal in the belief systems of the pioneers of social work.

Niebuhr made several recommendations for social workers related to the dangers of sentimentality. First, the unstable, transient nature of the sympathy which motivates a benevolent vocation should be connected with a vision of an ultimate value. Second, the "shrewder insights" of a religion, which understands the human personality to be paradoxically God-like yet finite, can defend against the sentimentality that an idealistic or personalized view of love fosters. Finally, he recommended that the Christian ideal of perfect love is "probably too high for the attainment of any nation" or any group, because groups will not sacrifice themselves to serve the interests of another group. Niebuhr concluded therefore, that groups should aspire to justice rather than to love. Implicitly, this suggests to social workers that they, even though motivated by sympathy, ought to seek justice rather than the impossible specter of an ideal self-sacrificing love.

Niebuhr speaks at length in *Contribution* and elsewhere of the dangers of sentimentality. But is sentimentality dangerous in social work? Three observations of social work trends confirms Niebuhr's hypothesis that sentimentality deteriorates and is therefore problematic for social work. The first observation is that the dual social work tradition from the COS and the Social Settlement movements are not equally represented in current social work practice. The individual-focused practices from the COS movement dominate the profession as evidenced by the debates regarding the "legitimacy" of private practice and the fact that the majority of current National Association of Social Work members do direct practice. Policy advocacy and groupwork, inherited from the Social Settlement pioneers, play minor roles in contemporary social work practice. Secondly, this narrowed focus has also privatized social work practice and its community roles. Social work roles in public welfare agencies are diminishing in all but management positions as incidence of private clinical social work is rising. The profession, rather than taking prominent roles in community advocacy, tends to look inward.

Niebuhr also recommended that social work subordinate its vocational aim to an ultimate ideal. Is this necessary? The risk of *not* having an ultimate guiding principle, implied by Niebuhr, is that an emotional and privatized motivation is not sturdy enough for the profession to weather expectable storms in its contact with the depths of human misery and social injustice. The decades of debate the profession has carried on regarding its identity, mission and values evidence analogous concern. Although the profession has grown (in size and sophistication) through these years of debate, no "ultimate value" has been settled upon. Social work's emotion-based motivation has survived. The problem is also that the debates over identity, mission and values all assume the same fundamentally sentimental presuppositions. Human beings are good. Period. They are finite and capable of great good; due to nature, nurture or some combination. When evil is encountered, the desire to, in language of the Social Settlement tradition, "turn the stray sheep back to the path," becomes the priority, and debate regarding the profession's aim resolves into debate about relative effectiveness of competing technique.[10] In addition, the field's tenacious defense of a principle of self-determination is seemingly due to the inability of the profession to articulate a secularized equivalent "doctrine of sin" to hold in tension with its generous estimation of human possibilities. This necessarily cursory review suggests that the act of debating professional identity may in fact lead the profession away from its intent to articulate its ultimate value, because it is predisposed to an image of human nature that is imbalanced.

Niebuhr's Critique of Social Work: A Useful Prescription for the Profession?

Niebuhr's theological conception of love is useful to illuminate and critique social work's tradition. *Contribution* was written during the historic period when the social work profession was seeking to synthesize its dual traditions. Niebuhr critiqued both theologies which were at the basis of each strand in the tradition—the COS's and the Settlement's. The outcome in the profession was the adoption of the practice from the COS tradition and the philosophy of the Social Settlement movement. This hybrid, while in theory would hold in tension the two conflicting theologies of which each is a product, in practice has given rise to interminable and seemingly irresolvable debate regarding the profession's mission, membership and values.[11] Given the overly positive estimation of human nature and the lack of agreement on an "ultimate" value to serve, the profession remains a conglomeration of factions. Unlike the Social Settlement workers who valued their role as "interpreters" of social conditions, current social workers tend to be embroiled in internal, professional disputes.

How might Niebuhr's insights assist? One resolution comes from paying closer attention to the historical moment in which *Contribution* appeared. As presented above, the theological differences between the COS and Settlement movements up into the post-W.W.I. period can be broadly construed as a conflict between an emphasis on sin and an emphasis on love. According to Niebuhr, sin is inevitable and love is "impossible." Given the tendency in social work to privilege one or the other, and the incumbent problems with this, something is needed to hold these two in fruitful tension. Drawing upon Niebuhr's recommendation, can *justice* serve this mediating function?

Niebuhr's realist approach to the individual in society holds in tension the "paradoxes of religion" (Niebuhr, 1932, p. 67). The primary paradox is the Christian insight that the human is both made in the image of God and is a sinner.

> This emphasis upon the sinfulness of man has been just as strong, in classical religion, as the emphasis upon his Godlikeness. It has *saved religion, at its best, from the sentimentality into which modern culture has fallen since the romantic period,* with its reaction to dogma of man's total depravity by its absurd insistence upon the natural goodness of man. The *real religious spirit has no illusions about human nature. It knows the heart of man to be sinful. It is therefore not subject to the cynical disillusion into which sentimentality degenerates when it comes into contact with the disappointing facts of human history* (p. 66, emphasis added).

From this perspective Niebuhr criticized both the classical or orthodox excessive attentiveness to human's sinful nature and the modern or liberal denial of sin. He chastised the likes of the charity organizers by indicting their moralism as counterproductive. Their excessive focus on the individual created blindness to the injustices of social conditions. He chastised the likes of the Settlement workers as hopelessly sentimental and therefore easily disillusioned and embittered. Consequently, Niebuhr urged upon the orthodox a greater measure of the loving forgiveness which the liberals prize as well as attention to social conditions; and he urged the liberals to greater mindfulness of the realities of sin. Proponents of both theologies easily succumb to self-righteousness. The orthodox charity worker who busily goes about the business of saving others' souls can easily forget the limitations of their own. The liberal who blithely confesses the sins of their group, from which they feel emancipated, is easily seduced by "the temptation to be humble and proud at the same time" (Niebuhr, 1957b, p. 120). Niebuhr commended to social work a moderate position which both acknowledges the realities of sin and posits human goodness while maintaining in tension the interaction between the individual and the group. Absent this, social conditions are not subject to critique, so reform of the structural causes of impoverishment and injustice is not possible. In sum, he cautioned social work to guard against the sentimentalism found among modern liberal religionists.

How might this critique and recommendation inform the understanding of historical social work? The pioneers of both the COS and the Settlement House movement represent poles along the continuum between "Sin" and "Love". In their attempts to eradicate human sinfulness and express divine love, respectively, they succumbed to the temptation to ignore the larger questions of social justice. By bridging the gap between love and sin with a strong critique of those who ignore social injustice, Niebuhr avoided the pitfalls of both extremes and oriented the discussion away from individual sin or love and toward the action of the whole. Contemporary social work would do well to follow his lead.

Notes

1 Examples include Josephine Shaw Lowell and Joseph Tuckerman. See (Howe, 1988). These Unitarians were among the theological liberals of their day. They rejected the more conservative evangelical "revivalists." Tuckerman believed, for example, that "a Calvinist preacher who went into the slums teaching predestination and depravity did more harm than good" (Howe, 1988, p. 242). Both Calvinist Puritans and Unitarian Puritans were active in public life. Most relevant to social work's tradition is the Unitarian theology, however, it co-existed in a society still very much influenced by Calvinism and undoubtedly in practice reflected these influences (Cole, 1954).

2 The city itself was also seen as fostering the conditions of sinfulness that led to pauperism. See Paine's 1893 text, "Pauperism in Great Cities: Its Four Chief Causes" for additional detail (Paine, 1964).

3 She followed Josephine Shaw Lowell's work quite closely.

4 Richmond uses the term "client" as early as 1917 in her classic text, *Social Diagnosis* (Richmond, 1917).

5 Taylor offers the text of a letter from a pastor who works on the streets as an example of the impossibility of saving an individual if sinful environments are left untouched. "'Dear Pastor, In the first place, when we try to help a fallen brother, the odds against us are too great. Last night I believe that man was in earnest. When he said, 'I am tired of sin,' he meant it....He went out from God's house, away from those commissioned to do his work. Where could he go but out into the cold, friendless streets of a great city? Then what? ....he was to shun the dram shop. He did this. He passed by seven, with the struggle which God only knows. The door of the eighth stood open. It did look warm and comfortable within. So he finally went in... Where could I have taken him? Cannot something be done to lessen these odds, to even things up, to give the Lord a fair show with a man who wants to be saved?'" (Taylor, (1913), p. 26).

6 For an excellent review of the general role the social gospel played in the social settlement movement see: (Carson, 1990).

7 Taylor is known to current social work students as the founder of the Chicago Commons settlement and the initiator of the social work courses that became institutionalized as the University of Chicago's School of Social Services Administration predecessor institution, the Chicago School of Civics and Philanthropy. Less known is the fact that Taylor was an ordained Protestant minister who accepted his teaching position at the Chicago Theological Seminary on the condition that he be allowed to set up a settlement house.

8 The second definition is offered by Ada Woolfolk.

9 One of Niebuhr's illustrations of this is of a good liberal minister in a Kentucky coal mining town who sided against the miners in a labor dispute on the grounds that strikes, because they were assertive, were contrary to Biblical love (Niebuhr, 1957a).

10 Ehrenreich makes this case regarding social work between 1920 and 1945; see: (Ehrenreich, 1985).

11 The inclusion of "membership" points to the mid-century debates regarding bachelor degree trained social workers and the earlier debates regarding volunteers and graduate-school trained social workers. See: (Popple, 1983). Specifics regarding the values debate fall beyond the scope of this study. For good summaries, see (Abbott, 1988; Berlin, 1990; Biestek, 1967; Faver, 1986; Gordon, 1965; Heineman, 1981; NASW, 1967; Reid & Popple, 1992; Timms, 1983; Weick, 1991).

References

Abbott, A. A. (1988). *Professional choices: Values at work*. National Association of Social Workers, Inc.

Addams, J. (1967). *Democracy and social ethics* (1902). New York: Macmillan Co.

Barnett, H. R. (1895a). Passionless reformers (1882). In S. A. Barnett & H. R. Barnett (Eds.), *Practicable socialism: Essays on social reform*. London: Longmans, Green & Co.

Barnett, H. R. (1895b). What has the Charity Organization Society to do with social reform? (1884). In S. A. Barnett & H. R. Barnett (Eds.), *Practicable socialism*. London: Longmans, Green & Co.

Berlin, S. B. (1990). Dichotomous and complex thinking. *Social Service Review*, 64(1), 64- 59.

Biestek, F. P. (1967). Problems in identifying social work values. In NASW (Eds.), *Values in social work: A re-examination*. Silver Spring, MD: National Association of Social Workers.

Brown, C. C. (1992). *Niebuhr and his age: Reinhold Niebuhr's prophetic role in the twentieth century*. Philadelphia: Trinity Press International.

Carson, M. J. (1990). *Settlement folk: Social thought and the American settlement movement 1885-1930*. Chicago: University of Chicago Press.

Cole, C. C. (1954). *The social ideals of the northern evangelists 1826-1860*. New York: Columbia University.

Cole, W. I. (1908). *Motives and results of the social settlement movement: Notes on an exhibit installed in the Social Museum of Harvard University*. Cambridge: Harvard University.

Ehrenreich, J. H. (1985). *The altruistic imagination: A history of social work and social policy in the United States*. Ithaca, NY: Cornell University Press.

Faver, C. A. (1986). Religion, research, and social work. *Social Thought*, *12*(3), 20-29.

Gordon, W. E. (1965). Knowledge and value: Their distinction and relationship in clarifying social work practice. *Social Work, 10*(3), 32-39.

Heineman, M. B. (1981). The obsolete scientific imperative in social work research. *Social Service Review, 55*(3), 371-396.

Howe, D. W. (1988). *The Unitarian conscience: Harvard moral philosophy 1805-1861*. Middletown, CT: Wesleyan University Press.

Kellogg, D. O., Rev. (1880). The principle and advantage of association in charities. *Journal of Social Science, XII*, 84-90.

Leiby, J. (1984). Charity Organization Reconsidered. *Social Service Review*, (December), 523-538.

Loch, C. S. (1904). If citizens be friends. In C. S. Loch (Ed.), *Methods of social advance: Short studies in social practice by various authors*. London: Macmillan and Company Limited.

Loch, S. C. S. (1892). *Charity organization* (2nd ed.). London: S. Sonnenschein & Co.

Marty, M. E. (1986). Modern American religion: The irony of it all 1893-1919. Chicago: The University of Chicago Press.

NASW (Ed.). (1967). *Values in social work: A re-examination*. Silver Spring, MD: National Association of Social Workers.

Niebuhr, R. (1932). *The contribution of religion to social work*. New York: Columbia University.

Niebuhr, R. (1957a). Religion and class war in Kentucky (1932). In D. B. Robertson (Ed.), *Love and Justice: Selections from the Shorter Writings of Reinhold Niebuhr*. Louisville, KY: Westminster/John Knox Press.

Niebuhr, R. (1957b). The confession of a tired radical (1928). In D. B. Robertson (Ed.), *Love and Justice: Selections from the Shorter Writings of Reinhold Niebuhr*. Louisville, KY: Westminster/John Knox Press.

Phillips, H. B. (1957). *The reminiscences of Reinhold Niebuhr [Microfilmed interview transcripts]*. New York: Oral History Research Office Columbia University.

Popple, P. R. (1983). Contexts of practice. In A. Rosenblatt & D. Waldfogel (Eds.), *Handbook of clinical social work*. San Francisco: Jossey-Bass.

Rauschenbusch, W. (1912). *Unto me*. Boston: The Pilgrim Press.

Reid, P. N., & Popple, P. R. (Eds.). (1992). *The moral purposes of social work: The character and intentions of a profession*. Chicago: Nelson-Hall.

Richmond, M. E. (1917). *Social diagnosis*. New York: Russell Sage Foundation.

Taylor, G. (1913). *Religion in social action*. New York: Dodd, Mead and Co.

Taylor, G. (1931). *Pioneering on social frontiers*. Chicago: University of Chicago Press.

Taylor, G. (1936). *Chicago Commons through forty years*. Chicago: Chicago Commons Association.

Taylor, G. (1937). Introduction: Mary McDowell—Citizen. In C. M. Hill (Ed.), *Mary McDowell and municipal housekeeping*. Chicago: Chicago Council of Social Agencies.

Timms, N. (1983). *Social work values: An enquiry*. London: Routledge & Kegan Paul.

Wade, L. C. (1964). *Graham Taylor: Pioneer for social justice, 1851-1938*. Chicago: University of Chicago Press.

Weick, A. (1991). The place of science in social work. *Journal of Sociology and Social Welfare, 18*(4), 13-34.

CHAPTER 5

GOOD NEWS FOR THE POOR: CHRISTIAN INFLUENCES ON SOCIAL WELFARE

Mary Anne Poe

For the United States of America, the wealthiest and most powerful country in the world, the question of what to do about the poor in our midst is a haunting question. How do the poor impact our economy and political system—our freedom and well-being—our rights and privileges? How does American prosperity affect the poor? The United States has to address the problem because of concern for the very ideals that are American. It also has to address the problem because widespread poverty leads inevitably to social unrest.

For Christians, the question of what to do about the poor raises even more critical concerns. How does God want the poor to be treated? What does the Bible say? What is our responsibility as individuals and as part of the church to our poor neighbors? How should Christians try to influence the political and economic systems?

Social welfare programs and policies are a response to questions that arise in each generation. Why should we care about the poor? How do we determine who deserves help and who does not? Should we attempt to change individual hearts or change social structures in order to alleviate poverty? Who is responsible for the poor? Programs and policies always reflect our values about the nature of poor people and our responsibility to them. What we do as a society about poverty, what programs and policies we develop, depends on how we answer these questions.

Like music in a symphony, there have been themes that recur in the relationship between programs and policies that serve the poor and the belief systems that inform them. The political, economic, and social context gives shape to particular programs and policies that emphasize specific beliefs that vary in different historic periods. Political, economic, and social conditions interact with belief systems in unpredictable ways at various times to influence views of poverty (Dobelstein, 1986). This chapter highlights some of those themes as they have been experienced through history and how Christian faith and practice have intersected with the public arena to address needs.

Biblical Principles Regarding the Poor

The Bible records God's revelation to people and how humans have responded to God. The biblical record, taken as a whole, supports specific principles about what it means to be human and how humans should relate to God, to other people, and to the environment. Some of the fundamental premises in the biblical record set the stage for social welfare history. These basic premises have been described in more detail by others (Keith-Lucas, 1989; Sider, 1999), but generally include the following:

- Humans are created beings designed for relationship with others. They are interdependent.
- God is concerned for justice and right relationships among people.
- In these relationships humans can do great good or great harm.
- Humans have the ability and responsibility to choose, perhaps not their particular life circumstances, but how they will respond to their life circumstances.
- Humans have value and dignity.
- Work is a natural part of human nature and contributes to one's sense of worth and dignity.
- The ability to create wealth is a gift.
- Material and environmental resources should be shared. They do not "belong" to any one person or group. Stewardship is the human responsibility to share resources fairly.
- God has a special concern for those who are disadvantaged.

The earliest biblical records reveal distinctive guidelines for the care of the poor. The guidelines are shaped by the covenant relationship of a people with their God who represented love and justice. If God is Creator, then all human life should be treated with respect and care. This is a way to honor God. The guidelines apply not only to individuals and families, but also to the larger community and society.

The ancient Hebrew idea of charity, *tsedekah*, is directly related to the concept of justice (Morris, 1986). The helper benefited from the act of charity as well as the one receiving help. It was a reciprocal benefit that balanced relationships between people. In the Scriptures, God specified the need for interdependent relationships and charity was an aspect of this. The prophet Micah summed up this principle by stating, "He has showed you, O people, what is good. And what does the Lord require of you? To act justly and to love mercy and to walk humbly with your God" (Micah 6:8). God intended that society benefit by sharing resources among all its members in a just and equitable way.

The Old Testament law specified how the community should provide care and to whom. God's people were supposed to be hospitable to strangers and foreigners (Exodus 22:21; Hebrews 13:2). The Sabbath and Jubilee years restored property and maintained a more equitable distribution of resources (Leviticus 25; Exodus 21: 1-11; Deuteronomy 15: 12-18). Those with wealth were supposed to leave grains in the fields for the poor (Leviticus 19: 9-10). Communities and families cared for widows and orphans (Deuteronomy 14: 28-29; 26:12). They were to offer kind treatment to slaves and debtors and provide a means for them to gain their freedom (Deuteronomy 15). Lenders were to make loans without charging interest (Exodus 22: 25; Deuteronomy 15: 1-11).

God is known for avenging the mistreatment of the weak (Psalm 9:8, 12, 16; 10: 17-18). The prophets railed against the people and nations that failed to behave mercifully and justly with the poor. They voiced words of judgment when the laws were ignored (Isaiah 59: 15; Ezekiel 34: 1-6; Amos 4: 1-3; Amos 5: 21-24; Zechariah 7: 8-14; Malachi 3:5). Those who could work were expected to do so, but the laws were aimed at the community and required the kind of compassion toward the poor that God himself had demonstrated. God's word strongly asserts that God is just and wants people to behave in a just and caring way toward one another, and especially toward the weak (Sider, 1999).

The New Testament added a new and more challenging idea to the care of the poor. Jesus' life serves as a model for all to follow. The four Gospels record the behavior of Jesus toward those who were disenfranchised. The message to those who will hear it is to "follow Jesus," do what Jesus did. Jesus asked his followers to love others as he loved. The reason to care about the poor is not simply the reciprocal benefit of charity or obedience to the Old Testament laws, but one's commitment to God. One cares about others, especially the poor, not because it brings benefit but because that person in need is made in the image of God: "Whatever you do for one of the least of these, you did for me" (Matthew 25:40).

The New Testament also proclaims God's concern for justice. Jesus announced his mission in his first public message in the synagogue in Nazareth. He read from the prophet Isaiah,

> The Spirit of the Lord is on me, because he has anointed me to preach good news to the poor. He has sent me to proclaim freedom for the prisoners and recovery of sight for the blind, to release the oppressed, to proclaim the year of the Lord's favor (Luke 4:18-19).

His ministry was characterized by attention to the weak and helpless and oppressed. The early church adopted the same standard of care so that "there was no poverty among them, because people who owned land or houses sold them and brought the money to the apostles to give to others in need" (Acts 4:34). The apostle James warned the church about unequal distribution of material resources (James 5: 1-6) and about prejudicial treatment based on one's social class (James 2: 1-17).

The Bible supports the value of work and the accompanying idea that one's ability to create wealth is a gift. Adam and Eve worked in the Garden even before their fall into sin. The story of Job shows that wealth can be transitory and is subject to God's control. Jesus himself worked as a carpenter. The apostle Paul admonishes believers to "settle down and get to work and earn your own living," and "whoever does not work should not eat" (II Thessalonians 3: 10-12).

Social Welfare History in Western Societies

Biblical principles about human relationships and God's will for humans have had a profound impact on social welfare history in the Western Hemisphere. The earliest records of church life reveal radical efforts to be sure that material and spiritual needs were met. The book of Acts states that material resources were shared in the community so that none were needy. The early church stressed the need to provide help to the poor even if some that were helped were not deserving of it. The church was a "haven of vital mutual aid within the pagan environment" (Troeltsch, 1960, p. 134).

The charity of the early church was formulated in small Christian communities that had little or no influence on the state in the early years under Roman rule. Christianity began with many, but not all, members from the poorer classes because most people were from these ranks (Stark, 1996). The aim was to show God's love. The church was not a political movement and thus not necessarily directed at prompting social reform.

The human tendency of those with sufficient means to try to distinguish the deserving from the undeserving emerged regularly and in contrast to the earliest biblical teachings. Some early Christian leaders responded to this human tendency toward judgment. Chrysostom of Antioch in the fourth century was a strong advocate for charity based on the need of the giver to share. He was concerned with the heart of the giver and the need for those who had sufficient means to share with those who did not. Gregory of Nanzianus believed that a lack of care for the poor was a greater sin than giving to the undeserving poor (Keith-Lucas, 1989). The tension between the idea of charity as a need of the giver's soul and charity to simply meet the needs of the poor has existed throughout social welfare history.

As Christianity spread through the Roman Empire and beyond, it began to exert more influence on political, economic, and social policies. Thus, by the time Constantine institutionalized Christianity as the "state" religion, biblical ideas of justice and charity held some political power. By the Middle Ages, the church and state were enmeshed with the church taking the lead role in the care of the poor as well as many other matters of political or economic interest. Over time the church's initial interest in showing God's care for the poor was overshadowed by interest in maintaining a seat of power in the political arena. After the Middle Ages, the church's power diminished. The Renaissance, the Industrial Revolution, the Enlightenment, and the Modern Era all had the effect of shifting political and economic power from the church to more secular entities. The locus of control for social welfare shifted as well.

Who Is Responsible for the Social Welfare?

A major theme through history has addressed the question of who is responsible for the poor. As Christianity developed and became more institutionalized, the social welfare system also developed. The church provided social services–not always with compassion or justice-but nevertheless motivated by biblical imperatives. It amassed an enormous amount of property after Constantine's rule and through the Middle Ages, some of which was to be used for the benefit of the poor. The bishop of each diocese was the patron for the poor (Troeltsch, 1960). Hospitals, hospices and sanctuary were typical services provided by the church for those who did not get aid through the feudal system (Keith-Lucas, 1989). Tithing was a prominent aspect of life in the church. Usually one-third of the tithe was designated for the care of the poor (Dolgoff, 1997). The giving of charity became a way to earn one's salvation.

The state was reluctant to assume responsibility for the poor early in western history. In England, The Statute of Labourers in 1349 was the first law enacted that gave government the responsibility. The value of work and a person's responsibility to provide for family dominated its formulation. The law's intent was less charitable than a means to control labor and the behaviors of poor people (Dolgoff, 1997). A series of Poor Laws followed the Statute of Labourers from its passage in 1349 to the mid-1800s. The shift had begun from church responsibility for the poor to government responsibility. Beginning with the Poor Laws, the state gradually accepted a role in oversight. The church and its biblical understandings, though, helped to shape the laws because the bishops sat in the House of Lords and government officials were drawn from the clergy. As government involvement increased, church acceptance of responsibility slowly abated (Popple and Leighninger, 1993). However, individual church members or clergy continued to provide leadership and personnel for the actual work of relief.

Social Control

The need for order has had great popularity during certain periods of time as a way to control the poor. Reasons and motives for helping the poor are numerous. On one extreme is the biblical imperative to love as God loved. Christian believers have Jesus as a model for how to care about the most marginalized and oppressed people. Biblical injunctions include doing justice, showing mercy, valuing every life regardless of circumstances, and personal responsibility and freedom to behave in a manner that contributes to the good of all. At the same time a reason for helping the poor developed out of a need to regulate the social and economic order, to encourage productive work and discourage dependency. The Poor Laws were, in part, designed to regulate labor and the migration of people from one community to another. Minimum wage laws and various tax laws are also a means to regulate poverty through control of the economic system (Piven & Cloward, 1971).

Reasons for helping the poor and efforts toward that end can begin with the best of intentions and after time become sidetracked. The poor can be hurt by the very efforts designed to help. Assistance given in the name of Christ but not in the spirit of Christ is perhaps capable of doing the greatest harm (Keith-Lucas, 1989; Perkins, 1993). Those who profess to help, yet are judgmental, patronizing, or cruel, do not reflect the manner of help prescribed by God. Some would argue that the emergence of state-operated "help" for the poor tended to shift the emphasis from one of charity as outlined by the model of Jesus to one of social control.

Personal Responsibility

During the period of the Protestant Reformation in the church, the culture changed from an agrarian one built on a communitarian spirit to an industrial society focused on individual rights and responsibility. Families were more isolated and less interdependent. Understanding of many biblical principles was shifting as well. Rather than the one Holy Catholic Church representing the biblical tradition and having authority to interpret biblical principles, the reform movement sanctioned individual responsibility to God for understanding and interpreting scripture and for how to live one's faith. Martin Luther, John Calvin, and the Anabaptists stressed personal salvation and church authority became less hierarchical. Anyone who had faith could relate to God and interpret the Bible. Though all Christian groups continued to give consideration to the poor, the emphasis on personal responsibility meant that the poor, too, were responsible to live holy lives. God would bless faithful believers (Keith-Lucas, 1989).

The reformers were outraged at the abuses of power perpetrated by the church. They decried the greed of the ecclesiastical establishment and sought to restore biblical concern for individual dignity and faith (Couture, 1991). The perspective on social welfare was also shifting. Biblical imperatives to show compassion and mercy had ebbed in relation to the need to urge the poor toward personal responsibility and labor. The "principle of less eligibility" established in the Poor Laws continued to ensure that those who labored would not have less material resources than those who received aid (Dolgoff, 1997, p. 61). Rigorous scrutiny and early means tests prevented those who were considered "undeserving" from enjoying the benefits of aid. The theology of the Protestant Reformation focused on personal salvation and holiness, challenged church authority as it had been practiced by Roman Catholics, and encouraged hard work and thriftiness. The Protestant work ethic became the standard applied to poor people and to social welfare programs.

The English Poor Laws crossed the Atlantic and shaped the social welfare system in the American colonies (Trattner, 1979; Axinn & Stern, 2001). Still, the Judeo-Christian tradition provided the philosophical basis for treatment of the poor (Hugen, 1998). Biblical principles, though often misconstrued in actual practice, remained the rationale for the system that existed. The biblical belief in the value of work and the responsibility to care for one's family became the dominant philosophical basis for almost all social welfare programs. Principles that were powerfully informed by the life and work of Jesus and the early church, however, were weakened by the traditions of church and society.

Personal Regeneration and Social Change

Two religious movements of the nineteenth century had particular influence on the administration of social welfare. The first of these was revivalism. The periods of the Great Awakenings stressed personal regeneration and holiness. Those transformed by the power of God were called to service in the world. The goal for the revivalist was dynamic Christian faith that would change society as a whole. George Whitefield and George Muller established orphanages. Jonathan Edwards advocated for American Indians who were being exploited by settlers. Many leaders of the abolitionist movement were products of revivals, including Harriet Beecher Stowe, John Woolman, and Charles

Finney (Cairns, 1986). Numerous social ministries emerged as a result of spiritual revivals. These included urban mission centers, abolitionist societies, the Salvation Army, the Young Men's Christian Association (YMCA), the Women's Christian Temperance Union (WCTU), and Volunteers of America (Timothy Smith, 1976; Maguson, 1977; Cairns, 1986). The revivals sparked concern for the spiritual salvation of souls and also for the overall welfare of society (Cairns, 1986; Poe, 2002).

The second religious trend affecting social welfare practices in the nineteenth century was the social gospel movement (Trattner, 1979). Theological liberalism of the nineteenth century was an attempt to make the Christian tradition congruent with the prevailing scientific naturalism of the day. Theologians like Walter Rauschenbusch and Washington Gladden articulated this theology for the academy. Charles Sheldon popularized it with his novel, *In His Steps*. Interestingly, a phrase from this book, "What would Jesus do?" re-emerged in evangelical Christian circles in the last decade of the twentieth century (Poe, 2002). The social gospel focused on building the kingdom of God on earth. It adopted the popular scientific methodologies of the day and hoped for social change based on humanitarian ideals rather than regenerate hearts.

This more liberal theology called into question long-standing "fundamentals" of the faith. The nature of Scripture and the doctrines of creation and Christology were subjected to scientific analysis. Liberal theologies minimized the supernatural aspects of faith while more conservative theologies emphasized them. The divergent theologies caused the two groups to disassociate from each other in their works of service in the world. Whereas liberal theologies contributed to the rise of the profession of social work and increased governmental oversight of social welfare (Wenocur & Reisch, 1989), conservative theologies focused on church growth, evangelism and the future kingdom of God, and distanced themselves from secular attempts to reform society by good works.

Philosophies dominant in the twentieth century in the United States—naturalism, materialism, and capitalism—do not necessarily reflect a Christian worldview that demands care for others because they are valued creations of God. These philosophies emphasize productivity, the value of work and wealth, and order in society. The profession of social work, though, espouses values of celebrating the worth and dignity of every person regardless of their circumstances. As David Sherwood asserts, it is only fair to ask of the profession "where did these values come from and what gives them moral authority?" (Sherwood, 1997, p. 122).

Social Casework and Social Reform

The growth of the profession of social work in the late nineteenth century illustrates another recurring dilemma. Can poverty be eliminated by helping one person at a time—the social casework method? Or is poverty best fought by social reform as reflected in the settlement house movement? Through history, both approaches have been used by church and state. The early church functioned as a community in which no one had need (Acts 4:32-34). The Great Awakenings of the nineteenth century resulted in organized efforts to change aspects of the social order such as abolishing slavery. At other times, the focus was on one individual poor person at a time. For many Christians, poverty is simply a spiritual matter healed by spiritual regeneration. As people are converted, society itself will be transformed. This thinking especially dominates some forms of evangelicalism. For other Christians, poverty is a reflection of an unjust society that needs reform. Conversion of individual souls is not the focus for these Christians, but rather social action.

The state also has approached aid to the poor by addressing individual needs for change as well as changing social structures. Income transfer programs are directed at individual poor people who deserve aid to enable them to rise above poverty level. Programs such as Head Start, though, reflect a broader institutional effort to change the nature of the poor community to allow more equal opportunity in the market place. The Personal Responsibility and Work Opportunity Reconciliation Act (PRWORA) of 1996 captured both of these methods to some extent, though the emphasis is clearly individual reform. In this Act, assistance is time-limited with expectations that the poor will enter the labor market quickly. Individuals can lose benefits if they do not comply with certain lifestyle rules. For example, a mother under age eighteen must live at her parents' home or in another adult-supervised setting and attend school. Welfare mothers must identify the fathers of their children and convicted drug felons need not apply. To encourage steady employment, states can use funds for employment supports like childcare. Tax laws and minimum wage laws are examples of addressing the economic system in order to reduce poverty. The Earned Income Tax Credit is an example of a policy that "helps the poor, rewards work, strengthens the family, and discourages welfare" (Sider, 1999, p. 103).

The Welfare State

The early twentieth century was a period of growth and prosperity for the nation, which was still relatively young. As the free market economy matured, the United States clearly represented the land of opportunity. Immigrants flooded the borders. Natural resources abounded for the consumption of the relatively small population and a political system based on liberty and justice for all created an environment in which anyone supposedly could succeed. By the twentieth century the state was established as the primary caretaker for the poor and in this role often overlooked the contributions made by faith-based organizations (Vanderwoerd, 2002).

A prosperous nation or person tends to have little tolerance for those who cannot or do not succeed. Though Judeo-Christian ideology was still a strong undercurrent for most American life at this time, the increasing strength of liberalism, materialism, and capitalism deeply impacted public welfare policy (Dobelstein, 1986). The American ideals of rugged individualism and hard work suggested that the poor simply needed the influence and advice of those who had succeeded. Material relief was viewed as more handicap than aid. Many felt that material relief and ill-informed charity promoted laziness and pauperism (Wilson, 1996).

The Depression of the 1930s presented an occasion to question views that held individuals alone responsible for their poverty. American society confronted the reality that poverty often was a consequence of the condition of the economic system rather than simply believing that poverty resulted from immoral living or unwise personal decisions. Congress responded with the Social Security Act in 1935 and other New Deal legislative acts that addressed economic needs. The Social Security Act assured aid to the elderly, the needy, the blind, and dependent children. The New Deal established responsibility for the poor firmly in the seat of government (Trattner, 1979; Levitan, Mangum, & Mangum, 1998).

While faith-based groups continued to provide much relief, the ultimate authority in American society for developing social welfare programming was given to government. What had begun to happen in the latter part of the Middle Ages and during the Industrial Revolution with the Poor Laws was complete. Certainly the philosophical basis for society paying attention to the poor still had some connection with the Judeo-Christian tradition of charity, but in reality the principle of stabilizing the economy and maintaining social order guided policy making. Government had decided that poverty would always be an issue and that it was the role of government to give oversight (Levitan, Mangum & Mangum, 1998).

Government policies and programs established rigorous means tests to determine a person's eligibility for aid. The presumption persisted that many recipients of aid were out to defraud the generosity of others. The "principle of less eligibility" remained. Aid provided subsistence support but nothing more. Processes for accessing aid were often designed to protect the system rather than serve the needs of the poor.

Social welfare had changed quite dramatically from that demonstrated by early Christian believers of the first few centuries after Christ.

Welfare policies since World War II have tended to sway back and forth in levels of generosity. During the Johnson era, the War on Poverty had the lofty vision of eradicating poverty. While its goals were hardly attained, there is some evidence that this era established a safety net for most of the poor (Trattner, 1979). At least most could be assured of having food and basic medical care. In this period, solving the problem of poverty involved adjusting social and economic systems and providing services to support families.

The Reagan/Bush years of the 1980's emphasized different priorities. Poverty was still a problem, but the goal was to eradicate dependency. Programs and services were designed to relieve the federal government of responsibility for the poor and to turn welfare recipients into full participants in the regular market economy. When Clinton became President the goal was to "end welfare as we know it." Welfare reform legislation passed in 1996 with the Personal Responsibility and Work Opportunity Reconciliation Act (PRWORA). This Act essentially ended the federal guarantee of help for poor families with dependent children (Mink, 1999; Dolgoff, 1997). It shifted the administration of relief from the federal government to states in block grants. The Act was predicated on the belief that poor relief could be better managed closer to home. The 1996 welfare reform legislation also assumed that the free market system was a level playing field where the poor could be motivated toward self-sufficiency (Wilson, 1996).

The Importance of Social, Political, and Economic Context

The years of the Depression that caused the nation to realize the need for a federalized system of public welfare had faded out of memory. Many people believed that the welfare system created in the 1930's spawned a different and dangerous set of values from the American ideals of work, independence, and family. Much in the United States had changed since the earliest European settlements. The economic system was mature and now dominated worldwide markets. Society had evolved from an agrarian one to an industrial one to a technological and global one. Furthermore, the nation that had begun with decidedly Judeo-Christian values had become more and more pluralistic and postmodern. These changes in culture influenced the treatment of the poor and the programs and policies formulated to address their needs. The evangelical Christian focus on personal salvation and holiness reinforced the American belief system that each person must be independent and self-sufficient. Conservative political and economic analysts, such as Charles Murray and Lawrence Mead, ascribed the ills of poverty to the "negative effects of welfare" (Wilson, 1996, p. 164).

The twentieth century had ushered in welfare states, both in the United States and in Europe. A difference in the social welfare systems is found in the fundamentally different premises of American and European thought and the very different political and economic contexts. The two contexts illustrated by the United States and Europe after World War II demonstrate the power of the political, economic, and social context in shaping social welfare policies. After World War II, Europe was devastated. The entire society needed to be rebuilt. The United States, in contrast, had not experienced as much loss during the war. The Depression that preceded the war had ended and American values of independence and productivity dominated. American welfare has tended to focus on particular groups, such as the aged, blind, disabled, or orphaned. The "doctrine of less eligibility" prevails and the valuing of rugged individualism dominates. The European system places more emphasis on a communitarian belief system. Consequently, social welfare in Europe tends to be more generous and more inclusive. Social benefits related to health care, housing, child care, employment, and income support tend to be applicable to the entire population rather than limited benefits targeted to particular groups as in the United States (Wilson, 1996; Pedersen, 1993).

Faith-Based Initiatives

George W. Bush came into office as President in 2000 with a call for "compassionate conservatism." Those with biblical faith have always been concerned for the poor, but with the rise of the modern welfare states in the United States and Europe, the church has not prioritized a corporate responsibility for social welfare policies and programs. Since welfare reform in 1996 and the election of George W. Bush, the state is revisiting the idea of collaboration. Charitable Choice provisions in the welfare reform legislation of 1996 opened possibilities again for partnerships between church and state in caring for the poor (Sider, 1999; Sherwood, 1998; Hodge, 2000).

In January 2001, President Bush established the White House Office of Faith-Based and Community Initiatives (OFBCI). He appealed to the old Judeo-Christian tradition of compassion and care for the poor and to the old economic and political view that the poor are often best helped by non-governmental services. The assignment for this office was to strengthen the collaboration of government with faith-based organizations providing social services. The Charitable Choice provisions of the PRWORA of 1996 had opened the doors to partnership between government and faith communities that had essentially been closed since the New Deal of the 1930's (Vanderwoerd, 2002; Sherwood, 1998; Sider, 1999; Hodge, 2000). This raised again the question of who is responsible to care for the poor and how is help best given.

Global Context

Christians believing the call to follow Jesus should be very concerned about global poverty. For the richest and most powerful nation on earth to be knowledgeable about devastating poverty in some nations and continue to live in its ease evokes the prophetic voice of the Old Testament: "Away with your hymns of praise! They are only noise to my ears. I will not listen to your music, no matter how lovely it is. Instead I want to see a mighty flood of justice, a river of righteous living that will never run dry" (Amos 5:23). "I despise the pride and false glory of Israel, and I hate their beautiful homes. I will give this city and everything in it to their enemies" (Amos 6:8).

Biblical faith calls Christians to practice good citizenship by being engaged in the public discourse about social welfare policies and programs and the impact of all policies on the poor in the world. The reality for the twenty-first century is a global economy. It is this political and economic context that will shape U.S. policy in the years ahead. Today, social welfare policies are inevitably linked to the global marketplace. Minimum wage laws, immigration laws, labor and trade laws will all influence how the poor are treated in the United States as well as around the world. The relationship of faith-based organizations and their provision of social services with the government system of social services will also continue to be a dominant theme.

Conclusion

The biblical narrative primarily challenges the non-poor to create conditions for the poor that are just and caring. God does not allow the prosperous to simply wallow in their comfort. In so doing, they become oppressors. Rather, God wants people to have open hands and hearts to the poor, to overflow with generosity and concern. The responsibility is given to family, friends, and community to offer "a liberal sufficiency so that their needs are met" (Sider, 1999, p. 70).

Details of time and place vary dramatically. Social, political, religious, and economic systems create contexts that warrant a variety of methods and approaches to dealing with poverty and influence understanding of the poor. The Bible says that we will have the poor with us always (Deuteronomy 15:11; Matthew 26:11). The biblical imperative to care for the poor and the weak in a manner that empowers them and values their worth and dignity as persons has not changed. What distinguishes followers of Christ is a fundamental commitment to continually work to support the most vulnerable members of society for all are God's children and made in God's image. Whether it is organizing a soup kitchen or challenging tax policies, the call of God for Christians is to bring good news to the poor. This is the mission for social workers as well.

References

Axinn, J. & Stern, M. (2001). *Social welfare: A history of the American response to need* (5th ed.). Boston: Allyn and Bacon.

Cairns, E. E. (1986). *An endless line of splendor: Revivals and their leaders from the Great Awakening to the present*. Wheaton, IL: Tyndale House.

Couture, P. D. (1991). *Blessed are the poor? Women's poverty, family policy, and practical theology*. Nashville, TN: Abingdon Press.

Dobelstein, A. W. (1986). *Politics, economics, and public welfare*. Englewood Cliffs, NJ: Prentice-Hall, Inc.

Dolgoff, R., Feldstein, D., & Skolnick, L. (1997). *Understanding social welfare* (4th ed.). White Plains, NY: Longman Publishers.

Hodge, D. R. (1998). Welfare reform and religious providers: An examination of the new paradigm. *Social Work and Christianity 25 (1)*, 24-48.

Hugen, B. (Ed.). (1998). *Christianity and social work: Readings on the integration of Christian faith and social work practice*. Botsford, CT: North American Association of Christians in Social Work.

Keith-Lucas, A. (1989). *The poor you have with you always: Concepts of aid to the poor in the western world from biblical times to the present*. St Davids, PA: North American Association of Christians in Social Work.

Levitan, S. A., G. L. Mangum, & S. L. Mangum (1998). *Programs in aid of the poor* (7th ed.). Baltimore: Johns Hopkins University Press.

Magnuson, N. (1977). *Salvation in the slums: Evangelical social work, 1865-1920*. Metuchen, NJ: Scarecrow Press.

Mink, G. (Ed.). (1999). *Whose welfare*? Ithaca, NY: Cornell University Press.

Morris, R. (1986). *Rethinking social welfare: Why care for the stranger?* New York: Longman.

Pedersen, S. (1993). *Family, dependence, and the origins of the welfare state: Britain and France, 1914-1945*. New York: Cambridge University Press.

Perkins, J. (1993). *Beyond charity: The call to Christian community development*. Grand Rapids, MI: Baker Books.

Piven, F. F. & R. A. Cloward (1971). *Regulating the poor: The functions of public welfare*. New York: Random House.

Poe, M. A. (2002). Christian worldview and social work. In D. S. Dockery & G. A. Thornbury (Eds.), *Shaping a Christian worldview: The foundations of Christian higher education* (pp. 317-334). Nashville, TN: Broadman & Holman.

Popple, P. R. & L. Leighninger (1993). *Social work, social welfare, and American society*. Boston: Allyn and Bacon.

Sherwood, D. A. (1997). The relationship between beliefs and values in social work practice: Worldviews make a difference, *Social Work and Christianity 24(2)*, 115-135.

Sherwood, D. A. (1998). Charitable choice: Opportunities and challenge for Christians in social work. *Social Work and Christianity 25(1)* 1-23.

Sider, R. J. (1999). *Just generosity: A new vision for overcoming poverty in America*. Grand Rapids, MI: Baker Books.

Smith, T. L. (1976). *Revivalism and social reform: American Protestantism on the eve of the Civil War.* Gloucester, MA: Peter Smith Publishing.

Stark, R. (1996). *The rise of Christianity: A sociologist reconsiders history*. Princeton, NJ: Princeton University Press.

Trattner, W. I. (1979). *From Poor Law to welfare state: A history of social welfare in America.* New York: The Free Press.

Troeltsch, E. (1960). *The social teaching of the Christian churches*. Chicago: University of Chicago Press.

Vanderwoerd, J. R. (Spring, 2002). Is the newer deal a better deal? Government funding of faith-based social services. *Christian Scholar's Review 31(3)*, 301-318.

Wenocur, S. & M. Reisch (1989). *From charity to enterprise: The development of American social work in a market economy*. Urbana, IL: University of Illinois Press.

Wilson, W. J. (1996). *When work disappears: The world of the new urban poor.* New York: Alfred A. Knopf.

CHAPTER 6

SOCIAL WORK'S LEGACY THE METHODIST SETTLEMENT MOVEMENT[1]

Sarah S. Kreutziger

Walter Trattner in his social welfare history *From Poor Law to Welfare State,* critically asserts that religious settlements were little more than "modified missions....bent on religious proselytizing, rigorous Americanization, and the imposition of social conformity on lower class clientele" (1976, p. 17). I believe he vastly underestimates the scope and positive impact of religious settlements on the more highly publicized Social Settlement Movement and on social work itself. Starting in the mid-nineteenth century, in response to the demands of the industrialization of American cities and towns, the religious settlement workers created, financed, and staffed outreach programs to the most marginalized inhabitants of the inner cities. They formed Bible classes, kindergartens, industrial schools, clubs, loan banks, job bureaus, dispensaries, reading rooms, and other programs that laid the groundwork for later social reforms. In the process, they created the foundation for the beginning of modern social work. Religious settlements strengthened the cause of women's rights and paved the way for women to enter careers in social welfare. And, in the South, religious settlers led the campaign for racial and ethnic equality.

Many denominations sponsored these specialized city missions, but perhaps none was as well organized and tenacious as the Methodist Episcopal Church (now the United Methodist Church) in spearheading this form of mission outreach. For that reason, an examination of the Methodist Religious Settlement Movement not only shows the work of religious settlers as part of the religious settlement movement, but highlights as well the tension between the ideologies of Christianity and the emerging tenets of enlightenment liberalism. This tension forms social work values today.

Origins of the Methodist Religious Settlement Movement

City Missions

The religious settlement movement in American Methodism began in New York City "on the 5th of July, 1819, [when] 'a number of females' met at the Wesleyan Seminary... for the purpose of forming an Auxiliary Society to the Missionary Society of the Methodist Episcopal Church, which had been formed the previous April" (Mason, 1870, p. 82). While their original purpose was to support missionaries to the North American Indians, their work gradually focused on problems closer to home. By 1850, "the ladies of the mission," united in evangelistic pragmatism, began their work in the notorious Five Points of New York City surrounded by:

> ...miserable-looking buildings, liquor stores innumerable, neglected children by scores, playing in rags and dirt, squalid-looking women, brutal men with black eyes and disfigured faces, proclaiming drunken brawls and fearful violence. (Mason, 1870, p. 33)

The Five Points Mission was the earliest city mission and the precursor of later settlement homes and community centers in the United States (Leiby, 1978; Magalis, 1973; Riis, 1962).

Led by evangelist Phoebe Palmer, one of the most famous women of her day, the ladies raised money for a building, appointed a paid missionary, and volunteered to conduct Sunday schools, church services, and a nursery for working women. Later, they opened a reading room as an enticement for men who habitually sought solace in taverns, started a medical dispensary, installed public baths for the tenement dwellers, and provided emergency food and shelter for the poor.

Another project of the Missionary Society was "rescue work." In 1833, the women formed the Moral Reform Society to help women who "were victims of sin and shame" (Ingraham, 1844, p. 39) find ways to support themselves other than prostitution. The Society hired city missionaries who were some of the first female social workers. The first and most famous was Margaret Pryor whose descriptions of her "walks of usefulness" became a best-selling book and did much to publicize their work.

Pryor's and Palmer's pleas to move into social reform were spoken in language of the "woman's sphere of action." This language can be appreciated best when we consider the assigned roles and relationships of that era. As homemakers whose responsibility was to build a "sanctified" (holy) society, women were exhorted by religious leaders to protect their homes and others' homes by instilling spiritual values and righteous living in their children and other members of the household. Their special providence was to take care of other women and children who did not have similar resources or religious beliefs. It followed then, that other rescue work was directed at children. Charles Loring Brace, founder of a massive foster care system for destitute children, began his career at Five Points Mission. His work there convinced him that "effective social reform must be done in the source and origin of evil,—in prevention, not cure" (Brace, 1973, p. 78). He founded the Children's Aid Society in 1853; an organization that relocated more than fifty-thousand children to rural homes to remove them from the real and perceived dangers of city life.

The Five Points Mission and similar agencies were part of a broader effort known as the City Mission Movement which had its roots in the New York Religious Tract Society. The tract societies distributed religious literature to convert the inner-city poor. In the 1830s, members of the Tract Society began holding prayer meetings and establishing Sunday schools for the children marked for evangelism (Smith-Rosenberg, 1971). As the volunteers became familiar with the living conditions of the residents, they carried food and clothing with them on their rounds and set up emergency funds. In time, they organized their welfare work into wards for distribution and created a new organization, the Society for the Relief of the Worthy Poor. This became the New York Association for Improving the Condition of the Poor. By 1870, forty full-time salaried missionaries were pioneering model tenements, summer camps for children, industrial training schools, and systematic "outdoor" relief. The Association was a forerunner of the New York Charity Organization Society, a pioneer of early professional social work.

The Institutional Churches

The rapid replication of the programs of the Five Points Mission was inspired by the challenge of the industrial age and the difficulties experienced by the men and women who immigrated to the United States to work in its factories. "Between 1860 and 1900, some fourteen million immigrants came to America and about another nine million, mainly from southern and eastern Europe... arrived between 1900 and 1910" (Trattner, 1979, p.135). The massive crowding, illnesses, and social problems created by the influx of largely unskilled, illiterate, foreign-speaking individuals was unparalleled in our history. In New York City, two-thirds of the population lived in tenements in 1890, while Chicago, then the fastest growing city in the world, packed inner-city residents near the putrid-smelling, unsanitary stockyards where slaughtered animal carcasses fouled water and air. Gangs and petty criminals, fortified by alcohol and other drugs, preyed on the new arrivals. The "urban frontier, like the rural frontier, was a dangerous place" (Seller, 1981, p. 50).

To the native-born Americans, the newcomers were dangerous in other ways. Their political attitudes, born out of feudal societies in which government was an agent of social control, provided a challenge to American democracy. In the slums, the immigrants turned to old-world political traditions such as the "padrone," or political boss, who would manipulate the system for personal gain in exchange for votes. American ideals of patriotic civic action on the basis of self-denial and responsibility clashed with these attitudes (Hofstadter, 1955).

Americans were also concerned about the breakdown of traditional Protestant religious customs and beliefs founded on Puritanism which portrayed the United States as a "holy experiment" destined to create a new society as a beacon to the rest of the world (Winthrop, 1960; Woodbridge, Noll, & Hatch, 1979). Living sin-free, disciplined, temperate, hard-working lives was crucial to this cause. The immigrants, mostly Roman Catholic, drank, brought "continental ideas of the Sabbath" with them, displayed nomadic living habits, and wore fancy dress (Strong, 1893, p. 210). These practices severely distressed city evangelists. Even worse for their cause was the reality that many in the mainline denominations were becoming indifferent to the plight of the poor and abandoning the inner city churches.

The solution to these changes was to set up a specialized form of city missions in these abandoned churches to Americanize, and hence Christianize, the new arrivals by offering them resources and support. These citadels against the onslaught of massive social problems were called Institutional Churches. Programs and activities developed in these "open" or "free" churches (because there was no charge for the pews) were adopted by the social settlers and others following in their footsteps (Bremner, 1956). These churches viewed themselves as "institutions" that ministered seven days a week to the physical and spiritual wants of all the people within their reach. They sponsored clinics, free Saturday night concerts, self-supporting restaurants and lodging houses, wood yards for the unemployed, "fresh air work" for women and children, and "gold-cure" establishments for drunkards. There was a marked emphasis on practical education. Institutional churches sponsored libraries and literary societies and carried on kindergartens, trade schools, and community colleges (McBride, 1983, p. xi).

Although these churches have been described as similar to the secularized social settlements because they adopted many methods and educational theories of the "new charity" (Abell, 1962, p. 164), there is much evidence that the primary mission of the institutional churches was evangelism. While their programs were similar to non-sectarian charities, their ideology was quite different. The Methodist women who supported institutional work were motivated by Scripture. They were to feed the hungry, care for the sick, and clothe the poor (Tatum, 1960).

Methodist women carried these ideals into their work with the religious settlements and supported all of these missions through the structure and activities of the Home Missionary Societies.

The Home Missionary Societies

Almost without exception, the Home Missionary Societies were made up of white, middle-class women, better educated than most of their female contemporaries and freed from time-consuming house chores by the same industrial revolution that was creating the massive social problems in the cities and towns. While many other denominations were ministering to poor and oppressed individuals, the Methodists were the most zealous and well-organized. By 1844, when the Methodist Episcopal Church separated into the southern and northern branches over slavery, there were already 360 missionaries in the United States and one mission in Liberia supported by these societies (Norwood, 1974).

After the Civil War, the local mission societies joined together to build national organizations within the two divisions. The northern church established its missionary societies first in 1869, followed by the southern church nine years later, to aid foreign missions. The Woman's Home Missionary Society was founded in 1880 in the northern Methodist Episcopal Church to support missions within the United States. Their support of missions in the South, especially for the recently freed slaves, led to the founding of the southern church's Home Mission Society in 1880 (*Home Missions*, 1930).

Much of the philosophy undergirding the mission societies' work came from a societal view of women as the moral guardians of the home. In the North, missionary society members organized under the banner of "evangelical domesticity," the notion that the natural spiritual superiority of women gave them the authority to protect their homes and children from the evil influences of society (Lee, 1981). Countless women echoed the belief that "in every well-regulated family their [sic] mother is the potent influence in molding the little ones committed to her sacred guidance" (*Women's Missionary Society*, 1884, p. 4). Much of the reform activity therefore, was directed toward helping other women and children create barriers against the evils that would destroy the sanctity of the home.

In the South, the drive to purify homes was made more difficult by antebellum ideology. The plantation mentality that enslaved black women kept white women in bondage as well. A rigid, tightly-knit, hierarchical social order demanded obedience and submissiveness. As a result, religious activities for women stressed personal piety rather than the "social holiness" of evangelical service that northern women had channeled into abolition, women's rights, and other reforms (Thompson, 1972; Scott, 1970). The Civil War, despite its devastation, liberated southern women for reform activities previously denied them. Consequently, they poured their energies into "their appointed sphere": the churches. In time, the wives, daughters, and sisters of former slave holders joined with the wives, daughters, and sisters of slaves to establish agencies and organizations that promoted racial harmony and reinforced the cause of women's rights (Hall, 1979; Scott, 1984). A significant product of their work was the Methodist Religious Settlement Movement.

The Religious Settlements

Activities and Staffing

Methodist settlements, like their predecessors, often began as child care facilities for working mothers and expanded into kindergartens, sewing clubs, domestic labor training, homemaker clubs, rescue work for prostitutes, boys' athletic clubs, classes in cooking, play grounds, and religious services. Although they also included reading rooms, public baths, English classes, night school, dispensaries, lectures, concerts, music lessons, bookkeeping and banking classes, military drills, gymnastics, milk stations, saving associations, libraries, and "improvement clubs for men,"—they were primarily geared to the needs of mothers and children (Woods & Kennedy, 1911).

The settlement houses were originally sponsored as an expanded mission project of the Women's Home Missionary Society (WHMS), the Chicago Training School for City, Home and Foreign Missions (CTS), and several independent associations. While the goal of the leaders of these organizations was still the sanctification of society through the changed lives of individuals, their work among the poor enlarged their vision of the difficulties that these individuals faced. City missionaries realized that society as a whole must be changed if their goal to evangelize the world was to be reached. Fed by the theology of the social gospel, which saw sin as systemic as well as individual, the city missionaries and their supporters created a broader, more far-reaching attack upon the barriers that kept all people from realizing their God-given potential.

Volunteers from the missionary societies and churches, along with a few paid city missionaries, ran many of the early missions; but the need for better training and education for their expanding work prompted missionary society leaders such as Lucy Rider Meyer, Jane Bancroft Robinson, and Belle Harris Bennett to advocate for biblically-trained women who would live in the neighborhoods among the disadvantaged in the same manner that foreign missionaries lived with citizens in the lands they served. After much planning, hard work, and many setbacks, the efforts of these women and others were realized by the 1880's in a new version of the home missionary: the deaconess.

Deaconesses were distinguished from the city missionaries by the clothing they wore, their communal living arrangements, their formal connection to the church, and their unsalaried service (*Deaconess Advocate*, February 1901). Easily recognized because of their dark dresses, starched bonnets tied with a large white bow, and brisk manner, the deaconesses took their calling seriously. Their task was to "minister to the poor, visit the sick, pray for the dying, care for the orphan, seek the wandering, comfort the sorrowing, [and] save the sinning..." (Thoburn & Leonard in Lee, 1963, p. 37). With the biblical deaconess Phoebe as their model, deaconesses went into the inner cities of the North and the factory towns and rural communities of the South as part of the twentieth century vanguard for the religious settlement movement. In the first thirty years of the Methodist diaconate, the Chicago Training School, founded by Lucy Rider Meyer, sent nearly 4,000 deaconesses and city missionaries to work in hospitals, schools, settlements, rescue homes, and churches. Forty of these institutions were started by CTS graduates (Brown, 1985).

In the Southern states, Methodist settlements constituted from 30% to 100% of all settlements when the first national listing was compiled in 1911 (Woods & Kennedy, 1911). Settlements that served white populations were called Wesley Houses, after Methodism's founder John Wesley, and settlements that served African-Americans were known as Bethlehem Houses (Tatum, 1960). Settlement leaders worked with white American cotton mill employees in Georgia, French-Arcadians families and Italian immigrants in Louisiana, African-American farms workers in Tennessee and Georgia, European seafood workers in Mississippi, and Hispanic migrant workers in Texas and Florida (Nelson, 1909). Many of the settlements were headed by deaconesses who lived in the neighborhoods they served. In 1910, there were six Methodist deaconess training schools and ninety social agencies staffed by 1,069 deaconesses (Glidden, in Dougherty, 1988).

The Deaconess Mother Heart

The religious basis of the beliefs and values of the deaconess sisterhood was the Puritan vision of America's spiritual manifest destiny: America as the beacon to the rest of the world. Deaconess values were also formed from Wesleyan ideals of "perfecting" society through service and mission, cultural definitions of women's position and place, enlightenment views of scientific reasoning, and the emerging social gospel. Their declared goal was the salvation of the "household of faith": American society. The evils of unchurched people, drunkenness, pauperism, and negative influences from foreigners could be wiped out, they believed, with a return to Christian ideals based on the earlier promise of God's covenant with the "New Jerusalem," the United States. This heavenly pattern, imprinted upon America, would ensure the salvation of the world. As deaconess educator Belle Horton declared, "we must 'save America for the world's sake'" (Horton, 1904, p. 41).

Justification for women's entry into this noble endeavor came from church tradition and the Bible as expressed through the metaphor of the Mother Heart. The Mother Heart, as described by Meyer, was the nurturing, caring, feminine side of God understood and possessed by women. Deaconess sisterhood, reinforced by communal living arrangements and church connection, readily integrated the holistic social gospel tenets into their ideological center. Since building the Kingdom of God on earth required the sanctification of each home, it was important for churches to include the work of women: those whose specific mission was the care of God's "unmothered children". This allowed the deaconesses, and by extension—all females—greater authority to be ministers to the whole of society. This expanded vision of women's role in the church and community helped set the stage for the ordination of women, suffrage, and other forms of women's rights. It also helped pave the way for women to enter paid careers as the profession of social work emerged from its two pioneer branches: the Charity Organization Societies and the Settlement Movements.

Religious Settlements and Social Settlements

The women who staffed the settlement homes and institutions were on the front lines of the home mission field. Because the early city mission and institutional churches had provided the model for service and intervention in the lives of the dispossessed for non-sectarian settlements and associated charities just as they had for the religious settlements, there was a great deal of exchange of information, ideas, education, and services. Meyer was a friend of social settlement leader Jane Addams and each knew and respected the other's work. Addams helped Meyer select the site for the CTS and was involved in the early plans. Meyer had wanted to put Addams on the School's Board of Trustees in 1892, but was voted down. Hull-House was just then drawing the fire of the churches because it had been thought necessary to eliminate any direct religious teaching from its program and one or two members of the Training School Board protested against the presence of this "unChristian enterprise" (Horton, 1928, p. 182).

Addams discussed this experience in *Twenty Years at Hull-House* (1981) and the embarrassment it caused, in her words, to "the open-minded head of the school" (p. 72). Addams compared the Training School favorably to the activities of the social settlements. Meyer and Addams continued to be friends throughout their careers and Meyer frequently spoke of Addam's work in the *Deaconess Advocate*, the journal of the CTS.

Despite opposition from church members who objected to the non-religious atmosphere of the social settlements, social settlement leaders continued to lecture regularly at the CTS and the students' field work included living as residents at Hull-House and other social settlements (Brown, 1985). By 1913, Meyers had supplemented the biblically-oriented lectures with textbooks by charity organization pioneers Edward J. Devine and Amos Warner (*Bulletin CTS*, January, 1914). By 1918, her students were working in the United Charities and Juvenile Protection Associations as "visitors" (*Bulletin CTS*, December, 1918), and were learning to think in the codified, scientific methods of the "new charity." Although religious motivation and language continued to be part of the curriculum, the new field of sociology and its promise of "perfecting" society through social engineering gradually supplanted the earlier emphasis on evangelism and proselytization in all the training schools. In time, it would become increasingly difficult to distinguish between the ideology and practices of those who graduated from the deaconess training schools and those who graduated from the university-based schools of social work. As deaconess education and values became less and less distinguishable from the values and methods of early professional social work, deaconess organizations began to lose the sponsorship of the church and other financial backers. Consequently, deaconess training schools were merged into schools of theology or schools of social work (Tatum, 1960; Nola Smee, telephone interview, July, 1995; address by Walter Athern, April 26, 1926, Boston University School of Theology Archives).

The Decline of the Methodist Religious Settlement Movement

While the movement toward non-sectarian liberalism characterized by scientifically-trained workers was initially moderated by the religious training of the settlers and other mission workers, the increasing centralization of reform activities and governmental intervention in social reform tipped the balance in favor of secularism. Additionally, "the spontaneous will to serve," so evident in earlier church volunteers, was subverted by the drive for professionalization. Previous values that had stressed compassion, emotional involvement, and vigorous love of humanity, according to social work historian Roy Lubove (1965), were "educated out" in preference for a "scientific trained intelligence and skillful application of technique" (p. 122). This new climate of professionalism at the beginning of the twentieth century changed the relationship between helper and those helped. Agencies became bureaucratic rather than evangelical, more contractual than spontaneous, and more removed from their clients.

One of the defining and continuing differences between the social settlements and the religious settlements was the pressure by churches on sectarian settlements to use their work for proselytizing (Doris Alexander, telephone interview, July, 1995; Davis, 1967). This pressure caused many of the settlements begun under religious auspices to sever their ties with their parent organizations. This was done to solicit community-wide support and to appeal to wealthy industrialists interested in ecumenical charities (Dubroca, 1955; Trolander, 1987). After World War I, with the rise of the Community Chest and other centralized social service funding, social settlement leaders were forced to answer to an organizational hierarchy that could dictate policy and programs. The net result was less emphasis on controversial community action (Trolander, 1987) and religious instruction. Funding from these centralized agencies also reinforced the drive to replace sectarian-trained workers with professional social workers.

Compounding these trends was social work's move into individual treatment and away from community development. Veterans of World War I suffering from battle-fatigue and shell shock required more than friendly neighborly relationships to help them cope with their personal and health-related problems. Red Cross workers treating military families discovered that Freudian psychoanalytic approaches and casework techniques developed by Mary Richmond, pioneer leader of the Charity Organizational Societies, were better suited to their needs. "Friendly visiting" gave way to therapeutic intervention as settlements were changed from community centers into mental health clinics.

This trend continued until by the early 1960's, professional social workers had replaced volunteers and religious settlement workers in many of the centers. The consequences of the move, according to one historian, led to greater emotional detachment between residents and the workers and less mutual concern and care. As she explained:

> In place of spontaneity and being available around the clock, [social workers] made appointments and 'treatment plans.' Instead of seeking to do *with* the neighborhood, they sought to do *for* the neighborhood. Their 'professional' detachment from the neighborhood was not only physical, it was psychological. (Trolander, 1987, p. 39)

While Methodists followed similar practices related to staffing, there were some differences. Methodist deaconesses continued to reside in the settlements until the mid 1980's (Nola Smee, telephone interview, July, 1995) which helped to maintain the physical as well as the symbolic presence and sense of involvement in the neighborhoods that is part of the settlement legacy. Even when the settlers moved out, it was not so much because of their lack of dedication as it was from church policy and changing attitudes. The decline of religious settlers paralleled the decline of the deaconess movement as deaconesses began to retire and fewer and fewer women were willing to expend the level of commitment required for the diaconate as other opportunities for ministry and employment opened to women. The success of the deaconess crusade, the right of women to participate fully in the church and community, in other words, contributed to its decline (Betty Purkey, telephone interview, July, 1995).

Implications for the Future

While the history of religious settlements has remained in the shadows of the highly publicized work of social settlements such as Jane Addam's Hull-House (Addams, 1981; Davis, 1967; Leiby, 1978), the fact remains that these sectarian-sponsored organizations contributed much to the origins and success of early social work. Overlooked by most social work chroniclers were the hundreds of religiously-committed women, backed by an army of loyal supporters, who also moved into inner-city and rural neighborhoods to share their talents and service with the less fortunate. Methodist settlement leaders were typical examples of these women and their dreams.

The Methodist religious settlers' vision of society began with evangelical hopes for a holy nation undergirded by mutual concern for each other and love of God. This vision inspired the work that built hundreds of social welfare institutions and provided the support and financial resources to run them. When these front-line city missionaries were forced by the overwhelming task and changing times to create new ways of thinking and practice, they lost part of the religious underpinning that defined their vision. Despite these challenges and the decline of the deaconess movement, many of the original settlement houses survive as community centers and urban outreach stations for the churches. As such, they serve as reminders of what the church is capable of doing when the call for commitment, dedication, and sacrifice is answered. When, in the words of Bellah et al., (1985), we seek "the recovery of our social ecology [that] would allow us to link interests with the common good" (p. 287).

The religious and social settlers faced a society reeling from the effects of "wrecked foundations of domesticity" (Addams, 1972, p. 47) and other problems of societal dislocation and despair. Many contemporary people would agree that this century's end brings similar challenges. Family disorganization, international disruptions, population shifts, some with tragic consequences, and continuing disagreements over race, class, and gender create disunity and loss of purpose. Our country, like religious institutions and other social service professions, seems to be searching for a renewed vision and mission. Social work leaders Harry Specht and Mark Courtney (1994) join others calling for the profession of social work to return to its defining mission in the tradition of the settlement movements and the strong belief in the improvement of society. The history of the Methodist Religious Settlement Movement offers one avenue to reclaim that charge.

Notes

This chapter was rewritten from information from the author's unpublished dissertation research for Tulane University and research from a paper submitted to the School of Divinity at Duke University.

References

Abell, A. I. (1962). *The urban impact on American Protestantism 1861-1900*. Hamden: Archon.

Addams, J. (1981). *Twenty years at Hull House*. Phillips Publishing Co., 1910; reprint, New York: Signet Classic.

Addams, J. (1972). *The spirit of youth and the city streets*. New York: MacMillan Co., 1909; reprint, Urbana: University of Chicago Press.

Bellah, R. N., Madsen R., Sullivan W. M., Swidler A. & Tipton S.M. (1985). *Habits of the Heart: Individualism and commitment in American life*. Berkeley: University of California Press.

Brace, C. L. (1973). *The dangerous class of New York*. New York: Wynkoop & Hollenbeck, Publisher, 1872; NASW Classic reprint, Washington, DC: NASW.

Bremner, R. H. (1956). *From the depths: The discovery of poverty in the United States*. New York: New York University Press.

Brown, I. C. (1985). *"In their times": A history of the Chicago Training School on the occasion of its centennial celebration, 1885-1985*. Evanston: Garrett Evangelical Theological Seminary.

Bulletin of the Chicago Training School for City, Home and Foreign Missions. (1914). 15(4).

Bulletin of the Chicago Training School for City, Home and Foreign Missions. (1918). 18(4).

Davis, A. F. (1967). *Spearheads for reform: The social settlements and the progressive movement 1890-1914*. New York: Oxford University Press.

Deaconess Advocate. Vols. 14-29, 1898-1914.

Dougherty, M. A. (1988). The Methodist Deaconess, 1885-1918: A study in religious feminism. Ph. D. diss., University of California, Davis.

Dubroca, I. (1955). *Good neighbor Eleanor McMain of Kingsley House*. New Orleans: Pelican Publishing Co.

Hall, J. D. (1979). *Revolt against chivalry: Jessie Daniel Ames and the women's campaign against lynching*. New York: Columbia University Press.

Hofstadter, R. (1955). *The age of reform*. New York: Alfred A. Knopf.

Home Missions. (1930). Nashville: Woman's Missionary Council, Methodist Episcopal Church, South.

Horton, I. (1904). *The burden of the city*. New York: Fleming H. Revell Company.

Horton, I. (1928). *High adventure—life of Lucy Rider Meyer*. New York: Methodist Book Concern.

Ingraham, S. R. (1844). *Walks of usefulness or reminiscences of Mrs. Margaret Prior*. New York: American Female Moral Reform Society.

Ladies of the Mission. (1854). *The old brewery and the new mission house at the Five Points*. New York: Stringer & Townsend.

Lee, E. M. (1963). *As among the Methodists: Deaconesses yesterday today and tomorrow*. New York: Woman's Division of Christian Service, Board of Missions, Methodist Church.

Lee, S. D. (1981). Evangelical domesticity: The Woman's Temperance Crusade of 1873-1874. In H. Thomas & R. S. Keller, (Eds.), *Women in new worlds*, (pp. 293-309). Nashville: Abingdon Press.

Leiby, J. (1978). *A history of social welfare and social work in the United States*. New York: Columbia University Press.

Lubove, R. (1965). *The professional altruist: The emergence of social work as a career 1880- 1930*. Cambridge: Harvard University Press.

Magalis, E. (1973). *Conduct becoming to a woman*. New York: Women's Division, Board of Global Ministries, The United Methodist Church.

Mason, M. (1870). *Consecrated talents: Or the life of Mrs. Mary W. Mason*. New York: Carlton & Lanahan.

McBride, E. B. (1983). *Open church: History of an idea*. U.S.A.: By the author.

Nelson, J. (1909). *Home mission fields of the Methodist Episcopal Church, South*. Home Department, Board of Missions, Methodist Episcopal Church, South.

Norwood, F. A. (1974). *The story of American Methodism*. Nashville: Abingdon Press.

Riis, J. A. (1962). *How the other half lives: Studies among the tenements of New York*. 1890. Reprint, American Century Series. New York: Hill & Wang.

Scott, A. Firor. (1970). *The southern lady: From pedestal to politics 1830-1930*. Chicago: University of Chicago Press.

Scott, A. Firor. (1984). *Making the invisible woman visible*. Urbana: University of Illinois Press.

Seller, M. S. (1981). *Immigrant women*. Philadelphia: Temple University Press.

Smith-Rosenberg, C. (1971). *Religion and the rise of the American city: The New York City Mission Movement, 1812-1870*. Ithaca: Cornell University Press.

Specht, H. & Courtney M. E. (1994). *Unfaithful angels: How social work has abandoned its mission*. New York: The Free Press.

Strong, J. (1893). *The new era or the coming kingdom*. New York: Baker & Taylor Co.

Tatum, N. D. (1960). *A crown of service: A story of women's work in the Methodist Episcopal Church, South, from 1878-1940*. Nashville: Parthenon Press.

Thompson, E. (1972). God and the southern plantation system. In Samuel Hill, (Ed.), *Religion and the solid South*, (pp. 57-91). Nashville: Abingdon Press.

Trattner, W. I. (1979). *From poor law to welfare state*. (2nd. ed.), New York: Free Press.

Trolander, J. A. (1987). *Professionalism and social change*. New York: Columbia University Press.

Winthrop, J. (1960). A model of Christian charity. In H. S. Smith, R. T. Handy, & L. A. Loetscher (Eds.), *American Christianity*, (pp. 98-102). New York: Charles Scribner's Sons.

Woman's Missionary Society of the Methodist Episcopal Church, South. (June): 1884.

Woodbridge, J. D., Noll M. A., & Hatch N. O. (1979). *The gospel in America*. Grand Rapids: Zondervan Publishing House.

Woods, R. A. & Kennedy A.J., (Eds). (1911). *Handbook of settlements*. New York: Charities Publication Committee.

Archives

Boston University School of Theology.
Special Collections, University Libraries,
Boston, Massachusetts

CHAPTER 7

WHEN SOCIAL WORK AND CHRISTIANITY CONFLICT

Lawrence E. Ressler

His name is Emory and he is a Christian. To be more specific, he is a Mennonite. He may not look like what you expect a Mennonite to look like, but he is. When Emory was young, his family followed more traditional customs. They drove only black cars, for example. His dad wore a plain coat and his mom wore a white bonnet and dark stockings. They had no radios or televisions. His relatives, who have remained committed to traditional Mennonite customs, would not approve of the mustache he now wears, the television, stereo, computers, and gold-colored car he has. What is more important to know about Emory, however, is that while he has abandoned many of the traditional customs, he still has the soul of a Mennonite. It is the framework that provides structure and purpose to his living. A story might help illustrate the influence that being Mennonite has on his life.

When Emory was about 13, he earned money by mowing lawns. One day, when he went to mow a lawn for a customer, he found another boy at the same house with a lawnmower. Emory informed the boy that he had been hired to do the mowing, to which the boy replied that he had been hired to do it. Emory insisted the job was his, and before he knew what happened, the other boy drew back and hit Emory squarely on the jaw, knocking him to the ground. Emory got up and did what he thought was proper. He turned his face to one side and said, "Here, do you want to hit this side too?" After all, Jesus had said, "Turn the other cheek." To Emory's surprise, the boy hit him a second time. Rather than fight about the lawn, Emory got up and went home. Even as an adolescent, Emory was guided by the Mennonite commitment to nonviolence.

Emory's personal sense of history begins in January 1525 when Conrad Grebel and Felix Mantz chose to be rebaptized as adults in Zurich, Switzerland. They did so based on their reading of the Bible. The choice to be a Christian, they believed, should be a voluntary adult decision rather than a procedure imposed on infants, as was the custom of the day. Such an idea ran counter to official church policy and the law that required infant baptism. This issue may not seem significant today, but at that time adult baptism was considered both heresy and treason.

Adult baptism was considered so egregious during the sixteenth and seventeenth centuries that it could result in capital punishment.

The adult baptisms of Grebel and Mantz marked the beginning of the Anabaptist (rebaptizer) movement which was an extension of the Protestant Reformation begun by Martin Luther in 1517. The word Mennonite was given to followers of Menno Simons, an Anabaptist leader in Holland in the latter part of the sixteenth century. Menno Simons and his followers were deeply committed Christians who desired to use the Bible as a guide to living, particularly the New Testament and the teaching of Jesus. Over the years, a distinctive Mennonite theology and life style developed. This included such things as nonconformist living, service to others, community accountability, and simple living. The visible application of this theology included dressing distinctively, rejecting some technology, a worldwide voluntary service system to help people in need, and living a modest lifestyle. Central to their belief system was a commitment to nonresistant love which was to be put into consistent and practical action. Love, following the teaching of Jesus, was to be extended even to one's enemies.

Anabaptists, including Mennonites, were so empowered by and committed to their faith, that while they would not kill to preserve their beliefs, they were willing to die for them. The commitment to their faith was put to the greatest of tests. Anabaptists were persecuted for several hundred years in Europe because of their beliefs and lifestyle, with over 3000 men, women, and children being burned to death, drowned, and beheaded (Bracht, 1837). Take Michael Sattler and his family who were rebaptized in 1525, for example: The Sattlers were arrested, tried, found guilty of heresy and treason, and instructed to recant. Because Michael would not, his tongue was cut out and red hot tongs were applied three times to his body. When he continued to refuse to abandon his beliefs, he was driven to the countryside and had red hot tongs applied five more times to his body. When he still would not renounce his Anabaptist beliefs, he was burned at the stake. His wife and sisters were later drowned because they also would not recant (Baergen, 1981).

In Emory's own direct family, his grandfather seven times removed was sentenced to prison in 1710 for his religious beliefs. The family, along with many other Mennonites, came to America in 1715 primarily in search of religious freedom. James Madison specifically mentions the "Menonists" in the influential apology for religious liberty written in 1785 entitled "Memorial and Remonstrance" (Gaustad, 1993, p. 145). For Emory's ancestors, the First Amendment to the Constitution was a welcome end to several hundred years of religious oppression.

Like his ancestors, Emory has no interest in killing to protect his rights. While Emory cannot state for certain that he would take persecution to the point of death for his beliefs, in his soul he would want to. Following Christ is as dear to Emory as it was to his ancestors.

Emory is also a social worker. He has worked with delinquent children, with individuals and families as a counselor, in rural and urban community development, and in a prison. He has been employed in both religious and secular settings and has attended or worked in social work educational institutions for two decades. Emory has also had leadership roles in the National Association of Social Workers (NASW), as well as the North American Association of Christians in Social Work (NACSW).

Emory is equally committed to his faith and the social work profession. He has found the social work profession to be a particularly meaningful vocation. This is not surprising since the social work profession has religious roots. For him, like the originators of social work a century ago, the motivation for helping those in need is related to being a faithful follower of Christ. I John provides a particularly clear connection between Emory's theology and his interest in social work:

> We know love by this, that he laid down his life for us—and we ought to lay down our lives for one another. How does God's love abide in anyone who has the world's goods and sees a brother or sister in need and yet refuses to help? Little children, let us love, not in word or speech, but in truth and action (I John 3:16-18).

Emory is an example of what can be called a Christian social worker. Emory didn't realize there was such a thing until he went to graduate school and his professor proudly introduced himself as a Radical social worker. Emory learned that a Radical social worker is one who accepts the thinking of Karl Marx and the ideals of Marxism. Emory did not become a Marxist, even though his professor wanted him to become one, but he did learn that one's worldview influences how he or she sees history, the world, problems, solutions, and how he or she does social work. He was inspired when he realized that Jesus Christ and Christianity was for him what Karl Marx and Marxism was for his professor. If there is a Radical social work, then there is a Christian social work, he thought. Emory appreciated the honesty of his professor and decided he would be as open about his belief system.

Emory was surprised a few years later, when he learned that a few social workers think you cannot be both Christian and a social worker. If you want to be a "real" social worker, they said, you have to let go of the Christianity since it is oppressive. Emory was startled, when he began to do research about religion and social work, to learn that social workers, students, and faculty who identify themselves as Christian experience religious discrimination in the profession. Emory was disheartened about how often it takes place in the profession when he learned that in one study half of the subjects who identified their theology as conservative said they had experienced religious discrimination because of it (Ressler, 2000). The NASW Code of Ethics includes religious groups among the list of people who deserve respect.

How can this discrimination be happening, he wondered? There are points of tension between social work and Christianity. The purpose of this chapter is to explore the reasons for these tensions and to offer several suggestions for reducing the tensions between the two.

Spirituality and Religion

To fully understand the tension between Christianity and social work, it is important to distinguish between spirituality and religion.

Definitions

Spirituality, in the popular social work use of the term, refers to "the basic human drive for meaning, purpose, and moral relatedness among people, with the universe, and with the ground of our being" (Canda, 1989, p. 573). Human beings from this perspective are viewed as more than physical beings determined by their basic drives as Freud suggested, by the economic system as Marx believed, or by the environment as Skinner argued. A spiritual perspective holds that at the core of the human being is a search for meaning, the desire to know, and the yearning to be connected. The spiritual aspect becomes especially clear where there is a crisis like the World Trade Center disaster in New York City. People were stunned and wanted to know why the carnage had happened. God-talk became a part of public discourse, and prayer became commonplace. The loss of life of nearly 3,000 people generated a compassionate response from millions who reached out to console and support those who lost loved ones. Just as a fallen power line reminds us of the electrical system that we generally take for granted, death and destruction exposes the spiritual part of human beings of which we are often unaware. Spirituality is just as inherent to human existence as biology, psychology, and sociology.

Spirituality is distinguished from religion which is defined as "an institutionally patterned system of beliefs, values, and rituals" (Canda, 1989, p. 573). Religion involves the organization of ideas about the relationship of the supernatural world and the natural world. It also includes the organization of activities and people that stem from an understanding of the supernatural and natural worlds. Whereas spirituality is largely philosophical in tone and speaks to human nature issues, religion is more sociological and theological. Spirituality is a personal phenomenon while religion is a social phenomenon.

A Typology

Using contemporary definitions, an analysis of spirituality and religion results in a fourfold typology. The first category could be called **Spiritual and Non-Religious**. This would include people who are actively engaged in a search for, or have found, meaning and connection in life. They do so, however, outside of a religious framework. They do not attend a church and are not involved in what is considered religious activities. Meaning in life and connectedness come from non-religious sources such as nature, a job, special relationships, or even the mundane aspects of daily living that are approached with a spiritual attitude. The second type could be designated **Religious and Disspirited**[1]. This would be typical of people who go to church, follow religious rituals, and even support the religious organization. Their life, however, has no meaning and they do not feel connected to others. They may be involved in religious activity, but it does not provide meaningful structure or purpose for life. The third classification could be referred to as **Disspirited and Non-Religious.** This would involve persons who are not consciously purposeful about life nor connected. They may well feel aimless and isolated from others. They also are not involved in religious activities, do not embrace a religious belief system, and are not part of a religious community. The fourth category could be called **Spiritual and Religious**. This would consist of persons whose meaning in life is related to their religious experience. Emory, described earlier, is in this category. The person of Jesus Christ and the Bible, as well as an awareness of the Holy Spirit, gives form and substance to his life. The Mennonite theology helps organize how he understands the world, history, and the future, and it influences how he lives. Going to church, reading the Bible, praying, singing, worshiping with others, and attending church conferences provide inspiration and motivation. His religion is a source of hope and strength. Radical social work would also be in this category even though Marxism is not a traditional religion.

Spirituality, Religion, and the Social Work Profession

After decades of neglect, the topic of spirituality has become increasingly popular in social work in recent years. Spirituality is being addressed more frequently in social work journals and in textbooks (e.g. Bullis, 1996; Ellor & Netting, 1999). Workshops at conferences include topics related to spirituality. Dozens of colleges and universities offer courses on spirituality. Spirituality has moved from being ignored to being in vogue.

The topic of religion, like spirituality, has been largely ignored in social work for the greater part of the twentieth century (Cnaan, 1997; Loewenberg, 1988). There is an interesting paradox with respect to religion, however. On the one hand, increasing recognition is being given to the importance of religion in the profession. This is evident in the revised 1996 NASW Code of Ethics where religious diversity has been given increased status. Religion is now included as one of the groups which social workers are implored to be sensitive to along with race, ethnicity, national origin, color, sex, sexual orientation, age, marital status, political belief, and mental or physical disability. Social workers are instructed in the NASW Code of Ethics to "obtain education about and seek to understand the nature of social diversity and oppression" related to religion as well as diverse groups (1.05). Social workers are further instructed to "avoid unwarranted negative criticism of colleagues" related to religion (2.01), to "not practice, condone, facilitate, or collaborate with any form of discrimination" on the basis of religion (4.02), and are required to "act to prevent and eliminate domination of, exploitation of, and discrimination against any person, group, or class" on the basis of religion (6.04). In other words, respect for religious diversity seems to be of equal importance to other types of diversity.

At the same time, there has been significant tension in the profession with respect to religion, especially when religion is an important source of meaning for clients and social workers, i.e., those who are in the Spiritual and Religious category. Alan Keith- Lucas highlighted the crux of the matter with this question in 1958, "What happens, then, to the social worker who is not content with religious generalizations and who really believes and acts by what he says in his creed?" (Keith-Lucas, 1958, p. 236). Keith-Lucas, who wrote prolifically about the integration of Christianity and social work for 50 years, believed that, with careful theology and a good understanding of social work, the two were compatible. He states,

> The task of beginning to make such a synthesis will not, however, be an easy one. It will require an exploration for those willing to undertake it, of what theology really teaches and not what most people take for granted that it teaches, or remember from Sunday School...It must be intellectually rigorous, con-

> ducted by people who are amateurs neither in religion nor social work. It will have to do with the 'hard paradoxes' rather than the 'easy correspondences' (p. 236).

Not everyone supports Keith-Lucas' argument that religion and social work are compatible. In spite of clear evidence that social workers do not feel adequately prepared to deal with religious issues which arise in social work practice (Joseph, 1988; Sheridan, 1992), some social workers are opposed to exploring and acknowledging the relationship of religion and social work. Clark (1994), for example, argues, "If we want the social work profession to maintain its political and technological gains, we must not move religion to a position of central importance" (p. 15). Increased attention to religion in social work, Clark argues, will place the profession on a "slippery slope."

Some social workers have gone so far as to try to eliminate religiously committed social workers or faith-based institutions from the profession. One of the most visible and volatile clashes in social work took place between the Council on Social Work Education (CSWE) and religiously-affiliated institutions in the 1990s. At the center of the conflict was an accreditation standard developed in 1982 that expanded nondiscrimination requirements. Proponents wanted to require every social work program to state that they would not discriminate on the basis of sexual orientation. This requirement conflicted with the state laws in some states as well as the religious beliefs of some schools. The religious institutions that objected to the expanded policy did not discriminate against students and faculty on the basis of their orientation, but they did insist on their right to establish codes of conduct that prohibited homosexual behavior just as they prohibited other types of behavior such as non-married or extra marital heterosexual intimacy, gambling, smoking, and use of alcohol. The opposing institutions refused to put the phrase "sexual orientation" in their nondiscrimination statements because proponents do not distinguish between orientation and behavior. For the Christian colleges, the non-compliance with the expanded policy was based on an important religious belief which they believed should have the same respect as that given to other groups.

From 1982 to 1995, the conflict was dormant because the policy was not enforced. That changed beginning in 1995 when a number of schools were told by representatives of the CSWE Commission on Accreditation that they would not be accredited if they did not comply with the standard. Some religiously-affiliated schools responded by threatening CSWE with a lawsuit on several grounds. First, the 1982 standard was viewed as a violation of the profession's commitment to religious diversity; and being denied accreditation was seen as a violation of the principle of social justice. Second, denying accreditation to religiously-affiliated institutions for policies related to their religious beliefs was interpreted as a violation of the First Amendment guarantee of religious freedom. Third, since eliminating religiously-affiliated institutions from accreditation would result in their students being ineligible for state licensure, anti-trust concerns were raised. Interestingly, CSWE acknowledged in a publicly distributed memorandum that the requirement concerning sexual orientation had been added with the knowledge that it violated the religious beliefs of some institutions (CSWE Commission on Accreditation, January 1996). The proponents of the policy saw the standard as enforcing justice. The opponents saw the standard as religious discrimination that violated the profession's commitment to diversity and opposing oppression and discrimination.

Two months later, a meeting was called to discuss the matter at the Annual Program Meeting of CSWE. An attorney employed by CSWE announced in the meeting that the 1982 policy was a violation of the law and would not stand up in court. The CSWE Commission on Accreditation (COA), forced to change the policy, made several attempts to find a solution that appeased both the proponents and opponents of the expanded non-discrimination policy. Finding a solution that was agreeable proved to be very difficult. After several proposed revisions, the 1982 standard was removed and a new one put in place that called for "specific, continuous efforts to provide a learning context in which understanding and respect for diversity (including age, color, disability, ethnicity, gender, national origin, race, religion, and sexual orientation) are practiced" (CSWE Commission on Accreditation, 1997). The standard was received favorably by many religiously-affiliated institutions but was resisted by advocates of gay and lesbian groups. These advocates insisted that the nondiscrimination policy must mention specifically sexual orientation. Despite opposition, The CSWE Board of Directors approved the statement by a narrow margin in June of 1997.

The conflict emerged again in 2000 when the Curriculum Policy Statement was revised into a new Educational Policy and Accreditation Standards (EPAS). The 1982 mandatory statement was proposed again and many religious institutions objected. Lawyers were consulted again and CSWE was informed again that the 1982 policy was illegal. CSWE returned to the 1997 standard, which was incorporated into the new EPAS. A great deal of tension remains just below the surface and the conflict has exposed a significant level of animosity among some social work educators and practitioners toward religious persons and institutions.

Recent studies have shed new light on the religious tensions in the profession. The conflict appears to be related to a clash of worldviews more than rejection of religion as a whole. One study (Ressler & Hodge, 2001) explored the experience of social workers by self-identified theological orientation. Four options (Very Conservative, Conservative, Liberal, and Very Liberal) were presented on a rating scale and respondents were asked to identify themselves. The results demonstrate that the tension increases as the theology becomes more conservative. Christian social workers who embraced a conservative theology reported 142% more discrimination than Christian social workers who embraced a liberal theology. In a follow-up qualitative study of Christians who identify their theology as conservative (Ressler & Hodge, 2001a), every respondent (N=12) indicated that they had experienced discrimination in the profession because of their faith. Respondents gave wide-ranging examples of discrimination including: not being hired for jobs, being fired, not being admitted to graduate school, being publicly ridiculed, receiving failing grades, and being denied tenure.

These studies support the sociological theory of Hunter (1991) who argues that a "culture war" is taking place in American society between those with what he calls a "progressive" worldview and those with an "orthodox" worldview, rough equivalents to the concepts of liberal and conservative. According to Hunter, one pole in the culture war is the conservative perspective, which anchors its epistemology in external, definable, transcendent authority. For Christians this authority is the Bible. Biblically based justice from an orthodox worldview involves divinely established, timeless principles. Justice is measured as conformity to right living as is defined in scripture. Right living includes both macro behavior of systems and micro behavior of individuals. On the other end of the continuum is the liberal perspective which anchors its epistemology in a more humanistic tradition with truth seen as an unfolding reality informed by the ethos of the current age. Justice is defined by the most recently enlightened understanding of inalienable rights and healthy behavior of systems. Empirical evidence and logic are the primary authorities in determining what justice is and is not.

The tension in social work, using Hunter's framework, is a conflict between progressive-minded social workers and orthodox-minded social workers (i.e. liberal and conservative) who define and work for justice based on very different understandings of what the good society looks like and how it functions. The heated debates about the issues of abortion, euthanasia, and sexual behavior are social fault lines around which the two worldviews clash. It follows that since the social work profession is dominated by progressive-minded supporters, religious devotees who embrace a more conservative theology experience significantly more prejudice and discrimination than liberally oriented religious devotees.

Why the Conflict Between Social Work and Christianity?

At one level, there seems to be a natural compatibility between Christianity and social work. Take the six core values and related ethical principles espoused in the NASW Code of Ethics, for example. Related to the value of **Service** is the following ethical principle, "Social workers' primary goal is to help people in need and to address social problems." For Christians, this brings to mind the statement of Jesus, "Whoever wishes to be great among you must be your servant, and whoever wishes to be first among you must be your slave just as the Son of Man came not to be served but to serve, and to give his life a ransom for many" (Matt 20:26-28). The value of service appears to be highly esteemed in both social work and Christianity.

The second of the social work values is **Social Justice** with the ethical principle stated as follows, "Social workers challenge social injustice." Some theologians, such as Donahue (1977) argue that justice is the central theme in the Bible. The admonition of Micah 6:8 seems to fit quite nicely with the NASW principle. "He has told you, O mortal, what is good; and what does the LORD require of you but to do justice, and to love kindness, and to walk humbly with your God."

The third social work value is **Dignity and Worth of the Person** and the fourth value is **Importance of Human Relationships**. The related ethical principles are that "Social workers respect the inherent dignity and worth of the person" and that "Social workers recognize the central importance of human relationships." Both of these principles appear to have striking Christian parallels. The most dominant symbol in Christianity, the cross, is a powerful reminder to Christians of God's unconditional love. The NASW commitment to social relationships seems compatible with Jesus' admonition to love your neighbor as yourself (Luke 10:27). Indeed, Christians are called to love one's enemies and to do good to those who hate them (Luke 6:27).

The fifth and sixth values are **Integrity** and **Competence** with the related ethical principles being "Social workers behave in a trustworthy manner" and "Social workers practice within their areas of competence and enhance their professional expertise." While the Bible does not speak to these issues directly, they would easily fit the Christian imperative to be holy (Ephesians 1:4) and to be above reproach (I Timothy 5:4).

In other words, at the principle level of the NASW Code of Ethics, there exists what appears to be an easy fit between social work and Christianity. At this level, social work appears to be a natural profession for Christians who want to help.

Incompatible Christian Issues

While similarities can be demonstrated between Christianity and social work at the value and ethical level, there are many areas of difference, some of which result in significant tension. Some of the tensions are rooted in Christian practices and beliefs that some people in the social work profession find problematic. This includes spiritual reductionism, unbalanced social work practice, and religious tyranny.

Spiritual Reductionism

One source of tension between social work and Christianity stems from a strain of thought I will call spiritual reductionism. Reductionism, according to Babbie (1995), is an overly strict limitation on the kinds of concepts and variables to be considered as causes in explaining a broad range of human behavior" (p. 93). Spiritual reductionism is rooted in the ancient Greek philosophy of gnosticism that embraced a dualistic view of the world. To oversimplify, the material world was seen as evil while the spiritual world was viewed as good. Gnostics believed they had secret knowledge which would lead people to return to the goodness found in the spiritual world.

In a similar way, contemporary Christian spiritual reductionism has a bifurcated view of existence. The material world, including the human body, is viewed as fallen, doomed, and temporary. The spiritual world, including the human soul, is eternal. Heaven and Hell are places where good and bad reign for eternity. The ultimate destiny of the soul depends on spiritual decisions made prior to death. Since the soul is viewed as eternal and the material world as temporary, saving a person's soul is the only action that really matters.

Spiritual reductionism can have a significant impact on how Christians conduct themselves. For example, shortly after I moved to a new house, two representatives from a local church knocked on my door. Bluntly they asked, "Are you a born-again Christian?" I was shocked by their directness and was speechless. I mumbled something, and they went away. The only issue that concerned them was my spiritual welfare. I suspect I said yes, and that seemed to be all they were concerned about.

This type of theology can also have a direct impact on attitudes about social work. For example, Dwight Moody and Billy Sunday, well-known evangelists of the early twentieth century, spoke out actively against social work arguing that it detracted from the more important work of saving souls (Loewenberg, 1988). Moberg (1977), in *The Great Reversal: Evangelism and Social Concern*, examines the split between "fundamentalists" and "social gospelers" that took place between 1910 and

1930. He describes in considerable detail the rejection of social welfare concerns by fundamentalists who embraced a gnostic-like theology.

Christian spiritual reductionism can impact the practice of social work as well. Food, clothing, or shelter, for example, may be used as a means to an end. Material needs may be addressed only as a way to get to the spiritual aspect of clients which is viewed as the more important aspect. Christian spiritual reductionism can also result in a myopic assessment of problems. Placing a higher value on the spiritual dimension than on other dimensions of a person may result in the belief that if spiritual problems are resolved, other problems will dissipate. It can also reduce intervention strategies to those which address spiritual issues. Furthermore, Christian spiritual reductionism can result in a dependence on religious language when working with clients. Not only may the social worker rely heavily on religious language when assessing problems, he or she may establish client use of religious language as a measure of success. Finally, working in contexts which prohibit the use of religious language for legal or other reasons, may lead to employment frustration for spiritual reductionistic social workers because of their inability to deal with what they consider to be the most important area of life.

Unbalanced Social Work Practice

A second tension between social work and Christianity stems from an understanding of evangelism that has the potential to clash with the profession's commitment to client self-determination. I received a letter once from a Christian social worker who shared this dilemma:

> It is the dying person who seems content without "religion" that truly frustrates me. I fear for his/her death based on my own spiritual beliefs that death without Jesus Christ equals Hell. Yet, I continue to practice my commitment to not force discussion about his/her spiritual apathy in honor of my professional value: self-determination. So I ask the following question: How can I profess to be a Christian and practice ethical social work? (personal correspondence, 1996)

The more a person's theology emphasizes evangelism and Hell, the more difficult it may be to remain committed to the social work value of self-determination. If one believes "death without Jesus Christ equals Hell," the most caring act one could engage in would be to lead the person into a saving knowledge of Christ and into eternal life. The more intense the conviction, the more extreme the measures may be to "save" people. Indeed, in its most extreme form, forcing someone to confess their sins is interpreted as a loving act even if causing pain is necessary. Sadly, some Christians have used beating, torture, drowning, and burning people to death in an effort to save their souls.

Christian social workers are sometimes linked to extremist groups who get media attention for their aggressive behaviors and message of judgement. Some of these groups base their actions on Christian theology and justify their abrasive behavior on Divine duty. The pro-life effort, Operation Rescue, noted for aggressive efforts to stop abortions, has as its byline, "Using Biblical truth to bring an end to the Holocaust of abortion." The anti-gay activist, Fred Phelps, notorious for demonstrating against homosexuality at the funeral for Matthew Shepherd, is a Baptist preacher from Topeka, Kansas. The website for his effort is www.godhatesfags.com. Some social workers may assume that these groups represent all Christians.

Religious Tyranny

A third source of tension between social work and Christianity results from a phenomenon I will call religious tyranny. Religious tyranny, like other types of tyranny, imposes one way of doing things on others. It ignores diverse perspectives and may even be threatened by them. Whether the social policies are unintentionally insensitive to diverse groups or intentionally controlling, the result is the same; a second class of citizenship results.

One form of religious tyranny stems from a belief that the United States is or should be a Christian nation. Elsen (1954) illustrates this conviction:

> Let us be honest. Our kind of democracy depends on religion. It depends on the Christian religion. Its ideas are Christian ideas. Its ideals are Christian ideals. Its goals are Christian goals. Allow Christian faith and practice to languish, and democracy as we know it begins to disintegrate. (p. 175)

Numerous American colonies in the eighteenth century (Connecticut, Delaware, Georgia, Maryland, Massachusetts, New Hampshire, New Jersey, North Carolina, Pennsylvania, South Carolina, and Vermont) had laws that were deferential to Christianity. The South Carolina constitution, for example, stated, "The Christian Protestant religion shall be deemed, and is hereby constituted and declared to be, the established religion of this State" (Gaustad, 1993, p. 171). Numerous colonies limited public offices to persons who would affirm Christianity. Pennsylvania, for example, required the following:

> Each member [of the legislature], before he takes his seat, shall make and subscribe to the following declaration, viz: 'I do believe in one God, the creator and governor of the universe, the rewarder to the good and punisher of the wicked. And I do acknowledge the Scriptures of the Old and New Testament to be given by Divine inspiration' (Gaustad, 1993, p. 170).

State-sponsored religion was declared illegal for the entire nation in 1868 when the Fourteenth Amendment to the Constitution was adopted[2]. The Fourteenth Amendment required that states honor the Constitutional bill of rights including freedom of religion in the First Amendment which states, "Congress shall make no law respecting an establishment of religion, or prohibiting the free exercise thereof" (Gaustad, 1993, p. 44).

Neither the First Amendment nor the Fourteenth Amendment, however, have eliminated the belief for some that Christianity should be the preferred religion and that laws and legislators need to be consistent with it. The most visible advocate in recent years is Pat Robertson, the president of the Christian Broadcast Network, who ran for president in 1992. He states in a recent book, "There is absolutely no way that government can operate successfully unless led by godly men and women operating under the laws of the God of Jacob" (Robertson, 1991, p. 227).

This issue is, for some Christian social workers, one of the most troubling dilemmas. The NASW Code of Ethics calls on social workers to be dually committed to clients and to the general welfare of society (e.g. NASW Code of Ethics, 1.01, 6.01). Consequently, if one believes that Christianity is the one true religion and that biblically supported lifestyles are necessary to achieve a healthy society, there is a sense of obligation to advocate for Christian ways of doing things. At the same time, the Code of Ethics calls for respect for diversity. These two standards result in a perplexing ethical dilemma for some.

It needs to be pointed out that this is not just a Christian dilemma. All social workers have a vision of what constitutes the general welfare of society. Each social worker must wrestle with the tension between the patterns which are consistent with this vision and ideas or practices that are at odds with it. This tension was illustrated most clearly at a seminar focused on religious fundamentalist families. A social worker convinced of the rightness of egalitarian family structure indicated that she would never be able to work with a family that had a hierarchical structure. Her vision of what constitutes a healthy family system was at odds with a model that others embrace. Her dilemma was fundamentally the same as that faced by many Christians.

Oppressive Aspects of Social Work

There is, however, another side to the social work and Christianity tension that is less frequently acknowledged in the profession. The tension between social work and Christianity can also stem from social work thought and action that is religiously oppressive and lacks commitment to religious diversity. Ironically, some social workers, in their attempt to pursue social justice for certain groups, condone prejudice and discrimination against certain religious groups with whom they disagree. Just as there are problematic areas that stem from Christian theology and practice, there are problematic ideologies and practices by some social workers in the profession. This includes social work secularism, religi-phobia, and social work tyranny.

Social Work Secularism

Secularism is a way of thinking that denies or ignores the spiritual dimension of life and discredits the value and contribution of religion. While there is widespread agreement that social work has a religious foundation (Niebuhr, 1932; Marty, 1980; Goldstein, 1987; Loewenberg, 1988; Midgley, 1989; Keith-Lucas, 1989), it is also clear that social work was significantly influenced by the progressive mindset of the late nineteenth century which promoted a positivist worldview and devalued spirituality and religion. Empirical evidence and logic, the twin pillars of science, were embraced in the social sciences as superior ways of knowing.

Karl Marx, Emile Durkheim, and Sigmund Freud, key social scientists upon which social work theory relied during much of the twentieth century, all viewed religion with suspicion and doubt. Religion for Marx was oppressive, for Durkheim was a social construction, and for Freud a neurotic impulse. With respect to social work, friendly visiting was replaced with scientific charity, while religiously motivated compassion and caring gave way to social diagnosis.

Evidence for the secular influence in social work is provided by Cnaan and Wineburg (1997). In reviewing papers given at the CSWE Annual Program Meeting, they found that only 30 out of 1500 (2%) papers given at the CSWE Annual Program Meeting from 1990–1994 dealt with religion and service delivery, with only 2 papers addressing "contemporary concerns of religiously-based social services" (p. 7). Their study found that, with few exceptions, the 20 most popular texts "made no mention of any congregational or sectarian aspect of social work with the exception of the obligatory Charity Organization Societies" (p. 8). Furthermore, their study found that only 10 of 50 social welfare syllabi reviewed mentioned religiously-affiliated social service provision.

Positive sentiments from social work pioneers about spirituality and religion have been largely expunged from historical accounts of social work. Seldom acknowledged, for example, is Jane Addams' view of the critical role of Christianity in the settlement house movement. Referring to Christian humanitarianism, she states, "Certain it is that spiritual force is found in the Settlement Movement, and it is also true that this force must be evoked and must be called into play before the success of any Settlement is assured" (Addams 1910: p.124, as quoted in Garland, 1994, p.81).

Likewise, little has been said about the positive attitude the renowned Mary Richmond had about the role of the church. She states:

> After all has been said in objection to past and present methods of church charity, we must realize that, if the poor are to be effectively helped by charity, the inspiration must come from the church. The church has always been and will continue to be the chief source of charitable energy; and I believe that, to an increasing degree, the church will be the leader in charitable experiment and in the extension of the scope of charitable endeavor...The church has always been the pioneer in such work. (Richmond, 1899, p. 174-175)

Cnaan and Wineburg (1997) conclude that a "bias of omission" related to religiously-based social service provision exists in social work.

A second aspect of social work secularism is related to the broader church/state legal issue. While there has been no Supreme Court decision that has directly addressed the relationship of religion and social work, the profession has been influenced by the secular philosophy advanced by the Supreme Court in other arenas, the most significant of which have taken place in education. The dominant church/state philosophy endorsed by the Supreme Court in the twentieth century was first articulated by Justice Black in 1947 when he wrote, "The First Amendment has erected a wall between church and state. That wall must be high and impregnable" (Eastland, 1993, p. 67). This philosophy has resulted in Supreme Court decisions that have consistently ruled against religion in the public arena. Carter (1993), in a recent bestseller about politics and religion, concludes that the law has trivialized religion and needs to move towards a more accommodating stance.

Since the growth of the social work profession has been closely correlated with the growth of the welfare state, the "high and impregnable wall" philosophy suggested by Justice Black has had a significant impact on how religion was dealt with by social workers. Namely, religion in publicly funded agencies has been treated as a phenomenon outside the purview of social work. In order to observe the "high wall" separation of church and state, religious issues, if acknowledged at all, were seen as best dealt with by religious representatives. While no study has been completed to document the impact of the "high wall" philosophy on social work, there is a wealth of anecdotal evidence from social workers in public agencies who report being strictly forbidden to address religious or spiritual issues, to use religious language, or to pray with clients even if it was in the client's best interest and desired by clients. While dealing with religious issues is surely a complicated professional matter, the principle strategy followed by the profession was to refuse to deal with them.

The secularization of social work practice has gone beyond social workers working in publicly funded agencies, however. Religion-free social work practice has been presented as the only responsible professional position. There have been individuals and organizations over the years that have explored and supported an accommodating philosophy of religion, but with little public acknowledgment and presented only in obscure literature. Most notable among those addressing the relationship of Christianity and social work is the North American Association of Christians in Social Work (NACSW), which has been in existence since 1950 and has published the journal *Social Work and Christianity* since 1974. As for individual contributions, Alan Keith-Lucas was by far the most productive writer on the integration of faith and social work (Ressler, 1992). In general, however, little attention has been given to the relationship of religion and social work even in private agencies not constrained by the First Amendment.

Religi-phobia and Religious Discrimination

Religious prejudice and discrimination are reported with surprising frequency by religiously active social workers. While no study has been completed to evaluate the full extent of the problem, one small study (Ressler, 1997) found that 12 of 18 persons (67%) who placed themselves in the **Spiritual** and **Religious** category had experienced prejudice or discrimination within the profession. For example, the respondents reported the following:

> They act like you are a fanatic if your religion permeates your life... In a board meeting, I heard someone talking about "those born-again" folks in a derogatory manner. There have been times that born-again [persons] are accused of extreme behaviors and portrayed as lunatics, when in fact, the person may have had

> difficulty without born-again affiliation. My religious values, especially my personal interpretation of scripture concerning homosexuality, resulted in my being told by a supervisor that I shouldn't be a therapist because I couldn't be objective enough to work with gay and lesbian clients. A vivid memory occurred as an undergraduate when a professor jumped on me in the classroom for including Scripture in a paper. A peer was ridiculed in the classroom for her faith by another instructor. Mostly subtle beliefs that Christian values are somehow different than those of others and should never be expressed.

Religious discrimination has made inroads into some social work institutions, which has resulted in screening out of students with certain religious belief systems. The social work faculty at St. Cloud State University, for instance, in 1992, developed a position paper entitled, "The S.C.S.U Social Work Department's Position on Attitudes Towards Gay and Lesbian People" (St. Cloud State University Department of Social Work, 1992). Referring to themselves as gatekeepers for the profession, the position statement attempted to outline what was expected of students related to gay and lesbian people. The initial paper stated,

> The only legitimate position of the social work profession is to abhor the oppression that is perpetuated in gay and lesbian people and to act personally and professionally to end the degradation in its many forms... Many of our students come from religious backgrounds that do not accept homosexuality...It is not okay in this case to "love the sinner and hate the sin"...Students who have predetermined negative attitudes towards gay and lesbian people, and who are not open to exploring these values, will not find this program very comfortable and should probably look elsewhere for a major (p. 2).

The social work program also required that student applicants participate in an admission interview that "made a point of examining students' attitudes towards homosexuality" (Hibbard, 1994, p. 1). With the support of the Christian Legal Society, the American Jewish Congress, American Jewish Committee, the Center for Individual Rights, the Intercollegiate Studies Institute, and the Minnesota Civil Liberties Union, the statement and interview was challenged by some students. As a result, the statement was revised and reference to a student's religion was dropped. The interview has been replaced with an "admissions meeting in which students 'formally introduce' themselves to the department" (p. 1).

Social Work Tyranny

Hidden in the question about religious values being in conflict with social work values is an issue which the social work profession needs to address. Some social workers advocate a form of professional tyranny with the notion that there is one correct social work worldview and one set of values in social work that all must agree with. Social workers, they believe, who do not accept this worldview and agree with the popular application of social work values should be censured or even banished from the profession.

This argument was made by the University of Buffalo with respect to the CSWE non-discrimination statement on sexual orientation described earlier. The faculty at the University of Buffalo signed a petition that stated,

> We, the faculty at the University of Buffalo, are disappointed and outraged at CSWE's proposal to exempt social work programs at religious institutions from nondiscrimination on the basis of sexual and political orientation... If these programs want to receive CSWE accreditation, they must be held to nondiscrimination policies (State University of New York at Buffalo, School of Social Work, 1996).

Linda Jones, in her argument against allowing religious institutions to be exempt from the sexual orientation non-discrimination standard, suggested that programs that did not comply should, among other things, be "explicitly identified by CSWE in its listing of accredited programs" and "should be monitored with particular diligence and asked to demonstrate their efforts in these areas at an additional time midpoint between accreditation site visits" (Parr & Jones, 1996, p. 310). Ironically, her recommendation that there be public identification of those who are different and that there be close monitoring of their behavior is a form of discrimination and oppression, the very behaviors they claim to be opposing. The tone in the NASW lesbian and gay issues policy is similarly intolerant. The policy statement reads,

> NASW affirms its commitment to work toward full social and legal acceptance and recognition of lesbian and gay people. To this end, NASW shall support legislation, regulations, policies, judicial review, political action changes in social work policy statements, the NASW Code of Ethics, and any other means necessary to establish and protect the equal rights of all people without regard to sexual orientation (NASW, 1994, p. 163).

There is no recognition of diversity among groups and no room for variation. The position is dictatorial.

Where to From Here

The current tension between social work and Christianity, in other words, has both a Christian aspect and a social work aspect. Reducing the tension involves adjustments from both the Christian community and the social work community.

Christian Adjustments

First, Christians need to embrace a wholistic Christian understanding of creation that acknowledges the spiritual dimension of life but with a balanced view of the world, including the psychological, social, biological, economic, political, and environmental aspects. Christians who have a wholistic theology will likely find much in common with the person in environment framework which undergirds social work.

Second, it is important for Christian social workers to develop a theology of evangelism that does not abandon self-determination. Most Christian theologies view self-determination as a basic human right and one that God has afforded to each of us. If, as most Christians believe, God provided humans with the ability and responsibility to choose, including the freedom to make bad decisions, surely Christian social workers need to allow clients to make their own choices. Self-determination is a sound Christian principle even for evangelicals, as well as a central social work value.

The self-determination dilemma may also involve a mistaken assumption about what self-determination in social work means. Self-determination does not mean that a social worker does not confront and cause discomfort when working with clients. Self-determination means that first, you do what you do with the awareness and consent of the client, and second, that you respect the right of clients to make their own decisions.

Third, Christian social workers will need to develop a confident understanding of their own role and the contribution of Christianity in society while remaining committed to diversity, even if laws and individual behavior do not fully support a Christian sense of morality. This begins with a Christian humility that acknowledges that we "see through a glass darkly" and that "all have sinned and fallen short of the glory of God." It further acknowledges that God permits humans to live in ways that violate His intended plans. Finally, the temptation to impose Christian values can be reduced by interpreting the Christian role as one of salt and light rather than conquerors.

Having said this, Christians need to be afforded the right of others to participate in public conversation about what constitutes the general welfare and to be involved in the political process.

Social Work Adjustments

There are adjustments that the social work profession can make as well to reduce the tension. This involves, first of all, adopting positions on social issues that are inclusive rather than exclusive. Interestingly, on the abortion and euthanasia issues, the social work profession has made a conscious effort to respect and accommodate diverse values. For example, on the abortion issue the 1996 NASW position statement relates that,

> In acknowledging and affirming social work's commitment to respecting diverse value systems in a pluralistic society, it is recognized that the issue of abortion is controversial because it reflects the different value systems of different groups. If the social worker chooses not to participate in abortion counseling, it is his or her responsibility to provide appropriate referral services to ensure that this option is available to clients (NASW, 1994, p. 3).

For the individual, diversity is acknowledged and honored. With respect to social policy, the position is moderate.

> In states where abortion services are not available as one option, those members of NASW who so desire may work toward legalization, planning, funding, and implementation of such services (p. 3).

With respect to the euthanasia position, the NASW policy states,

> In acknowledging and affirming social work's commitment to respecting diverse value systems in a pluralistic society, end of life issues are recognized as controversial because they reflect the varied value systems of different groups. Social workers should be free to participate or not participate in discussion about assisted-suicide or other discussion concerning end of life decisions depending on their own beliefs, attitudes, and value systems (p. 59).

Social worker diversity is respected individually. With respect to social policy, the position is conservative.

> It is inappropriate for social workers to deliver, supply, or personally participate in commission of an act of assisted suicide when acting in a professional role (p. 60).

Furthermore, if the profession is going to respect religious beliefs, then it will have to allow for diversity among institutions. This is the position that the Commission on Higher Education has taken in a publication that states,

> The Commission respects and honors the diversity of institutions it accredits and recognizes institutional limits created by law, government, or religious tenets. It does not find the diversity of its member institutions incompatible with the principles of equity and diversity within those institutions (Commission on Higher Education, April 1996, p. 1).

Toward a Common Agenda

The fact that there are differences between Christianity and social work should not be a surprise to either Christians or social workers. For Christians, the very nature of the created world assumes differences between people and groups by extension. The belief in sin and redemption, the Kingdom of God and the Kingdom of this world presumes differences between the Christian and non-Christian. Likewise, the social work profession supports the notion of differences through its concept of diversity. Differences are to be expected.

Furthermore, neither Christians nor social workers should be surprised that some differences result in tension. Jesus warned His disciples many times of the likelihood of conflict (e.g. John 15:18-19). Likewise, the NASW Code of Ethics acknowledges the reality of tension between social workers with different points of view. The Purpose of the NASW Code of Ethics includes this statement, "Reasonable differences of opinion can and do exist among social workers with respect to the ways in which values, ethical principles, and ethical standards should be rank ordered when they conflict."

The reality of tension does not need to lead to destructive interaction, however. Christians are called to live at peace with everyone as much as is possible (Romans 12:18) and to pray for leaders so that "we may live peaceful and quiet lives in all godliness and holiness" (I Timothy 2:1-2). The social work profession, for its part, has a section in the NASW Code of Ethics that requires responsible handling of conflict between colleagues (2.03, 2.04).

Tensions exist in part because the differences reflect differing values. Tensions also reflect the fact that not all things are of equal worth, and policies and actions make a difference in the lives of people in society. Tensions exist over differences because things matter. The goal, therefore, is not to eliminate all differences, since this is impossible. The goal is not even to eliminate all tension, since this, too, is not possible. The goal is to reduce the tension as much as possible and to avoid oppressive behavior while making room for as much freedom as possible.

Reducing tension requires that differing parties respect each other and engage in dialogue about the differences we see and the tensions we feel. It is particularly critical to listen to those who see injustice and feel oppressed. Listening, it needs to be pointed out, does not mean one agrees; nor does it necessarily resolve the tensions. It does, however, provide information, which may lead to wiser, healthier, and more empathic decisions.

Christians must insist on their right to live according to their faith, but they must extend the same right to others. The goal is to find solutions that make room for as many opinions as possible. This can only happen when people with differences learn to work together to find solutions. Resolving conflict in a way that brings people together is a great challenge of life. How can we be one and yet many? How can we find unity in our diversity? These are not simple questions, and there are no simple answers. It seems that social workers and Christians ought to be among those best able to model constructive conflict management. Trying to accomplish this will surely get us closer to living in peace.

Notes

1 Since philosophically, all people are viewed as spiritual much like they are sociological and psychological, the term disspirited is used rather than non-spiritual. The fact that a person has no meaning in life or feels unconnected does not mean they are non-spiritual. It rather indicates a negative spirituality.

2 There is a debate among Constitutional scholars as to whether the First Amendment prohibits favoring religion in general or one particular state- favored religion. The majority on the Supreme Courts since 1947 have favored the religion in general point of view. There has been a minority point of view that argues the intent of the First Amendment was to prohibit one state- authorized religion.

References

Babbie, E. (1995). *The practice of social research.* Belmont, CA: Wadsworth.

Baergen, R. (1981). *The Mennonite story.* Newton, KS: Faith and Life Press.

Bracht, T. (1837). *Martyrs' Mirror.* Lancaster, PA: D. Miller.

Bullis, R. K. (1996). *Spirituality in social work practice.* Washington, D. C.; London: Taylor & Frances.

Canda, E. (1989). Response: Religion and social work: It's not that simple. *Social Casework, 70,* 572-574.

Carter, S. (1993). *The culture of disbelief: How American law and politics trivialize religious devotion.* NY: Basic Books.

Clark, J. (1994). Should social work address religious issues? No! *Journal of Social Work Education, 30*(1), 13-15.

Cnaan, R. &., Wineburg. (1997, March 7). Social work and the role of the religious community. Council on Social Work Education. Chicago.

Commission on Higher Education. (April 1996). *Statement concerning the application of equity and diversity principles in the accreditation process.* 3624 Market Street, Philadelphia, PA 19104: Middle States Association of Colleges and Schools.

CSWE Commission on Accreditation, J. N., Chair. (1996, January 22). [Proposed Changes in Accreditation Standards] (Memorandum to Deans and Directors). 1600 Duke Street, Alexandria, VA 22314.

CSWE Commission on Accreditation, J. N., Chair. (1997, February 20). [Proposed Revision to Standard 3.0] (Memorandum to Deans and Directors of Schools of Social Work). 1600 Duke Street, Alexandria, VA 22314.

Donahue, J. (1977). Biblical perspectives on justice. In John Haughty (Ed.), *The faith that does justice*, 68-112.

Eastland, T. (1993). *Religious liberty in the supreme court: The cases that define the debate over church and state.* Washington, DC: Ethics and Public Policy Center.

Ellor, J., Netting, E. . (1999). *Religious and Spiritual Aspects of Human Service Practice.* Columbia, SC: University of South Carolina Press.

Elsen, E. (1954). *America's spiritual recovery.* Westwood, NJ: Fleming H. Revell.

Garland, D. (1994). *Church agencies: Caring for children and families in crisis.* Washington, D.C.: Child Welfare League of America.

Gaustad, E. (1993). *Neither king nor prelate: Religion and the new world 1776-1826.* Grand Rapids, MI: Eerdmans.

Goldstein, H. (1987). The neglected moral link in social work practice. *Social Work, 32*(3), 181-186.

Hibbard, J. A., Jungman. (1994). St. Cloud Drops "Attitude" Screening. *The Minnesota Scholar.*

Joseph, M. (1988). Religion and social work practice. *Social Casework, 69*(7), 443-452.

Keith-Lucas, A. (1989). Southern comfort. *Social Services Insight, 4*(8), 1-5.

Keith-Lucas, A. (1958). Readers comments. *Social Casework,* 236-238.

Loewenberg, F. M. (1988). *Religion and social work practice in contemporary American society.* New York: Columbia University Press.

Marty, M. E. (1980). Social service: Godly and godless. *Social Service Review, 54*(4).

Midgley, J., Sanzenbach. (1989). Social work, religion and the global challenge of fundamentalism. *International Social Work, 32*(4), 273-287.

Moberg, D. (1977). *The great reversal: Evangelism and social concern.* NY: Holman.

NASW. (1994). *NASW Speaks: NASW Policy Statements.* Silver Spring, MD: Author.

Niebuhr, R. 1. (1932). *The contribution of religion to social work.* New York: Pub. for the New York School of Social Work by Columbia University Press.

Parr, R. &., Jones. (1996). Should CSWE allow social work programs in religious institutions an exemption from the accreditation nondiscrimination standard related to sexual orientation. *Journal on Social Work Education*, 32(3), 297-313.

Ressler, L., Hodge, D. (2001). Religious Discrimination in Social Work: An Exploratory Study." Accepted for publication by *Social Thought*.

Ressler, L., Hodge, D. (2001a). Silenced Voices: The Narrative of Conservative Christians in Social Work. Accepted for publication by *Social Thought*.

Ressler, L. (2000). *Religious Discrimination in Social Work: An International Survey of Christian Social Workers. Social Work and Christianity, 27, no 1*, 49-70.

Ressler, L. (1992). Theologically enriched social work: Alan Keith-Lucas's approach to social work and religion. *Spirituality and Social Work Journal*, 3(2), 14-20.

Ressler, L. (1997). Spirituality and religion [A survey of 90 MSW students]. Roberts Wesleyan College.

Richmond, M. (1899). *Friendly visiting among the poor.* Montclair, NJ: Patterson Smith.

Robertson, P. (1991).*The new world order.* Dallas: Word.

Sheridan, M., Bullis. (1992). Practitioners' personal and professional attitudes and behaviors toward religion and spirituality: Issues for education and practice. *Journal of Social Work Education*, *28*(2), 190-203.

St. Cloud State University Department of Social Work. (1992, April 29). [The S.C.S.U. Social Work Department's Position on Attitudes Towards Gay and Lesbian People]. St. Cloud, MN.

State University of New York at Buffalo School of Social Work. (1996, February 17, 1996). Petition to the CSWE Board of Directors distributed publicly at the Council on Social Work Education Annual Program Meeting. Washington D.C.

CHAPTER 8

FAMILIES AND THEIR FAITH[1]

Diana R. Garland

Congregations often look to social workers as staff members or consultants to provide leadership for congregational ministries with families (Garland, 1999). Goals for family ministry include helping families strengthen the faith dimension of their family life, participate in a community where they are supported and provide support and service to others, and develop strength and resilience in their relationships so that they can face life challenges. These goals are mutually reinforcing. A significant body of research has demonstrated that families that are strong, especially in the face of adversity, have an active spiritual dimension to their life together. They are involved in a community of faith (Brody, Stoneman, & McCrary, 1994; Call & Heaton, 1997; Deveaux, 1996; McCubbin & McCubbin, 1988; Walsh, 1999). For example, a group of researchers have discovered that regular attendance at religious services is inversely associated with domestic violence (Ellison, Bartkowski, & Anderson, 1999).

The research thus far has not described the variables of faith and religion in family life sufficiently for congregations to know *how* they can strengthen this dimension of family life, however. This question is not only of interest to social workers in congregations, but also to social workers in all kinds of settings whose work includes both preventing family distress by helping families to develop strength and resilience, as well as helping families in distress find effective coping strategies. Every crisis in life is by definition at some level a crisis of faith. Spirituality is a dimension of life that needs attention whatever the problem or circumstance that brings a family to seek help.

From a social systems perspective, it is commonly accepted that families have shared beliefs, values, and practices, although these frameworks of meaning have not been called "family faith." For example, Hamilton McCubbin and his colleagues studied the strength and resilience of families in many circumstances, including families in wartime who have lost loved ones or who have confronted the ongoing stressor of having a family member "missing in action." McCubbin concluded that families have what he called "a family schema." He defined a family schema as "a set of beliefs, values, goals, priorities, and expectations about themselves in relationship to each other, and about their family in relationship to the community and the social system beyond its boundaries" (McCubbin & McCubbin, 1993, p. 154). McCubbin has seen the family schema as relatively stable, "a point of reference, a guide or standard against which situational and stressor level appraisals are compared and shaped" (McCubbin & McCubbin, 1993, p. 154). McCubbin's research describes families developing within the family unit a shared understanding, trust and acceptance, "usually with the assistance of their spiritual beliefs, thus making the difficulties comprehensible and meaningful" (McCubbin & McCubbin, 1986, p. 71). "Family faith" is an alternative definitional frame for studying family schema in religious families.

Biblical Narratives and Family Faith

When working with a congregation, the effective church social worker draws the connections from the social science research and theory to the language and concerns of the church, sometimes by connecting current concerns with the biblical themes and narratives of Christian faith. Bible stories provide a shared spiritual heritage for the faith community; they are stories that shape our understanding of God and our world and ourselves. The meaning of biblical narratives is not always transparent or uni-dimensional, providing rich opportunity for community conversation, conflict, and deeper understanding over time. Biblical texts that address the role of faith and spirituality in families provide such a framework for conversation about social work research and practice with families in congregations. The story of Lydia provides a fascinating place to begin this connection from social science research today to stories now 2000 years old.

When the head of the household became a Christian in the church of the first century, so did everyone else in the household. Lydia, a business woman and a household head, must have been remarkable in her patriarchal first-century Roman world. When Paul and Silas showed up and preached where the women in town gathered by the river to pray, Lydia was there and experienced God "opening her heart. " In response, Lydia had the apostles baptize her whole household (Acts 16: 13-15). She then persuaded Paul and Silas to come eat and stay with her family.

Sometime later, Paul and Silas were arrested. While they were in prison, singing hymns and praying through the night, a violent earthquake shook the foundations of the prison and opened all the prison doors. The jailer, afraid that all the prisoners had escaped, prepared to run himself through with his sword, but Paul stopped him, shouting, "Don't harm yourself! We are all here!" (Acts 16:25-29). In response, the jailer asked what he must do to be saved. Paul's response was "Believe in the Lord Jesus, and you will be saved—you and your household" (Acts 16:31). In response, the jailer and his family were baptized "immediately" (Acts 16:33). The story concludes, like the story of Lydia, with Paul and Silas going home with the jailer for a meal with the family, the jailer "filled with joy because he had come to believe in God—he and his whole family" (Acts 16:34; see also 1 Cor. 1:16).

In the United States in the 21st Century, deciding to take up one religion or another is largely a personal choice. If a husband or wife makes a decision to become a Christian, we don't round up their spouse, children, sisters and brothers, and anybody else living in the household, and dunk or sprinkle them with baptismal waters (depending on the baptismal traditions of the particular faith community). Did Lydia's family take a vote about whether or not they wanted to be baptized? The jailer's wife had not even been at the prison to hear the Paul and Silas' impromptu prayer meeting. Did her husband even ask her first if she wanted to be baptized? What is more, Paul told the jailer that if he believed in the Lord Jesus, he *and his household* would be saved.

Clearly, cultural differences create these questions for us. In the patriarchal Roman culture of the early church, householders controlled the religious expression of the household. Households had their own gods and their own altars, and joining a household meant joining that household's religious practices. Christians adopted this household model for the early churches. Churches did not have land and buildings; they met in private houses. The earliest missionaries tried to win over one household, which then became the base for reaching out to other households in the community (Lampe, 1992; Straughan, 2002). We do not have any way of knowing the extent to which all members of the household understood, much less chose, the faith they were adopting (Osiek, 1996).

It is too easy to dismiss the concept of faith belonging to the household or family as a first-century cultural artifact, however. In a research project studying the faith of families, I visited with 120 American families for about two hours each and learned about the faith of American families in four different regions of the country and in four different Protestant denominations: United Methodist, National Baptist, Presbyterian USA, and Southern Baptist (Garland, 2001; 2002a). The project used grounded theory methodology (Glaser & Strauss, 1967; Miles & Huberman, 1994; Rubin & Rubin, 1995; Weiss, 1994). The analysis of more than 240 hours of transcribed interviews has led to a model for understanding faith as a dimension of family life that has significance alongside and influencing the other dimensions of family life social workers consider in their assessment of families, such as communication, roles, power distribution, and subsystem boundaries. This model has grown from the study of Christian Protestant families and has yet to be explored with families belonging to other faith traditions.

Religion, Spirituality, and Faith

The three terms religion, spirituality, and faith are interrelated but can be distinguished from one another. Religion refers to a *shared culture* of beliefs, values, and rules for behaving and relating to others and to God. Religion is thus an aspect of a group or a culture. Often that culture becomes formalized in organizations; in the Christian church, those organizations include congregations, denominations, and parachurch and ecumenical organizations.

Religious behaviors are often expressed in rituals that are rich with meaning because they express the beliefs and values shared by a people. The individual is not alone but is a part of and connected with a believing community that reinforces, challenges, and shapes individual faith. Prayers recited together, "passing the peace," baptism, and partaking of communion together are rituals rich with meanings that connect us to God and to the community of faith. Religion is for a community or culture, then, what faith is for the individual, and it is also in dynamic interaction with individual faith when the individual is a part of a religious community or organization. For those persons who are a part of a religious group or community, religion thus provides an environment in which faith develops and is nurtured and challenged. But religious organizations and communities are not any person's entire environment; many persons develop faith totally independent of and unrelated to formal religion. Even persons who are deeply religious—deeply committed to their church or religious traditions—are influenced by the other groups and cultures to which they belong. Faith develops in response to and in interaction with the person's whole physical and interpersonal environment, not just those contexts that are overtly religious. The nature of the faith of those who are significant to one also has an enormous influence on the shape of one's own faith.

Spirituality refers to the individual, interpersonal, and transcendental *behaviors and experiences* through which we express and develop faith. Spirituality, then, is the behavioral component, that which we do because of our beliefs and understanding of God or the power that transcends our own. Sometimes spirituality is overtly religious, such as in rituals, and sometimes it is not. Persons can be spiritual without being a part of a religious group or tradition. In Christian religion, spirituality is often expressed in what have been called "practices" or "spiritual disciplines." These practices include such activities as worship, prayer, meditation, study of Scripture, singing, confession of failures to others, forgiveness of others, listening compassionately to others, hospitality, giving of one's financial and other resources, service to others, and working for social justice.(Anderson & Foley, 1998; Bass & Dykstra, 1997; Bender, 1995; Brother Lawrence of the Resurrection, 1977; Dykstra, 1997; Foster, 1978; D. R. Garland, 2002b; Lee, 1990; Nelson, 1990).

Because of the interrelationship and sometimes overlapping nature of religion and spirituality, people often do not distinguish between them (Zinnbauer & al., 1997). In fact, Charles Joanide found that Christians are uncomfortable at trying to discuss spirituality and religion as though they are separate entities, insisting that they are profoundly interrelated; "religion is likened to 'a bonding agent' that connected them to God, their neighbor (neighbor referring to people in their social network) and to their cultural and ancestral past" (Joanides, 1997, p. 72). He concluded that "faith" is a term that communicates more effectively with persons who are Christians than either religion or spirituality. As we are using the term, "faith" includes the highly individualized and internalized beliefs, sense of trust, actions, and experiences of individuals. It can also refer to the shared beliefs and behaviors of a group of people (a family) or a whole community (a congregation).

What is Faith?

David and Darlene have been married for ten years. They each brought a son and a different religious tradition to their marriage. David has continued to be involved in the Catholic church with his son Pete, and Darlene is active in the Presbyterian church with her son Paul. When I asked Darlene's family what faith means to them, she answered, "I guess faith is the belief that Jesus was here and real and died for us and we have eternal life through Him."

For Darlene, faith is *belief* about who God is and how God relates to persons. Faith has to do with the answers we have come to as we have wondered about the big questions of our lives. Faith is something that involves our minds, our thinking, our pondering and deciding on what we believe to be the truth.

Belief leads to *trust*, a second facet of faith. Another word for trust is *confidence*. The beliefs we hold increase our trust, our confidence that we can face life's challenges. Shamika is a young wife and only child of her widowed African-American mother and her deceased Anglo-American father. She answered the same question, "what does the word faith mean to you?" by saying,

> It seems like faith is so much a part of me, but it's not conscious. It's inside me. It's like a thread in fabric. It's a thread that runs all through that you don't see but if you pull it out all the other threads fall out. My faith doesn't really hold my family together but I think it's definitely something that holds me together. I rely on it and then I don't worry so much about things that I can't control. I believe in God—that He loves me; that I can't control everything. I can't do everything by myself. I think my faith makes me stronger for the rest of my family.

Shamika not only *believes in God,* but she believes that *God loves her and acts* on that love by making her strong. She trusts God to hold her together. Her faith does not keep her from worrying, but it keeps her from worrying "so much." And it seems that it prepares her for the demands of family life. If belief has to do with our thoughts and minds, then trust has to do with our emotions, our heart.

Beth and Tom have been married 40 years. Their daughter Misty is 25 and has always lived with them; their two grown sons live in other cities in the state. Misty works full time in a hospital and also is the youth minister for the youth in their church. She is carrying on what she has watched her parents do all her life—work in the church. Beth told me, "Most of our activities have been in the church; that's where we've met people and had friends." They have done renovation of the church building, carpentry and painting. And they have been leaders in various programs of their Methodist congregation, teaching adult Sunday School classes and leading children's groups. Misty said, "I can't remember ever a time in my life that the church was not there and a very active part of my life and our family's life." Currently, however, Beth is discouraged and angry over a conflict in their congregation and has not been attending. "It's the most traumatic experience I've ever been through," she said. Even so, they are still busy serving. Beth and Tom are running a food drive for an ecumenical community ministries agency. Tom repairs bicycles for the church to give to poor children. And they deliver Meals on Wheels. Here is how Beth defined faith for me:

> Two things best describe God. One of them is a quick story about a little boy and little girl, and I'm this way about my faith. They are late for school and the little boy says, 'Let's stop and pray,' and the little girl says, 'Let's run and pray.' That's kind of my faith. I've got a faith that God is there. I talk to Him. I pray for the guidance. 'Just show me, guide me, and help me be aware that you are guiding me.' The other thing is that I guess my faith is too simple. To me there are just two verses in the Bible that are

> really important. "Love your neighbor as yourself" and "God so loved the world He gave his only son." And the third one is where Jesus said, "In my father's house are many mansions. I go to prepare a place for you." That's good enough for me.

Beth says her faith is "too simple;" she simply believes that God is there and listens to her prayers. She trusts that Heaven will be there and she does not have to worry about it. But she actually begins her definition of faith with action—she believes in running while she is praying. She does not simply leave it to God to work out problems. The three scriptures she refers to touch on three aspects of faith: belief ("God so loved the world."), trust ("I go to prepare a place for you"), and action ("Love your neighbor as yourself").

People's actions flow from belief about what is real and what is important. Jesus taught us to be active, storing up treasures for ourselves in heaven, not on earth, where moth and rust destroy. "For where your treasure is, there your heart will be also" (Matt. 6:21). We treasure that which we value. That treasure is what we give our hearts to, what we trust. In other words, action not only grows out of our faith, but action also turns around and shapes our faith. What happens if we believe that God answers prayers if we believe and trust in him, and we do believe and trust and still the sick child for whom we are praying so fervently and confidently dies? Sometimes the outcomes of our attempts to live faithfully deepen and confirm our faith. But other times, our faith is shaken and changed (Nelson, 1992). Faith is thus a cycle that begins with belief about God and our world and our place in it—the "meaning" of our lives and our experiences. Those beliefs lead to trust (or a lack of trust), which leads to actions, and the outcomes of those actions in turn have an impact on our understanding, our beliefs.

Figure 1. Faith as a dynamic cycle.

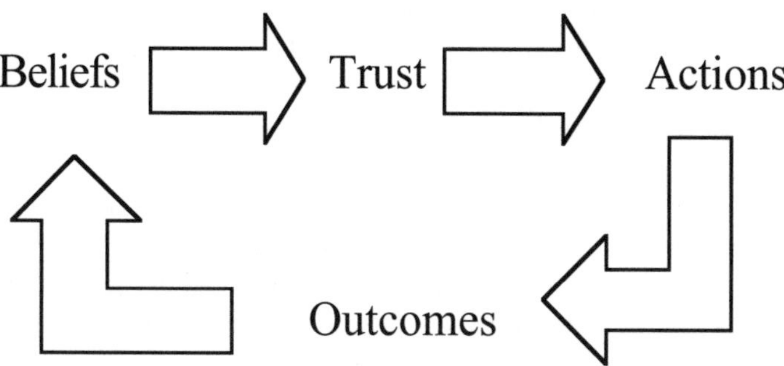

To truly understand a person's faith, we need to know more than a summary statement of beliefs, or even what that person values and trusts. We need to know how they are living their faith day by day in response to those beliefs. The stories of daily living are not simply illustrations; they *are* the embodied beliefs of persons, the lived experiences that are more than simple belief statements can say. Those actions are the person's identity as a person of faith. We need to know the stories of how they came to their beliefs, what they are committed to, and the stories of living those commitments. Craig Dykstra has argued that to study persons' faith, we need to look for the intentions that shape how they approach life. What are the person's life stories, the themes, events, and experiences that say "this is who I am?" Rather than assigning persons to stages of faith development, the approach James Fowler has taken (Fowler, 1981, 1991), this approach suggests that social workers need to learn about persons' faith biographies, the stories that represent persons' faith in all its complexity (Dykstra, 1986).

Faith is particularly significant in social work practice because of the profession's focus on person-in-environment. Faith points us to the client's ultimate environment (Fowler, 1981). It identifies the powers and influences on persons' behavior that otherwise might be hidden to us. Viktor Frankl pointed out, for example, the unseen powers of hope and faith and meaning-in-the-midst-of suffering that had a significant impact on the survival of some concentration camp prisoners during the Holocaust (Frankl, 1969). The beliefs derived from one's faith identify the meaning of experiences, a meaning quite unlike what others would experience in similar situations. Stories provide a medium through which families develop and share their faith in the telling of their own family stories. These stories often tell more than the words and events used to tell the story; underneath and carrying the words are the meaning and purpose of their shared lives, and the faith they have—in one another, in what they value together, in God. Stories say to others and to the family itself, "This is who we are." Because of that underlying melody of meaning, stories give families a sense of identity and of belonging (Garland, 2003).

Family as the Crucible for Our Personal Faith

Family life provides a crucible for individuals to learn faith. For example, research has shown that parents directly and indirectly impact God-images in children. When parents are perceived as nurturing and powerful, especially when mother is perceived as powerful and father is perceived as nurturing, children perceive God as both nurturing and powerful (Dickie et al., 1997).

Adults, too, have their faith shaped by family life. Family experiences test, shape, and deepen our faith. A step-mother described faith to me this way:

> Real issues of living a Christian life are more difficult in an intimate relationship with your family than they are with anybody else. I mean, people can go out and serve food in a soup kitchen and think they're doing this Christian deed and then not understand how to nurture or help somebody in their family who is starving for some other thing. I am not getting along with my step-daughter. Last Sunday, I sat in church and listened to the sermon and I just kept thinking, "This is horrible; I am not treating her in the way I would think of myself as a Christian." It tortured me to try to figure that out. I didn't get any further than that. A lot of people are looking for very simplistic guidance instead of having to suffer the pain of wrestling with things. The family represents a working path to get there.

Families Shape Personal Beliefs

Conversations about faith in families commonly take place in response to family life events or discussion of ideas and experiences to which members are exposed. Shamika's father worked at an automobile factory when he and Sheryl married. Because he was White and marrying a Black woman, other men at the plant began to harass him, and this continued for more than a year, until after Shamika's birth. Sometimes he ignored the taunts and threats, but when it got to him, he would lash back. Shamika's father ended up dead, his murder still unsolved. Shamika said:

> You never think that someone would be that prejudiced and that narrow minded that they would actually want to take another person's life. But it does happen. And it had happened in that town before. They knew of other cases where black men got together and killed a white person because they felt like you don't need to be with our women, or white men did it. It went both ways. When I was 13 or 14, it just hit me. I was looking through my photo albums one day. I don't know why, but I just couldn't handle it any more. I felt so alone. I was really depressed for a while, and my mom asked, "What's wrong?" I finally just broke down and started sobbing and she said, "You're not by yourself. Remember how I used to tell you when you were little that he's still watching you up there. He knows what's going on with you." She also told me that my dad was such a good person

> that he was just too good for the world. When I got married it came back again because I thought, 'Why can't I have my dad walk me down the aisle?' There are questions that come up that there is no answer for. There's no why. It's not something you can stop yourself from asking and it's very difficult for me.

Shamika went on to say that faith has meant believing that she can leave justice in God's hands, as her grandmother taught: "My grandmother always used to tell my mother, 'What goes around comes around. Don't worry about it. God sees it.'"

Instead of thinking about revenge, she believes that God will dispense judgment on those who take care of people who don't do what they're supposed to do.

> It's not up to me to decide it or find them or try and bring justice. That's not my job. God takes care of people who do things right and who do things wrong and I have to believe that. I have to let my hands not touch that one. It's almost evil hating something like that. I shouldn't be this angry. It's something I have to work through and I have to let it go and it's very hard. I think if I didn't have my faith, if I didn't believe in God, I don't think I would come out of it.

Growing up with the reality of her father's murder has created significant challenges for Shamika's beliefs about God and justice. The family has not just been the context for the challenge, however; it has also provided ways of thinking about it and emotional support for dealing with the challenge. Mother is there, sensitive enough to see through the moods of a 14-year-old that "something is wrong," and then offering presence and a comforting belief that her father is still with her. Grandmother offers a belief system that there will be justice, that Shamika can put her trust in God.

Families Teach People to Trust—or Not

Families also provide a context for persons—both children and adults—to learn to trust—trust one another and trust God. When family relationships are not trustworthy, then faith in God may also be shaken, for adults as well as for children. Erik Erikson describes the first task of human beings as the establishment of basic trust (Erikson, 1968). But this does not happen, if at all, merely once and for all (Parks, 1992). Persons repeatedly find anchors of trust shaken loose and then reestablished, often and especially in family relationships.

Jacob and Kate are parents of two sons David (age 9), and Douglas (age 7). Twenty years ago, Jacob and Kate met in college, fell in love, and married when they graduated. Both parents sing in their church choir. Also, Jacob directs and Kate plays the piano for their children's choir in which David and Douglas sing enthusiastically. They all go to Sunday School and worship every Sunday. It all sounds so "John and Mary Church family," until they talk about the tragedy that has shaped their life together and their understanding of God's ways.

Kate grew up Catholic and Jacob grew up in a National Baptist church. Their different faith traditions were not important when they met and married, though, because church was not important to either of them. Kate remembers being one of only two African-American families in the church of her childhood, and how uncomfortable and unwelcome she felt there. Jacob became disillusioned with the church when his pastor's daughter became pregnant and, because of the pregnancy, the pastor refused to allow her a church wedding.

> I thought to myself, "Here you're teaching us forgiveness. Are you really learning any of what you're telling us?" After a while I just found myself saying the heck with it. We'd read the paper in bed on Sunday mornings instead of getting up and going to church.

Their first son, Mark, was born when they had been married three years. Their lives revolved around him, a happy child with big smiles and dancing feet that entertained their extended family. He was the first grandchild. When Mark was three years old, Kate began having nightmares that something terrible was going to happen. "Does God send dreams?" she still wonders. Jacob describes what began as an average day, with Kate rushing to take Mark to the babysitter on her way to work.

> I remember the expression on Mark's face. He had his coat on and he looked at me and said, "Bye!" and he had this expression on his face like, "See ya. Everything's fine." I often wonder if children communicate with God more than adults do. He came back and gave me a kiss good-bye. He hadn't done that in a while. I still remember.

While they were both working, Kate told me,

> There was a fire at the babysitter's house and he died from acute carbon monoxide poisoning. The flames didn't get him...

Jacob interrupted her,

> Smoke inhalation. He was asleep at the time. They said that it was painless. He probably just took a deep breath and never woke up. Our pain never stops.

Their world fell apart. Both of them were angry—at God, at one another, at the world in general—because the loss was so terribly painful. They struggled to hold on to one another. Two more sons were born. But they were growing apart in their search for meaning in the seeming senselessness of Mark's death. Kate was desperate:

> I went to see spiritualists and they said, "You need to pray more." They gave me some suggestions and I went to the library and I was looking at different books. I came across the dream books and I came across meditation and one thing just led to another. I was into searching, so I looked at a lot of different things. Channeling, and all that. What is everything about? This was my thing. Strictly my thing. I tried to share it a little bit with Jacob, but he wasn't into it. I didn't want to impose.

As Jacob said, "We just took different paths." They occasionally visited churches together, because Jacob was looking for more "traditional" answers to his grief. No place felt right, and they never attended the same church twice. Seven years after their son's death, the pastor of a little Baptist church in their community came to visit them and said something they had never heard before from a church leader, "Is there anything we can do for you?" He held their hands and prayed with them, and they went to church with him to find a delightful mix of Anglo and African-American families worshipping together. They felt at home. The congregation did not try to salve their grief or tell them why their son had died but gave them a safe place to grieve and struggle together. It has been almost ten years since their son's death, and even today it is still difficult for them to talk about.

They still don't agree on what it means. Jacob believes that somehow God needed his son:

> When Mark passed, I'd just get up every morning and think, 'Well, there's a plan out there. Nobody consulted me when He thought it up, but there must be a plan out there for something like this to happen.' He was three. At every family gathering he'd dance. And I just believe that there must be somebody out there that needed whatever that spirit could provide more than us. I have to think that there's a reason why. It's got to be because somebody else must have been going through some serious deprivation in their life and it was time for them to feel good too. I think I'm a much better parent now.

Kate disagrees.

> I don't have the same feelings. Mark was an extremely intelligent little boy. I was just beginning to teach him to read and spell words and he could do it. I'll never forget that. I remember a couple of days before he passed away, I was bragging to somebody at work about how smart my boy was. It just blows me away. I think everybody is part of a plan. His death pushed me to grow spiritually. I don't know if he was still here if we would be going to church. I really don't know.

Jacob added,

> I've never thought about that, but it's true.

Kate continued:

> I like to think I would have. God doesn't give you burdens that you can't bear. It was real traumatic when that happened. We survived it. We've moved on. We've progressed. We did not go backwards.

Clearly, their faith has been shaped by their shared experience, and they both think they have grown spiritually as a consequence. The account of their son's death that they had shared earlier is a family story, told to me in the typical tag team story-telling of families. It is clear, however, that they have not talked much about their attempts to understand the *meaning* of their son's death, indicated when Jacob says, "I've never thought about that." They do agree about trusting that God allowed this tragedy to occur for a reason, though they do not agree on what that reason is. They both describe the resulting spiritual growth they have experienced, but they use the word "me" not "we." Although they do not necessarily agree on the meaning of their son's death, putting their lives together afterwards has clearly been a family experience. As Kate says, "We survived it. We did not go backwards."

With all their unanswered questions and even fundamental differences in their understanding of God's ways, they celebrate their survival. They had lived in their house three months when Mark died. For Jacob, the house has come to symbolize their life since his death:

> I think this house pictures the way that things have been with us. It looks great now. But if you had seen what it was like before we got hold of it, you wouldn't have believed it. I put the floor down. Kate and I patched and sanded and primed and painted those walls. I put the moldings up. Whatever you see here is

> because we did it. Sometimes people come in those rooms and say, "Oh this is beautiful!" and I feel like saying, "Do you want to see the scars? Do you want to see how it got to look beautiful?"

Their family is "beautiful" because they have survived. They may never agree on the meaning of their son's death. Many in their church community probably would not agree with either one of them. Does God cause the death of children because their spirits are needed elsewhere? Or to shake their parents into a spiritual journey? Perhaps senseless, evil things happen outside of God's control, and God grieves with us and is present to us as we grief. But if God does not cause such things to happen, then is God not in control? Why do bad things happen?

No one who loves others is spared such questions. Every family has or will someday face life-shaking tragedy. Perhaps it will not be Kate and Jacob's kind of tragedy, but it will be a tragedy nevertheless. In families, we confront the most fundamental issues of life and death and faith. We learn faith here, and we are shattered here, and we struggle—whether together or in isolation—to make sense of it all here. Often the families whom social workers serve are dealing with such fundamental issues; death, unemployment, disabling illness, addictions, and all the other crises of family life are fundamentally crises of life's meaning and thus of faith. For Kate and Jacob, this has been a lonely path because they found different answers. And yet they did so in one another's arms, and in the arms of a community of faith. They held on to one another, gave one another room to struggle and, at the same time, did not leave one another alone in the struggle. They remodeled their house—together.

Family as the Context for Action

Families provide multiple opportunities in both the mundane and the extraordinary experiences of life for acting on faith. Parents overwhelmed by the responsibilities of parenting pray and find strength greater than what they believe they could muster without God's help. The actions of reading the Bible and praying provide a sense of peace even in the most difficult of times. In a time of great financial crisis, the community of faith provides help that carries a family through and deepens their trust in God and the people of faith. At other times, however, the expected outcomes of their faith-based action are not forthcoming. Faith is challenged and sometimes reshaped. Corrine described the crisis of faith she experienced that began with a routine surgery on one of her sons shortly after her conversion.

> I had my newborn faith. I felt like I had been born again and was

> trying to be a little bit too rigid in my behavior. I thought, 'I'm not going to cuss and I'm not going to think bad thoughts.' I had my little checklist and thought if I did all these things I would be okay with God. And I prayed every day for 45 minutes for all these people on my list. I thought if I did this, I would be okay with God. Kurt (the younger son) had all these warts on his hand. They said they could remove them with laser surgery, and just give him a general anesthesia. That's pretty traumatic to give a little seven-year-old. So while Kurt was in recovery and I looked across the street and I saw the cross and I started praying. I said, 'God I know that this is a sign that everything is going to be just fine. Thank you Lord that you protected my child just like I had been praying so hard for. And thank you for letting him come out and they say everything will be fine.'

Everything was not fine, however. Her son developed a rare infection and almost died. Afterward he developed other major problems that have continued to threaten his health and have challenged his mother's faith:

> Some churches teach that if you pray those prayers of protection and if you do everything right things will be right in your life. And I thought, "Why?" I even went to a Bible study called "Trusting God." My next-door neighbor took me. She said, "I think this will help you." It left me even more spiritually devastated because I felt like they were pointing a finger at me: "This must have happened for a reason. Did God do this to you to bring you closer to Him?" And I thought, "He would not use a child! These things don't happen to bring me or my husband to the Lord." I will never go back to that. I don't try to fit theology in little neat boxes any more. I just say that I don't understand. We're just supposed to help each other through it. I will never go back to those churches again. I love my church because they would soothe, they would comfort, but they weren't pushy like we had to get in and solve this today. They were just there.

This family experience challenged her beliefs about how God responds to faith practices. In fact, she rejected those beliefs. In the resulting crisis of faith, she sought out and joined a new faith community and, in the process, redefined her understanding of God. When the results of being faithful have are not what we expect, our beliefs often change and the cycle of belief, trust, behavior and outcomes continues.

Up to this point, we have been looking at ways that families provide a context for shaping, challenging, and reshaping the faith of individuals. In addition, however, families have sacred stories that tell about their experiences *as a family*.

Narratives of Family Faith

James and Marianne brought four children to their marriage from their previous marriages. James' son Corey has severe developmental and physical challenges and uses a wheel chair. Corey works part-time at a sheltered workshop. Marianne has two daughters, Sasha (16) and Sandi (11). Last year, the "ours" baby, Ariah, was born. They live on the edge of poverty, both economically and physically. Both of them are working at low-wage jobs to support their four children. The two-story home they proudly own is located in the inner city on a quiet street but not far from the public housing projects where James works as a maintenance man. The area is inhabited by gangs and has a high rate of violence. James sees the projects as his mission field. Whenever he goes into an apartment to fix a leaky faucet or broken appliance, he prays. He doesn't pray for protection. He prays instead that he will care for the resident as he would care for Jesus. It is Marianne who is praying for protection for him!

It has not always been this was. Soon after their marriage, James became unemployed and; in discouragement, slipped into alcohol and drug abuse, sometimes not coming home at night. Marianne hung on, praying for God to help her husband. Now he is recovering and has had a profound conversion experience. They are proud that they are becoming an anchor family in their struggling community. James loves their congregation and their pastor, and he is in training to become a deacon. As we talked about their faith, Marianne told me that she identifies with Moses' wife:

> She just stuck with him with him being gone up to the mountain and coming back down. That's how I look at myself. Through thick and thin. That's my husband. It got close, because I kept thinking when we were going through it, "I'm just going to tell him to get out, to leave." And then I thought, "No, because if I tell him that, he'll really do it. If I tell him to leave, he won't come home." Through all of what was happening, I kept praying and praying and praying. It just made me stronger. It was something that I needed to increase my faith and to make me strong.

Sandi, the eleven-year old, picked up on the earlier statement that her mother identifies with Moses' wife. Sandi said her favorite Bible story is of the boy David,

> Because he fought Goliath with only five stones. And Goliath had a sword and shield, and David killed Goliath with just one stone. I think I'm as strong as David and I can do anything with Christ.

This is a story of strength, and a child learning strength from parents who have "been through" and persevered.

Family Belief and Trust

Peggy and Bill are in their 70s, married more than 50 years. They raised four sons, and the story of their life that overshadows all others is that of losing Chris. Chris was in the military, stationed in Puerto Rico. They knew that Chris and his wife were have marital troubles, but they didn't know how serious. Chris became depressed. As they told the story to me, they interrupted and verbally tumbled over one another, both of them with tears in their eyes through most of the story. First, they received a call that Chris was "missing in action" from his military unit. During those same days, Bill's elderly mother became ill and died. The funerals were in the same week.

As Bill began to relate how, that same weekend, one of their grown sons came for a visit, Peggy interrupted "Let me tell this," she said. "The Lord just takes care of you because Grant (oldest son) was here and the day that they came to tell us that Chris' body had washed ashore. Grant and his wife came."

Bill picked up the story again,

> Daddy we have some folks here." It was about this time in the afternoon. He said, "We have some folks here that want to see you; are you up to seeing them?" I said, "Sure I want to see them." He said, "They're from the military." I said, "Are they here to tell me they found Chris' body?" He said, "Yes, sir." I don't believe there is any way you can do something like this without the Lord. For three days, knowing your son is missing and not knowing where he is, all you do is pray and talk to God about it every waking minute and you wonder how you sleep but I slept like a baby.

Peggy interrupted him,

> On Tuesday—that's the day that they came out to tell us that they had found his body—well, by that time all of us were getting anxious and didn't know what to do. Thousands of miles away and he's missing. So each one, Bill and all three of our other sons had gone to see their pastors.

Bill explained,

> I went to talk to Brother Tim and said, "Preacher I don't know how to take it." I just told him about Chris being missing and I just talked to him about 30 minutes. Well, Grant in (another town) went and talked to his preacher that day, Marty in (another town) talked to his preacher that day and Bart over in (another state) went and talked to his preacher that day. All four of us talked to our preachers that day.

Peggy said,

> A kind of peace came over me, and I just sort of relaxed and when they came and told us the news you know, I was still calm. I didn't go to pieces or anything. I guess we had been prepared. Bill told me that he went and talked to his preacher and they mostly prayed for me. So I felt like that's what happened.

Bill agreed,

> A peace comes over you that is unexplainable. During this time we have a swing that is on the back lot and in the four days time—I wasn't working because I had just had a heart attack—and I'd just sit in that swing and mope and dread and cry my heart out and talk to the Lord. In it I told the Lord that day if he'd help me find Chris (crying), I'd try to live my life to suit him. And I'm trying to do it.

Peggy went on with the story: "The lady that came from the base, she was a psychologist that came and talked to us. She had told us that if a storm had not come up his body would never have washed ashore."

The details of Peggy and Bill's story turn what seems like a senseless tragedy into a story of God at work in their lives during this terrible time. Their oldest son happened to be in their home because of his grandmother's death when the news came of his brother's body being found. Peggy cited this detail as evidence that "the Lord takes care of you"; Grant was there to support and comfort them. They credit Peggy's sense of peace to the fact that the three remaining sons and Bill all independently consulted their pastors on the same day and prayed for her, and it was at that time that she found a new sense of peace in the midst of the crisis. The father had prayed for searchers to find his son, presumed dead by that point, pledging to live a more "suitable life" if God would help. When he adds, tears rolling down his face, that he's "trying to do it," his wife explains. A storm washed their son's body ashore, or he would never have been found. She implies that God sent the storm as an answer to the father's prayer. They have suffered tremendous grief. But the story is one that communicates not chaos and meaningless but quite the opposite. Through the presence of others orchestrated by God, and through a storm many miles away, they trace orderliness and experience these events as God's care for them. Together, telling the story confirms the meaning they have found together in these events.

You met Darlene and her second husband David earlier. They have two sons from previous marriages, his son Pete (age 14) and her son Paul (age 11). When were talking about what faith means to them, Paul said that for him,

> Faith means living the life that I think God would want me to live and believing that He is our creator and nothing happens without God having a plan. I was talking to my mom about it in the car just a few days ago about how every bad thing ends up with a good thing. When my mom moved here, she probably thought it was going to be the end of the world because she didn't know anybody or about anything that goes on down here [in the Deep South]. But if she hadn't done that she wouldn't have met my dad and chances are she wouldn't have had me. And another example is if my mom hadn't gotten divorced, I wouldn't have Pete [stepbrother] or my Dad [stepdad].

Paul takes two crises in his mother's life—her move to the South and her divorce—and traces how God used them for good. These must be family stories he has been told, because all of this happened before he was born or can remember. He does not simply tell the story but further develops it, pointing out that without the move, she would not have met his father (and had him!), and without the divorce, he would not have his stepfather and stepbrother. Notice, too, that he had this conversation with his mother "in the car just a few days ago." Conversation about faith and other matters of importance often come when families are on our way to somewhere else, not when they plan for them.

Family faith stories are not all sweetness and good feelings. Paul later recounts a rather frightening incident for him. I had asked the family if they had ever experienced a time when God seemed absent. Paul began hesitantly, casting his eyes at his parents,

> Paul: I don't know if I should say this about this cause it was a real bad time.
>
> Mom: Go for it. That you felt God's absence? When?!

Paul: Well I know He wasn't absent but I remember one time at our old house my mom had accidentally sat some of my dad's file papers next to the water, the sink and I think I might have bumped them into the sink and the water dripped all over them.

Dad (interrupting): At the old house?

Paul continues: And you got real mad cause your case was tomorrow.

Everyone began talking at once, and Paul said, louder than the others, "I remember this one."

Dad: Did they get really wet?

Paul: The ink went all over and you couldn't read anything.

Dad: (laughing) I don't remember this.

Paul pressed on: You thought Mama did it and she didn't and I kept trying to tell you that and you were so mad that you got Mamas' jewelry box and threw it out the door.

Pete: I remember that.

Mom: I don't remember this.

Pete: I remember that. I don't know if it was papers, though.

Paul, steadily eying his stepfather: I felt like, "God why didn't you." I tried to tell you that but you were too busy yelling at Mom.

The parents agree in not remembering this incident and seem to be considerably embarrassed at the telling of it. It is a poignant scene as the older stepbrother powerfully sides with the younger child by affirming over and over that he also remembers this event his parents claim to have forgotten, yet at the same time softening the tension of the moment just a bit by questioning one of the details of the story (whether or not it was papers that got wet). Paul frames his story as a time when he felt God's absence, even though he "knew" God was still there. His trust was shaken, even though his belief did not change. He had been through the divorce of his parents, although he did not remember it because he was a baby. But here is his step-father, the man he knows as father, throwing his mother's belongings out the back door, perhaps sending a frightening warning to him that his mom and he might also be thrown out of the family.

It is doubtful that the parents would have considered this to be a faith-shaping experience for their children. But now they cannot escape it, because the story has been told, affirmed by the older step-brother and told in the context of the son's understanding of God. The story is now a part of the family's narrative about God and faith and themselves.

Stories often take on a life and develop meanings that were not apparent when they "actually" happened. In fact, they are continuing to "actually happen" as the family tells the story as an illustration of their life together. The story of the angry stepfather above is such a recollection. The story "happens" all over again as the 11-year-old links this memory to his understanding of God, bringing the past into the present as they process it together and frame it as a story of faith. As frightening as this event is, it is a story of faith and trust. The stepson feels secure and trusting enough to tell it these years later, with his mother's encouragement, and the family has survived what may have felt like a rending of relationships at the time. It was just a jewelry box after all. The family survived. And now they can laugh about it, although the parents are clearly unsettled at this revelation of what their children remember. Even so, what once felt so shaky is now secure, now trustworthy. What does that mean to this child's understanding of God?

Family Outcomes

Families have stories of how "things work out"—or not—as a result of their shared faith. Jan and Harold live in the back of a very large old home in a downtown neighborhood in a Southern city. Their divorced daughter and their two grandsons live upstairs. They are not totally happy about this arrangement, but they are trying to help their daughter through some difficult times. They have a large sitting area and living space in their bedroom. These are their "private" quarters; the rest of the house is shared. Jan is a schoolteacher and takes care of her daughter's two sons in the after school hours. In addition, her elderly mother lives about three houses away. They also have three other grown children and several other grandchildren. Their son Martin has been a particular source of challenge and grief, having been involved with using and selling drugs for almost a decade. Their relationship with their son has been the most significant context in which their faith has been tested and shaped. Harold said,

> I figured if I set him down and tried to talk to him the way you and I are talking, I could convince him. You can't do it. The drugs are stronger. Lying upstairs, I said my prayers, I said, "All right God, he's yours. I've done all I can do." God intervened. I had taken out a $40 a month insurance policy on him, kept it for

> a year and it paid $12,000 for treatment. That took care of the whole thing for a while, then he got back into it and he disappeared. God intervened again. Martin went to the beach, found a friend, and the friend said, "If you stay drug-free, you can live with me until you get on your feet." He met his wife, and she straightened him out. God has come in so many times.

Jan added,

> That's the only time we ever had results. It was when we told God that he was no longer ours anymore.

Harold went on,

> Jan said he got a child on drugs and he was working right over there by the school. I wanted him in a pine box in the ground. (Their son sold drugs to a schoolchild, and Harold wanted him dead as a consequence.) We got to the point that, although we didn't plan the funeral, we knew that if it happened, we were all right. When I turned him over to God that night you cannot imagine the doors that started opening.

This story began as Harold's but quickly became a family story of faith as Jan added her thoughts. When Harold said, "I said my prayers, I said, "All right God, he's yours," Jan responded, "It was when *we* told God that he was no longer ours anymore." She has broadened the story; this is no longer simply the story of a grief-stricken father. This is *their* story. He is not alone in it. And he affirms what she has just said, by continuing, "We know." Undoubtedly, they have talked over these experiences many times before. Each of them has thought about it, trying to make sense of it. But they have also talked it over together, constructing this shared understanding of their experience. Even so, Harold ends this segment by returning to his private prayer, "And when I turned him over to God that night." The individual's faith experience is not lost in the family's experience. Rather, the two interact with one another.

Implications for Social Work

Every family provides a context in which faith develops and is challenged. Family life may provide the context for the individual's faith experience, such as Shamika's struggle to trust God to deal justly with those who murdered her father. Both children and adults have their faith shaped in the transactional life of families, as these family stories demonstrate. The family's life offers multiple crises that challenge and/

or affirm the faith of family members. In turn, as these stories are told and retold, they become family stories, stories in which individuals participate in a story of faith that belongs to the family group, such as the story of Jan and Harold's wrestling with their son's drug addiction. As social workers listen to the stories of families who are wrestling with different life circumstances, they need to tune into how family's understand and find meaning in those experiences, what they believe to be "truth" and how they make sense of their life experiences both as individuals and as a family.

Belief and trust lead to actions based on faith, and those actions have consequences. In turn, the consequences give us more to ponder, confirming, challenging, and sometimes modifying beliefs and trust. When Corrine's prayers for her son's safety during minor surgery were met instead with life threatening illness that is still affecting his health, her beliefs and trust were thrown into disarray. When their infant son died in a fire, Jacob and Kate spent years struggling to find answers for themselves. Family life can be a safe haven, but it can also present faith-threatening challenges.

Social workers often find themselves thrust into the stream of client family's experiences and need to learn much more about that family than whether they are Catholic or Lutheran or Buddhist or Unitarian Universalist. They need to know the faith stories of their lives, and the crisis that concurrently confronts them in the context of that narrative. Even more significantly, families need to tell their stories to one another. Stories are how families say who they are; they deepen family celebrations; and give families ways to cling to one another in hard times. As important as it is to tell stories to one another in families, families also need to share their stories with others, to pass them on and share them and compare them with those of a larger community of people who confirm, challenge, and deepen the narratives of a family's faith journey, connecting the family's story to the great stories of religious faith. If a congregation is truly a community of faith, then it is a place where people and families know one another not just by name but also by their stories.

Note

1 Adapted from Garland, D. (2003) *Sacred stories of ordinary families: Living the faith everyday.* San Francisco: Jossey-Bass.

References

Anderson, H., & Foley, E. (1998). *Mighty stories, dangerous rituals: Weaving together the human and the divine*. San Francisco: Jossey-Bass.

Bass, D. C., & Dykstra, C. (1997). Growing in the practices of faith. In D. C. Bass (Ed.), *Practicing our faith: A way of life for a searching people* (pp. 195-204). San Francisco: Jossey-Bass.

Bender, C. (1995). *The meals are the message: The growth and congestion of an AIDS service in organization's mission multiple institutional fields*. New Haven, Conn: Program on Non-Profit Organizations, Institution for Social and Policy Studies, Yale University.

Brody, Gene H., Stoneman, Douglas F., & McCrary, Chris (1994). Religion's role in organizing family relationships: Family process in rural, two-parent African American families. Journal of Marriage and the Family, 56(4), 878-888.

Brother Lawrence of the Resurrection. (1977). *The practice of the presence of God* (J. Delaney, Trans.). Garden City, NY: Doubleday.

Call, Vaughn R. A., & Heaton, Tim B. (1997). Religious influence on marital stability. Journal for the Scientific Study of Religion, 36(3), 382-392.

Deveaux, William. P. (1996). African Methodist Episcopal: Nurturing a sense of "somebodyness". In P. D. Airhart, and Bendroth, Margaret Lamberts (Ed.), Faith traditions & the family (pp. 73-84). Louisville: Westminster/John Knox.

Dickie, J. R., Eshleman, A. K., Merasco, D. M., Shepard, A., Vander Wilt, M., & Johnson, M. (1997). Parent-child relationships and children's images of God. *Journal for the Scientific Study of Religion, 36*(1), 25-43.

Dykstra, C. (1986). What is faith?: An experiment in the hypothetical mode. In C. Dykstra & S. Parks (Eds.), *Faith development and Fowler* (pp. 45-64). Birmingham: Religious Education Press.

Dykstra, C., and Bass, Dorothy C. (1997). Times of yearning, practices of faith. In D. C. Bass (Ed.), *Practicing our faith: A way of life for a searching people* (pp. 1-12). San Francisco: Jossey-Bass.

Ellison, C. G., Bartkowski, J. P., & Anderson, K. L. (1999). Are there religious variations in domestic violence? *Journal of Family Issues?, 20*(1), 87-113.

Erikson, E. H. (1968). *Identity: Youth and crisis*. NY: W.W. Norton & Co.

Foster, R. (1978). *The celebration of discipline*. New York: Harper & Row.

Fowler, J. W. (1981). *Stages of faith: The psychology of human development and the quest for meaning*. San Francisco: Harper & Row.

Fowler, J. W. (1991). *Weaving the new creation: Stages of faith and the public church*. San Francisco: Harper.

Frankl, V. E. (1969). *The will to meaning: Foundations and applications of logotherapy*. London: Souvenir Press.

Garland, D. R. (1999). *Family ministry: A comprehensive guide*. Grand Rapids: Intervarsity Press.

Garland, D. R. (2001). The faith dimension of family life. *Social Work & Christianity, 28*(1 (Spring)), 6-26.

Garland, D. R. (2002a). Faith narratives of congregants and their families. *Review of Religious Research, 44*(1), 68-91.

Garland, D. R. (2002b). Family ministry: Defining perspectives. *Family Ministry: Empowering Through Faith, 16*(2).

Garland, D. R. (2003). *Sacred stories of ordinary families: Living the faith everyday*. San Francisco: Jossey-Bass.

Glaser, B. G., & Strauss, A. L. (1967). *The discovery of grounded theory*. Chicago: Aldine.

Joanides, C. (1997). A qualitative investigation of the meaning of religion and spirituality to a group of orthodox Christians: Implications for marriage and family therapy. *Journal of Family Social Work*, 2(4), 59-75.

Lampe, P. (1992). "Family" in church and society of New Testament times. *Affirmation: Union Tehological Seminary in Virginia*, 5(1 (Spring)), 1-19.

Lee, J. M. (Ed.). (1990). *Handbook of faith*. Birmingham: Religious Education Press.

McCubbin, Hamilton I., & McCubbin, Marilyn A. (1988). Typologies of resilient families: Emerging roles of social class and ethnicity. Family Relations, 37(3), 247-254.

Miles, M. l. B., & Huberman, A. M. (1994). *Qualitative data analysis* (2 ed.). Thousand Oaks: Sage.

Nelson, C. E. (1992). Does faith develop? An evaluation of Fowler's position. In J. Astley & L. Francis (Eds.), *Christian perspectives on faith development* (pp. 62-76). Grand Rapids: Eerdmans.

Nelson, R. A. (1990). Facilitating growth in faith through social ministry. In

M. Lee (Ed.), *Handbook of faith*. Birmingham: Religious Education Press.

Osiek, C. (1996). The family in early Christianity: "Family values" revisited. *The Catholic Biblical Quarterly*, 58, 1-24.

Parks, S. D. (1992). Faith development in a changing world. In J. Astley & L. Francis (Eds.), *Christian perspectives on faith development* (pp. 92-106). Grand Rapids: Eerdmans.

Rubin, H. J., & Rubin, I. S. (1995). *Qualitative interviewing: The art of hearing data*. Thousand Oaks: Sage.

Straughan, H. H. (2002). Spiritual development, *Christianity and Social Work* (2nd ed.): NACSW.

Walsh, Froma (Ed.). (1999). Spiritual resources in family therapy. NY: Guilford Press.

Weiss, R. S. (1994). *Learning from strangers: The art and method of qualitative interview studies*. New York: Free Press.

Zinnbauer, B. J., & al., e. (1997). Religion and spirituality: Unfuzzying the fuzzy. *Journal for the Scientific Study of Religion*, 36(4), 549-564.

CHAPTER 9

SPIRITUAL DEVELOPMENT

Hope Haslam Straughan

Within the social work profession, there is a growing movement affirming that spirituality and religious beliefs are integral to the nature of the person and have a vital influence on human behavior (Hugen, 1998). Canda (1988) identifies spirituality as a basic aspect of human experience, both within and outside the context of religious institutions. If a social worker is going to approach a person in a holistic manner, he or she must be willing to consider each person as a wondrous compilation of bio-psycho-social-spiritual elements. In this way, workers will have an extremely broad base from which to approach the strength and resiliency in the people with whom they interact. Spiritual development, a component of this broad understanding of a person, seems to occur both in a measurable, outward, predictable manner, as well as in a less tangible, personal journey. These complex and intertwined spiritual growth markers will be explored within this chapter, primarily from a Christian point of view.

Smith (1997-1998) claims that Christians are 'meaning makers,' taking "the raw material of lived experience—the gladness and the sorrows—and trying to seek the deeper meaning, see the larger picture, understand the levels and layers of life in all its fullness and intensity. We live, and then in faith we try to discover meaning" (p. 2). Spiritual deepening, or development then, is about becoming more consciously aware—being attentive, staying alert, and paying attention to life as we seek meaning.

The Council on Social Work Education (2000) has recently added the concept of spirituality to the required list to be addressed within the curriculum of accredited schools of social work. There are many important ways in which to incorporate this information in the overall social work curriculum. For instance, the role of religious institutions in society can be investigated, while considering the impact of their presence, and the potential natural support networks such entities might lend for some persons. In addition, techniques utilized by social workers that value a variety of possible religious experiences or spiritual beliefs might be explored in a practice course. One aspect of the growing self-awareness of social work students might be focused on their personal faith or spiritual experiences, including awareness of their own beliefs, and the impact of these on the people and their environments with which students will interact. Finally, one might argue that spiritual development content must be included in a course in which community is considered, as many religious traditions feature a strong cultural and communal identity and experience.

Incorporating spirituality within the Human Behavior and Social Environment life span content is a foundational attempt to honor holistic personal development. One can consider the development of an individual's spirituality from gestation through the years of life to death, while considering the socioeconomic, political, racial, ethnic, and greater societal influences impacting a person's faith journey. This approach is based on a clear assumption that an individual's spiritual capacity is not stagnant, but indeed develops, changes, and potentially increases. This type of thinking immediately causes us to consider whether spiritual information is best presented utilizing a traditional stage-based theoretical approach, or if the concepts lend themselves to a more fluid consideration in which particular themes are revisited throughout life. James Fowler (1981) has drawn from a deep psychological understanding of human development and crafted a model of spiritual development containing a pre-stage, and six subsequent stages of faith, which holds true to many of the assumptions of the traditional stage-models. Joan Borysenko (1996) and others have proposed more fluid approaches to spiritual development and have recognized that spiritual themes may be re-occurring throughout the life span. This concept is consistent with the spiral approach to growth and development. These ideas, often building upon the familiar concepts of the stage-based developmental patterns, will be presented in a later portion of this chapter.

Social workers commonly work within community-serving agencies, while seeking to help people who often have few choices about the conditions under which essential human needs are met. In this role, we must ensure that every protection is given the client and that his or her helplessness is not exploited (Spencer, 1961). "Certainly, in the light of the high value the social work profession has always placed upon the client's right to solve his [or her] own problems in the way that seems right to him [or her], it is assumed that any considerations of the social worker's role in the area of religion would be set in this context" (pp. 519-520).

Definitions

The roots of social work contain many religious and spiritually based components, lending motivation, direction, foundation, and location for social service provision. When approaching the issue of spiritual development and the impact of this on an individual, family, group, community or organization, it is crucial to define the terms that create the backbone for this important discussion. Sue Spencer (1961) was one of the first to attempt to define religion and spirituality from the perspective of a social worker. She identified three major hurdles experienced by those desiring to discuss spirituality and social work. "The first of these is the wide variety of religious beliefs held by individuals and by organized church bodies" (p. 519). The second hurdle is the difficulty of looking at the issue of religion and spirituality in an objective, yet comfortable and sympathetic way, as any discussion of religion is likely to be colored by considerable feeling and emotion that often stem from one's early experiences with organized religion. The third difficulty is found in our cultural bias, which celebrates the freedom to express religious impulses and to meet religious needs as persons see fit. This hurdle thereby cautions persons against infringing upon the right of religious freedom of others.

"From the rain dances of Native Americans to the celebratory dances of Hasidic Jews, from the whirling dervishes of Islam to the meditating monks of Zen Buddhism, from the ecstatic worship services of charismatic churches to the solemn, silent meetings of the Quakers, spirituality takes on many expressions" (Elkins, 1999, p. 45). Given the hurdles identified by Spencer, and the rich descriptions of spiritual expression listed by Elkins, it is crucial that when discussing spirituality and social work practice, we define terms consistently and clarify what is meant by spirituality. Edward Canda (1988), a social work educator who has made significant contributions to conversations about spirituality and practice has provided a definition that will serve as the cornerstone for this chapter and be continually integrated with our discussion of spiritual development. Canda suggests an understanding of spirituality that encompasses human activities of moral decision making, searching for a sense of meaning and purpose in life, and striving for mutually fulfilling relationships among individuals, society, and ultimate reality (however that is conceptualized by the client). "In that these aspects of human activity are common to all people, they are necessarily relevant to all areas of social work practice" (p. 238). Canda further delineates this spiritual component, by stating that the "professional helping relationship must be a genuine expression of the social worker's spiritual commitment to compassion and social justice—an 'I' who empathically relates with a 'Thou'" (p. 245). Though Canda does not limit his approach to a particular religious tradition, such as Christianity, the focus of this chapter is that of Christian faith and a Christian understanding of God.

Approaches to Thinking about Spiritual Development

Schriver (2001) utilizes a very helpful delineation of traditional and alternative paradigms as a way to structure thinking about people and their environments. The traditional paradigm, characterized in this chapter as those theories based on stage-based, predictable, ladder-oriented development, has sometimes led to a belief in only one route to only one answer rather than many routes to many answers. These theories have offered very important concepts that are often utilized and expanded within broader or alternative ways of thinking about development. "Alternative ways of viewing the world such as interpretive, consensual, non-Eurocentric, and feminist perspectives can add much to what we know and what we need to know to *do* social work" (p. xiv). Building on these assumptions, the remainder of the chapter will be organized in such a way as to demarcate particular spiritual development approaches. These approaches will be divided between those which seem to follow traditional paradigms, and those which lend themselves to alternative processes of understanding the spiritual journey of people, all the while acknowledging the crucial and unique role of their environments.

Traditional Ways of Thinking about Spiritual Development

Many researchers have found that a stage-based model of development, whether psychosocial, cognitive, spiritual, or moral, is descriptive and informative when considering the normal development of human beings. The work of two such researchers, Erik Erikson and Lawrence Kohlberg, will be considered in this chapter in relation to James Fowler's proposed stages of spiritual development. Erik Erikson (1950) proposed a theory of psychosocial development comprising eight stages. The key component in Erikson's work is the development of the sense of self by going through a series of crises. He proposes that the society within which one lives makes certain psychic demands at each stage of development, and that the individual must adjust to the stresses and conflicts involved in these crises in order to move to the next stage of development. Lawrence Kohlberg (1969) proposed a series of six stages through which people progress as they develop their moral framework. A summary of the stages presented by Erikson, Kohlberg, and Fowler can be seen in Table 1., on pages 146-147. A summary of James Fowler's (1981) stages of faith development across the lifespan will be utilized as a point of reference for a discussion of spirituality as it relates to Erikson's and Kohlberg's research.

James Fowler: Stages of Faith

Perhaps the most recognized contributor to the stage-theory approach to considering spiritual development is James Fowler (1981). A theologian and religious psychologist, Fowler set off a new wave of thinking about faith based on the work of such renowned developmental psychologists as Erik Erikson, Jean Piaget and Lawrence Kohlberg. "He claimed that faith, like life itself, goes through distinct stages as a person matures" (Kropf, 1991, p. 12). Fowler's term 'faith' is closely linked to the concepts Canda (1988) presents in his definition of spirituality. Canda's definition is broad enough to allow us to subsume Fowler's concept of 'faith' as a part of a sense of meaning and purpose in life, as well as the belief in an ultimate reality. Fowler considers the interface of the religious/spiritual dimension with other psychosocial aspects of the person (Joseph, 1988). Marra (2000) describes this phenomenon as developing sequentially. As in other stage-based developmental theories, it is possible to accelerate growth, or impede it, but steps cannot be skipped. Fowler (1981) discerns six stages in faith development. A pre-stage called Undifferentiated Faith is reflective of the infant up to about one and a half years of age, and is unavailable to empirical research (see Table 1). The faith of early infancy is characterized by the mutuality between infant and nurturers (Helminiak, 1987). "The emergent strength of faith in this stage is the bond of basic trust and the relational experience of mutuality with the one(s) providing primary love and care" (Fowler, p. 121). Looking at Table 1, we can see obvious similarities in the descriptions of Erikson's Stage-1 of psychosocial development, Basic Trust versus Basic Mistrust, and Fowler's pre-stage. Both researchers identify the most important task during the first 18 months of life as the development of trust due to the infants' needs being met by nurturers. Erikson discusses religion and notes that children may not need a religious upbringing. But, says Erikson (1950), they do need a sense of basic trust, a feeling not only that their fundamental bodily needs will be met and that their parents love them and will take care of them, but also that they have not been abandoned to the empty haphazardness of existence. The trust of the infant in the parents finds its parallel - and takes its mature form - in the parents' trust in God (Brandt, 1991).

Fowler (1986) states that "faith begins in relationship. Faith implies trust in—reliance upon another; a counting upon or dependence upon another" (p. 16). If one is to accept the basis for Erikson's stage progression, crisis completion, it raises a basic question related to spiritual development. At this early point in one's life, what impact would a child's inability to successfully reach basic trust or mutuality have on

Table 1: Stages of Psychosocial, Moral, and Spiritual Development
Erikson, Kohlberg, and Fowler

Erik Erikson's Eight Stages of Man (Psychosocial Development)		Lawrence Kohlberg's Six Stages of Moral Development		James Fowler's Six stages of Faith Development	
Stage/Age	Description	Stage/Age	Description	Stage/Age	Description
Stage 1: **Basic trust vs. basic mistrust** Birth-12/18 months	Infant develops trust, as he or she understands that some people or things can be depended on.			Pre-Stage: **Undifferentiated Faith** Birth-1 ½ years	Faith characterized by mutuality between infant and nurturers. First pre-images of God are formed prior to language & are feeling-oriented, not reason-oriented.
Stage 2: **Autonomy vs. Shame & Doubt** 18 months – 3 yr.	Accomplishing various tasks/ activities provides children with feelings of self-worth and self-confidence.				
Stage 3: **Initiative vs. Guilt** 3-6 years	Preschoolers encouraged to take initiative to explore & learn are likely to feel confident in initiating relationships, & pursue career objectives later in life. Preschoolers consistently restricted, or punished, are more likely to experience emotional guilt, & most often follow the lead of others.	Level 1-Preconventional 4-10 years Stage 1: **Punishment & Obedience Orientation** Controls are external. Behavior governed by receiving rewards/punishments. Decisions concerning what is good/bad are made in order to avoid receiving punishment. Stage 2: **Naïve Instrumental Hedonism** Rules are obeyed in order to receive rewards. Often favors are exchanged.		Stage 1: **Intuitive-Projective Faith** 3-7 years	Child constructs ever-shifting world of imitation, fantasy, & imagination. Child thinks only literally. Sees God as person yet realizes imagery falls short.
Stage 4: **Industry vs. Inferiority** 6-12 years	These children need to be productive & succeed in play and school activities.	Level 2 – Conventional 10-13 years Stage 3: **"Good Boy/Girl Morality"** Behavior governed by conforming to social expectations. Good behavior is considered to be what pleases others. Stage 4: **Authority-Maintaining Morality** Belief in law & order is strong. Behavior conforms to law & higher authority. Social order is important.		Stage 2: **Mythic-Literal Faith** 6-12 years	Emergence of concrete operational thinking precipitates the transition to this stage, as a child is able to see the world from more than 1 perspective. Child's world is simple, orderly, temporally linear, and dependable.

Stage 5: **Identity vs. Role Confusion** Adolescence	This transition period from childhood to adulthood is when a person examines the various roles they play, & integrate these roles into a perception of self, or identity.	Level 3 – Post Conventional (many persons never move to Level 3) Late adolescence Stage 5: **Morality of Contract, of Individual Rights, & of Democratically Accepted Law** Moral decisions internally controlled. Morality involves higher level principles beyond law & self-interest. Laws considered necessary, subject to rational thought & interpretation.	Stage 3: **Synthetic-Conventional Faith** 12-beyond	Emergence of formal operational thinking allows critical reflection on myths central to Stage 2. See God as personal & relational, holding great value to religious symbols.
Stage 6: **Intimacy vs. Isolation** Young adult	Young adulthood is characterized by a quest of intimacy. Persons not attaining intimacy are likely to suffer isolation, & were likely to resolve some of the crises of earlier psychosocial development.	Adulthood	Stage 4: **Individuate-Reflective Faith** Young adulthood or beyond (many persons stay between Stage 3 & 4)	Physical separation from home & encounter with new environment; authority moves from outside to inside person. Perception of God similar to Stage 3.
Stage 7: **Generativity vs. Stagnation** Maturity	People are concerned with helping, producing for, or guiding the following generation. People lacking generativity become self-absorbed and inward.	Stage 6: **Morality of Individual Principles & Conscience** Behavior based on internal ethical principles. Decisions made according to what is right vs. what is written into law.	Stage 5: **Conjunctive Faith** mid-life or beyond	Person must have known life experiences of grief/confusion; deepest truths are inconsistent; sweeter spirit than Stages 3 & 4; lives with ambiguity; views faith from perspective of others; open to change.
Stage 8: **Ego Integrity vs. Despair** Old Age	People look back over life & reflect, taking stock in their decisions. For some this leads to a sense of peace (ego integrity) & for others to a sense of sadness and despair.		Stage 6: **Universalizing Faith** Adulthood (exceptionally rare)	Characterized by brotherhood of all; focus on love, peace & justice; religion is relational, not conceptual; a radical absorption with unity of all people.

Table 1.

his or her spiritual development? Canda (1988), too, defines spiritual development partially as striving for mutually fulfilling relationships among individuals, society, and ultimate reality.

For Fowler, transition to Stage-1 begins with the convergence of thought and language, opening up the use of symbols in speech and ritual play. Stage-1 Faith, called Intuitive-Projective Faith, typical of the child of three to seven, involves a child thinking of God only in literal terms. For example, if an adult says "God is always with us," then the child sitting at the table may want to move over and give God half of his or her seat. Kohlberg (1969) describes the moral development of children at this age as motivated by avoidance of punishment. In many Protestant religious traditions, children are taught that God is love and lives in heaven with those who love God, while persons not loving God will go to hell. Due to a child's literal understanding at this age, he or she is often concerned with avoiding hell, or ultimate punishment.

Stage-2 Faith, Mythic-Literal Faith, is normative for children from the age of six to twelve, but as with all the subsequent stages of faith, they may remain in that stage throughout life. Children accept the stories and symbols of their community's beliefs in a one-dimensional, literal way, because at this stage they are cognitively unable to step back from the flow of the stories and critically formulate their meaning. Robert Coles (1990) asked a class of fifth graders to respond to the following question: "Tell me, as best you can, who you are" (p. 308). One boy wrote that "I was put here by God, and I hope to stay until He says OK, enough, come back" (p. 312). A Puerto Rican girl who usually didn't say much responded with:

> Well, how *does* He decide? How can He possibly keep track of everyone? I asked our priest, and he said all kids want to know, and you just have to have faith, and if you don't, then you're in trouble, and besides, you'll never know, because that's God's secret. He can do things and we think they are impossible, but He does them, anyway. But I still can't see how God can keep His eyes on everyone, and my uncle says it's all a lot of nonsense (p. 312).

These children were focused on the very concrete issue of God keeping track of so many persons, and could not get beyond that incomprehensible idea without the stories and words of their families, faith communities, and spiritual leaders.

Stage-3 Faith, Synthetic-Conventional Faith, can begin to evolve at adolescence (age twelve and beyond). Persons in this stage tend to see God as personal and relational, and in a more spiritual sense than before, assigning great value to religious symbols. A teen in this stage of faith may find great attachment to a cross necklace, as a symbol of his or her beliefs. A teen might find value in the Lord's Supper or communion, even if he or she is unable to specify the deep connection through words.

Fowler's Stage-3 corresponds with Erikson's Stage-5, identity versus role confusion, at least in terms of possible age identified as adolescence, or twelve and beyond. Erikson (1950) describes adolescence as a transition period from childhood to adulthood, when people examine the various roles they play, and integrate these roles into a perception of self, or identity. Fowler assumes that the teen has an ability to think abstractly which allows for a new level of thinking critically in relation to the stories and myths that one has been told in relation to one's belief. In Kohlberg's (1969) Stage-5, Morality of Contract, of Individual Rights, and of Democratically Accepted Law, the adolescent is moving to an internally controlled morality which parallels Fowler's and Erikson's stages. A person at this stage in life is making the significant shift from looking to others to define him or herself, to identify what is right or wrong, and to lead out in appropriate expressions of faith, to a more internally driven, and personally informed way of living. The tension is great in the adolescent years, as teens are struggling to establish their own identity and to be accepted by society at the same time. As a teen engages in critical thinking over time, he or she is able to move into a space that allows his or her own motivation and understanding to direct decisions, actions, and faith activities.

Consequently, developmental factors that lead to Stage-4 Faith include beginning to clash with external authority (most often parents in this case); encounters with life experiences and perspectives that force persons to examine belief structures; leaving home physically and/or emotionally, causing the examination of self and theology; and the influence of adult models at Stage-4. The optimum time to enter Stage-4 is during the traditional college years, age 18-22. Typically, life situations encountered during these years cause a person to think about his or her religious and spiritual identity and beliefs. Cognitively, the power of reason and critical analysis comes to the forefront, and this often is the case in a person's quest for understanding related to his or her spiritual self as well. Reason is held sacred above all else, often due to one's unwillingness to live with mystery. Persons in this stage are often open to seriously consider the views of others through study (reason), but not be open to being changed by them.

In Stage-4 Faith, Individuate-Reflective Faith, both the interruption of reliance on an external authority and the relocation of authority within the self, the "executive self" are required (Fowler, 1981, p. 79). Concurrently, Kohlberg (1969) identifies the center for moral decision making during adulthood, Stage-6, Morality of Individual Principles and Conscience, as internal ethical principles. Decisions made from this perspective are made according to what is right versus what is written into law, honoring this newly relocated authority within the self, as Fowler described.

Reaching Stage-5 Faith, Conjunctive Faith—formerly called Paradoxical-Consolidative Faith—is rare before middle age. This is largely due to an emerging awareness that reality is more complex than what one's Stage-4, highly rationalized view can contain (Helminiak, 1987). Externally, Conjunctive Faith realizes the validity of systems other than one's own and so moves away from seeing a situation as a dichotomy, as seen in Stage 4's either-or thinking. Persons using Conjunctive Faith realize that the deepest truths are inconsistent, resulting in what is often described by others as a sweeter spirit than previous stages. Erikson (1950) describes Stage-7, Generativity versus Stagnation, which is concurrent in the lifespan with Fowler's Stage-5, as a time when a person is concerned with helping, producing for, or guiding the following generation. Both theorists emphasize the external focus of this stage of life. Canda (1988) suggests an understanding of spirituality that encompasses searching for meaning and purpose in life. During this stage of life, this type of meaning and purpose often culminates in the extension of oneself for the support and development of others. Still, a person in Stage-5 "remains divided" (Helminiak, p. 198). People in Stage-5 faith are living in an untransformed world while experiencing visions of transformation. In some few cases this division leads to radical actualization called Stage 6 faith.

During later adulthood, changes associated with psychological and cognitive development impel a person to focus on the inner or spiritual self (Mulqueen, & Elisa, 2000). Exceedingly rare, according to Fowler, Stage-6, Universalizing Faith, incarnates and actualizes the spirit of an inclusive and fulfilled human community, drawn to the familihood of all people (Marra, 2000). This stage constructs an ultimate environment that includes and cherishes all beings (Fowler, 1981). For persons reaching this rare stage of faith development, Fowler suggests that they would be beyond mid-life. Erikson (1950) describes persons of old age as being in a crisis of Ego Integrity versus Despair. Persons in this stage, Stage-8, are looking back over their lives, reflecting, and taking stock of their decisions. For some persons this review leads to a sense of peace, but for others, to a sense of sadness and despair. Persons working out this crisis and reaching a point of peace or ego integrity might find that they are more open to the inclusion of all beings, as Fowler suggests.

Therefore, traditional ways of considering spiritual development draw on the assumptions of general human development. According to stage-based theorists, this growth in authentic self-transcendence that results from the individual's taking responsibility for himself or herself, "moves from infant, impulse-dominated self-centeredness to a conformist identity with one's social group and finally to post-conventional self-determination and integration of internal and external reality" (Helminiak, 1987, p. 77). Helminiak proposes Fowler's extensive work around stages of spiritual development as *the* stages of spiritual development, "at least within middle-class American and equivalent cultures" (p. 84). As has been demonstrated above, it can be useful to consider Fowler's stages of faith in light of other types of development across the lifespan, in order to gain a greater understanding of the common crises, cognitive abilities, conceptual frameworks, and worldviews.

One of the "criticisms leveled at general stage theories is that such theories are merely descriptions of how specific people change, and that such models are only valid for the one culture out of which they have emerged. The patterns are chiefly due to cultural factors, expectations, roles, and conditioning, or else economics, and do not reflect universal tendencies of human nature outside of the society portrayed" (Irwin, 2002, p. 30). Other specific critique of Kohlberg's and sometimes Erikson's work includes potential cultural biases inherent in the categorization, limitations imposed by children's limited vocabulary and expression of their ideas, the lack of clear-cut divisions between one category and another, and the idea that the stages must occur in an absolute order.

Dykstra (1981) questions the very foundation of Kohlberg's work. Though he finds Kohlberg to be quite clear about what he thinks morality is and what it takes to be a moral person, Dykstra questions the judgement-based or juridical ethics upon which this image of a moral person is derived. Dykstra contrasts Kohlberg's form of ethics which provides a clear guide for action through its rules and principles for decision making with 'visional ethics'. Dykstra's visional ethics focus on questioning what we see and what it is that enables human beings to see more realistically. For visional ethics, action follows vision, and vision depends upon character—"a person thinking, reasoning, believing, feeling, willing, and acting as a whole" (p. 59). Fowler (1986) himself contends that the contributions of Kohlberg and others are useful only to a point when addressing conceptually the last relational step of faith. This is primarily because Kohlberg favors an objectifying, technical reasoning, which has no room for freedom, risk, passion, and subjectivity, all central in Fowler's final stage of faith development.

Alternative Ways of Thinking about Spiritual Development

As social workers, concerning ourselves with "what and how we actually live in this world" can lead to a variety of approaches for defining and understanding spiritual development within ourselves and for those with whom we work (Marra, 2000, p. 72). While recognizing the worth and unique contribution of the stage-based approaches, a number of researchers have proposed expanded or additional ways of considering spiritual development. Carol Gilligan, Joan Borysenko, Matthew Fox and others have approached development from a largely feminist perspective and offer some additional useful ideas for thinking about spiritual development. In addition, Wendy Haight incorporates some broader cultural implications for considering the importance of the role of spirituality within the lives of children and all individuals. And, finally, Craig Dykstra's unique process critique, which focuses on the practices and behaviors that he identifies as inherent in spiritual development, will be discussed.

Gilligan, Borysenko, & Fox: Feminist Approaches to Development

An alternative way of thinking invites the participation of voices of those persons often unheard, including persons other than the young, white, heterosexual, Judeo-Christian, able-bodied, male, with sufficient resources and power (Schriver, 2001). Carol Gilligan and others (Taylor, Gilligan, & Sullivan, 1985) have examined the research and findings of many traditional theorists, and concluded that generally the experience of girls and women at best are treated with curiosity, and a brief description inferring 'otherness' in comparison to the 'norm,' defined as or assumed to be boys and men. Gilligan proposes a look at girls as "'different,' mainly to hold it apart from its common mistranslation, 'deficient'" (p. 2). She suggests that to listen to the voices of women is to learn a great deal about what is necessary for more completely understanding the meaning of individual development for both women and men (Gilligan, 1982). Additionally, persons in many minority groups hold a worldview emphasizing the inter-relatedness of the self or the individual with other systems in the person's environment such as families, households, communities, and the ethnic group as a whole. "In addition to and in conjunction with the family, religious and spiritual institutions hold and pass along the philosophical standpoints or worldview of the people" (p. 355). It is useful to review approaches that embrace a communal spiritual developmental process.

The bio-psycho-*spiritual* model that Joan Borysenko (1996) proposes expands the more traditionally accepted bio-psycho-social understanding of individual development. An assumption present within Borysenko's work is that a person's spiritual development is integrally connected to his/her cognitive, physical, and psychosocial learning and transformation. Borysenko, utilizing the bio-psycho-spiritual feedback

Table 2: The Feminine Life Cycle – in Seven Year Cycles Joan Borysenko	
Quadrant One: Childhood and Adolescence	Early Childhood 1st Period: Ages 0-7 From Empathy to Interdependence
	Middle Childhood 2nd Period: Ages 7-14 The Logic of the Heart
	Adolescence 3rd Period: Ages 14-21 Snow While Falls Asleep, But Awakens to Herself
Quadrant Two: Young Adulthood	A Home of One's Own 4th Period: Ages 21-28 The Psychobiology of Mating and Motherhood
	The Age 30 Transition 5th Period: Ages 28-35 New Realities, New Plans
	Healing and Balance 6th Period: Ages 35-42 Spinning Straw into Gold
Quadrant Three: Midlife	The Midlife Metamorphosis 7th Period: Ages 42-49 Authenticity, Power, and the Emergence of the Guardian
	From Herbs to HRT 8th Period: Ages 49-56 A Mindful Approach to Menopause
	The Heart of a Woman 9th Period: Ages 56-63 Feminine Power and Social Action
Quadrant Four: Elder Years	Wisdom's Daughters 10th Period: Ages 63-70 Creating a New Integral Culture
	The Gifts of Change 11th Period: Ages 70-77 Resiliency, Loss, and Growth
	Recapitulating Our Lives 12th Period: Ages 77-84 and Beyond Generativity, Retrospection, and Transcendence
Death	The Ultimate Act of Renewal & Growth

Table 2.

loop, describes this spiral-formation of development through 12 seven-year cycles of renewal and metamorphosis, each one preparing for the next (See Table 2). There are three such cycles in each 'quadrant.' The four quadrants are broadly defined as childhood and adolescence, young adulthood, midlife, and late adulthood. The thirteenth part of the life cycle, death, is perhaps the ultimate act of renewal and growth.

Borysenko explains the evolving capacities of each period, traces the waxing and waning of feminine consciousness, and assures women that midlife is a stage, not a crisis. Thomas (2001) cites similar findings, as she describes a "renewal of spirituality" for many women, as their lives changed the moment they gave birth (p. 93). Though Borysenko's work is grouped within linear age-related stages, her approach is largely focused on the recurring themes of the inter-connectedness between people, nature, and things. A person living in such a way as to embrace the ideals set out by Borysenko would recognize that true intimacy based on respect and love is the measure of a life well lived. This often plays out in the choices made by a person related to work, leisure, living arrangements, and social commitments, as well as forming the underlying motivation for all relationships. As the person grows older, Borysenko (1996) suggests that "this innate female spirituality underlies an often unspoken commitment to protect our world from the ravages of greed and violence" (p. 3). This presentation gives a wonderful example of the spiral-model of spiritual development (see Table 2).

A spiritual metaphor for traditional and alternative paradigms may be found in the familiar themes of 'Climbing Jacob's Ladder' and 'Dancing Sarah's Circle.' Climbing Jacob's ladder is a "male-dominated mystical teaching in Western Christianity," a metaphor based on Jacob's dream recorded in the twenty-eighth chapter of Genesis (Fox, 1990, p. 37). This text has been utilized to describe the faith journey as one symbolic of fleeing the earth in an upward climb to God. In this model or metaphor, Fox suggests that "we climb to God by contemplation and descend to neighbor by compassion. Thus compassion is descent; it is also an after-thought, a luxury that one can afford only after a very long lifetime of contemplative ascending" (p. 40). According to Fox, a spiritual developmental understanding based on this traditional, hierarchical, competitive, independent, and linear approach to growth will necessarily embrace distinct, clearly defined, and restrictive patterns. Openness to the visual and theoretical understanding of dancing Sarah's circle allows for a wide variety of spiritual experiences, explanations, and attachments of meaning for persons on this journey.

Borysenko (1999) replaces the heroic model of step-by-step progress up Jacob's ladder with the image of women walking and dancing Sarah's circle. She suggests that, like all women, the mother of Isaac came to know herself in the deep, intuitive way through the medium of her relationships rather than strictly in terms of a relationship with a transcendent God. Dancing Sarah's Circle is based on the biblical text found in Genesis 18-21, culminating in Sarah, at the age of ninety, giving birth to a surprise son she named Isaac, meaning "God has smiled, God has been kind" (Fox, 1990, p.44). Thus, a spirituality of Dancing Sarah's circle is one of laughter and joy. Sarah could be surprised, filled with unexpected wonder, and able to laugh. Sarah, then, is a symbol of laughter, creativity, and shalom.

An understanding of spiritual development based on this alternative notion including a shared experience/ecstasy, interdependence, nurture, circle-like welcome of others, culminating in a love of neighbor that *is* love of God, will necessarily embrace a broader, fluid, circular, dynamic, shared pattern of spiritual growth. Jesus' supper times with his disciples can be seen as a Sarah circle kind of intimacy and his Last Supper experience rings especially true to this dynamic. The sacrament of washing the feet that meant so much to Jesus the night before he died is a patent example of a Sarah circle dynamic. Jesus both washed his disciples' feet *and* had his feet washed with ointment by a woman willing to dry them with her long hair. "Sarah's entire circle dynamic is as much receiving as giving" (Fox, 1990, p. 56).

Within alternative approaches to understanding spirituality and spiritual development, certain concepts are central, such as mutuality, cooperation, harmony between persons, the earth, and God, and participating in significant life events. These are the main tenets of Sarah's Circle. One example of persons working together within this understanding of spirituality is a liberation group. Persons in these groups come together to share their pain of oppression and discrimination thus building a bond, and striving for mutual empowerment. Person's embracing the Sarah-Circle dynamic might take part in cooperatives such as food or clothing or housing, expanding the options, resources and flexibility of all involved. Living in harmony with the environment through interest in solar, wind and water energy systems is another example of people living Sarah's Circle within society. Finally, parents who insist on natural childbirth wherein their child will be welcomed eye to eye by a circle of fully conscious and celebrating, wonder-struck family, offer another way in which persons may choose to live out the tenets held within Sarah's circle, in full participation of important life events.

Borysenko (1996) acknowledges in the introduction to her book that although it is written primarily for women, she hopes that it will be equally enlightening to men. For whether we are biologically male or female, each of us contains aspects of the other. Her focus is the critical factor that unites women in a deeply spiritual perspective, transcending differences in religious beliefs. "From a spiritual vantage point our major life task is much larger than making money, finding a mate, having a career, raising children, looking beautiful, achieving psychological health, or defying aging, illness, and death. It is recognition of the sacred in daily life—a deep gratitude for the wonders of the world and the delicate web of inter-connectedness between people, nature and things" (p. 3). Borysenko's description of the spiritual realm of a person's life parallels nicely with Canda's (1988) emphasis on seeking a sense of meaning and purpose in life, and striving for mutual fulfilling relationships among individuals, society, and ultimate reality. Both authors are largely focusing on the relational aspects of persons, including connections with other persons, nature, things, and ultimate reality.

A significant difference between the growth of persons in Borysenko's understanding and Fowler's is that each previous type of interaction, personal experience, and belief process is cherished and viewed as critical, remaining a part of a person's whole, rather than an emphasis on leaving a particular stage behind for another, higher one. Bohannan (1992) comes to a similar conclusion. She states that women experience the sacred as immanent rather than as transcendent, living their lives in the awareness of the sacred around them, and practicing grace and love in the here and now. This rhythmic approach to the understanding of a woman's body, mind, and spirit, is interdependent, creative, and dynamic.

Wendy Haight: Cultural Implications for Spiritual Development

Spiritual socialization can be central to children's healthy development. Haight (1998) found that for some African American children, this foundation is directly tied to resiliency. Despite profound, ongoing stressors, her research found significant strength within African American children, their families and communities, often tied to the role of the church in their lives, and of a generally shared spiritual connection. Neumark (1998) suggests that spiritual development cannot be taught or managed, but "children can be encouraged to develop spiritually through being given the opportunity to consider, reflect, dream, and challenge" (p. 22).

Ancestral worldviews are reflected throughout the social institutions responsible for imparting the beliefs and values of the group such as the family, and religious and spiritual institutions. In addition to and in conjunction with the family, religious and spiritual institutions hold and pass along the philosophical standpoints or worldviews of the people (Schriver, 2001). The African-American community, like others, has a rich traditions and history that uplifts the hurt, comforts the struggling, and celebrates the soul. Church leaders rise to significance in the daily moral life of families and communities. "Individuals, families, and neighborhoods seek their counsel and support, guidance and inspiration. The church is also a fulcrum of much of the social life in the community and exists as a staging area for political and social activism" (Saleebey, 2001, p. 315).

A Rabbi working as a community organizer found that the lives of many low- to moderate-income people of color and working-class ethnic whites revolve around their religious and spiritual beliefs (ben Asher, 2001). Many African Americans hold a worldview with roots in an African philosophical position that stresses collectivism rather than individualism. The worldviews of many Native Americans perceive all aspects of life as interrelated and of religious significance although there is no single dominant religion among the many Native American cultures. Asian/Pacific American families stress a belief system in which harmony is a core value. Latino religious beliefs reinforce a belief system in which the role of the family is a central tenet (Harrison, Wilson, Pine, Chan, & Buriel, 1990). Such worldviews as these suggest much more in common with the core concerns of social work. The principles of social systems and ecological thinking found in these worldviews compliment the growing emphasis on spirituality and religion within social work practice.

The church often plays an important and supportive role for families of color. Church provides a sense of community and inter-relatedness for many individuals and families. Family and church are so intertwined for some African Americans, for example, that church members may refer to other members as their 'church family.' One's church family may provide such important supports as role models for young family members and assistance with child rearing. Even for African American families that do not belong to a formal church, spirituality may play a significant role. This spirituality is often a strength and a survival mechanism for African American families that can be tapped, particularly in times of death and dying, illness, loss, and bereavement (Boyd-Franklin, 1993). It is important to acknowledge the cultural implications of spiritual development, and the unique roles, meaning, and expectations found within each faith community.

Craig Dykstra: A Process Critique of Spiritual Development

Craig Dykstra (1999) embraces a certain 'strangeness,' a 'peculiarity' of Christian practice, as an asset, not a handicap. He accents the role of families, however defined, and youth, however attracted, in such settings which is a similar focus to Haight's findings related to some African American communities. This openness to 'strangeness' or other ways of thinking about and understanding certain life events, and ascribing meaning to them, fits well within an alternative approach to thinking about spiritual development. Dykstra's approach leaves more room for less traditional ways of expressing one's spiritual journey, which can include meditation, the acknowledgement of a particular geographic space which serves as a spiritual oasis, and the honoring of the God-given life and worth in all living beings.

Dykstra (1999) believes that the development of Christian nurture, rather than following formal 'stages,' relates to themes integral to the Christian story itself, focusing on ways of being and thinking and doing. If one considers spiritual development as a spiral-shaped experience, drawing from the recurring realities of a circle, but honoring the assumed growth and movement that a ladder suggests, it is possible to begin to understand a more thematic approach to this process. Dykstra identifies hunger, life, practices, places, and signs as broad themes recurring in our lives, embracing the mystery or depth of Christian faith, and a variety of methods for practicing this faith.

William Hull (1991) describes Christian salvation as a dynamic process—we were saved, we are being saved, and we will be saved. This somewhat subtle shift from the ladder image to a re-visiting process in cyclical form is quite profound, as the spiral-formation of growth allows one to re-engage with themes throughout life. This approach mirrors our own yearly reliving of the significant events on the liturgical calendar including communion, Lent, Easter, Pentecost, Advent, Christmas, and Epiphany. The process of re-experiencing these pivotal celebrations allows us to find the extraordinary in the 'ordinary.' As we continue to grow, change, understand ourselves, others, and God in different ways, our experiencing of these events is repetitive, yet new.

These alternative approaches to understanding spiritual development allow for the impact of greater societal, political, racial, ethnic, socioeconomic, physical, and emotional factors throughout this life process. Helminiak (1996) argues that if the needs of organisms are not met, the higher levels of psyche and spirit are adversely affected. Inversely, a sick spirit impacts psyche and organism negatively. Young, Cashwell, and Shcherbakova (2000) conclude that spirituality seems to provide a buffer from stressful life events that are perceived as negative, further supporting the value of the spiral-formed developmental impact.

Conclusion

The spiritual development approaches discussed in this chapter support the central tenet that "important religious beliefs, rituals, and social structures can play key roles as individuals and families move through the life cycle" (Hugen, 2001, p. 13). Some of the elements identified as significant dimensions of spiritual development are creativity, contemplation, commitment and quest or search for meaning (Halstead, 1992). In short, "spirituality is essential to human happiness and mental health" (Elkins, 1999, p. 44).

What occurs between the client and the social worker involves not only the traditional interventions, methods, and skills the social worker applies, but also a two-way exchange of ideas, feelings, beliefs, and values that may or may not be directly addressed or acknowledged. "Whether professionals are 'believers' in the spiritual dimension is important. 'Nonbelievers' may not be fully able to accept clients who consider spirituality and religion to be meaningful and useful within the context of their life experiences" (Sermabeikian, 1994, pp. 178-79). Social workers, therefore, should develop self-understanding regarding personal biases, their own experiences that lead to strong assumptions about others, existential issues and spiritual growth (Canda, 1988; & Schriver, 2001). "Self-inquiry must be a disciplined and consistent process of personal and professional growth. Social workers should examine their beliefs, motivations, values, and activities and consider the impact of these factors upon the client's spirituality" (Canda, p. 245).

A spiritual bias can be just as harmful as racism or sexism. When considering the issue of spirit, spiritual, and spirituality, a social worker must also consider his or her assumptions about the process of growth, deepening awareness and the meanings attached to this spiritual development. Whether the philosophical tenets of climbing Jacob's ladder or those supporting dancing Sarah's circle are embraced, social workers must enter into an awareness of the sacred for themselves and for the persons with whom they work.

References

ben Asher, M. (2001). Spirituality and religion in social work practice. *Social Work Today, 1*(7), 15-18.

Bohannan, H. (1992). Quest-tioning tradition: Spiritual transformation images in women's narratives and 'housekeeping.' *Western Folklore, 51*(1), 65-80.

Borysenko, J. (1996). *A woman's book of life: The biology, psychology, and spirituality of the feminine life cycle*. New York: Riverhead Books.

Borysenko, J. (1999). *A woman's journey to God: Finding the feminine path*. New York: Riverhead Books.

Boyd-Franklin, N. (1993). Race, class and poverty. In *Normal family processes*, Walsh, F. (Ed.). New York: Guilford.

Brandt, A. (1991). Do kids need religion? *Utne Reader*, 43, 84-88.

Canda, E.R. (1988). Spirituality, religious diversity, and social work practice. *Social Casework: The Journal of Contemporary Social Work*, 238-247.

Coles, R. (1990). *The spiritual life of children*. Boston: Houghton Mifflin.

Council on Social Work Education. (2000). Curriculum policy statement for master's degree program in social work education. Alexandria, VA: Author.

Dykstra, C. (1999). *Growing in the life of faith: Education and Christian practice*. Louisville, KY: Geneva Press.

Dykstra, C.R. (1981). *Vision and character: A Christian educator's alternative to Kohlberg*. New York: Paulist Press.

Elkins, D.N. (1999). Spirituality. *Psychology Today, 32*(5), 44-50.

Erikson, E. (1950). *Childhood and society*. New York: Norton.

Fowler, J. (1981). *Stages of faith: The psychology of human development and the quest for meaning*. San Francisco: Harper Collins.

Fowler, J. (1986). Faith and the structuring of meaning. In C. Dykstra, & S. Parks (Eds.), *Faith development and Fowler* (pp. 15-44). Birmingham, AL: Religious Education Press.

Fox, M. (1990). *A spirituality named compassion*. San Francisco: HarperCollins.

Gilligan, C. (1982). *In a different voice: Psychological theory and women's development*. Cambridge: Harvard University Press.

Haight, W.L. (1998). "Gathering the Spirit" at First Baptist Church: Spirituality as a protective factor in the lives of African American children. *Social Work, 43*(3), 213-21.

Halstead, M. (1992). The final frontier: Spiritual education is now subject to official scrutiny. *Times Educational Supplement, 3990*, I.

Harrison, A., Wilson, M., Pine, C., Chan, S., & Buriel, R. (1990). Family ecologies of ethnic minority children. *Child Development, 61*, 347-362.

Helminiak, D.A. (1987). *Spiritual development: An interdisciplinary study*. Chicago: Loyola University Press.

Helminiak, D.A. (1996). *The human core of spirituality: Mind as psyche and spirit*. Albany, N.Y.: State University of New York Press.

Hugen, B., (Ed.). (1998). *Christianity and social work: Readings on the integration of Christian faith and social work practice*. Botsford, CT: North American Association of Christians in Social Work.

Hugen, B. (2001). Spirituality and religion in social work practice: A conceptual model. In Van Hook, M., Hugen, B., & Aguilar, M. (Eds.), *Spirituality within religious traditions in social work practice* (pp. 9-17). Pacific Grove, CA: Brooks/Cole.

Hull, W.E. (1991). *The Christian experience of salvation*. Nashville: Broadman & Holman Publishers.

Irwin, R.R. (2002). *Human development and the spiritual life: How consciousness grows toward transformation*. New York: Kluwer Academic/Plenum Publishers.

Joseph, M.V. (1988). Religion and social work practice. *Social Casework: The Journal of Contemporary Social Work*, 443-449.

Kohlberg, L. (1969). *Stages in the development of moral thought and action*. New York: Holt, Rinehart & Winston.

Kropf, R. (1991). Faith's last stage may well be leap in the dark. *National Catholic Reporter, 28*(9), 12.

Marra, R. (2000). What do you mean, "spirituality"? *Journal of Pastoral Counseling, 22*, 67-79.

Mulqueen, J., & Elias, J.L. (2000). Understanding spiritual development through cognitive development. *Journal of Pastoral Counseling, Annual*, 99-113.

Neumark, V. (1998). Hole makes whole. *Times Educational Supplement, 4272*, pp. 22-24.

Saleebey, D. (2001). *Human behavior and social environments: A biopsychosocial approach.* New York: Columbia University.

Schriver, J.M. (2001). *Human behavior and the social environment: Shifting paradigms in essential knowledge for social work practice* (3rd ed.). Boston: Allyn & Bacon.

Sermabeikian, P. (1994). Our clients, ourselves: The spiritual perspective and social work practice. *Social Work, 39*(3), 178-83.

Smith, M.H. (1997-1998). Embodied wisdom, embodied faith: Bio-spirituality. *Hungryhearts,1*(3-4), 1-7.

Spencer, S.W. (1961). What place has religion in social work education? *Social Work*, 161-170.

Taylor, J.M., Gilligan, C., & Sullivan, A.M. (1985). *Between voice and silence: Women and girls, race and relationship*. Cambridge, MA: Harvard University Press.

Thomas, T. (2001). Becoming a mother: Matrescence as spiritual formation. *Religious Education, 96*(1), 88-105.

Young, J.S., Cashwell, C.S., & Shcherbakova, J. (2000). The moderating relationship of spirituality on negative life events and psychological adjustment. *Counseling and Values, 45*(1), 49-60.

CHAPTER 10

SPIRITUAL ASSESSMENT: A REVIEW OF COMPLEMENTARY ASSESSMENT MODELS

David R. Hodge and Crystal Holtrop

Assessment is considered by many to be an underdeveloped area in social work (Mattaini & Kirk, 1991). The lack of development is particularly acute in the area of spiritual assessment (Bullis, 1996; Sherwood, 1998). For instance, numerous studies have found that most social workers have received no training in the area of spiritual assessment (Bullis, 1996; Canda & Furman, 1999; Derezotes, 1995; Sheridan & Amato-von Hemert, 1999; Furman & Canda, 1994). The lack of attention devoted to spiritual assessment represents a significant oversight. Four issues, ontology, ethics, strengths, and autonomy will be discussed in brief to highlight the importance of spiritual assessment in social work.

Spirituality is often central to clients' personal ontology, meaning it may be the essence of their personhood. Spirituality may inform attitudes and practices in such areas as child rearing, diet, marriage, medical care, military participation, recreation, schooling, social interactions, as well as many other dimensions of life (DiBlasio, 1988; Rey, 1997). For one third of the general population, religion is the most important facet of their lives and over 50% consider it to be a very important aspect of their lives (Gallup & Lindsay, 1999; Walsh, 1999). Further, for African Americans, Hispanics, women, the elderly, the poor, and many other populations of significance to social workers, spirituality is even more salient (Gallup & Lindsay, 1999; Pargament, 1997). The provision of respectful services to these groups is often contingent upon practitioners' awareness of clients' spiritually based beliefs and practices. In order to provide effective services, social workers must develop some understanding of clients' spiritual worldview.

A second factor stems from the profession's ethical mandates. Spirituality is often expressed in distinct traditions or faith-based cultures (Fellin, 2000; Talbot, 2000). The NASW Code of Ethics (1999) stipulates that social workers are to demonstrate competence and sensitivity toward faith based cultures (1.05b) and recognizes the strengths that exist among such groups (1.05a). Ethically sound practice entails obtaining the knowledge to exhibit spiritual sensitivity to clients.

Social workers are increasingly recognizing the importance of strengths (Cowger, 1994; Hwang & Cowger, 1998; Saleebey, 1997). Reviews have consistently found a generally positive association between spirituality and a wide number of beneficial characteristics (Ellison & Levin, 1998; Gartner, Larson & Allen, 1991; Koenig, McCullough & Larson, 2001; Pargament, 1997). More specifically, various dimensions of spirituality have been associated with recovery from addiction (Turner, O' Dell & Weaver, 1999), depression (Propst, 1996), divorce (Nathanson, 1995), homelessness (Lindsey, Kurtz, Jarvis, Williams & Nackerud, 2000; Montgomery, 1994), serious mental illness (Sullivan, 1997), sexual assault (Kennedy, Davis & Talyor, 1998) as well as empowerment (Calhoun-Brown, 1998; Maton & Salem, 1995) and healing (Maton & Wells, 1995; McRae, Thompson & Cooper, 1999). While spirituality is often an important client asset, unfortunately, these strengths often lie dormant (Saleebey, 1997). To tap clients' spiritual assets for the purposes of ameliorating problems, practitioners must use methods designed to identify clients' strengths (Ronnau & Poertner, 1993).

Finally, there is the issue of client autonomy. Many clients desire to integrate their spiritual beliefs and values into the helping relationship (Privette, Quackenbos & Bundrick, 1994). According to Gallup data reported by Bart (1998), 66% of the general public would prefer to see a professional counselor with spiritual values and beliefs and 81% wanted to have their own values and beliefs integrated into the counseling process. Further, research suggests that spirituality tends to become more salient during difficult situations (Ferraro & Kelley-Moore, 2000; Pargament, 1997), when individuals may be more likely to encounter social workers.

In sum, spiritual assessment provides social workers with a means to understand clients' spiritual strengths, beliefs, and values—in short—their worldview. Not only is such knowledge often critical for culturally competent practice, in many instances it is an ethical imperative. Spiritual assessment provides a mechanism to identify clients' spiritual resources and honor their desire to integrate their beliefs and values into the clinical dialogue.

In light of the importance of spiritual assessment, this chapter reviews a number of recently developed assessment approaches and provides examples of how they may be applied in practice with Christian clients. Our intent is not to provide an exhaustive review of various assessment methods, but rather to review a specific series of assessment instruments. These four instruments were developed to complement one another in the hopes of providing social workers with a set of assessment tools for use in numerous settings with a variety of clients. Rather than being interchangeable, one approach may be ideal in one context while another tool may be better suited to address a different client-to-practitioner interface. Readers are encouraged to obtain the original articles in which the instruments first appeared and to become familiar with the strengths and limitations of each assessment instrument. The assessment tools may be used with a variety of different religious traditions, but here we will be applying a Christian point of view and using examples from practice with Christian clients.

After defining spiritual assessment, spirituality, and religion, four assessment instruments are reviewed—spiritual genograms (Hodge, 2001b), spiritual lifemaps (Hodge, in press), spiritual histories (Hodge, 2001a), and spiritual eco-maps (Hodge, 2000; Hodge & Williams, in press). A brief overview of the assets and limitations of each method is provided and, for the three diagrammatic instruments, case examples are provided to familiarize the reader with the instrument. A brief discussion on conducting an assessment concludes the chapter.

Definitions

Spiritual assessment is defined as the process of gathering and organizing spiritually based data into a coherent format that provides the basis for interventions (Hodge, 2001a; Rauch, 1993). The subsequent interventions may or may not be spiritually based. As implied above, a spiritual assessment may be conducted for the purposes of using traditional, non-spiritual, interventions in a manner that is more congruent with clients' beliefs and values.

Spirituality is defined as an existential relationship with God (or perceived transcendence) (Hodge, 2001a). Religion flows from spirituality, expressing the spiritual relationship in particular beliefs, forms, and practices that have been developed in community with other individuals who share similar spiritual experiences (Hodge, 2000). Accordingly, spirituality and religion are overlapping but distinct constructs (Canda, 1997; Carroll, 1997).

Spiritual Genograms

In a manner analogous to traditional genograms, spiritual genograms provide social workers with a tangible graphic representation of spirituality across at least three generations (Hodge, 2001b). Through the use of what is essentially a modified family tree, they help both practitioners and clients understand the flow of historically rooted patterns through time. In short, spiritual genograms are a blueprint of complex intergenerational spiritual interactions.

In keeping with standard genogram conventions (McGoldrick, Gerson & Shellenberger, 1999; Stanion, Papadopoulos & Bor, 1997), the basic family structure is commonly delineated across at least three generations. Typically, squares represent males and circles denote females. In some cases, triangles or other geometric shapes can be used to designate individuals who have played major spiritual roles but are not members of the immediate biological family (Hodge, 2001b).

To indicate clients' spiritual tradition, colored drawing pencils can be used to shade in the circles and squares (Hodge, 2001b). Color coding provides a graphic "color snapshot" of the overall spiritual composition of the family system (Hardy & Laszloffy, 1995). Various colors can be used to signify religious preference (Buddhist, Christian, Hindu, Jewish, Muslim, New Age, none, etc.), or more specifically when the information is known, denomination (Assemblies of God, Brethren, Catholic, Southern Baptist, Presbyterian, etc.). For example, a circle representing a female Southern Baptist could be colored red, a member of the Assemblies of God might be colored orange, a Muslim might be colored brown, and an individual whose affiliation and beliefs are unknown could be left uncolored. A change in an adult's religious orientation can be signified by listing the date of the change beside a circle which is drawn outside the figure and filling in the space between the circle and the figure with the appropriate color, a procedure which indicates the stability or fluidity of the person's beliefs over time. Using a similar approach, changes in orientation might also be noted by coloring the vertical segment connecting the child with the parents.

If needed, the color scheme can also be used to incorporate information on commitment (devout vs. nominal) and theology (conservative vs. liberal) (Hodge, 2001b). For example, yellow might be used to signify a devout, conservative Methodist while gray could be used for a nominal Methodist. Alternatively, symbols, which are placed beside the appropriate circle or square, could be used to indicate the degree of commitment or theological orientation. An open set of scriptures, for instance, might be used to indicate a devout person. Social workers should explain the options to clients and allow them to select the colors and symbols that they perceive best express their worldview.

Spiritually meaningful events should also be incorporated, such as water and spirit baptisms, confirmations, church memberships, and bar mitzvahs (Hodge, 2001b). Symbols drawn from the client's spiritual journey can be used to signify these events. For instance, a cross might be used by a Christian to indicate reaching a point of conversion, a dove might be used by a Pentecostal to depict a deeper work of the Holy Spirit, or a sunbeam might used by a New Age adherent to symbolize a time of profound spiritual enlightenment. In addition, short summary statements can be used to denote significant events or personal strengths.

In addition to depicting religious beliefs, it is also possible to include an affective component (Hodge, 2001b). In other words, felt spiritual closeness between family members can be illustrated on spiritual genograms. Lines with double-headed arrows [⟷] can be used to symbolize a relationship in which individuals experience a close reciprocal spiritual bond. The thickness of the line can indicate the intimacy or strength of the relationship. In situations where the relationship is more hierarchical and less reciprocal—as might occur with a grandparent mentoring a grandchild—a single arrowhead can be used to depict the flow of spiritual resources. Finally, spiritual conflict can be portrayed with a jagged line, similar to a lightening bolt, drawn between the two individuals.

Case Example

Diagram 1 (following page) indicates what a relatively straightforward spiritual genogram might look like for a couple, Mark and Beth, who are experiencing marital problems. In place of the colors that would normally be used with a spiritual genogram, patterns (for example, dots, diagonals, waves) are employed to depict various denominations.

After three years of marriage, Mark, 26, and Beth, 23, requested counseling after the recent birth of their daughter, Megan. Her birth renewed their interest in church attendance as they both desired to raise Megan with spiritual values and to have her baptized. However, they disagreed on practically everything else—how to spend money, parent their daughter, where to go to church, and how to accomplish household tasks. Mark and Beth's inability to resolve conflict was due to a power struggle over whose family of origin's rules they were going to follow. Due to their conflict over which church to attend, the therapist developed a spiritual genogram to enhance their traditional genogram.

During Mark's childhood, his nuclear family and his paternal grandparents attended the Baptist church that was 3 blocks away from their house. His family shared a tradition of going to Mark's paternal grandparents' house every Sunday after church. Although Mark knew that Aunt Betty and Uncle Joe attended a Lutheran church regularly, he had never heard them talk openly about their faith at family gatherings and was unsure how important it was to them. His maternal grandmother attended an Assemblies of God church before she was placed in the nursing home. He recalled his grandmother sharing a story about how she prayed for 30 years that her husband would become a Christian, and that her prayers were answered shortly before her husband died.

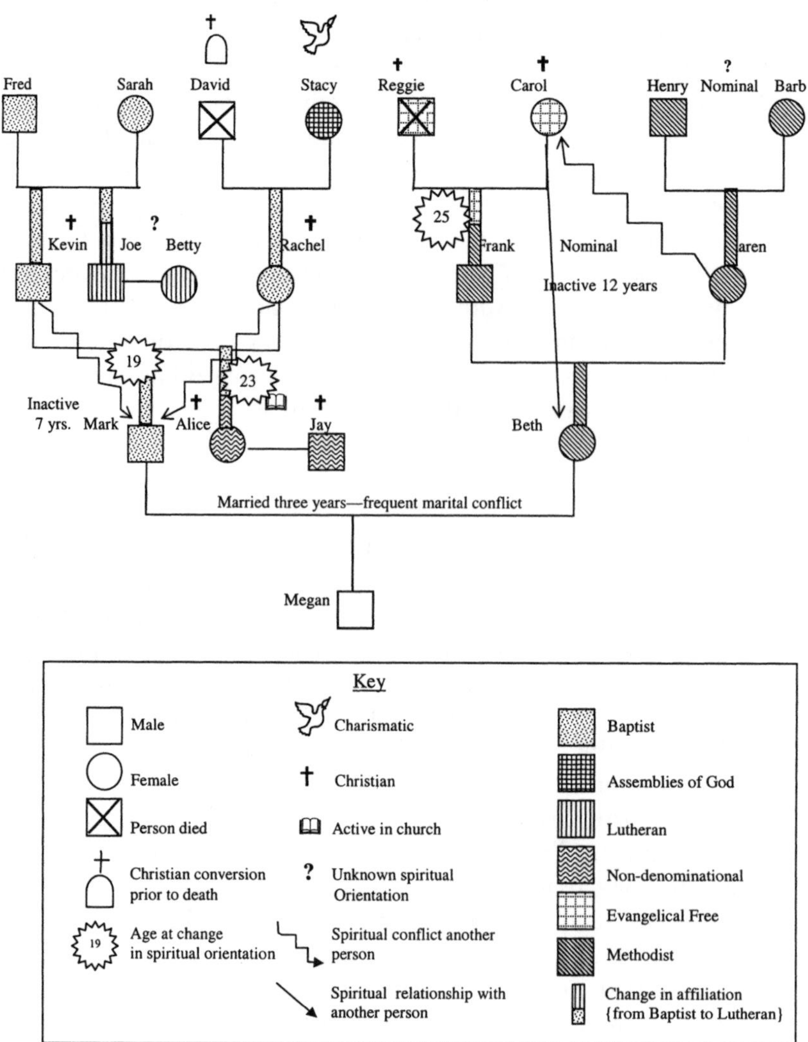

Diagram 1.

During his adolescence, Mark perceived his parents' rules as old-fashioned and rigid and rebelled against them. As soon as he left home, Mark stopped attending church, much to his parents' chagrin. His sister, Alice, left the Baptist church when she was 23 years old and started attending a non-denominational church where she met her husband, Jay. Alice and Jay are still actively involved in this church and frequently share information with Mark and Beth about family activities that are occurring there. As

Mark shared this information, the therapist drew a cross by the names of his parents, paternal grandparents, maternal grandmother, sister, and brother-in-law to indicate that they were Christians. She put a question mark next to his aunt and uncle due to Mark's lack of clarity about their level of commitment to their faith. In order to signify Alice and Jay's devout faith and active participation in their church, the therapist drew an open Bible near their names. She colored their circles and squares different colors to indicate the various denominations represented in Mark's family. Uncle Joe's and Alice's rectangles that attach them to their respective parents have two colors, indicating that they switched from attending the Baptist church to a different denomination.

Beth's family attended a Methodist church when she was young. However, their attendance dwindled to Easter and Christmas as Beth became active in school activities. She knew that her parents both believed in God, but did not see this belief influencing their lives. However, Beth had fond memories of sitting on her paternal grandmother's lap as she listened to her grandmother, Carol, read Bible stories to her. She also recalled attending Vacation Bible school which was sponsored by the Evangelical Free church her grandmother attended. She assumed that "Grandma Carol" was a committed Christian because she overheard her mother complain about "how religious Grandma Carol was" and observed her mother rebuff Grandma Carol whenever she offered to pray for the family. To signify Beth's mother's underlying conflict towards Grandma Carol over spiritual matters, the therapist drew a jagged arrow between their circles. Although her paternal grandfather died before Beth was born, she recalled her Grandma Carol fondly referring to her husband as "a fine man who loved people and the Lord."

Although Beth stated she believes in God, she acknowledged that she presently refers to God primarily when she is swearing angrily at Mark. However, as the conflict between Beth and Mark continued to escalate, she started contemplating "giving God a try." She was open to attending a church as long as it was not Mark's parents' church. She thought his mother already interfered with their marriage far too much. The therapist colored Beth's maternal grandparents' and parents' circles and squares red to represent the Methodist denomination. Due to their nominal interest in spiritual matters, Beth and Mark agreed that the therapist should not draw a cross by their names. She did draw a cross by Grandma Carol's name and by her paternal grandfather's name, and also drew an arrow from her Grandmother Carol to Beth, indicating the spiritual influence she had on Beth.

With the multi-colored spiritual genogram directly in front of them, Mark and Beth were struck by the diversity of denominations represented in their extended families. This new perspective helped them see beyond their original, narrowly defined choices of Baptist vs. Methodist that Mark and Beth clung to out of loyalty to their families of origin. The therapist encouraged the couple to interview members of their extended family, asking questions concerning their faith, their religious practices, and the strengths and limitations of their church and denomination. Beth and Mark discovered that the new perspectives gained from the interviews helped them be more evaluative in their decision-making process and moved them beyond their stalemate.

Assets and Limitations

Although spiritual genograms can be effective assessment instruments in a number of situations, they may be particularly useful when the family system plays an especially salient role in the client's life or when the client presents with problems involving family members or family of origin issues (Hodge, 2001b). For example, spiritual genograms might be used with interfaith couples experiencing spiritually based barriers to intimacy to expose areas of difference and potential conflict as well to highlight the respective spiritual strengths each person brings to the relationship. Similarly, spiritual genograms could also be used with couples from similar backgrounds to increase their level of intimacy.

Conversely, spiritual genograms may be an inappropriate assessment instrument in situations where historical influences are of minor importance. Further, even in situations where generational influences are pertinent, many clients do not connect past events with current difficulties. Accordingly, clients may view genogram construction and between-session tasks as an ineffective use of time. As Kuehl (1995) notes, proceeding with such interventions before clients appreciate their usefulness can reduce treatment adherence and jeopardize outcomes. Consequently, in some contexts it may be best to use assessment approaches that do not focus on the generational aspects of spirituality.

Spiritual Lifemaps

While spiritual genograms chart the flow of spirituality across at least three generations, spiritual lifemaps depict clients' personal spiritual life-story (Hodge, in press). More specifically, spiritual lifemaps are a pictorial delineation of a client's spiritual journey. In a manner analogous to renowned African writer Augustine's (354-430/1991) *Confessions*, spiritual lifemaps are an illustrated account of clients' relationship with God over time—a map of their spiritual life.

At its most basic level, a drawing pencil is used to sketch various spiritually significant life events on paper (Hodge, in press). The method is similar to various approaches drawn from art and family therapy in which a client's history is depicted on a "lifeline" (Tracz & Gehart-Brooks, 1999). Much like road maps, spiritual lifemaps tell us where we have come from, where we are now, and where we are going.

To assist clients in the creative expression of their spiritual journeys, it is usually best to use a large sheet of paper (e.g., 24" x 36") on which to sketch the map (Hodge, in press). Providing drawing instruments of different sizes and colors are also helpful as is offering a selection of various types and colors of construction paper and popular periodicals. Providing these items, in conjunction with scissors, glue sticks, and rulers, allows clients to clip and paste items onto the lifemap.

Spiritually significant events are depicted on a path, a roadway, or a single line that represents clients' spiritual sojourn (Hodge, in press). Typically, the path proceeds chronologically, from birth through to the present. Frequently the path continues on to death and the client's transition to the afterlife. Hand drawn symbols, cut out pictures, and other representations are used to mark key events along the journey. In keeping with many spiritual traditions, which conceive material existence to be an extension of the sacred reality, it is common to depict important lifestage events on the lifemap (for example, marriage, birth of a child, death of a close friend or relative, or loss of a job). While it is often necessary to provide clients with general guidelines, client creativity and self-expression should be encouraged.

To fully operationalize the potential of the instrument, it is important to ask clients to incorporate the various crises they have faced into their lifemaps along with the spiritual resources they have used to overcome those trials (Hodge, in press). Symbols such as hills, bumps and potholes, rain, clouds, and lightning can be used to portray difficult life situations. Delineating successful strategies that clients have used in the past frequently suggests options for overcoming present struggles.

Case Example

Diagram 2 (folowing page) provides an example of what a spiritual lifemap might look like on a smaller scale. Tyrone, a 42 year-old black male, was recently diagnosed with terminal cancer. The doctor confirmed his worst fears that the cancer was inoperable, and predicted that Tyrone had approximately 6 months to live. A medical social worker on the oncology ward met with Tyrone to help him process the shock of his prognosis and prepare for what appeared to be a premature death.

Shortly into their conversation, the social worker discovered that Tyrone was actively involved in the Third Missionary Baptist Church. Tyrone's eyes lit up as he shared that he began playing guitar in the church's music ministry 10 years ago, a couple of years after he became a Christian. It soon became clear to the social worker that Tyrone's faith was a significant strength and could help him cope with his present crisis. In order to help Tyrone identify effective coping strategies, the social worker encouraged Tyrone to develop a spiritual lifemap. Tyrone's creativity and musical interests seemed to indicate that this assignment would be a good fit for his personality.

Tyrone's parents divorced when he was 9 years old. He and his 2 older sisters lived with his mother and periodically visited his father. His mother was actively involved in a Pentecostal church and sang in the church choir. When Tyrone reached adolescence, his anger toward his absent father began to mount and was acted out in rebellion toward his mother. Out of desperation, his mother arranged guitar lessons for Tyrone to creatively redirect his anger and build his self-esteem. Tyrone established a lifelong mentoring relationship with his guitar teacher, Jerome, who consistently believed in him and spawned a passion for a variety of musical styles including blues, jazz, gospel, and rock. When he graduated from high school, he joined a band and played in clubs for the next 9 years. Disillusioned with God for not answering his childhood prayers for his father, Tyrone started experimenting with drugs and alcohol to numb his emptiness inside.

By age 27, Tyrone had successfully recorded a CD with his band and was gaining local notoriety. Life was good. He was doing well financially and he enjoyed dating several different women. However, this season was short-lived. By age 30, he was significantly in debt and was emotionally broken. After 3 years of dating, Tyrone's girlfriend, Janet concluded that Tyrone was more committed to his band than to her and she broke up with him. He coped by increasing his alcohol consumption, which hurt his performance and created conflict with his band members. After a particularly heated argument, Tyrone sought solace from Jerome, his former guitar teacher. Through this renewed friendship, Tyrone began examining his life, his priorities, and the source of his emptiness and bitterness. He forgave God for what he perceived to be abandonment (a replication of his father's abandonment) and he experienced a profound sense of God's love and acceptance. Tyrone soon realized that it was he, not God, who had abandoned divine and human love out of bitterness and despair.

Tyrone started attending the Third Missionary Baptist church. Upon Jerome's advice, Tyrone took a break from playing guitar and immersed

Diagram 2.

himself in Bible study, prayer, and Christian books to help him sort out his unresolved hurts, develop effective anger management skills, and evaluate his life goals. He also developed significant relationships with other men in a Promise Keepers group. He watched several men in the group weather severe trials by clinging onto God's promises and by receiving love and support from their friends. He gradually learned that no matter what happens in life, God is good, faithful, and in control.

After a 2-year hiatus, Tyrone began playing guitar in church. Using his talents to worship God gave him a sense of meaning and joy that was deeper than any he had experienced before. Completing the spiritual lifemap helped Tyrone reflect on his life, his pit and peak experiences, the lessons he had learned, and the people who had blest him. Most importantly, he identified key people that would support him through his present illness and pray for God to heal him. While discussing the lifemap with his social worker, Tyrone began to clarify the goals he still wanted to accomplish, like mentoring some young boys in church who were growing up in single parent homes. Through this reflective assignment, he also made the decision to write some songs as a creative way to express his pain, cry out to God, and receive strength and comfort.

Assets and Limitations

Of the assessment methods reviewed in this chapter, spiritual lifemaps are perhaps the most client-directed. Consequently, there are a number of unique advantages associated with the use of this diagrammatic model (Hodge, in press). By placing a client-constructed media at the center of assessment, the message is implicitly communicated that the client is a competent, pro-active, self-directed, fully engaged participant in the therapeutic process. Additionally, individuals who are not verbally oriented may find pictorial expression more conducive to their personal communication styles (McNiff, 1992).

The relatively secondary role that social workers play during assessment also offers important advantages. For many clients, spirituality is a highly personal, sensitive, and important area. Most social workers have had limited training about various spiritual worldviews, in spite of the central role spirituality plays in human behavior. (Canda & Furman, 1999). Consequently, there is the distinct risk that social workers may offend clients and jeopardize the therapeutic relationship through comments that are inadvertently offensive, especially with the use of more practitioner-centered, verbally-based assessment approaches. The pictorial lifemap affords practitioners the opportunity to learn more about the client's worldview while focusing on building therapeutic rapport by providing an atmosphere that is accepting, nonjudgmental, and supportive during assessment (Kahn, 1999).

In terms of limitations, some social workers may feel so removed from the process that this assessment approach makes poor use of therapeutic time. Indeed, in the time constrained, managed care world in which many practitioners work, in some cases it may be advisable to use the lifemap as a homework assignment (Hodge, in press). Another significant limitation is that many clients, such as those who are more verbal, those that are uncomfortable with drawing, or those who prefer more direct practitioner and client involvement, may find the use of a largely non-verbal, pictorial instrument to be a poor fit.

Spiritual Histories

A spiritual history represents a narrative alternative to a spiritual lifemap (Hodge, 2001a). Instead of relating the client's spiritual sojourn in a diagrammatic format, the client's spiritual story is related verbally. In a process that is analogous to conducting a family history, the client is provided an interactive forum to share his or her spiritual life story.

To guide the conversation, a two-part framework is used (Hodge, 2001a). As can been seen in Table 1, the first part consists of an initial narrative framework. The purpose of these questions is to provide practitioners with some tools for structuring the assessment. The aim is to help clients tell their stories, typically moving from childhood to the present.

It should also be noted that the questions delineated in Table 1 are offered as suggestions (Hodge, 2001a). Social workers should not view them as a rigid template that must be applied in every situation, but rather as a fluid framework that should be tailored to the needs of each individual client. In other words, the questions provide a number of possible options that can be used to facilitate the movement of the narrative and to elicit important information.

The second part of Table 1 consists of an interpretive framework (Hodge, 2001a) based on the anthropological understandings of Chinese spirituality writer Watchman Nee (1968). In addition to soma, Nee envisions a soul, comprised of affect, will, and cognition, and a spirit, comprised of communion, conscience, and intuition. Although human beings are an integrated unity and, consequently, the six dimensions interact with and influence one another, it is possible to distinguish each dimension. As is the case with other human dimensions, such as affect, behavior, and cognition, the dimensions of the spirit also can be discussed individually.

Communion refers to a spiritually based relationship. More specifically, it denotes the ability to bond with and relate to God. Conscience relates to one's ability to sense right and wrong. Beyond a person's cognitively held values, conscience conveys moral knowledge about the appropriateness of a given set of choices. Intuition refers to the ability to know—to come up with insights that by-pass cognitively based, information-processing channels.

As is apparent in Table 1, the questions in the interpretive anthropological framework are designed to elicit information about each of

Table I. Guidelines for conducting spiritual histories

Initial Narrative Framework

1. Describe the religious/spiritual tradition you grew up in. How did your family express its spiritual beliefs? How important was spirituality to your family? Extended family?

2. What sort of personal experiences (practices) stand out to you during your years at home? What made these experiences special? How have they informed your later life?

3. How have you transitioned or matured from those experiences? How would you describe your current spiritual/religious orientation? Is your spirituality a personal strength? If so, how?

Interpretive Anthropological Framework

1. Affect: What aspects of your spiritual life give you pleasure? What role does your spirituality play in handling life's sorrows? Enhancing its joys? Coping with its pain? How does your spirituality give you hope for the future? What do you wish to accomplish in the future?

2. Behavior: Are there particular spiritual rituals or practices that help you deal with life's obstacles? What is your level of involvement in faith-based communities? How are they supportive? Are there spiritually encouraging individuals that you maintain contact with?

3. Cognitive: What are your current religious/spiritual beliefs? What are they based upon? What beliefs do you find particularly meaningful? What does your faith say about trials? How does this belief help you overcome obstacles? How do your beliefs affect your health practices?

4. Communion: Describe your relationship to the Ultimate. What has been your experience of the Ultimate? How does the Ultimate communicate with you? How have these experiences encouraged you? Have there been times of deep spiritual intimacy? How does your relationship help you face life challenges? How would the Ultimate describe you?

5. Conscience: How do you determine right and wrong? What are your key values? How does your spirituality help you deal with guilt (sin)? What role does forgiveness play in your life?

6. Intuition: To what extent do you experience intuitive hunches (flashes of creative insight, premonitions, spiritual insights)? Have these insights been a strength in your life? If so, how?

Table from Hodge (2001)

the six dimensions. The questions are not meant to be asked in any specific order. Rather, they are provided to help social workers draw out the richness of clients' spiritual stories. As clients relate their spiritual narrative, they may tend to touch upon some of the dimensions listed in the interpretive anthropological framework. Social workers can pose questions drawn from the framework to more fully explore clients' spiritual reality in the natural flow of the therapeutic dialogue.

Assets and Limitations

There is a considerable amount of evidence that information is stored and organized narratively in the mind (Strickland, 1994). Accordingly, assessment methods that are congruent with this reality work with, rather than against, clients' mental thought processes. Indeed, for verbally oriented persons, spiritual histories may provide the best assessment method. The non-structured format allows clients to relate their stories in a direct, unfiltered manner. For example, whereas genograms require clients to circumscribe their spiritual reality upon a generational chart, assessment with spiritual histories allows clients to choose the relevant material to be shared.

However, not all clients are verbally oriented and some may find that a narrative assessment places too much attention on them in light of the sensitive, personal nature of spirituality. Some clients find it helpful to have a specific framework. Given the amorphous, subjective nature of spirituality, physical depiction may help concretize the client's strengths (Hodge, 2000). In other words, the process of conceptualizing and depicting one's spiritual journey may help to focus and objectify spiritual assets, which can then be discussed and marshaled to address problems. Still another limitation is the time spent exploring portions of the client's spiritual history that may have limited utility in terms of addressing the present problem the client is wrestling with.

Spiritual Eco-maps

In contrast to the above assessment tools, spiritual eco-maps focus on clients' current spiritual relationships (Hodge, 2000; Hodge & Williams, in press). The assessment instruments previously are united in the sense that they all are designed to tap some portion of clients' spiritual story as it exists through time. Spiritual genograms, lifemaps and histories typically cover one to three generations of a client's spiritual narrative. Spiritual eco-maps, on the other hand, focus on that portion of clients' spiritual story that exists in space. In other words, this assessment approach highlights clients' present relationships to various spiritual assets.

In keeping with traditional eco-gram construction (Hartman, 1995) the immediate family system is typically portrayed as a circle in the center of a piece of paper. Household family members can be sketched inside the circle, with squares depicting males and circles representing females (Hodge, 2000). Alternatively, separate eco-maps can be drawn for each individual (Hodge & Williams, in press).

Significant spiritual systems or domains are depicted as circles on the outskirts of the paper, with the names of the respective systems written inside the circles. The circles are placed in a radius around the family circle, which may consist of a single figure representing the client. While clients should be encouraged to depict the domains that are most relevant to their spiritual worldviews, there are a number of spiritual systems that are strengths in particular spiritual traditions.

More specifically, social workers should generally seek to explore clients' relationships with God, rituals, faith communities and encounters with angels, demons, and other spiritual visitations (Hodge, 2000). One's relationship with God is widely regarded as a key strength, as are rituals, or codified spiritual practices such as devotional reading, meditation, prayer, scripture study, singing hymns, worship, "practicing the presence" of God by focusing on God's presence and active involvement in daily affairs. Faith communities refer to various church and parachurch communities that individuals may associate with on a regular basis, such as church services, fellowship groups, mid-week Bible studies, youth groups, and singles associations.

As suggested above, social workers should also seek to incorporate into the eco-map any spiritual system that has meaning to the client (Hodge, 2000). For example, one may wish to explore clients' relationship to their parents' spiritual traditions or their relationship to individuals who hold a position of significant spiritual leadership in their lives, such as a pastor, spiritual mentor or elder. The goal should be to delineate on the eco-map all the spiritual systems that are relevant to the client's present spirituality.

The heart of the spiritual eco-map is the depiction of relationships between the family system and the spiritual systems, which are represented by various types of sketched lines (Hodge, 2000). Thicker lines represent stronger or more powerful relationships. A dashed line represents the most tenuous relationship, while a jagged line denotes a conflicted one. An arrow is drawn on the line to indicate the flow of energy, resources, or interest. As is the case with the other diagrammatic instruments profiled above, short, descriptive encapsulations, significant dates, or other creative depictions, can also be incorporated onto the map to provide more information about relational dynamics.

When using eco-maps with individuals, the appropriate type of line is drawn in between the family system (the figure representing the client) and the spiritual systems. When working with families, lines are drawn to the family system as a unit when the family shares a particular relationship in common, or more frequently, connections are drawn to individual family members depicting the various unique relationships between each family member and various spiritual systems.

A Case Example

In an abbreviated manner, Diagram 3 (following page) depicts how a spiritual eco-map might be used with the Martinez family, consisting of Miguel and Maria, and their two children, Angie, 16, and Tony, 10. The Martinez family sought counseling as part of a relapse prevention plan for Angie who had recently been released from an in-patient alcohol treatment program. The goal of counseling was to reduce the conflict and distrust that existed between Angie and her parents. Angie thought her parents were overly strict, and her parents felt betrayed by Angie's chronic lying. In addition, Miguel and Maria removed Angie from public school and enrolled her in a Christian school in an attempt to prevent her from associating with her peer group that frequently abused alcohol.

Angie and her parents were embroiled in a heated conflict as Angie complained that the Alcoholic's Anonymous (AA) groups that her parents insisted she attend were "stupid and a waste of time." Due to Angie's prior deceitfulness and poor decision-making, her parents did not trust Angie's assessment of the AA groups and were adamant that she needed to continue attending two groups per week to help her maintain her sobriety. In order to address this dilemma, the therapist developed a spiritual eco-map with the family to explore the family's spiritual worldview and resources and identify spiritually based alternatives to AA attendance. The family was receptive to this because AA had substantiated the benefits of spirituality in treating alcoholism.

The Martinez family was currently attending St. Vincent's parish. Maria had grown up in this parish and knew many of the parishioners. She and Miguel had attended Cursillo, a weekend retreat that guided participants as they explored a deeper relationship with God, and they continued to participate in Cursillo's on-going groups. Maria, in particular, stated that she had received a great deal of support and prayer from this group when she and Miguel discovered Angie's struggle with alcoholism. Tony had been an altar boy for a couple years and looked forward to seeing his friends at his Christian education class. In the past, Angie had viewed attending mass with disdain and thought that

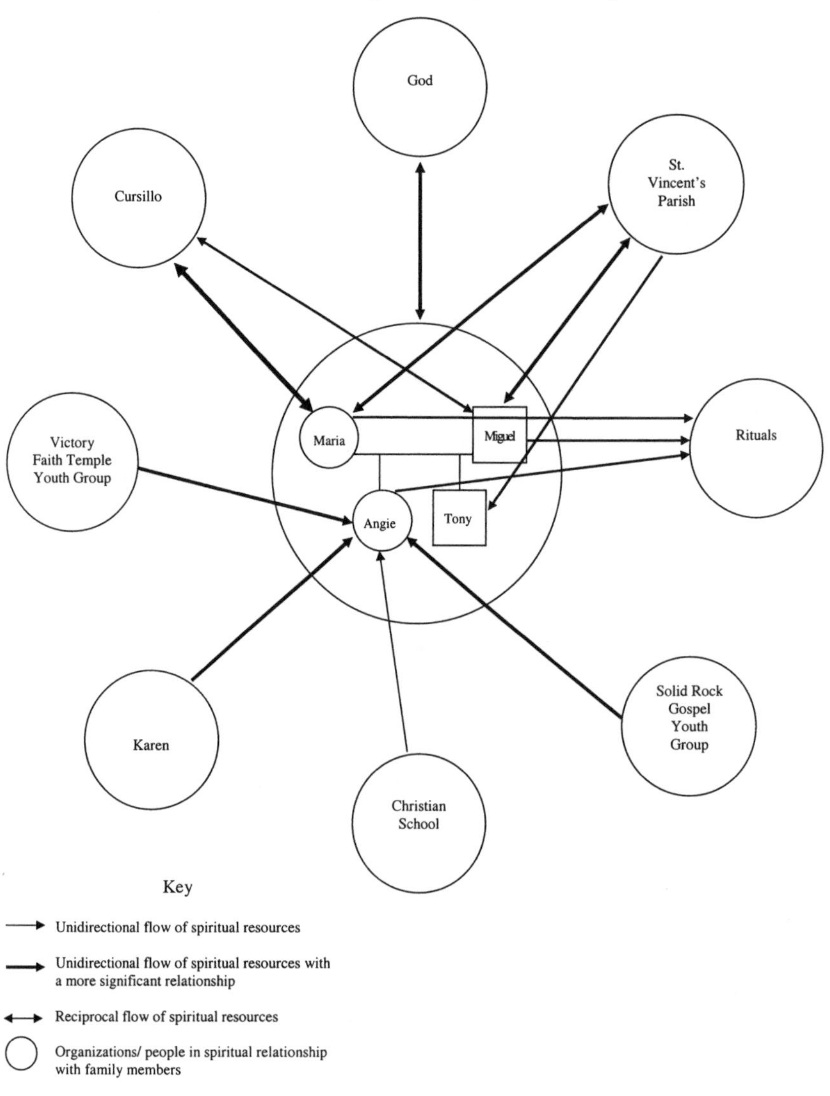

Diagram 3.

her peers at their parish were "stale." However, after attending in-patient treatment and switching to the Christian school, Angie slowly began to develop an interest in spirituality. Upon invitation from her new friends at school, Angie attended several local youth groups. Specifically, she enjoyed the "cool music" at Solid Rock Gospel Church, and liked the youth pastor, Dan, and his wife, Karen, at Victory Faith Temple.

The therapist asked Miguel and Maria if they would be comfortable replacing the AA groups with the youth groups. Although they both wished Angie would attend the Catholic youth group at their parish, they agreed to give it a try and the family contracted to evaluate the youth groups' effectiveness in two months.

The therapist asked the Martinez family if they practiced any family rituals at home. Maria stated that she and Miguel each individually spent some time reading scripture and praying. Angie surprised her parents by stating that, after a conversation with Karen, she had recently started reading a devotional book when she felt upset and praying when she felt tempted to drink. Miguel shared that they discontinued their attempt at family devotions a year ago after a major fight arose between Angie and him. The therapist asked if they would be interested in initiating family devotions again. However, in order to break the conflictual pattern of the parents lecturing and Angie bristling at their rigid rules, the therapist encouraged structuring the family devotional time as an open forum in which all family members would be free to share their perspectives and struggles. Miguel and Maria might share how their faith guides their decision-making and helps them deal with life's pain and hardships. Angie and Tony might share what they were learning in youth group, school, and Christian education class. This weekly ritual could potentially reassure Miguel and Maria that Angie was learning productive coping skills, build trust between family members, and help them forgive past grievances.

In congruence with the AA model, the therapist asked Angie if she could identify anyone on the spiritual eco-map that she respected and would like to be her sponsor who would provide support, guidance, and accountability for her. Angie stated that Karen had shared her life story in youth group, and was sure that Karen would be understanding, nonjudgmental, and helpful to her.

By developing the spiritual eco-map, the therapist was able to use the Martinez family's current spiritual resources to help them identify new solutions to their problems. Before this counseling session, Miguel and Maria had briefly heard Angie mention Karen's name, but their distrust and concern that the youth groups were not Catholic had prevented them from hearing the positive influence Karen and the groups were having in Angie's life. The process of developing the spiritual eco-map allowed Angie to openly share for the first time that her new-found faith was helping her stay sober and that the youth groups were helping her grow spiritually. As a result, the family moved past their stalemate, broke down barriers to communication, and began establishing trust.

Assets and Limitations

The main asset of spiritual eco-maps is that they focus upon clients' current spiritual strengths (Hodge, 2000). For social workers seeking to operationalize clients' spiritual assets to help clients solve their problems, this assessment approach may be ideal. The time spent in assessment is focused upon tapping into present spiritual resources.

In some cases, clients may find it less threatening to have a concrete object that functions as the focus of subsequent conversation. As is the case with all diagrammatic instruments, spiritual eco-maps provide an object that can serve as the focal point of discussion. The design of eco-maps, however, with their focus on environmental systems rather than, for example, clients' life stories, helps remove the emphasis from the client as an individual. In short, while other approaches may implicitly emphasize clients, devoid of their contexts, spiritual eco-maps explicitly stress the spiritual systems in clients' environments (Hartman, 1995).

Spiritual eco-maps suffer from the same limitations as other diagrammatic instruments relative to verbally based spiritual histories. In addition, in at least some situations, the focus on current spiritual assets may result in a limited assessment that overlooks salient historical factors. In other words, in some contexts an approach that allows social workers to explore current and historical resources may be useful.

Conducting an Assessment

Knowledge in terms of how to conduct an assessment is also important. Developing familiarity with assessment tools is only part of the assessment process. Practitioners must also know how to use these tools in an appropriate, spiritually sensitive manner. Although a detailed discussion of the mechanics of conducting a spiritual assessment is beyond the scope of this chapter, a few important points will be highlighted.

Social workers should be aware that many clients may be hesitant to trust practitioners due to concerns that practitioners will not treat with honor that which is held to be sacred (Furman, Perry & Goldale, 1996; Richards & Bergin, 2000). Consequently, due to the highly personal nature of spirituality, it is appropriate to procure clients' consent before engaging in a spiritual assessment. Additionally, social workers should explain a particular assessment instrument to ensure that the client is comfortable with the particular approach before engaging in an assessment.

To a great extent, clients' apprehension can be alleviated by expressing genuine support. Adopting an attitude of interest and curiosity toward the client's belief system is an appropriate therapeutic stance

(Patterson, Hayworth, Turner Christie & Raskin, 2000).

Social workers can also demonstrate spiritual sensitivity by obtaining knowledge of common spiritual traditions. For example, if one works in an area where Mormons and Pentecostals are prominent spiritual traditions, then seeking out information on Mormonism (Ulrich, Richards & Bergin, 2000) and Pentecostalism (Dobbins, 2000) can assist social workers in exhibiting spiritual sensitivity with these populations. Ideally, in the process of attempting to understand clients' spiritual worldviews, social workers should seek to envision life through the particular worldview of the client.

In their attempts to understand the worldviews of clients, social workers should develop their understanding of the oppression people of faith often experience in the largely secular culture. It is important for social workers to recognize that the dominant secular culture often marginalizes or otherwise de-legitimizes devout faith in such influential forms as television (Skill & Robinson, 1994; Skill, Robinson, Lyons & Larson, 1994), popular periodicals (Perkins, 1984), and high school (Sewall, 1995; Vitz, 1986; Vitz, 1998) and college level textbooks (Cnaan, 1999; Glenn, 1997; Lehr & Spilka, 1989). Social workers should reflect on how living in a culture that often ignores, devalues, and even ridicules believers' most cherished beliefs and values affects the psychology of people of faith.

Developing their understanding of clients' worldviews can assist social workers in respecting clients' spiritual autonomy. The focus of practice should not be on determining whether clients' spiritual beliefs are right or wrong, but rather on how their values animate their lives and assist them in coping with difficulties. The social worker's job is not to accept or reject clients' spiritual values but to understand them and help them use their beliefs and practices to assist clients in overcoming their problems (Fitchett & Handzo, 1998).

In some cases, however, social workers may perceive that clients' spiritual beliefs may be problematic. In such situations, social workers should not attempt to change clients' values in an area that lies outside the realm of their professional competence. Rather, practitioners should collaborate with or refer such clients to clergy (Johnson, Ridley & Nielsen, 2000). Given that this is the clergy's area of professional competency, pastors, priests, and other spiritual specialists are better equipped to ascertain the appropriateness of a given set of beliefs and practices. It is critical, however, that practitioners respect clients' spiritual autonomy by forming collaborative relationships with clergy that share the same denominational and theological orientation as the client. It would be unethical to covertly attempt to subvert clients' values by, for example, referring a client who holds conservative beliefs to a liberal pastor.

In keeping with their roles as social workers, practitioners should remain focused on empowering clients to address their problems. During the assessment process, social workers should keep two questions in mind. First, during past difficulties, how have clients culled from their spiritual frameworks, various resources to address their problems? Second, what types of unaccessed resources are available in this framework that can be marshaled to address current problems? Social workers can attempt to link clients with untapped resources to help them solve their problems. Practitioners might, for example, suggest particular interventions either drawn from, or consistent with, clients' spiritual worldviews.

More specifically, social workers might employ a modified form of cognitive therapy in which unhealthy beliefs are identified and replaced with positive beliefs drawn from the individual's spiritual belief system (Backus, 1985; Propst, 1996). Similarly, practitioners may explore the possibility of reframing current problems as opportunities for spiritual growth (Pargament, 1997). In attempting to foster the adoption of more productive patterns of behaviors, spiritual rituals may be employed as "exceptions" to unproductive behavioral patterns (Hodge, 2000). Decision-based forgiveness interventions may be useful in some contexts (DiBlasio, 1998) while existential, brevity of life interventions may be appropriate in other situations (Hodge, in press). In each individual setting, the unique spiritual beliefs of the clients and the theoretical orientation of the social worker will indicate which interventions are selected. In any setting, however, the goal should be to help clients use their spiritual strengths to address their issues and concerns.

Conclusion

In order to provide services that are sensitive to clients' spiritual worldviews, social workers must conduct spiritual assessments to have some awareness of clients' spiritual realities. Similarly, to help clients tap into their spiritual strengths to address the problems they wrestle with, it is necessary to undertake an assessment of clients' strengths. A single assessment approach, however, is unlikely to be ideal in all situations; diverse needs call for a variety of approaches. If the profession of social work is to take seriously its mandate to provide culturally sensitive services that build upon clients' unique strengths, then in many cases performing a spiritual assessment is an imperative.

References

Augustine. (354-430/1991). *Confessions* (H. Chadwick, Trans.). New York: Oxford University Press.

Backus, W. (1985). *Telling the truth to troubled people.* Minneapolis, MN: Bethany House.

Bart, M. (1998). Spirituality in counseling finding believers. *Counseling Today, 41*(6), 1, 6.

Bullis, R. K. (1996). *Spirituality in social work practice.* Washington, DC: Taylor & Francis.

Calhoun-Brown, A. (1998). While marching to Zion: Otherworldliness and racial empowerment in the black community. *Journal for the Scientific Study of Religion, 37*(3), 427-439.

Canda, E. R. (1997). Spirituality. In R. L. Edwards (Ed.), *Encyclopedia of social work* (19th ed., pp. 299-309). Washington, DC: NASW Press.

Canda, E. R., & Furman, L. D. (1999). *Spiritual diversity in social work practice.* New York: The Free Press.

Carroll, M. M. (1997). Spirituality and clinical social work: Implications of past and current perspectives. *Arete, 22*(1), 25-34.

Cnaan, R. A. (1999). *The newer deal.* New York: Columbia University Press.

Cowger, C. D. (1994). Assessing client strengths: Clinical assessments for client empowerment. *Social Work, 39*(3), 262-268.

Derezotes, D. S. (1995). Spirituality and religiosity: Neglected factors in social work practice. *Arete, 20*(1), 1-15.

DiBlasio, F. A. (1988). Integrative strategies for family therapy with Evangelical Christians. *Journal of Psychology and Theology, 16*(2), 127-134.

DiBlasio, F. A. (1998). The use of a decision-based forgiveness intervention within intergenerational family therapy. *Journal of Family Therapy, 20*(1), 77-94.

Dobbins, R. D. (2000). Psychotherapy with Pentecostal Protestants. In P. S. Richards & A. E. Bergin (Eds.), *Handbook of psychotherapy and religious diversity* (pp. 155-184). Washington, DC: American Psychological Association.

Ellison, C. G., & Levin, J. S. (1998). The religion-health connection: Evidence, theory, and future directions. *Health Education and Behavior, 25*(6), 700-720.

Fellin, P. (2000). Revisiting multiculturalism in social work. *Journal of Social Work Education, 36*(2), 261-278.

Ferraro, K. F., & Kelley-Moore, J. A. (2000). Religious consolation among men and women: Do health problems spur seeking? *Journal of the Scientific Study of Religion, 39*(2), 220-234.

Fitchett, G., & Handzo, G. (1998). Spiritual assessment, screening, and intervention. In J. C. Holland (Ed.), *Psycho-oncology* (pp. 790-808). New York: Oxford University Press.

Furman, L. D., & Canda, J. M. (1994). Religion and spirituality: A long-neglected cultural component of rural social work practice. *Human Services in the Rural Environment, 17*(3/4), 21-26.

Furman, L. D., Perry, D., & Goldale, T. (1996). Interaction of Evangelical Christians and social workers in the rural environment. *Human Services in the Rural Environment, 19*(3), 5-8.

Gallup, G. J., & Lindsay, D. M. (1999). *Surveying the religious landscape.* Harrisburg, PA: Morehouse Publishing.

Gartner, J., Larson, D. B., & Allen, G. D. (1991). Religious commitment and mental health: A review of the literature. *Journal of Psychology and Theology, 19*(1), 6-25.

Glenn, N. (1997). *Closed hearts, closed minds: The textbook story of marriage*. New York: Institute for American Values.

Hardy, K. V., & Laszloffy, T. A. (1995). The cultural genogram: Key to training culturally competent family therapists. *Journal of Marital and Family Therapy, 21*(3), 227-237.

Hartman, A. (1995). Diagrammatic assessment of family relationships. *Families in Society, 76*(2), 111-122.

Hodge, D. R. (2000). Spiritual ecomaps: A new diagrammatic tool for assessing marital and family spirituality. *Journal of Marital and Family Therapy, 26*(1), 229-240.

Hodge, D. R. (2001a). Spiritual assessment: A review of major qualitative methods and a new framework for assessing spirituality. *Social Work, 46*(3), 203-214.

Hodge, D. R. (2001b). Spiritual genograms: A generational approach to assessing spirituality. *Families in Society, 82*(1), 35-48.

Hodge, D. R. (In press). Spiritual lifemaps: A client-centered pictorial instrument for spiritual assessment, planning, and intervention. *Social Work*.

Hodge, D. R., & Williams, T. R. (In press). Assessing African American spirituality with spiritual eco-maps. *Families in Society*.

Hwang, S.-C., & Cowger, C., D. (1998). Utilizing strengths in assessment. *Families in Society, 79*(1), 25-31.

Johnson, W. B., Ridley, C. R., & Nielsen, S. L. (2000). Religiously sensitive rational emotive behavior therapy: Elegant solutions and ethical risks. *Professional Psychology: Research and Practice, 31*(1), 14-20.

Kahn, B. B. (1999). Art therapy with adolescents: Making it work for school counselors. *Professional School Counseling, 2*(4), 291-298.

Kennedy, J. E., Davis, R. C., & Talyor, B. G. (1998). Changes in spirituality and well-being among victims of sexual assault. *Journal for the Scientific Study of Religion, 37*(2), 322-328.

Koenig, H. G., McCullough, M. E., & Larson, D. B. (2001). *Handbook of religion and health*. New York: Oxford University Press.

Kuehl, B. (1995). The solution-oriented genogram: A collaborative approach. *Journal of Marital and Family Therapy, 21*(3), 239-250.

Lehr, E., & Spilka, B. (1989). Religion in the introductory psychology textbook: A comparison of three decades. *Journal for the Scientific Study of Religion, 28*(3), 366-371.

Lindsey, E. W., Kurtz, P. D., Jarvis, S., Williams, N. R., & Nackerud, L. (2000). How runaway and homeless youth navigate troubled waters: Personal strengths and resources. *Child and Adolescent Social Work Journal, 17*(2), 115-140.

Maton, K. I., & Salem, D. A. (1995). Organizational characteristics of empowering community settings: A multiple case study approach. *American Journal of Community Practice, 23*(5), 631-656.

Maton, K. I., & Wells, E. A. (1995). Religion as a community resource for well-being: Prevention, healing, and empowerment pathways. *Journal of Social Issues, 51*(2), 177-193.

Mattaini, M. A., & Kirk, S. A. (1991). Assessing assessment in social work. *Social Work, 36*(3), 260-266.

McGoldrick, M., Gerson, R., & Shellenberger. (1999). *Genograms: Assessment and intervention* (2nd ed.). New York: W.W. Norton & Company.

McNiff, S. (1992). *Art as medicine*. Boston: Shambhala.

McRae, M. B., Thompson, D. A., & Cooper, S. (1999). Black churches as therapeutic groups. *Journal of Multicultural Counseling and Development, 27*(1), 207-220.

Montgomery, C. (1994). Swimming upstream: The strengths of women who survive homelessness. *Advances in Nursing Science, 16*(3), 34-45.

NASW Code of Ethics. (1999). Available: www.naswdc.org/Code/ethics.htm (Accessed 1/20/00).

Nathanson, I., G. (1995). Divorce and women's spirituality. *Journal of Divorce and Remarriage, 22*(3/4), 179-188.

Nee, W. (1968). *The spiritual man.* (Vols. 1-3). New York: Christian Fellowship Publishers.

Pargament, K. I. (1997). *The psychology of religion and coping.* New York: Guilford Press.

Patterson, J., Hayworth, M., Turner Christie, & Raskin, M. (2000). Spiritual issues in family therapy: A graduate-level course. *Journal of Martial and Family Therapy, 26*(2), 199-210.

Perkins, H. W. (1984). Religious content in American, British, and Canadian popular publications from 1937 to 1979. *Sociological Analysis, 45*(2), 159-165.

Privette, G., Quackenbos, S., & Bundrick, C. M. (1994). Preferences for religious and nonreligious counseling and psychotherapy. *Psychological Reports, 75,* 539-547.

Propst, L. R. (1996). Cognitive-behavioral therapy and the religious person. In E. P. Shafranske (Ed.), *Religion and the clinical practice of psychology* (pp. 391-407). Washington, DC: American Psychological Association.

Rauch, J. B. (1993). *Assessment: A sourcebook for social work practice.* Milwaukee: Families International.

Rey, L. D. (1997). Religion as invisible culture: Knowing about and knowing with. *Journal of Family Social Work, 2*(2), 159-177.

Richards, P. S., & Bergin, A. E. (Editors). (2000). *Handbook of psychotherapy and religious diversity.* Washington, DC: American Psychological Association.

Ronnau, J., & Poertner, J. (1993). Identification and use of strengths: A family system approach. *Children Today, 22*(2), 20-23.

Saleebey, D. (Editor). (1997). *The strengths perspective in social work practice* (2nd ed.). White Plains, NY: Longman.

Sewall, G. T. (1995). *Religion in the classroom: What the textbooks tell us.* New York: American Textbook Council.

Sheridan, M. J., & Amato-von Hemert, K. (1999). The role of religion and spirituality in social work education and practice: A survey of student views and experiences. *Journal of Social Work Education, 35*(1), 125-141.

Sherwood, D. A. (1998). Charitable choice: Opportunity and challenge for Christians in social work. *Social Work and Christianity, 25*(3), 1-23.

Skill, T., & Robinson, J. D. (1994). The image of Christian leaders in fictional television programs. *Sociology of Religion, 55*(1), 75-84.

Skill, T., Robinson, J. D., Lyons, J. S., & Larson, D. (1994). The portrayal of religion and spirituality on fictional network television. *Review of the Religious Research, 35*(3), 251-267.

Stanion, P., Papadopoulos, L., & Bor, R. (1997). Genograms in counseling practice: Constructing a genogram (part 2). *Counseling Psychology Quarterly, 10*(2), 139-148.

Strickland, L. (1994). Autobiographical interviewing and narrative analysis: An approach to psychosocial assessment. *Clinical Social Work Journal, 22*(1), 27-41.

Sullivan, W. P. (1997). On strengths, niches, and recovery from serious mental illness. In D. Saleebey (Ed.), *The strengths perspective in social work practice* (pp. 183-199). White Plains, NY: Longman.

Talbot, M. (2000, February 27). A mighty fortress. *The New York Times Magazine*, 34-41, 66-8, 84-5.

Tracz, S. M., & Gehart-Brooks, D. R. (1999). The lifeline: Using art to illustrate history. *Journal of Family Psychotherapy, 10*(3), 61-63.

Turner, N. H., O' Dell, K. J., & Weaver, G. D. (1999). Religion and the recovery of addicted women. *Journal of Religion and Health, 38*(2), 137-148.

Ulrich, W. L., Richards, P. S., & Bergin, A. E. (2000). Psychotherapy with Latter-day Saints. In P. S. Richards & A. E. Bergin (Eds.), *Handbook of psychotherapy and religious diversity* (pp. 185-209). Washington, DC: American Psychological Association.

Vitz, P. C. (1986). *Censorship: Evidence of bias in our children's textbooks.* Ann Arbor, MI: Servant Books.

Vitz, P. C. (1998). *The course of true love: Marriage in high school textbooks*. New York: Institute for American Values.

Walsh, F. (1999). Religion and spirituality. In F. Walsh (Ed.), *Spiritual resources in family therapy* (pp. 3-27). New York: Gilford Press.

CHAPTER 11

CHRISTIANITY AND THE TREATMENT OF ADDICTION: AN ECOLOGICAL APPROACH FOR SOCIAL WORKERS

Jason Pittman and Scott W. Taylor

Most people can describe at least one instance of how alcohol and drug addiction has had a negative impact on their own lives or the lives of people they love. Children today, regardless of age or ethnicity, grow up in a society where access to drugs and alcohol is extremely easy. Parents who misuse alcohol and drugs also influence how their children perceive and understand the use of alcohol and drugs. At a Christian ministry conference recently, participants were asked to share how drugs and alcohol had personally affected their lives, or the lives of people they know. Nearly everyone in attendance shared stories about their sons and daughters, aunts and uncles, mothers and fathers, and grandparents whose lives were negatively impacted by addiction.

According to the National Council on Alcohol and Drug Addiction (2000), 10,000 deaths annually were attributed to alcohol abuse, as well as an additional 10,000 deaths to illegal drug use, making alcohol and drug addiction the third leading cause of preventable mortality in the United States. Furthermore, Gallup (1999) suggested that addiction is a common issue involved in most of the following social problems: "murder and lawlessness, highway deaths, suicides, accidental deaths, injustices, hospitalizations, poor school performance and dropout, job absenteeism, child and spouse abuse, low self-esteem, and depression" (p. xi). Addiction is a serious problem, and it is imperative that we continue to try to understand its impact, not only in the United States, but in the entire world.

Professionals working in the field of addiction treatment and laypersons helping from a Christian perspective have struggled with how best to assist addicts. For example, Gray (1995) noted that most people dealing with addiction are also struggling in many other areas of life. Social workers need to advocate for an eclectic approach that involves the contributions of many disciplines. An eclectic approach includes "models of interventions strategies and approaches, modalities of intervention, organized conceptualizations of client problems or of practice, sets of practice principles, practice wisdom, and even philosophies of practice" (Abbott, 2000, p. 27).

This chapter attempts to provide insight into the main issues regarding an informed eclectic approach. In the first section, we discuss the general field of addiction treatment, define addiction for the purpose of this chapter, provide a summary of addiction etiology theories, and discuss relevant treatment interventions. The second section is a discussion concerning the interaction of Christianity and addiction historically, with particular emphasis on the contribution of pastoral theology and Christian treatment programs. The chapter concludes by emphasizing that social workers should utilize an eclectic approach when helping addicts, while integrating the contributions of addiction etiology theories and treatment interventions.

Brief History

In the United States, the nation's first settlers had to deal with issues related to drug and alcohol abuse. They drank more beer than water because of the lack of safe drinking water (Van Wormer, 1995). In the eighteenth century, distilled spirits became available to the masses and contributed to drunkenness at all class levels. People viewed alcohol and drug addiction as a moral problem, resulting from sinful behavior and moral weakness in the individual. Society treated addicts very poorly, and they faced condemnation, guilt, shame, and many times ostracism (Morgan, 1999, p. 4). The term "alcoholic" was first used by the Swedish physician Magnus Huss in 1849. He defined alcoholism as "the state of chronic alcohol intoxication that was characterized by severe physical pathology and disruption of social functioning" (White, 1998, p. xiv).

Within the last hundred years, we have seen a major shift in how society perceives addiction. During the temperance and prohibition movements people tried to eliminate alcohol completely, believing that if alcohol were illegal, then addiction would cease to exist. Later, with the help of scientific research, the medical field began identifying addiction as a disease, considering the etiology to be strictly biological (Van Wormer, 1995). It was during the early 1900s when Huss's term "alcoholic" began to be circulated within professional circles, and in the 1930's, Alcoholics Anonymous (AA) launched the term into widespread use.

By 1944, the U.S. Public Health Service identified addiction as the fourth largest health concern in the nation (Strung, Priyadarsini, & Hyman, 1986). The professional, medical, and research communities began to mobilize and to create the new field of addiction treatment through the following: work of pioneers like E.M. Jellinek and Mark Keller; organizations such as the National Committee for Education on Alcoholism, Research Council on Problems of Alcohol; the Summer School of Alcohol Studies at Yale; and volunteers like Marty Mann and her National Council on Alcoholism (Morgan, 1999; Royce, 1981; White, 1998). The first major step in shaping the field of addiction treatment and counseling occurred when the American Medical Association accepted the disease concept of alcoholism in 1956. One year later, the World Health Organization accepted the concept of alcoholism as a pathological condition.

By 1960, society began debating how best to define alcoholism while over 200 definitions circulated in various helping arenas (White, 1998). Professionals began to include other drugs and behaviors besides alcohol in the field of addiction, causing the debates to continue through the end of the 20th century. Today, the American Psychiatric Association (APA) uses the term "substance related disorders" to be inclusive of a broad range of problems associated with alcohol and drug usage (American Psychiatric Association, 2000). In this chapter, we will use the term addiction earlier defined by APA as the state of being "compulsively and physiologically dependent on a habit-forming substance" (McNeece & DiNitto, 1998, p. 23).

Addiction Etiology Theories

The 1960s-1980s was a time of growing research and development concerning addiction studies in the broad areas of psychology, psychiatry, and social work. Today, there are a number of theories to explain addiction, and these theories are as varied as the number of definitions of addiction (McNeece & DiNitto, 1998). We will provide a brief summary of the following broad areas of etiology theory: moral, biological, psychological, sociocultural, and multi-causal.

Historically, the moral theory has described addiction as a result of "humankind's sinful nature" (McNeece & DiNitto, 1998). Fingarette and Peele (as cited in McNeece & DiNitto) provide the contemporary equivalent of the moral theory. These theorists, however, do not suggest that addiction is caused by sinful nature; instead, addiction is a result of bad choices. We place these theorists in the moral model because their primary premise is that addiction is cured by the simple choice of abstinence.

Biological theories assume addicts are "constitutionally predisposed to develop a dependence on alcohol or drugs" (McNeece & DiNitto, 1998, p.27). These theories emphasize the physiological sources of addiction such as genetics or neurochemistry. Genetic research is not suggesting that people are genetically determined to be addicts. Instead, it points toward people as being predisposed to addiction. Neurochemistry is divided into two theories: brain dysfunction and brain chemistry. These theories argue that biochemical changes taking place in addicts may cause irreversible loss of control during the use of alcohol or drugs. Research suggests that certain people have the propensity to be unable to control their usage once they start. This lack of control may be due to heredity or actual changes that occur within the body because of the drug interacting with the brain (Clinebell, 1990; Leshner, 2001).

Psychological theories include a broad range of theories that have very different outlooks on the cause of addiction. For example, cognitive-behavioral theories suggest several reasons for addicts taking drugs: to experience variety, desire to experience pleasure, or avoidance of withdrawal symptoms (McNeece & DiNitto, 1998). In addition, psychodynamic and personality theories look to underlying personality issues, hoping to explain the causes of addiction. These explanations vary greatly and may consist of coping with painful experiences, guilt, loneliness, conflict, or low self-esteem (Clinebell, 1990).

Sociocultural theories emphasize the importance of social attitudes toward addiction and link those attitudes surrounding alcohol and drugs as being the cause of many people's decision to start abusing drugs or alcohol (Ciarrocchi, 1993). Theorists categorize sociocultural theories into three areas that focus on different environmental factors found in society and culture (McNeece & DiNitto, 1998). For example, theorists argue that European countries have a much lower rate of alcoholism as compared to the U.S. because of their tolerant views on drinking and intolerant views on drunkenness.

Addiction is a very complex disorder that affects all aspects of one's life. Professionals in the last sixty years have provided extensive research and literature in the field, attempting to explain the root causes of addiction. Unfortunately, research does not provide one simple cause of addiction. Theorists, however, have proposed two models that attempt to include multiple etiology theories of addiction. Pattison and Kaufman (as cited in McNeece & DiNitto, 1998) offered a multivariate model in the early 1980s that encompassed a multitude of causes of addiction. Health care and human service professionals, however, have advocated for the public health model. This model attempts to encompass many different possible causes of addiction and involves looking at the interaction of the agent, host, and environment.

Addiction Treatment Interventions

There are a variety of interventions available to treat individuals suffering from addiction. For this chapter, intervention is conceptualized in three ways: self-help groups, professional treatment programs, and counseling techniques. Alcoholic Anonymous (AA) is an example of a spiritual based self-help. They have attempted to bypass the problems of etiology and move into offering to alcoholics and helpers a pragmatic program of recovery that is based on the person's spiritual life and understanding of a higher power. Therefore, many people today mistakenly refer to AA as a treatment program instead of a self-help group. AA started in the 1930s by two alcoholics trying to help each other stop drinking. It was one of the pioneering self-help groups and quickly became a widespread movement. In addition, AA was instrumental in promoting the labeling of alcoholism as a disease. However, AA itself did not advocate a strict disease model. It was simply a fellowship of people with a common desire to stop using alcohol and drugs, and finding sobriety by "working" through a twelve-step program.

As of January 2001, AA reported over 100,000 groups worldwide with membership totaling over 2.1 million people (General Service Office, 2001). Although one of the hallmarks of AA is non-professional treatment, most professional treatment centers have integrated AA's ideas into the core of their addiction treatment programs (Van Wormer, 1995). In fact, Brown, Peterson, and Cunningham (1988) reported 95% of U.S. treatment centers are requiring, or have access to, AA meetings in their treatment programs.

Interventions can also include professional treatment programs such as outpatient or inpatient clinics or hospitals as well as long-term residential facilities. In the U.S., alcohol and drug treatment systems provided over 15,000 federal, state, local, and private programs that served 760,721 clients in 1999 (Office of Applied Studies, 1999). The Minnesota model of treatment, introduced by the Hazelden Treatment Center in Minnesota in the 1940s, combined AA's twelve-steps with psychologically based group therapy (Van Wormer, 1995). This model gained popularity in the 1970s and is the predominant model used in treatment centers today.

There are a multitude of interventions available to clinicians treating addicts based on counseling techniques and theories, many of which are based on the etiology theories discussed in the previous section. Similar to how researchers have proposed that one etiology theory is not sufficient, they have also suggested that there are strengths in many of the counseling interventions. In fact, Miller, et al. (1995) argued in their methodological analysis of outcome studies that "there does not seem to be any one treatment approach adequate to the task of treating all individuals with alcohol problems" (p. 32).

Transtheoretical Model

Prochaska, DiClemente, and Norcross (1992) began to study how people change in psychotherapy. They realized that the hundreds of outcome studies did not offer insight into the common principles that were allowing the change to occur. These researchers spent years analyzing and researching the processes that people go through when they change and the corresponding processes therapists use to facilitate that change. They developed the Transtheoretical Model that consists of two important interrelated theories for practice: the stages of change and the processes of change.

In the first part, Prochaska, et al. (1992) suggested that the stages of change (see table 1.0) do not necessarily progress in a linear nature, but because of how common relapse is in addiction, addicts usually follow a spiral pattern of change. Abbott (2000) noted that, "not every one completes the cycle. Some recycle numerous times; others stay in one or more stages of change, never exiting" (p. 117). Prochaska, et al. explained that "the stage of change scores were the best predictors of outcome; they were better predictors than age, socioeconomic status, problem severity and duration, goals and expectations, self-efficacy, and social support" (p. 116).

The Transtheoretical Model also stresses the importance of matching the processes of change to the stage of change. Prochaska, et al. (1992) noted that past addiction treatment's poor success rates were in part due to treatment centers not having tailored their therapeutic approach to match the clients' stage of change (see table 1.0). Abbott (2000) suggested that when the social worker is choosing a process of change and accompanying methods and techniques, it is best to consider the client's "age, personality characteristics, cultural factors, lifestyle, previous experiences with therapy, the severity of the ATOD [alcohol, tobacco, other drugs] problem, and available environmental resources" (p. 120).

Christian Approaches to Etiology and Intervention

This section explores the development of Christian approaches to etiology and treatment of addiction. We will also highlight the significance of Christianity in the development of Alcoholic Anonymous. Christianity has struggled with the topic of addiction, because it has historically characterized addiction as simply a sinful choice. This has created barriers between Christians attempting to provide a theological contribution to the field of addiction treatment and the secular community.

In the late 1800s, a religious experience was viewed as the antidote for addiction (White, 1998). Many addicts were proclaiming that

Table 1[1]
Stages of Change in Which Particular Change Processes are Most Useful

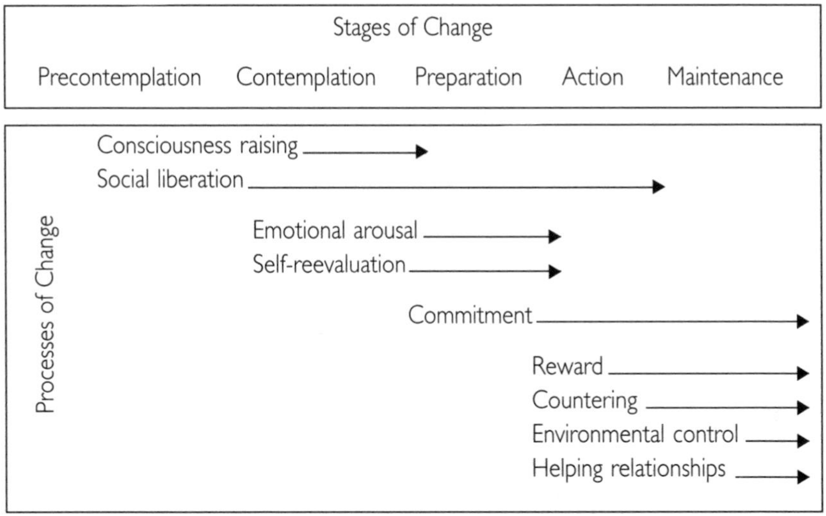

1 Source: Table 1 from Changing for Good (1994) by James O. Prochaska, John C. Norcross and Carlo C. Diclemente. Reprinted by permission of Harper Collins Publishers Inc.

God took away their addiction in religious revivals. These revivals provided entrance for addicts into other social groups such as lodges, churches, tent meetings, missions, and informal helping resources. The emergence of an urban society significantly contributed to the increase in the numbers of Christian approaches to alcoholism recovery. The areas in cities where vagrants and destitute alcoholics made their homes were labeled "Skid Rows" (p. 72). These areas were becoming major problems for civic leaders, and chronic addiction was seen as the primary problem.

In 1826, David Nasmith started a rescue mission in Glasgow, Scotland. The name "rescue mission" implied that the organization would rescue persons from "Skid Rows" by providing temporary shelter, food, and other assistance. Jerry McAuley and Samuel Hadley started similar rescue missions in the U.S. to address the problems associated with addiction and "Skid Rows" (White, 1998). These pioneers were heavily influenced by protestant evangelists who preached that addiction was a sin and emphasized the conversion experience as the cure for addiction. By the early 1900s, the rescue mission movement had spread to most of the major cities in the U.S. (Bakke, 1995). Currently, there are almost 200 rescue missions in the U.S. that have treatment programs.

Salvation Army became the most extensive urban Christian approach in helping addicts (White, 1998). William Booth started Salvation Army in 1865 in London, England, and the organization expanded to the U.S. in 1880. Booth attracted addicts by providing them with food and shelter and suggested that the cure for addiction would involve "Christian salvation and moral education in a wholesome environment" (White, p. 74). By 1900, Salvation Army had spread to over 700 U.S. cities. Today, Salvation Army has 152 centers in the U.S. serving over 15,000 addicts annually (Peters, 1980; Salvation Army, 2002).

The early 20th century also saw an emergence of professional views on religion and addiction recovery. In 1902, William James, a Harvard psychologist and medical doctor, wrote *The Varieties of Religious Experiences* (White, 1998). This book explored the role of religious conversion as the cure for addiction, describing religious transformation as being either a sudden or a gradual process. James wrote about the power that conversion has on removing the cravings for alcohol and providing a new perspective or outlook for the addict's life. These ideas highly influenced the later developments of AA.

Another example of a Christian presence in the addiction field was seen when the Emmanuel Church Clinic in Boston opened in 1906 for the treatment of various psychological disorders (White, 1998). These early clinicians attempted to integrate religion, medicine, and psychology in their treatment for addiction. This program was quite different from Salvation Army or rescue missions. Emmanuel's treatment was the first to focus on psychologically based group and individual counseling. White suggested that this program "foreshadows the current use of spirituality in addiction treatment" (p. 100). Their use of self-inventory and confession was influential in the development of the Oxford Group, a Christian evangelical group, and later AA. The Emmanuel clinic discontinued its treatment program after the death of one of the primary founders, Rev. Dr. Elwood Worcester, in the 1940s.

Alcoholics Anonymous is one of the most influential approaches rooted in Christianity. AA does not align itself with any religious group, church, or organization, it understands addiction to have biological, psychological, and social influences, but primarily offers a spiritual approach to recovery (Hester & Miller, 1995). Christian concepts, however, are inherent in AA's twelve-steps, and these concepts have had a large impact on the development of various twelve-step programs.

The founders of AA, Bill Wilson and Dr. Bob Smith, began as members of the Oxford Group (White, 1998). The Oxford Group movement began on college campuses in England and spread quickly in the U.S. Clinebell (1998) suggested "it was an attempt to bring vital, first-century Christianity into the lives of people, challenging them to live by certain ethical absolutes and motivating them to change others" (p. 273). The Oxford Group used six steps to accomplish this purpose. In 1939, Wilson and "Dr. Bob" took the ideas from these six steps and adapted them specifically to the needs of alcoholics, thereby, creating the twelve-steps of AA.

The idea of AA's Twelve-Steps is that alcoholics cannot overcome addiction on their own. They must turn their lives over to a higher power and seek a spiritual path to recovery as the only way to gain control of their addiction (Hester & Miller, 1995). It is important to note that the Twelve-Steps are not a requirement for AA membership; they are the steps the founding AA members took to obtain and maintain sobriety and are "suggested as a program of recovery" In addition, AA stresses that these principles are primarily "guides to progress" and members "claim spiritual progress rather than spiritual perfection" (Alcoholics Anonymous, pp.59- 60).

Step one suggests that alcoholics should admit they are "powerless over alcohol – that [their] lives had become unmanageable." Step two begins the process of believing that a Higher Power can help them, while Step three suggests they need to make a "decision to turn [their] will and [their] lives over to the care of God as [they] understand Him." In Step four, alcoholics make a "searching and fearless moral inventory of [themselves]" (Alcoholics Anonymous, p. 58). Then, Step five suggests that alcoholics should admit to "God, to themselves and to another human being the exact nature of their wrongs." Step six asks alcoholics to be ready for God to help them with their character defects, and Step seven encourages alcoholics to ask "Him to remove [their] shortcomings." In Step eight, alcoholics make "a list of all persons we had harmed, and become willing to make amends to them all" (Alcoholics Anonymous, pp. 58-59). Subsequently, Step nine encourages members to make amends with those people.

The final three maintenance steps provide suggestions for alcoholics to maintain sobriety. Step ten requires alcoholics to be continually responsible for their negative behavior and promptly admit when they are wrong. Step eleven emphasizes that alcoholics must continue in spiritual growth through prayer and meditation with the goal of being knowledgeable of God's will for their lives and the "power to carry that [will] out." Finally, in Step twelve, once alcoholics have completed the other steps and have had a "spiritual awakening," they are encouraged to help other alcoholics through that same process (Alcoholics Anonymous, pp. 58-60).

When Wilson and "Dr. Bob" created the twelve steps, they purposely avoided any direct reference to Jesus Christ, and this omission upset many Christians (Hardin, 1994). They thought that the anonymity of God in the twelve steps was strategically important. This generic form of spirituality and the traditions of AA have kept it from being an organized religion. However, it is important to note that both AA and organized religions share a "moral and transcendent perspective; an emphasis on repentance; ultimate dependence and conversion experience; scriptures and a creed; rituals; and a communal life" (Peteet, 1993, p. 263-267). Christians should not let the lack of direct references deter them from utilizing AA.

The success and rapid growth of AA had an effect on the development of Salvation Army's addiction treatment programs. By the 1940s, Salvation Army began to separate their addiction treatment centers from their homeless shelters (White, 1998). They changed their programs in order to include "a broadening approach to treating alcoholism that integrated medical assistance, professional counseling, Alcoholics Anonymous, and Christian Salvation" (White, p. 75). Salvation Army officers were also involved in the initial Summer School of Alcohol Studies at Yale University, and, by the 1950s, Salvation Army was hiring social workers to help implement a more professional structured therapy program.

Rescue missions and Salvation Army historically have received the most criticism for their moralistic views on addiction, viewing that addicts just need to "get saved" (Clinebell, 1998). As described above, however, Salvation Army has attempted to integrate clinical models with a Christian perspective. Furthermore, research has shown that Salvation Army has comparable success rates to other secular treatment centers (Bromet, Moos, Wuthmann, & Bliss, 1977; Gauntlett, 1991; Katz, 1966; Moss, 1996; Zlotnick & Agnew, 1997).

In recent years, rescue missions have also begun to integrate clinical models with their Christian perspective. Rescue missions, overall, still emphasize Christian conversion as the primary solution to recovery more than does the Salvation Army. Additionally, Salvation Army primarily uses AA while the association of rescue missions is a sponsor of Alcoholics Victorious, a network of explicitly Christian twelve-step support groups. Unfortunately, little research has been conducted on the evaluation or treatment approach of rescue missions (See Fagan, 1986).

In 1958, David Wilkerson, a Pentecostal preacher, started Teen Challenge, a more explicitly Christian salvific approach to addiction treatment. In his book, *The Cross and the Switchblade,* Wilkerson shares his experiences in ministering to the youth and the gangs in New York City. Teen Challenge views addiction as primarily an issue of sin, and the solution is a conversion experience where the person is "'born again' by accepting Jesus Christ as 'personal Savior'" (Muffler, Langrod, & Larson, 1997, p. 587). Teen Challenge currently operates 120 centers in the U.S. and 250 centers worldwide for its 12 to 18 month residential program (Teen Challenge, 2000). Ironically, only six Teen Challenge centers serve teenagers. Many programs also have changed their name to be more inclusive for all ages (e.g., Life Challenge in Dallas, TX). Interestingly, Muffler, Langrod, & Larson (1997) argued that the rates of success for Teen Challenge have been grossly over stated; instead of 86%, they suggest that success rates are closer to 18.3%, similar to the 15% success rates of secular therapeutic communities.

Other arenas of Christian treatment have developed over the years. Saint Marr's Clinic in Chicago, the Christian Reformed Church's Addicts Rehabilitation Center in New York, Episcopal Astoria Consultation Service in New York, and East Harlem Protestant Parish's Exodus House (White, 1998) are some examples. Muffler, et al. (1997) noted that Protestants and Catholics address addiction at the denominational or diocesan level through organizations like Catholic Charities or Lutheran Social Services. Also, there are Christian treatment programs located within hospital settings (e.g., Rapha) or outpatient clinics (e.g., New Life Clinics or Minirth Myer Clinics) designed for individuals with insurance or other means to pay for treatment.

In addition, there are thousands of smaller Christian treatment programs throughout the U.S. In the state of Texas, for example, of the approximately 115 registered faith-based providers, the larger Christian organizations mentioned in the paragraph above account for fewer than ten of the providers. The majority of the remaining organizations are local Christian treatment facilities. Furthermore, the Christians in Recovery's (2002) database contains over 2500 Christian ministries, organizations, local groups and meetings worldwide that deal with addiction. The Substance Abuse and Mental Health Services Administration, a government agency, does not track faith-based or Christian programs in their database of over 15,000 treatment facilities. In fact, they claimed it was difficult to even define faith-based programs because a facility may be funded by a religious organization, but not have inherently religious teachings (L. Henderson, personal communication, April 15, 2002).

Pastoral Theology's Contribution

Christian approaches to addiction treatment vary based on their theological interpretation of Biblical passages. Furthermore, a dichotomy in addiction treatment developed based on those particular theological approaches to addiction. Some approaches have focused on addiction simply as sin, and "getting saved" was the primary solution. Other groups took a more liberal approach to addiction as some theologians were beginning to shift their thoughts to what the Bible says about human nature, our relationship with God, and God's purpose for our lives and applying it to addiction treatment. A full historical account of the development of pastoral theology's contribution to the addiction treatment field is not within the scope of this section. However, a brief historical summary is provided with particular emphasis on several theologians' contributions to the understanding of addiction.

Protestant pastoral theology began in the 1800s in Germany, but the American pastoral theology movement, which focused more on the psychology of religion, emerged in the 1930s with pioneers such as Anton Boisen, Richard Cabot, and Russell Dicks (Burck & Hunter, 1990). They provided insight into the relationship between religion and health and contributed a large amount of literature concerning psychological pastoral care and counseling to the field. These pioneers drew from the work of Paul Tillich and other neo-orthodox theologians.

Clinebell's (1998) textbook presented his pastoral approach to addiction. Originally published in 1956, it was the first major work on addiction by a pastoral theologian. Clinebell (1994) argued that religious factors rooted in the addicts' handling of existential anxiety are crucial to understanding both the etiology and the treatment of addiction. He suggested that addicts are trying to "satisfy religious needs by a nonreligious means—alcohol" (p. 267). A Christian holistic view of addiction, from a pastoral theological view, does not suggest that people are "sinful because they are addicted… rather, disharmonious existence is a state of being indigenous to the human condition and requires intervention by a power greater than ourselves" (Morgan, 1998, p. 27).

One can trace this theology back to existential philosophers and theologians such as Heidegger, Kierkergaard, Tillich, and Moore (Morgan & Jordan, 1999). Existentialism is primarily concerned with questions regarding the meaning and value of human life (Evans, 1984). Existentialists argue that all humans are finite beings, and we all experience "a sense of limits, restlessness, and estrangement" (Morgan & Jordan, p. 265). Tillich (1991) described estrangement as separation from God and said it was a part of our "essential nature" (p. 187).

Clinebell (1998) applied this theology to understanding addiction and argued that this estrangement causes us to have anxiety, and we seek to soothe our anxiety in inappropriate ways. Hunter (1990) suggested that this anxiety leads to inner conflict that cuts off the person from growth and development. This experience of aloneness and feeling isolated, not just from others, but also from self, makes us vulnerable to addiction. Clinebell (1998) wrote that as we begin to crave the "anxiety-deadening effects" of drugs and alcohol we are attempting to soothe the anxiety through artificial means (p. 30).

It is important to understand that dealing with issues of meaning and the finite nature of human life is basic to everyone. We all struggle with who we are psychologically and spiritually (Morgan & Jordan, 1999). For addicts, coping takes the form of addiction and has the psychological function to "compensate for missing or inadequately developed psychological functions of self-care, self-soothing, and self-regulation" (Hopson & Moses, 1996, p.10). Temporarily, this form of coping will suffice to numb the anxiety. Eventually, however, it is not enough to stop the deep psychological and spiritual need for meaning and purpose. In fact, as addicts continue to use drugs and alcohol, life becomes even more meaningless, hopeless, and spiritually empty (Clinebell, 1998). The American Psychiatric Association (as cited by Miller, 1998) described addiction as "a phenomenon that slowly takes over a person's life, displacing all else" (p. 34). Addicts position alcohol and drugs in the place of God, attempting to fill the void of estrangement. The theological term for this process is idolatry (Romans 1; Isaiah 42:8).

Surrender and Sanctification

Continuing with pastoral theology's contributions to the addiction field, we take the next step to see how confronting the idolatry helps in the recovery process. Addicts begin to deal with the idolatry in their lives when they confront and deal with their existential anxiety (i.e., the void of not knowing what the purpose in life is). As they begin to ask for help, a Christian spirituality can offer addicts a "nonchemical means" of soothing their anxiety (Clinebell, 1998, p. 283). This process of spirituality begins with surrendering, a process that addicts go through when they begin to realize they cannot control their addiction. AA identifies this process as "hitting bottom." It may occur during different points in life for each addict, and the common thread between addicts is a realization that they have lost their freedom in addiction, realizing that alcohol and drugs are not God.

Christians have a rich theological history from which they can draw ideas relating to this idea of surrender. Saint Augustine, an early theologian, wrote that until the human heart rests in God, the restlessness in our lives would not cease (Morgan & Jordan, 1999). Writing about human pursuit of happiness and the need to soothe the anxiety, Augustine argued that people would only find emptiness until they come to a place of surrender, allowing God to fill the void that only God can fill. Augustine emphasized the bondage of the will by describing it as "the force of habit, by which the mind is swept along and held fast even against its will" (Stone & Clements, 1991, p. 260).

Dietrich Bonhoeffer (1995), a twentieth century theologian, wrote that the first step for maturing Christians is to cut off ties from the previous life. He added that single-minded obedience is how God calls people in the Scripture; one only needs to deny oneself in order to be a disciple of Christ. Jurgon Motlmann (1999), a contemporary theologian, said that when Christians deny themselves, they become weak, but it is in this weakness where they will find their strength. As they surrender, they find meaning and purpose in God.

Albers (1997) described the process of surrender as "experienced, but never totally explained; accepted for what it is, but never totally accounted for; observable, but not objectively definable in conventional scientific categories" (p. 25). Interestingly enough, secular scientists have some understanding and appreciation of this process. Tiebout, a pioneer psychiatrist in the field of addiction, looked at this process of conversion in alcoholics involved in AA and concluded that surrender and the process of spiritual transformation is the key to change for addicts (Tiebout, 1951; 1994).

Let it be noted that surrender is not an instantaneous event that cures addiction. Addicts may not be seeking to soothe the anxiety with drugs, but addicts are still "addict(s) in the therapeutic sense" (Limeta, 1993, p. 40). In many ways, this is when the difficult work begins; Christian theology terms this process sanctification. Once addicts surrender and begin a relationship with the divine, the process of sanctification assists the believers as they seek to mature in their faith.

Discussion of Theories and Treatment Interventions

McNeece and DiNitto (1998) noted, "a significant advance in the study of addiction is the realization that it is probably not a unitary disease" (p. 32). However, practitioners may become very dogmatic in their application of one theory for all types of cases. This approach of taking from only one theory is not supported by the literature, and therefore, it has the possibility of not providing the best treatment. Abbott (2000) warned that the wrong use of theory in social work practice could lead to ineffective treatment for clients.

The National Association of Social Workers (as cited in Abbott, 2000) suggested that social workers should take into consideration that "social, economic, and environmental factors contribute to alcohol, tobacco, and other drug abuse " (p. xi). Goodman (1995), a psychiatrist, wrote that one of the problems in addiction treatment is that it encompasses biological, behavioral, social-interpersonal, and psychodynamic issues; and most treatment providers are only trained in one or two of those areas. Social workers are trained in all of these areas and bring valuable skills and education to the addiction treatment field.

Van Wormer (1995) noted that the ecological framework provides the best paradigm in capturing the complexities of addiction and offers assistance when conceptualizing and treating addiction. A major advantage of the ecological framework is that "it can subsume within its framework other theoretical models and treatment orientations. There is not an either-or with this formulation – viewing the person in the situation includes the total biopsychosocial reality" (Van Wormer, 1995, p. 18). Social workers need to appreciate the contributions each of the etiological theories of addiction provides to understanding the problem, while realizing that only one model is insufficient for total recovery.

The Transtheoretical Model, a good example of an ecological model, is one of the most promising and helpful research and practice tools in the addiction field. Dunn (2000) suggested that social workers should adopt this model for addiction treatment not only because of the strong empirical research supporting it, but also for its "compatibility with the mission, values, and problem solving orientation of social work practice" (p. 143). The Transtheoretical Model provides the tools necessary to assess the client's stage of change, as well as the means by which to select and implement an eclectic counseling intervention. It also will allow social workers to be effective in their pursuit of helping addicts through the problem solving process. Furthermore, the model lends itself to effective social work practice that is designed and tested to work with diverse client populations.

Although the Transtheoretical Model is not inherently based upon Christian principles, many of the techniques and processes can be adapted to and integrated with Christian beliefs. For example, the model is very insistent about the idea that change from addiction occurs over time and should not always be construed as a one-time event; surrender is just the beginning of the process of healing for addicts (Velicer, Prochaska, Fava, Norman, & Redding, 1988). In fact, all the stages of change can be applied to assisting addicts in changing or maturing in their spiritual lives.

Despite the clear congruence between social work and proven empirical evidence for the Transtheoretical Model, it is not the only tool social workers should be utilizing. Social workers must be committed to looking at whole persons in their environments. One of the most powerful tools to help addicts is to provide them with the opportunity to build a community of support and fellowship. Churches can help fill this void for addicts. Many times, however, there is the need to be around people struggling with the same issues; addicts can find this encouragement and support in AA.

Clinebell (as cited in Albers, 1999) positively stated, "in all the long, dark, dismal history of the problem of alcoholism, the brightest ray of hope and help is Alcoholics Anonymous" (p. 1). Davis and Jansen (1998) argued that there is a gap in recent social work literature regarding AA. Researchers have debated the efficacy of AA, but Emerick's (as cited in Davis & Jansen) recent review of AA studies and outcome evaluations suggested that AA is successful in treating addiction, at least for a large number of addicts. In response to this success, social workers need to be aware of the workings of AA and how many of the concepts of AA can be understood through Christian theology. According to Haller (1998), social workers need to understand the spiritual nature of AA because it allows social workers to be better listeners and helpers when understanding popular AA terminology.

Social workers should also assist in translating these concepts for other social workers. Our dual roles can be used to assist in educating others about the spirituality emphasis in AA, dispelling the prevalent myths (e.g., Davis & Jansen, 1998). Social workers must make the connection that both the profession of social work, in regard to the NASW Code of Ethics, and AA "embrace empowerment, connectedness, and interdependence, and most important, the principle that people can change, regardless of how oppressed they find themselves by their circumstances" (Davis & Jansen, p. 180).

In addition, there is mounting evidence that AA's emphasis on surrender and powerlessness are problematic for African Americans (Morgan & Jordan, 1999). Critics believe these flaws are because of the influence of the founders of AA, white middle class men heavily influenced by the conservative evangelical Oxford Group. The work of the Black Extended Family Project, a partnership with Haight Ashbury Free Clinics and Cecil Williams at Glide United Methodist Church (as cited in Smith & Seymour, 1999) has helped to bridge this gap. They offer an alternative and innovative Christian spiritual program for African Americans that takes into consideration these legitimate concerns.

Feminists have been especially critical of AA for these reasons and for AA's use of a male God (Van Wormer, 1995). Others have countered that AA encourages a personal understanding of a Higher Power that does not dictate a male or female God.

Some social workers have resisted the disease theory implications of addiction because it contradicts the strengths perspective or systems framework (Rhodes & Johnson, 1996; Spense & DiNitto, 2002). Van Wormer (1995) argued that the disease model is simply "a mere explanation and not a theory or framework at all" (p. 18). Furthermore, social workers have suggested that the disease concept emphasizes the pathological nature of addiction and assumes that addicts do not accept responsibility for their addiction.

However, the disease model is particularly useful in moving society's view of addiction from a previous moralistic stance to encompass a broader understanding of addiction. It allows addiction to be understood as a progressive and potentially life-threatening problem, if it is not treated. In addition, Morgan (1998) suggests that the disease model assists in reducing "the church's tendency to objectify evil as external to itself" (p. 36). Although the disease theory should not be used exclusively, it does provide a tool for the clinician when working with addicts.

Many Christian treatment programs attempt to integrate the addiction etiology theories and treatment interventions previously discussed with Christian teaching. Good research on these organizations, however, is not present at this time. The literature is lacking in both empirical outcome studies and descriptive studies on Christian treatment interventions. We have just a few studies on Christian treatment programs such as Salvation Army, Teen Challenge, and rescue missions. Although these studies, at a basic level, suggest Christian programs are successful, most of those conducted, and particularly the Teen Challenge studies, do not hold up to empirical standards. Furthermore, we have only limited information on what individual centers do in their programs. Literature suggests that the only reason these organization help is that they provide a salvation experience for struggling addicts.

There are several reasons for the lack of research literature on Christianity and addiction treatment. Science has long ignored the efficacy of Christian approaches, and even the very popular AA has not received the rigorous studies that other treatment modalities have received. Most secular sources categorize AA in the moral category, when in reality it is a spiritually based program. In addition, there is difficulty in empirically testing such concepts as estrangement or idolatry. It may not be easy, but that does not mean that the ideas are invalid.

Conclusion

McNeece and DiNitto (1998) note that "the major definitional issue concerning addiction is whether it is a bad habit, a disease, or a form of moral turpitude" (p. 4). On one end of the spectrum, we have addiction treatment programs that have built their intervention model around the idea that "faith is both the starting and end point in recovery. It is the healing power of Jesus Christ, in the Church, and not the intervention of behavioral science, that brings about and maintains the individual's rehabilitation" (Muffler et al., 1997, p. 587). On the other end of the spectrum, we have addiction treatment programs that have moved so far away from their evangelical roots that their programs are hardly distinguishable from secular programs.

Christian social workers, drawing on their ecological framework, should advocate for an approach to addiction that attempts to balance theological beliefs regarding addiction with the growing scientific knowledge and theories available. Social workers should provide leadership in developing, evaluating, and implementing holistic models for addiction treatment. Social workers practicing in a Christian addiction treatment environment need to embrace all that theology and science have to offer in order to provide the best care possible for those suffering from addiction.

References

Abbott, A. A. (Ed.). (2000). *Alcohol, tobacco, and other drugs: Challenging myths, assessing theories, individualizing*. Washington, DC: National Association of Social Workers.

Albers, R. H. (1997). Transformation: The key to recovery. *Journal of Ministry in Addiction & Recovery, 4*(1), 23-37.

Albers, R. H. (1999). Editorial: The spirit and spirituality of twelve step groups. *Journal of Ministry in Addiction & Recovery, 6*(1), 1-7.

Alcoholics Anonymous. (2001). *Alcoholics anonymous: The story of how many thousands of men and women have recovered from alcoholism* (4th ed.). New York: Alcoholics Anonymous World Services.

American Psychiatric Association. (2000). *Diagnostic and statistical manual of mental disorders* (4th ed.). Washington, DC: American Psychiatric Association.

Bakke, R. (1995). New faces of rescue missions [Electronic version]. *City Voices, Summer*.

Bonhoeffer, D. (1995). *The cost of discipleship* (1st Touchstone ed.). New York: Touchstone.

Bromet, E., Moos, R., Wuthmann, C., & Bliss, F. (1977). Treatment experiences of alcoholic patients: An analysis of five residential alcoholism programs. *International Journal of the Addictions, 12*(7), 953-958.

Brown, H. P., Peterson, J. H., & Cunningham, O. (1988). A behavioral/cognitive spiritual model for a chemical dependency aftercare program. *Alcoholism Treatment Quarterly, 5*(1-2), 153-175.

Burck, J. R., & Hunter, R. J. (1990). Pastoral theology: Protestant. In R. J. Hunter (Ed.), *Dictionary of pastoral care and counseling* (pp. 867-872). Nashville, TN: Abingdon Press.

Christians in Recovery. (2002). *Recovery ministry database*. Retrieved April 24, 2002, from http://christians-in-recovery.org/db

Ciarrocchi, J. (1993). *A minister's handbook of mental disorders*. New York: Paulist Press.

Clinebell, H. J. (1990). Alcohol abuse, addiction, and therapy. In R. J. Hunter (Ed.), *Dictionary of pastoral care and counseling* (pp. 18-22). Nashville, TN: Abingdon Press.

Clinebell, H. J. (1994). Philosophical-religious factors in the etiology and treatment of alcoholism. *Journal of Ministry in Addiction & Recovery, 1*(2), 29-46.

Clinebell, H. J. (1998). *Understanding and counseling persons with alcohol, drug, and behavioral addictions: Counseling for recovery and prevention using psychology and religions* (Rev. ed.). New York: Abingdon Press.

Davis, D. R., & Jansen, G. G. (1998). Making meaning of Alcoholics Anonymous for social workers: Myths, metaphors, and realities. *Social Work, 43*(2), 169-182.

Dunn, P. C. (2000). The stages and processes of change model: Implications for social work ATOD practice. In A. A. Abbott (Ed.), *Alcohol, tobacco, and other drugs: Challenging myths, assessing theories, individualizing* (pp.111-143). Washington, DC: National Association of Social Workers.

Evans, C. S. (1984). *Existentialism: The philosophy of despair and the quest for hope.* Grand Rapids, MI: Zondervan

Fagan, R.W. (1998). Religious nonprofit organizations: An examination of rescue missions and the homeless. *Social Thought, 18*(4), 21-48.

Gallup, G. H. J. (1999). Preface. In O. J. Morgan & M. R. Jordan (Eds.), *Addiction and spirituality: A multidisciplinary approach* (pp.xi-xii). St. Louis, MI: Chalice Press.

Gauntlett, S. L. (1991). Drug abuse control and the Salvation Army. *Bulletin on Narcotics, xiii*(1), 17-27.

General Service Office. (2001). *Estimated AA membership and group information.* Retrieved April 21, 2002, from http://www.aa.org/english/E_FactFile/M-24_d4.html

Goodman, A. (1995). Addictive disorders: An integrated approach: Part one - An integrated understanding. *Journal of Ministry in Addiction & Recovery, 2*(2), 33-75.

Gray, M. C. (1995). Drug abuse. In Richard L. Edwards (Ed.), *Encyclopedia of social work* (Vol. 1, pp. 795-803). Washington, DC: National Association of Social Workers.

Haller, D. J. (1998). Alcoholics Anonymous and spirituality. *Social Work and Christianity, 25*(2), 101-114.

Hardin, M. (1994). Let God be God: A theological justification for the anonymity of God in the 12 step program. *Journal of Ministry in Addiction & Recovery, 1*(2), 9-22.

Hester, R. K., & Miller, W. R. (1995). *Handbook of alcoholism treatment approaches: Effective alternatives* (2nd ed.). Boston: Allyn and Bacon.

Hopson, R. E., & Moses, M. J. (1996). Theology of paradox: A Pauline contribution to the understanding and treatment of addictions. *Journal of Ministry and Addiction, 3*(1), 7-47.

Hunter, R. J. (1990). *Dictionary of pastoral care and counseling.* Nashville, TN: Abingdon Press.

Katz, L. (1966). The Salvation Army's men's social center. *Quarterly Journal of Studies on Alcohol, 27*(4), 636-547.

Leshner, A. I. (2001). Addiction is a brain disease: Issues in science and technology online. Retrieved November 10, 2001, from http://www.nap.edu/issues/17.3/leshner.htm.

Limeta, M. (1993). *A guide to effective rescue mission recovery programs.* Kansas City, MO: International Union of Gospel Missions.

McNeece, C. A., & DiNitto, D. M. (1998). *Chemical dependency: A systems approach* (2nd ed.). Boston: Allyn and Bacon.

Miller, W. R. (1998). Researching the spiritual dimensions of alcohol and other drug problems. *Addiction, 93*(7), 979-990.

Miller, W. R., Brown, J. M., Simpson, T. L., Handmaker, N. S., Bien, T. H., Luckie, L. F., et al. (1995). What works? A methodological analysis of the alcohol treatment outcome literature. In R. K. Hester (Ed.), *Handbook of alcoholism treatment approaches: Effective alternatives* (pp. 12-44). Needham Heights, MA: Allyn & Bacon Inc.

Moltmann, J. (1999). *God for a secular society: The public relevance of theology.* London: SCM Press.

Morgan, O. J. (1998). Practical theology, alcohol abuse and alcoholism: Methodological and biblical considerations. *Journal of Ministry in Addiction & Recovery, 5*(2), 33-63.

Morgan, O. J. (1999). Addiction and spirituality in context. In O. J. Morgan & M. R. Jordan (Eds.), *Addiction and spirituality: A multidisciplinary approach* (pp. 3-30). St. Louis, MI: Chalice Press.

Morgan, O. J., & Jordan, M. R. (Eds.). (1999). *Addiction and spirituality: A multidisciplinary approach*. St. Louis, MI: Chalice Press.

Moss, B. G. (1996). Perceptions of church leaders regarding the role of the church in combating juvenile delinquency in San Antonio, Texas: Implications for church and community-based programs. *Dissertation Abstracts International: Section B: The Sciences and Engineering, 57*(6-B), 4036.

Muffler, J., Langrod, J. G., & Larson, D. B. (1997). There is a balm in Gilead: Religion and substance abuse treatment. In J. W. Lowinson (Ed.), *Substance abuse: A comprehensive guide* (pp.584-595). Baltimore: Williams &Wilkins.

National Council on Alcoholism and Drug Addiction. (2000). *Alcoholism and alcohol related problems*. Retrieved February 10, 2002, from www.ncadd.org

Office of Applied Studies. (1999). *Uniform facility data set (UFDS)*. Washington, DC: Substance Abuse and Mental Health Services, Department of Health and Human Services.

Peteet, J. (1993). A closer look at the role of a spiritual approach in addictions treatment. *Journal of Substance Abuse Treatment, 10*, 263-267.

Peters, T. K. (1980). *An investigation into the role of religious experience and commitment as a therapeutic factor in the treatment and rehabilitation of selected drug addicts from Teen Challenge: A follow up study*. Unpublished doctoral dissertation, New York University, New York.

Prochaska, J. O., DiClemente, C. C., & Norcross, J. C. (1992). In search of how people change: Applications to addictive behaviors. *American Psychologist, 47*(9), 1102-1113.

Prochaska, J. O., Norcross, J. C., & DiClemente, C. C. (1994). *Changing for good: The revolutionary program that explains the six stages of change and teaches you how to free yourself from bad habits* (1st ed.). New York: W. Morrow.

Rhodes, R., & Johnson, A. D. (1996). Social work and substance abuse treatment: A challenge for the profession. *Families in Society, 77*(3), 182-185.

Royce, J. E. (1981). *Alcohol problems and alcoholism: A comprehensive survey*. New York: Free Press.

Salvation Army. (2002). *What we do*. Retrieved March 10, 2002, from http://www.salvationarmy.org

Smith, D. E., & Seymour, R. B. (1999). Overcoming cultural points of resistance to spirituality in the practice of addiction medicine. In O. J. Morgan & M. R. Jordan (Eds.), *Addiction and spirituality: A multidisciplinary approach* (pp.95-110). St. Louis, MI: Chalice Press.

Spense, R. T., & DiNitto, D. M. (2002). Introduction. *Journal of Social Work Practice in the Addictions, 1*(3), 1-5.

Stone, H. W., & Clements, W. M. (1991). *Handbook for basic types of pastoral care and counseling*. Nashville: Abingdon Press.

Strung, D. L., Priyadarsini, S., & Hyman, M. M. (Eds.). (1986). *Alcohol interventions: Historical and sociocultural approaches*. New York: The Haworth Press.

Teen Challenge. (2000). *About Teen Challenge*. Retrieved May 1, 2000, from www.teenchalleng.com

Tiebout, H. (1951). Surrender as a psychological event. *American Journal of Psychoanalysis, 11*, 84-85.

Tiebout, H. M. (1994). The ego factors in surrender in alcoholism. Northvale, NJ: Jason Aronson Inc.

Tillich, P., & Taylor, M. L. (1991). *Paul Tillich: Theologian of the boundaries*. Minneapolis, MN: Fortress Press.

Van Wormer, K. (1995). *Alcoholism treatment: A social work perspective*. Chicago: Nelson-Hall Publishers.

Velicer, W. F., Prochaska, J. O., Fava, J. L., Norman, G. J., & Redding, C. A. (1988). Applications of the transtheoretical model of behavior change [Electronic Version]. *Homeostasis, 38*, 216-233.

White, W. L. (1998). *Slaying the dragon: The history of addiction treatment and recovery*. Bloomington, IL: Chestnut Health Systems/Lighthouse Institute.

Zlotnick, C., & Agnew, J. (1997). Neuropsychological function and psychosocial status of alcohol rehabilitation program residents. *Addictive Behaviors, 22*(2), 183-194.

CHAPTER 12

SPIRITUAL AND RELIGIOUS DIMENSIONS OF MENTAL ILLNESS RECOVERY NARRATIVES[1]

Roger D. Fallot

Theorists in many fields of inquiry have examined the importance of narrative in structuring human experience. Philosophers of religion (Crites, 1971), theologians (Goldberg, 1982), personality theorists (McAdams, 1993), psychoanalysts (Spence, 1982; Schafer, 1983), and psychiatric rehabilitation specialists (Harris and others, 1997), among others, have demonstrated the many ways in which stories may provide coherence, meaning, and direction to self-understanding. McAdams (1993) claims that each of us "naturally constructs [a story] to bring together the different parts of ourselves and our lives into a purposeful and convincing whole" (p. 13). In the last decade, this line of thinking has come to include the stories people tell of their experiences with illness and suffering: their "illness narratives" (Kleinman, 1988; Frank, 1995). Focusing on the spiritual and religious dimensions of stories, this chapter explores a narrative approach to the experiences of people who have been diagnosed with severe mental illness and discusses the roles such stories may play in recovery.

The stories people tell about their lives call attention to the need to make sense of—to discover or construct meaning in response to—life events and circumstances. Personal narratives have the power not only to disclose the individual's core values and implicit philosophies but to shape ongoing life activities—to open up some possibilities and to constrict others. For instance, if a particular story, overtly or covertly, prioritizes constancy and minimizes change, the individual's motivation for maintaining stability may be paramount, and exploring alternatives may be correspondingly foreshortened.

Like all stories, personal narratives may be viewed through the lens of literary criticism. Theme, plot and subplot, characterization, activity, tone, movement, and voice are among the listener's descriptive and interpretive tools. Frank (1995), writing primarily about chronic physical illnesses, offers a typology of illness narratives. *Restitution* narratives, he claims, convey a central movement motif—from a state of health through one of illness to restored well-being. In distinct contrast, *chaos* narratives lack clear, linear movement. They are more reactive to momentary stress than they are reflective; they hold little hope that life will get better. Finally, Frank notes, is the *quest* narrative—the type most commonly seen in published illness stories. Here the teller accepts the illness and holds to the belief that something may be gained through its experience. The illness becomes the occasion for discovering and enacting some purpose on the quest.

Led by consumers, the mental health field has come, in the last decade, to place increasing emphasis on the concept of recovery (Anthony, 1993; Spaniol, Koehler, & Hutchinson, 1994). In fact, many of the writings by consumers (Cooke, 1997; Deegan, 1988; Unzicker, 1989) spurring this new emphasis may be thought of *as recovery narratives*. By this I mean that writers often frame their personal stories of mental illness, its impact, and its aftermath in recovery terms; they acknowledge both the reality of mental illness and its effects, yet develop a sense of meaning and direction that supports their moving beyond the limitations imposed by the illness and by societal responses to it. Recovery, in this context, involves narrative themes of challenge and hope, of stigma and assertiveness, of limitations and new possibilities, of struggle and empowerment.

Published recovery narratives in mental illness have drawn primarily, then, on elements of Frank's quest narratives, whereas restitution and times of acknowledged chaos are secondary. The reality of most persistent and recurring mental illnesses is a cyclical one that "complicates enormously the problem of establishing new identities, new purposes, and new meanings" (Hatfield & Lefley, 1993, p. 186), as well as new personal narratives. When the very illness around which recovery is sought may function to disturb mood or to cloud cognitive clarity, the process of consistent meaning-making is itself at risk. So it becomes all the more important for many consumers to weave a self-story encompassing disruption, stability, and growth.

From this perspective, mental illness recovery narratives reflect a particular set of values and related motifs that place the individual in relationship to her or his immediate and larger contexts. They provide a general orienting system in which specific coping techniques may find particular salience. Because of this overarching function of recovery narratives, religious and spiritual themes may be of great importance for many individuals. Spiritual commitments may dispose people to make sense of their experience in ways consistent with their religious beliefs, to draw on religious resources for both more general and more specific coping (Pargament, 1997), and to construct further narrative development so that they take spiritual realities into consideration. So, although recovery narratives may serve as coping mechanisms for dealing with the stressors related to mental illness, they do so primarily by offering a more comprehensive scheme for understanding, adapting to, and overcoming the challenges of severe mental disorders—a scheme that for many individuals includes religious and spiritual dimensions.

This is not to say, of course, that spirituality always plays a positive role in these narratives and in their associated coping styles. Religious and spiritual concerns may become part of the problem as well as part of the recovery. Some people have experienced organized religion, for example, as a source of pain or guilt or oppression. Rather than being a positive resource for recovery, religion in this sense may merely deepen and complicate the need for recovery. Alongside those who experience the faith community as welcoming and hospitable are those who find it stigmatizing and rejecting. Alongside those who feel uplifted by spiritual activities are those who feel burdened by them. And alongside those who find comfort and strength in religiousness are those who find disappointment and demoralization. Given the relative neglect of religious issues in the mental health field, however, and given a history of overemphasis on the difficulties associated with religion, it is important to see that for many people with severe mental illnesses, spirituality is a core element in the narrative context for recovery.

Key Religious and Spiritual Themes in Recovery Narratives

In spiritual discussion groups, psychotherapy sessions, consumer satisfaction interviews, trauma recovery groups, clinical interviews, and numerous consultations at Community Connections, individuals have shared parts of their personal recovery stories. Before turning to certain themes distilled from these interactions, it is important to indicate some of the characteristics of these consumers. Consumers at Community Connections have all been diagnosed with a severe mental illness at one time. They are predominantly African American and largely identify themselves as Christians, mostly Protestant. Significant histories of substance abuse, physical and sexual abuse, homelessness, and poverty are also prevalent in this inner-city population. Recovery in this setting is thus not focused only on the experience of mental illness but is a multidimensional process that responds to broadly based experiences of marginalization and victimization.

Theme One: Whole-Person Recovery Takes Whole-Person Involvement. For many people, recovery narratives may draw on a somewhat paradoxical image of spirituality: it is at once the most profound center of one's life and the most encompassing whole. In a survey at Community Connections, nearly half of the participants agreed or strongly agreed with this statement: "My whole approach to life is based on religion" (Fallot & Azrin, 1995). This sort of affirmation—that spirituality lies at the heart of recovery and that it forms the basis for other dimensions of growth—is common. It may be rooted in the beliefs and rituals of organized religion, in twelve-step programs that emphasize the centrality of a higher power, or in a personal conviction that the self is most clearly defined by its spiritual expression. But whatever its foundation, *spirituality* as the core of identity stands as a sharp contrast and frequent antidote to *mental illness* as a core identity. People who incorporate in their recovery an understanding of themselves as children of God or as being an integral part of the larger world often adopt a more positive and hopeful tone about their place and roles in the community.

When consumers say, then, that "spirituality has been the most important part of my recovery," they are often referring to this whole-person orientation. Usually such comments are not intended to minimize the value of psychiatric medications nor of psychotherapeutic relationships nor of other rehabilitative supports. But they do claim a holism that points beyond the biopsychosocial dimensions to an ultimate source of meaning and identity.

Theme Two: True Recovery Is a Long-Term and Often Effortful Journey. Many religious traditions and spiritual movements offer avenues to healing. The image of spiritual growth as a journey or pilgrimage is a prominent one. Recovery narratives drawing on this theme differ significantly from those calling for a quick and all-encompassing solution to the problems attending mental illness. One spiritual discussion group, for instance, explored the distinctions between *magic* and *healing*. Some individuals held out hope for a "magic pill" or life-transforming moment that would relieve them of their struggles, whereas others talked about their own experiences with healing and recovery as a journey that requires considerable time and effort. The latter group strongly opposed the notion that some human or divine intervention would instantly change their lives. Rather, they emphasized their own responsibility and activity while simultaneously drawing on the sustenance of divine support. This stance, they claimed, led to greater fulfillment and less disappointment than passively waiting for miracles.

Theme Three: Hope Is an Essential Ingredient for Continuing Recovery. The recurrent nature of most severe mental disorders is often demoralizing for consumers, families, friends, and professionals. Given such cyclical problems, the maintenance of a hopeful position is difficult. Yet, according to many consumers, it is also essential to sustained recovery. Spirituality and religion are prime resources for hope. Some consumers build hopeful elements of their recovery narratives around beliefs in God and God's benevolence ("God's purposes are for the best" or "God will never give me more than I can handle" or "God wants the best for my life"). Christians reported drawing on scriptural stories of hope in the face of apparently overwhelming obstacles (the account of God's deliverance of the Hebrew people from Egypt, for example). The idea of a force in the universe that is allied with good and opposed to evil was voiced by some individuals who did not see themselves as connected to organized religion. Being in tune with this positive power then became a reason for hopefulness.

Many recovery narratives struggle with the difference between realistic hope and blind optimism. More realistically hopeful stories acknowledge the difficulties posed by mental illness and by societal responses to it but find hope in spite of these problems. Other narratives minimized or deny them, asserting that all will somehow work out for the best. Spiritual and religious dimensions of hope, then, place it in its ultimate context of divine or universal purposes. Personal narratives may draw on this ultimacy to sustain hope necessary for the journey.

Theme Four: Recovery Depends on the Experience of Loving Relationships. Many stories include the importance of divine love in strengthening and sustaining recovery. This experience of relationship with God, often nurtured in religious practice, may have affirming and valuing motifs—that God truly cares for each person as an individual and that God is deeply interested in each person's welfare. When a personal God-image is less prominent, a sacred quality of love may still be acknowledged. Some research has supported the idea that relationships with "divine others" may be related to psychological aspects of well-being (Pollner, 1989). In qualitative terms, stories that describe the self as strengthened by this relationship seem to involve greater confidence, capacity to tolerate stress, and willingness to take initiative. One woman talked about how her relationship with God had given her inner strength so that she could face more directly the pain of her trauma history and mental illness.

Some recovery narratives give a prominent place to reciprocal caring; one must give as well as receive love in order to feel whole. One man described his struggles, for example, with the idea of loving your enemies. This was hardly an abstract concern for him, as it directly affected how he chose to handle conflicts with roommates and other acquaintances. How tolerant or how confrontational should he be? Other people recounted the vitalizing importance of caring for their children. Especially when such care had been disrupted by psychiatric or substance abuse problems, recovery of these connections focused not simply on renewed contact with their children but on re-establishing ongoing loving relationships. For many consumers, the love found in human relationships is a reflection of the sacred—a further expression of divine love. For others, it is a primary animating force, giving direction and purpose to daily life.

Theme Five: The "Serenity Prayer" Expresses a Key Process in Recovery. It is perhaps not surprising in a population with extensive substance abuse and twelve-step experience that Reinhold Niebuhr's ([1943] 1980) "Serenity Prayer" should have a prominent place in many recovery narratives: "God, give us grace to accept with serenity the things that cannot be changed, the courage to change the things which should be changed, and the wisdom to distinguish the one from the other" (p. 823). Yet the images involved in this prayer are by no means limited in applicability to those with addictive disorders. When applied to coping with the apparent vagaries of mental illness, disability, societal stigma, and discrimination, such wisdom is indeed highly valued. Many consumers have built some version of this sentiment into their spiritual understanding and practice. Each phrase has a unique part to play in recovery.

Simply deciding which goal to pursue or which problem to address is daunting for many individuals with mental disorders. Choosing to focus on those over which the individual has or can develop greater control is often portrayed as a key step in recovery. Having devoted too much effort to attempts to change other people or to meet unrealistic expectations or to conquer psychiatric symptoms by using will power, consumers here describe the tremendous relief, hopefulness, and confidence that may grow from identifying goals over which they can exert at least some significant control. Rather than feeling aimless in their recovery attempts, they feel an enhanced ability to channel energy toward arenas in which their efforts are likely to make a difference. So the "wisdom to know the difference" is often recognized as a turning point in recovery stories.

Second, many consumers recount their attempts to accept aspects of their lives that cannot be changed. Most commonly, the stories of their personal, sometimes painful, pasts pose special challenges in this regard. Some expressions capture specific, religiously framed variations of this process: "Letting go and letting God" or "I turned that over [to God]" or "I left that in God's hands." Others rely on twelve-step acknowledgments of powerlessness and reliance on a higher power than the self. There may be struggles around the apparent intractability of the consumer's problems. In some recovery narratives, the ability to accept periodic symptoms without accepting the demoralizing idea of begin chronically and permanently disabled led to significantly greater motivation. Recognizing that the acknowledgment of their mental illness did not require them to renounce meaningful life goals was in fact energizing rather than depleting.

Finally, the "courage to change the things I can" takes on special significance in many recovery stories. The importance of developing assertiveness and the experience of empowerment can hardly be overstated in this context. Empowerment is both the central value and central goal of the recovery movement for many consumers. Developing or renewing a sense of power in solving personal problems and pursuing meaningful life goals is a corollary of this principle. Mental illness recovery stories often highlight learnings around symptom management, including the importance of medication, ways to minimize intrusive thoughts or hallucinations, and methods for coping with identified stressors. Developing and enhancing skills in interpersonal, educational, or vocational domains contribute to a sense of empowerment, as does the ability to define one's own needs and hopes and actively seek to fulfill them. Consumers report that having a more effective voice and becoming an active collaborator in their own service planning and evaluation is often one of the main shifts toward greater personal strength. Many understand this empowerment in terms that reflect spiritual or religious convictions in addition to any psychosocial ones. The divine or sacred can be a resounding source of personal power, which can be expressed as follows: being uplifted or given courage, feeling valued enough not to settle for less than one deserves, being freed to follow one's own life course, and cultivating the belief that God wants each person to live a life of abundant wholeness.

Yet empowerment to change what can be changed may include not only immediate personal and interpersonal spheres but public and political ones as well. Although for many consumers this is a secularly informed concern, for many others it has distinctly religious and spiritual meanings. Some consumers talk of their involvement in advocacy or in public policy (as well as in personal choices) as a *mission* or a *vocation*. Both of these terms may carry traditional religious implications. The consumer's story is being allied with a larger sacred story, and his or her purpose is being allied with larger, often divinely construed, purposes. This is precisely where some mental health professionals become skeptical about the use of religious language. For example, does talking about "doing God's will" necessarily point to some delusional process? Only a careful assessment of the meaning of such language—

both in that individual's overall functioning and in any relevant faith community context—can provide answers to this question. But for many people with severe mental illnesses, such a claim does not differ from that made in spiritual or religious contexts by innumerable believers. Their faith entails developing a sense of their unique role (a calling, perhaps) in bringing into reality certain core values.

It is certainly true that for some individuals the "Serenity Prayer" is useful primarily as a cognitive-behavioral framing; it serves to distinguish the controllable from the inevitable and to focus change efforts in the most potentially responsive arenas. For many others, however, the fact that it is offered as a prayer is essential to its power. Its petitionary form places the serenity, courage, and wisdom sought in the context of the individual's relationship with God (and often that of a faith community as well). For believers, this is especially relevant. Bringing such fundamental requests to God acknowledges in process what is stated in content: that these virtues may not be entirely at the individual's disposal and that they may be more properly experienced as gifts than as achievements.

Theme Six: Recovery Is a Journey Toward Genuineness and Authenticity. One of Frank's (1995) primary interpretive categories for illness narratives is the extent to which the teller's unique voice finds clear expression. In the accounts of people recovering from mental illness, this experience is also central and often enormously complex. Many metaphors reflect this process: discovering—or rediscovering—one's "true self"; feeling that one is "centered" or "grounded"; recognizing moments when action emerges from what is "really me" or truly "spontaneous"; becoming more regularly in consonance with "who I really am." Some frame this as a journey of return; its imagery involves "getting back to the person I was" (usually before the trauma or substance abuse or symptoms of mental illness) and thus draws on restitution themes. Some view it as a journey forward; the emerging self is being both discovered and created along the way, incorporating many struggles as well as achievements in its composition. Although consumers in either case often report the challenges of recognizing and consolidating a consistent sense of self in light of complicating psychiatric symptoms, there remains a fundamental motive to do so.

In some frameworks, the development of greater authenticity is inherently and implicitly a spiritual concern. Nothing is more fundamental to human existence than the achievement of genuine selfhood. In others, this connection to the spiritual or religious is explicit. Being "the self that one is meant to be" points to a sense of ultimacy, or underlying direction and coherence that transcends that self. Many religious people place this ultimacy in relationship to a personal God or to a faith community in which one's genuine identity is formed and finds fulfillment. Many recovery stories place authentic self-expression, then, in the context of spiritual and religious life. Here the "true self" emerges not only in dialogue with one's own history and one's own relational context but with the most basic questions of identity, meaning, and purpose.

Theme Seven: Recovery Is a Story of Action and Pragmatism as Well as Conviction. Many of the previous themes have emphasized the kinds of understandings and beliefs that characterize spirituality in recovery narratives of people with mental illness. But virtually all of these stories have concrete implications for daily living. Some examples will demonstrate the more immediate functions of these activities.

Faith communities. Religious groups can be a profound source of affirmation, comfort, and belonging in the lives of individuals who have often experienced stigma, rejection, and exclusion. One woman who had returned to church after many years of homelessness and isolation talked about her surprise and gratification that she could once again join others in worship, that she could be accepted—even welcomed—by such a community, and that she could begin to fit in with a group that represented key values in her life. Others describe the ways in which faith communities have extended themselves to meet some specific need—for transportation or food or emotional support. For people whose sense of themselves as marginal and unworthy is frequently reinforced by the larger society, religious groups may play a powerful role in reasserting their value and place in the wider community and in offering social, emotional, and tangible supports.

Prayer and meditation. Meditative time may deepen a sense of connection to self and, in prayer, to God. But mental illness recovery narratives often recount other, more tangible benefits as well. Some stories emphasize prayer or meditation as a very specific mode of self-soothing—a calming, relaxing, and reassuring response to external or internal stress, including hallucinations. Others focus more on its problem-solving functions: talking things over with God helps to sort through options and make better decisions; prayer reinforces motivation to abstinence from drugs and alcohol; meditating or praying puts things back in perspective and helps control emotional over-reaction. Still others describe how prayer improves mood. It may renew hope and expand the range of personal possibilities, or it may cultivate a sense of gratitude and draw attention to the positive aspects of some individuals' lives, or it may clarify a sense of purpose. Whether one considers their more abstract or more concrete effects, prayer and meditation often play an active role in these recovery narratives.

Religious literature and music. Both devotional materials and scripture appear frequently in the stories of people recovering from mental illness. Over half of the Community Connections participants in a recent survey said that they read scripture at least once a month (Fallot & Azrin, 1995). In addition to the general deepening of spiritual life this literature offers, it may also be responsive to specific individual needs. For example, certain biblical passages (such as many of the Psalms) are deeply reassuring and comforting. They may be read repeatedly as a steady source of strength or may be drawn on in particular moments of stress. Other passages speak directly to God's concern for the sick and the marginalized and serve as distinct reminders of God's care. Consumers read still others as challenges to use all of their talents and strengths as fully as possible.

Listening to religious music has in some ways very similar functions in recovery stories: comforting, strengthening, reminding, and challenging. African American spirituals, for instance, have special significance for many believers. This music expresses a wide and deep emotional range, engaging listeners in both the painful reality of suffering and the comfort, hope, and joy available to the faithful. And actively participating in the singing and movement of religious music may offer social and emotional benefits beyond that of listening. A gospel music group at Community Connections has played an important role for people (re)discovering musical interests and abilities. It has encouraged many people who are usually withdrawn and isolated to join in making music and in sharing their talents publicly. Culturally as well as musically, singing has helped many group members re-establish active roles in an important community.

Ritual. For many people with severe mental illness, disorganization has characterized a great deal of their daily lives. It is not surprising, then, that rituals associated with religion or spirituality are highly valued by consumers who prize their structure, regularity, and predictability. Whether these are rituals built around personal practice (for example, prayer at regular times, devotional readings, listening to music, watching worship services on television) or they constitute participation in formally structured activities of a faith community (worship, community service, making music), many recovery narratives describe the important capacity of such rituals to organize experience, provide meaning, offer trustworthy and safe social engagement, and express core beliefs.

Conclusion

These themes are intended to be an illustrative rather than exhaustive compilation of the ways spirituality and religion may serve as resources in the stories people tell of their ongoing recovery from mental illness. Such stories present important opportunities for mental health professionals working with this group of people. First, service providers may serve as accepting and empathic hearers of these stories, including their religious and spiritual dimensions. Rather than ignoring or minimizing references to spirituality in recovery and rehabilitation, these domains should be explored seriously. And, if an assessment supports the value of religion in a particular consumer's recovery, clinicians should be prepared to support collaboratively the consumer's convictions and practices. Second, professionals may play a very important role in the further development and elaboration of recovery narratives. Recovery stories do not emerge in a vacuum. They are created out of the teller's relationships and conversations with important others and from available social and cultural resources. By actively engaging with the consumer's story, the clinician offers new perspectives, challenges limits, and affirms strengths. Being respectfully open to expression of spiritual beliefs and activities is one of the keys to facilitating the telling and living of many consumers' recovery stories.

Note

1 This chapter was first published in 1998 in *New Directions for Mental Health Services*, 80, 35-44. © Jossey-Bass. This chapter is used by the permission of John Wiley & Sons, Inc.

References

Anthony, W. A. (1993). Recovery from mental illness: The guiding vision of the mental health service system in the 1990s. *Psychosocial Rehabilitation Journal*, 16(4), 11-23.

Cooke, A. M. (1997). The long journey back. *Psychiatric Rehabilitation Skills*, 2(1), 33-36.

Crites, S. (1971). The narrative quality of experience. *Journal of the American Academy of Religion*, 39, 291-311.

Deegan, P. E. (1998). Recovery: The lived experience of rehabilitation. *Psychosocial Rehabilitation Journal*, 11(4), 11-19.

Fallot, R. D., & Azrin, S. T. (1955) "Consumer Satisfaction: Findings from a Case Management Program Evaluation Study." Paper presented at the Annual Conference of the International Association of Psychosocial Rehabilitation Services, Boston, June 1995.

Frank, A. W. (1995). *The wounded storyteller: Body, illness, and ethics*. Chicago: University of Chicago Press.

Goldberg, M. (1982). *Theology and narrative.* Nashville: Abingdon Press.

Harris, M., Bebout, R. R., Freeman, D. W., Hobbs, M. D., Kline, J. D., Miller, S. L., & Vanasse, L. D. (1997). Work stories: Psychological responses to work in a population of dually diagnosed adults. *Psychiatric Quarterly*, 68(2), 131-153.

Hatfield, A. B., & Lefley, H. P. (1993). *Surviving mental illness: Stress, coping, and adaptation.* New York: Guilford Press.

Kleinman, A. (1988). *The illness narratives: Suffering, healing, and the human condition.* New York: Basic Books.

McAdams, D. P. (1993). *Stories we live by: Personal myths and the making of the self.* New York: Morrow.

Niebuhr, R. (1980). The serenity prayer. In E. M. Beck (ed.), *Bartlett's familiar quotations.* (15th ed.) Boston: Little, Brown.

Pargament, K. I. (1997). *The psychology of religion and coping: Theory, research, and practice.* New York: Guilford Press.

Pollner, M. (1989). Divine relations, social relations, and well-being. *Journal of Health and Social Behavior*, 30, 92-104.

Schafer, R. (1983). *The analytic attitude.* New York: Basic Books.

Spaniol, L., Koehler, M., & Hutchinson, D. (1994). *The recovery workbook: Practical coping and empowerment strategies for people with psychiatric disability.* Boston: Center for Psychiatric Rehabilitation.

Spence, D. P. (1982). *Narrative truth and historical truth: Meaning and interpretation in psychoanalysis.* New York: Norton.

Unzicker, R. (1989). On my own: A personal journey through madness and re-emergence. *Psychosocial Rehabilitation Journal*, *13*(1), 71-77.

CHAPTER 13

SPIRITUALITY, END-OF-LIFE CARE, AND AGING

Cheryl K. Brandsen

Social workers interested in spirituality, palliative and end-of-life care, and gerontology no doubt find this to be a thought-provoking and demanding moment in the profession.[1] Each of these three areas presently receives much attention in the social work profession and literature.[2] The work is stimulating and energizing, yet difficult and, at times, overwhelming. In this chapter, I will do three things: First, I will identify several challenges social workers face in their efforts to integrate spirituality into end-of-life care for older adults. Second, I will review models of human development, of spirituality, and of end-of-life care with an eye toward understanding the needs and experiences of dying older adults with respect to spirituality. These models of spirituality are congruent with Christian faith. Third, given the challenges Christian social workers face, I will propose a model for practice.

Conceptual and Pragmatic Challenges for Social Work Practitioners

Social workers who take seriously the challenge to address spirituality with aged and dying persons encounter large conceptual and pragmatic difficulties. Conceptual challenges include the heterogeneity of older adults, lack of conceptual models for end-of-life care, and ambiguity about definitions of spirituality and religion. Pragmatic challenges include concerns with delivery of care in nursing homes, hospices, and acute care hospitals.

Heterogeneity of older adults: Conceptually, older adults are not easily defined. Given entitlement criteria attached to Social Security and Medicare policies, we often think of older adults as being about 65 years of age or older. However, there is tremendous heterogeneity of aging with respect to physical and psychological variables. Consequently age tells us little about who is an older adult. When speaking of frail elders, older persons with significant physical and mental health problems, Kaufman (1999/2000) notes that no cultural models exist for slow decline and its concerns and sufferings. In American society, says Kaufman, "there is no narrative about what is good for the patient when the patient is an old person in decline" (p. 81).

Frameworks for end-of-life care: Delivering quality end-of-life care is hampered by the lack of a conceptual model for what constitutes such care. Singer, Martin, and Kelner (1999) observe that only experts have been included in conceptualizing end-of-life care while models based on patients' perspectives are missing.[3] Furthermore, clarity is lacking about when the dying process begins. Physicians have far less prognostic confidence than the general public realizes, and lack accurate prediction models for the multi-system diseases and declines of older adults. Deaths that have a clear terminal diagnosis, a staged trajectory of dying (such as AIDS or cancer), and an aware and expressive person making complex health care decisions are not typical in later life (Kaufman, 1999/2000; Seale, 1998). Rather, a trajectory of slow and uneven decline shaped by various chronic diseases result in a sense that death will not happen *this time*; another hospitalization and further life-prolonging treatments can always be tried. Thus, until we begin to pay attention to the "living-dying interval," that is "the period of time between the knowledge of one's impending death and death itself" (Engle, 1998, p. 1172), we are without useful practice models for supporting or assisting the dying process when older adults are frail, cognitively impaired, and unable or unwilling to direct treatment decisions.

Defining spirituality: Defining spirituality in a way that is useful to practitioners is also challenging. The health care and social science literature, including social work, does not lack thoughtful deliberations with respect to defining spirituality. Such considerations often contrast spirituality with religion, and to a lesser extent, faith.

For the purposes of this chapter, Canda and Furman's (1999) understanding of religion and spirituality form the basis for our discussion. These social workers have spent much of their professional lives addressing these issues, and their definitions build from and on the work of others. In their review of definitions, Canda and Furman identify six common attributes of spirituality. These include:

1. An essential or holistic quality of a person that is considered inherently valuable or sacred and irreducible.
2. An aspect of a person or group dealing with a search for meaning, moral frameworks, and relationships with others, including ultimate reality.
3. Particular experiences of a transpersonal nature.
4. A developmental process of moving toward a sense of wholeness

in oneself and with others.

5. Participation in spiritual support groups that may or may not be formally religious.
6. Engagement in particular beliefs and behaviors, such as prayer or meditation, in a spiritual or religious context (pp. 44–45).

In coming to a working definition of spirituality, Canda and Furman (1999) suggest that spirituality "relates to a universal and fundamental aspect of what it is to be human–to search for a sense of meaning, of purpose, and moral frameworks for relating with self, others, and the ultimate reality... Spirituality may express through religious forms, or it may be independent of them" (p. 37). In contrast, religion is "an institutionalized pattern of beliefs, behaviors, and experiences, oriented toward spiritual concerns, and shared by a community and transmitted over time in traditions" (p. 37).

While these understandings of spirituality and religion underlie the discussion here, it is important to recognize that at the practice level, the clients with whom we work may hold very different understandings of these terms. Thus the challenge for practitioners is not only to arrive at explicit definitions so that further research about the impacts of spirituality and religion can occur, but also to assess carefully and respectfully the multiple meanings clients attach to these terms (Zinnbauer, Pargment, Cole, Rye, et al., 1997).

Nursing home care: In addition to conceptual challenges, social workers also face serious pragmatic difficulties in addressing spirituality with clients. Some of these are related in part to the site of death, and in particular, when sites of death are nursing home facilities, hospice care, or acute care hospitals. With respect to nursing homes, the Omnibus Budget Reconciliation Act of 1987 (OBRA 1987) contained within it nursing home regulations that emerged from a series of nursing home reforms in the 1980s. Among other things, OBRA 1987 mandated the development and use of the Resident Assessment Instrument (RAI) to collect uniform data about each resident for individualized care planning. The RAI includes both the Minimum Data Set (MDS) for resident assessment and the Resident Assessment Protocols (RAPs) for standardized care planning that are triggered by selected MDS items. While in theory, this process makes sense, the RAI has been criticized for several significant shortcomings. The 500-question MDS administered to new residents contains only one question assessing religious needs, and residents' responses to that question do not trigger further formal care planning through the Resident Assessment Protocol (RAP). Thus spiritual needs may well be overlooked in formal care planning even though other studies report that nursing home residents find religion and spiritual care to offer much comfort and assistance in coping (Engle, 1998; Engle, Fox-Hill, & Graney, 1998; Koenig, 1994).

Hospice care: Difficulties in addressing spirituality with Hospice clients are well documented in the professional literature. Hospice practitioners, like social workers in general, are unclear about how to define spiritual care. McGrath (1997) notes that in spite of the centrality of spirituality in hospice ideology, it is the ignored dimension. Individual programs tend to make their own decisions about the role of spirituality (Millison, 1995). Although recognized as an important aspect of patient services in the Medicare code, the federal guidelines for spiritual care are vague and unclear. The regulations do not define what is within the parameters of the requirements made. Specifications such as what spiritual counseling is to address, how it is to be delivered, and how it is to be reimbursed, are not discussed (Babler, 1997).

Additional documented challenges with addressing spirituality in hospice sites include uncertainty about disciplinary domains, lack of knowledge among staff, and lack of clarity about assessment. Although clergy receive the most intentional training in spiritual care, no consensus exists that this domain belongs to clergy alone (Derrikson, 1996; Reese & Brown, 1997; Welk, 1998). With respect to staff knowledge, hospice staff, like many other social workers and health care personnel, report they lack knowledge of how to assess and address spirituality concerns (Canda & Furman, 1999; Hay, 1989; Piles, 1990). Definitional, domain, and knowledge concerns about spirituality result in lack of clarity about meaningful criteria on which to base spiritual assessment (Millison, 1995). No standard spiritual assessment exists except for a lengthy list of over 50 triggers that might indicate the possible existence of a spiritual need. Timing issues are also a concern. Spiritual assessment is emphasized at intake, but no ongoing assessment mechanisms are in place. Furthermore, addressing spiritual care assumes a time period of up to six months, but in reality the median hospice stay is 15 days.

Acute care hospitals: A large body of empirical research documents serious shortcomings in end-of-life care with respect to comfort, communicating with patients and families, honoring preferences for treatment or lack thereof, and basic medical care (Field & Cassell, 1997). The Study to Understand Prognosis and Preferences for Outcomes and Risks of Treatments (SUPPORT), a major investigation into end-of-life care in prestigious teaching hospitals found that pain and physical suffering among dying patients was inadequately assessed and treated; family members reported moderate to severe pain for at least half of the time for 50 percent of patients who died in the hospital. Furthermore, patient preferences for care, including do-not-resuscitate orders, were routinely ignored. Additionally, families incurred devastating financial bills. One-third of families of dying persons reported losing most or all of the family's major source of income, one-third reported losing life savings, and one-fifth of families had to delay or cancel significant personal events, such as a job, an education, or needed medical care (Knaus, Lynn, & Teno, 1995).

Conceptual Models for Social Workers

Given the challenges social workers face in addressing spirituality with older adults in end-of-life care, it is useful to remind ourselves of existing human development models that include older adults, explicit models for understanding spirituality, and models for understanding end-of-life care. From these we glean understanding about the tasks and themes that need to be explored.

Human development theories: Erik Erikson's psychosocial development theory is familiar to most social workers. Focusing on his eighth and final stage of life for person's age 65 and older, Erikson suggests that the last task to be completed is achieving integrity. Erikson defines integrity as certainty about the meaning and order of life, a love of the human ego (not of the self) that demonstrates "some world order and spiritual sense," and an "acceptance of one's one and only life cycle as something that, by necessity, permitted no substitutions" (1950, p. 232). Despair points to a lack of ego integration resulting in fear of death, a rejection of one's life accomplishments and practices, and a feeling that no further time is available for achieving integrity. The central process by which one achieves integrity, says Erikson, is through a process of life review.

Lars Tornstam (1999), in collaboration with Joan Erikson (1997), Erik Erikson's widow, and Erikson himself before death, identifies a ninth stage of development for Erikson's theory. This stage, called gerotranscendence, explores how "aged people face the deterioration of their bodies and faculties" (Erikson, 1997, p. 123). Tornstam describes this stage as a "shift in metaperspective from a materialistic and pragmatic view of the world to a more cosmic and transcendent one, normally accompanied by an increase in life satisfaction" (p. 178). It differs from Erikson's stage of ego integrity in that it is more forward moving and focused on the cosmic or transcendent dimensions of life. These dimensions include a preoccupation with generational interconnections, relations between life and death, reflections on the mystery of life, and may include a decreased interest in material things and a greater need for solitude.

Critiques of these developmental theories abound. Yet their continued utility in the professional literature, in case studies, and as frameworks for research in emotional and cognitive changes as we age suggests that the themes and tasks of achieving integrity, of redefining oneself in the face of decline, of connections with other people and with a higher Being, and of writing a coherent story with our lives requires that we pay attention to these perspectives.

Models for conceptualizing spirituality: In addition to these theories of human development, explicit frameworks for conceptualizing spirituality also exist. Here, several social work-based models are summarized.

Ellor, Netting, and Thibault (1999) present a holistic model—a Whole Person model—for conceptualizing spirituality grounded in what is meaningful to the client (in contrast to a particular theoretical paradigm or personal theology of a given practitioner). This model pays attention to the physical, emotional, social, and spiritual self. Each self can be understood as a separate domain in theory, and perhaps treated separately in practice, but to do so is reductionistic, say the authors. The Whole Person model consists of parallel spheres. The lower sphere constitutes traditional clinical distinctions of emotional, social, and physical domains. The overlay of the spiritual sphere consists of affective, behavioral, and cognitive sub-domains. These sub-domains "overlap and interact in a dynamic interplay which results in the person's unique religious or spiritual identity" (p. 117). In addition, the spiritual sphere is conceptualized as a potentially integrative structure with the sphere of traditional clinical dimensions. The authors affirm that the model is:

> highly dynamic.... The correlation between the various subdimensions of spirituality will be different from one person to the next and within the same individual over time. Like a top spinning on a platter, the spiritual domain can touch other single domains, but most frequently it moves, encompassing some or even all of the several domains in the holistic views of the person (p. 118).

Canda and Furman (1999) present both a holistic model and an operational model for conceptualizing spirituality. The holistic model is conceptualized as three concentric circles. In the center circle, spirituality is understood as the center of a person, "a quality of a human being that is not reducible to any part" (p. 47). The second circle is divided into four quadrants each describing a particular aspect of human beings: biological, psychological, sociological, and spiritual. The outer circle, spirituality as wholeness of the person in relation with all, moves one beyond a sense of personal integrity and wholeness to a transpersonal self—one that is "in relation to other people, other beings, and the ground of being itself" (p. 48).

Canda and Furman's (1999) operational model of spirituality can help support more precise operationalization of concepts for practice and research. They identify six interrelated categories of manifestations: spiritual drives; spiritual experiences; functions of spirituality; spiritual development; contents of spiritual perspectives; and religious expressions in individuals and groups. Operationalization of spirituality here, they claim, "is much less murky" (p.56).

Moving closer to conceptualizations of spirituality and end-of-life care, Dona Reese (formerly Ita, 1995) proposes a causal model of death acceptance using a theoretical framework based on Erik Erikson's work where dying is seen as an additional life stage with its own psychosocial tasks, and spiritual issues are central to these tasks. Reese (1999) defines spirituality as a two-dimensional construct: transcendence in purpose in life and transcendence in sense of connection to an ultimate reality. Each construct raises important issues that dying persons consider. Concerns that illustrate the sense of purpose in life construct include (1) a search for meaning about why one has become ill and the meaning of one's life; (2) death anxiety and fears of the unknown, of suffering, of loneliness, and of extinction; and (3) unfinished business that keeps one from recognizing the positive purposes fulfilled in life and meeting unrealized goals. Concerns that map onto the sense of connection construct include (1) facing one's relationship with God and understanding how God works; (2) isolation and the interpersonal and structural factors that contribute to this as one is dying; and (3) paranormal experiences such as visions of deceased loved ones and religious visions. These are viewed as a connection with an ultimate reality and generally are not disturbing to dying persons.

There are also conceptual models for addressing spirituality at the end-of-life that are less developed, but nevertheless useful in recognizing important themes and tasks in dying. Dunbar, Mueller, and Medina (1998) present a model of psychological and spiritual growth at the end-of-life that includes five components important for growth: reckoning with death, life affirmation, creation of meaning, self-affirmation, and redefining relationships. Derrikson (1996), based on work with hospice patients, suggests four tasks that frame spiritual care: (1) remembering, where patients come to understand the meaning of their lives; (2) reassessing, where patients consider how they have defined themselves and their worth in the world; (3) reconciliation, where patients consider unfinished business with others; and (4) reunion, where patients report visions of deceased loved ones who come to accompany their passing from this world to the spirit world.

From this brief discussion of spirituality models, it is important that the reader remember the following points as we move forward. First, the notion of spirituality is wholistic; it is not an "add-on" but rather foundational to whom we are as unique human beings. Metaphorically, spirituality is akin to roots that nourish a tree, or a network of capillaries that course through our bodies and sustains life. Second and closely related, although not stated as such in the models summarized above, is the idea that spirituality is embodied in human beings. When we suffer, when we are isolated, or when we experience forgiveness and reconciliation with a loved one, for instance, we experience these through our bodies. Third, spirituality is dynamic. It is not something we understand in linear, cause-and-effect terms; rather "the working of spirituality in motion is dynamic, nonlinear, and multilevel" (O'Brien, 1992, p. 4). Fourth, spirituality is understood, experienced, and expressed by human beings in particular and unique ways. Ellor, Netting, and Thibault (1999) are especially clear about this, and recognize that practitioners must find ways to assess clients' unique understandings of spirituality grounded in what is meaningful to clients, not practitioners. Finally, all of these models are compatible with Christianity. Themes of finding purpose and meaning in life, making connections and experiencing a sense of belonging with others and to someone greater than ourselves, and giving and receiving forgiveness are central Biblical themes.

Models for conceptualizing end-of-life care: Earlier the point was made that delivering quality end-of-life care is hampered by the lack of a conceptual model for what constitutes such care from the perspectives of patients (Singer, Martin, & Kelner, 1999). Working from a developmental perspective, physician Ira Byock (1996) conceptualizes dying as the last stage in a continuum of developmental stages. Like other stages of life, dying has its own "characteristic challenges, or developmental landmarks" that "may develop a sense of completion, satisfaction, and even a sense of mastery within areas of life that are of subjective importance (p. 247). Paying attention to these themes and addressing them as they arise reduce suffering. These developmental landmarks include:

(1) sense of completion with worldly affairs;
(2) sense of completion in relationships with the community;
(3) sense of meaning about one's life (through life review, telling on one's stories, and transmission of knowledge and wisdom);
(4) experience love of self (self-acknowledgement, self-forgiveness);
(5) experiencing love of others and being able to express love and gratitude;
(6) sense of completion in relationship with family and friends;

(7) acceptance of the finality of one's life, including total dependency through finding a connection with some enduring construct;
(8) sense of new self beyond personal loss;
(9) sense of meaning about life in general; and
(10) letting go, including for some surrender to the Transcendent (Staton, Shuy, & Byock, 2001, p. 260).

These developmental landmarks in dying are congruent with developmental tasks in models of human behavior and themes in constructs of spirituality discussed earlier.

How Best to Help: A Model for Practice Congruent with Christian Faith

This brief review highlights that bringing spirituality, end-of-life care, and older adults together as a focus for social work assessment and intervention is complex and multi-layered, mediated broadly by practice settings and related organizational and public policies, culture, the experiences we have, and the meanings we attach to our experiences. Furthermore, the developmental and spiritual themes that are relevant for aging and dying seem to be, for many, all-encompassing, dynamic, and particularistic. Consequently, competent social workers need a practice model that can accommodate such variability and diversity.

Competent, Christian practitioners also require such a practice model. Additionally, they are concerned that the work they do with aging, dying persons is faithful to God. Working from Bouma, Diekema, Langerak, Rottman, and Verhey (1989) in the context of health care, I suggest three guidelines for Christian social workers to keep in mind; these three suggestions have implications for practice models selected by practitioners.

Bouma et al. (1989) suggest that having faith in God the Provider means, in large part, that "God's care is the world's constant companion" (p. 9). When people suffer, as they often do in later life, Christian people respond by being present with those who suffer, thereby assuring them that they do not suffer alone and are not abandoned in their suffering. A caring response to suffering will include competent medical and non-medical care, recognizing that suffering can be greater than physical pain, and may well include spiritual suffering. The practice model Christian social workers use should be one that communicates a willingness to suffer with aged, dying persons.

Also, because God's care is the world's constant companion, we must treasure and preserve the freedom in life. Working from an Augustinian understanding of freedom, Bouma et al. (1989) define freedom not as the option to do one thing one moment and another the next, but rather "the freedom to establish an identity and to maintain integrity" (p. 15). God invites us to establish ourselves in faithfulness to God and there find our freedom. Paradoxically, being free means that some will establish an identity apart from God. God's providence:

> respects and preserves it [freedom] even when that freedom is culpably and paradoxically used against God and its own fulfillment. And faithfulness to God the provider will dispose us to respect and preserve the freedom God gives even when, in terrifying mystery, it denies God's claims and cause (p. 14).

Subsequently, practice models used by Christian practitioners must be ones that, even in old age, assist clients to make choices congruent with identities constructed over a lifetime and preserve integrity.

Finally, what makes life "fundamentally good is caring relationships—relationships with God, with other people, with creation, and with ourselves" (Bouma et. al., 1989, p. 274). These relationships shape our identities, mold our commitments and responsibilities, and allow us to be with others in authentic ways. Subsequently, the practice model used by Christian practitioners must be one that values the importance of relationships in the lives of aged, dying persons.

Social Constructionism

Given what competent, Christian social workers must pay attention to with respect to spirituality and older persons who are dying, social constructionism provides a helpful theoretical framework. As a theoretical perspective, social constructionism questions modernist assumptions that knowledge is gained objectively and mirrors reality. Instead, social constructionism holds that our sense of what is real, and the meanings we attach to our experiences, is constructed in and through interactions with others, and is deeply influenced by the social, political, and historical contexts in which we live our lives (Allen, 1993; De Jong & Berg, 2002; Thayne, 1997; Weick, 1993). We create ways to understand the world, and these interpretations become part of the frameworks that govern everyday practices, seemingly unrecognized as structures that could be changed. Implicit here is the notion that we construct meaning not only as an individual exercise, but also with regard for and to others.

Given developmental tasks and themes of achieving integrity and gerotranscendence, of understanding the role and function of spirituality in one's life, and of negotiating quality end-of-life care, practice models grounded in social constructionism are well-suited to explore intersections between spirituality, aging, and end-of-life care. Together practitioner and client can co-construct the next stage of life, a stage congruent with one's identity over the lifespan, and which maintains one's integrity.

Narrative Practice: Narrative practice models are one example of practice models that emerge from social constructionist frameworks. Narrative methods, borrowed from literary fields, pay attention to life stories, how the story is told (structure), key themes, and ascribed meanings. Mohrman (1995), a physician, notes that "there is much to be learned from the way patients tell their own tales of suffering: What they emphasize, the chronology as they have experienced it, the side events that sound unrelated to us but clearly are not to them, what they fear it all means" (p. 67). Through attentive listening to patient stories, we restore the sufferer to "full personhood," and help them complete their lives in a way that is congruent with their identity and with the way in which they have lived their lives thus far.

Narrative assessment occurs frequently in the social science literature, and includes addressing issues related to end-of-life care, spirituality, and aging.[4] Although practitioners can simply invite clients to tell their stories, certain framing questions can be useful for telling the story. Ellor, Netting, and Thibault (1999) offer the following basic components for completing a spiritual assessment. In summary form, these include:

(1) taking a spiritual life history;
(2) determining how important religion and spirituality are to the client;
(3) determining how spiritually autonomous or institutionally or community-connected the client is;
(4) determining whether the client's spiritual and religious beliefs and practices are positively transformative, adaptive, or maladaptive;
(5) determining whether spiritual or religious pathology exists;
(6) determining if and why the client's spirituality is in conflict with the spirituality of his or her significant others;
(7) determining how spiritual and religious beliefs are translated into or influence the physical, psychological, interpersonal, societal, and environmental activities of daily life;
(8) determining how spirituality helps or hinders the client when thinking about or experiencing suffering and dying;
(9) determining what the client's spiritual goals are;
(10) determining what part spirituality plays in the overall therapeutic process; and
(11) determining whether the provider is the most appropriate source of intervention or if the client should be referred (p. 93).[5]

Strengths-based, Solution-focused Practice: Strengths-based, solution-focused (SBSF) practice is also congruent with social constructionist perspectives.[6] Although used in a wide variety of practice settings, its use in working with dying persons or with respect to spirituality does not appear in the professional literature.

Broadly, SBSF questions help persons create well-formed goals within their own frames of reference and develop solutions out of existing strengths and successes (De Jong & Berg, 2002). Solution-focused conversations often begin with asking persons, "How can I be useful to you?" What follows is often a description of problems. Rather than exploring the who, what, where, when, and why of these concerns in detail, solution-focused interviewers respectfully turn the conversation toward developing goals, listening carefully for who and what is important to a person, and what that person wants different in his or her life. A question such as "When things are better for you, what will be different?" invites persons to think about future possibilities and what they would like different when current problems do not exist.

What follows are excerpts from an initial interview with a hospice client where SBSF practice is employed. The client did not request this interview; rather it is part of the intake process, so it cannot be assumed that the client has any interest in meeting, or has anything that he wishes were different in his life. The interview was conducted by an MSW; a hospice nurse was also present. The client was an 80-year old man, Joe, who moved into a hospice residence about 48 hours before the interview was conducted. Joe's spouse of 53 years had died two years before, and only one of his seven children lived nearby. Joe had chronic obstructive pulmonary disease (COPD). He had pneumonia and lung infections frequently over the past 5 years. Joe lived several months longer than anticipated after his move into the residential program. Having his oxygen levels and medications monitored more closely than he was able to do at home alone resulted in an increased level of energy and quality of life. While unknown at the time of the interview, Joe lived for nearly six months in the hospice residence.

Pieces of the initial interview relevant to spirituality are transcribed below. We join the interview after introductions have been made and roles have been explained.

Social Worker (SW): So Joe, we understand from speaking with your doctor that this decision you made to move to the residence was a difficult one for you to make. How are you finding things to be here?

Joe: It was a huge decision. I didn't know what to do. I didn't want to burden my kids. And at first doing this felt like I was walking out on life. I'm not a quitter, and making this decision felt like quitting at first.

SW: I can only imagine how huge a decision this must have been for you, especially if it seems like walking out on life. How did you go about making this decision?

Joe: Mostly I did a lot of thinking. I talked to my doctor a bit. But mostly I sat on my porch and just thought.

SW: So you're a thinker, huh? How is thinking helpful to you? What's different after you spend time thinking?

Joe: (long pause) Well, I just sort things out in my head and things get clearer. I talk to my wife, who passed two years ago, and ask her what she thinks. Of course, she doesn't really answer me… I'm not going crazy and hearing voices… don't worry (laughs). But I imagine what she would say to me.

SW: So when you talked in your head with your wife about what you should do about coming here, what did your wife say?

Joe: She said, "Joe, don't be such a stubborn cuss. You're 80 years old. You had a good life and you worked hard. You took good care of me and the family. You served your country. You were kind and generous, even if you did drink too much and watch a few too many football games. There's no shame in dying, and there's no shame in needing some help now."

SW: Wow, she had lots of good things to say to you… a good husband and father, that you weren't a quitter…

Joe: (nodding and laughing) Yes, I married a smart lady. I made a good choice there.

SW: Sounds like it. It seems like you are really good at facing these big decisions that need to be made in life—who to marry, how to decide about moving here. Have you always been good at that, or did you have to work hard at learning that along the way?

Several things are happening here. First, the practitioner is exploring how Joe made the decision to come to the hospice residence. With COPD, the disease trajectory toward death is not clear cut, and there were several times earlier in Joe's life where he could have chosen to receive hospice care but did not. He has entered the "living–dying interval" discussed earlier (Engle, 1998). Second, the practitioner is working toward identifying strengths and resources. Several emerge quickly: Joe is a thinker; he is not a quitter; he is a hard worker and a good provider; and he has been a good husband. The practitioner compliments him about these. Third, Joe introduced his wife into the discussion. The worker uses this opportunity to ask relationship questions and better understand the context of Joe's life. Recall that relationship questions are central for Christian practitioners to explore, integral to social constructionism, and a key theme in spirituality models summarized earlier. A few minutes later, the conversation returns to how Joe is a thinker.

SW: You mentioned earlier that thinking is helpful to you in making big decisions because it helps you sort things out in your head. You talked with your wife about moving here. Did you talk with anyone else in your head about this?

Joe: I talked to God about this too. I asked him whether things were enough in order for me to have a spot in heaven. God said they could find room for even a defunct Catholic like me. Somewhere I remember someone telling me that you didn't need to be perfect to get into heaven, because heaven is where you get perfected. But I don't know if that's right. . .

SW: So how was this for you when you imagined God's response to whether you should come here now?

Joe: I'm not a feeling type of person. Never have been. But I cried a little bit when I thought about God saying that to me. It made me feel real good. But I don't know if it's true. I wish I knew if it was true. If I knew it was true, then I could go in peace. It's ok with my wife to go. She doesn't see me as a quitter. I'm just not sure about God and whether God would take me in.

SW: So being sure about God is a big thing to you? (Joe nods). Help me understand this. What will be different for you if you were sure about God—if you were sure God had a place in heaven for a defunct Catholic like yourself?

Joe: I could go in peace.

SW: Ah, and if you were going in peace, what would we notice about you that says "Joe is going in peace."

Joe: I would be sleeping better at night. Right now I wake up in a sweat, and get all confused about whether I am living or whether I've died. I'd sleep better.

SW: So you would be sleeping better. What else would we notice that tells us you are going in peace?

Joe: Hmmm (long pause). I would read my Bible again, and maybe even call a priest to talk with me. I don't do either of those things now because I keep thinking I will read something or the priest will say something that tells me there is no hope for me. So I just avoid those things... you know, what do you people call it, denial?

SW: So if you were reading your Bible or talking with a priest, we would know then that you were at peace? Anything else?

In these interactions, the practitioner continues to understand the meanings Joe attaches to his move to the residence. Notice how smoothly spirituality issues enter the conversation. In discussing how he made the decision to move, Joe offers some poignant commentary on his relationship to God, and it becomes clear that he is anxious about dying because he is not sure God will accept him into heaven. If he had such assurance, he could "go in peace." Practitioners using Ellor, Netting, and Thibault's (1999) spiritual assessment (summarized earlier) already have useful data for further exploration. The practitioner and Joe are also discussing themes noted earlier in models of spirituality. Notice also how the practitioner works toward preserving Joe's identity. Being a thinker and not being a quitter have emerged as qualities Joe values. The practitioner could have, at several points, offered assurances and given advice. She refrains from doing this, honoring Joe's ability to think this through. Finally, notice how the practitioner uses Joe's words and works at getting as clear an understanding as possible about what she and other staff would notice if Joe were "going in peace." This clear picture of going in peace will be useful in caring for Joe in the way he wishes to be cared for, for figuring out what needs to happen so that Joe can "go in peace," and for evaluation purposes, that is, to what extent Joe did "go in peace."

After a few more minutes of discussion on this subject (including a series of relationship questions about what other people would notice), the practitioner asks a scaling question.[7] Note that the practitioner could have returned to asking whether Joe talked with anyone else about the move to the hospice residence. Instead, she chooses to follow the idea of dying in peace.

SW: Here is an odd question for you, Joe. On a scale of 1 to 10, where one stands for you being in the worst kind of turmoil and fear about where you stand with God, and 10 stands for perfect peace knowing that you stand on solid ground with God, what number would you give yourself today?

Joe: A three, no, a four… a three. Three. Definitely a three.

SW: Ok, definitely a three. Now, with all you are going through—the COPD, moving here to this place—why a three? Why not a one or a two? How did you get to a three?

Joe: (looking puzzled). I don't usually think this way. (laughing). But this is better than all those damn paper and pencil tests you people seem so fond of giving... Well, things were a lot worse right after my wife died. I think she died because taking care of me was such hard work. I went through a really bad spell about 3 or 4 years ago, and could hardly get around. The doctor suggested hospice then, but I couldn't see it. Chrissy took good care of me, never complained, and then one night, she died in her sleep. A heart attack. I couldn't help but think that if I hadn't been such a stubborn cuss, as Chrissy called me, and gone into hospice back then, that she wouldn't be dead. I was feeling really guilty.

SW: That is a lot to live with. How did you cope with all that guilt?

Joe: Lots of thinking again. I knew Chrissy wouldn't want me feeling guilty. She would have said, "Joe, I married you for life, in sickness and health. There's no better way I would want to pass than taking care of you."

SW: It sounds like Chrissy loved you a lot.

Joe: That she did, and I loved her too, but one thing else I do know that Chrissy would tell me to do. Get things straightened out with Kate, our daughter. She's the youngest, always been a devil. Got pregnant at 16, moved out, lived with the bum, kicked him out, raised the baby on her own. She was doing a damn good job of it too, but I was just always too stubborn to be nice to her again. It always bothered Chrissy that I was so mad at Kate. So I knew when Chrissy died, I had to get things right with Kate. For Chrissy's sake, and for my sake, because then I was really scared I might die in my sleep too, and then I was really sure I wasn't right with God because of how I treated Kate. That is why I'm not at a 1 or 2 now.

SW: You are not a 1 or 2 now because you got things right with Kate? (Joe nods). Wow, was that hard for you to do? (Joe nods). How did you do this—get things right with Kate?

Joe: Kate did most of it. A week or so after the funeral, she came over to get a ring that was Chrissy's. I'm not a big talker, but I did say, "Kate, I'm sorry for everything." Kate took over from there. She's got a big heart, which is why she probably got into trouble in the first place. She didn't make me grovel. She said, "I know you're sorry. You're just a stubborn old man."

SW: So you got things worked out?

Joe: Sort of. We didn't ever talk about anything. But I started to act differently—talk to her when she came over—and she started to come over more. Danny, her boy, came over too. We'd watch football together. It's comfortable now. No, it's good, very good now.

SW: This is amazing. You wanted to get things right with Kate and you took the first step. And now things are very good. Some people find apologies very hard. And yet you did it.

Joe: I'm not a quitter. At my core, I'm a family man. It had to happen.

In the process of scaling, the practitioner here learns a great deal about what Joe has already done to lessen his fears about dying and get right with God. Again, returning to themes of importance noted earlier in spirituality (Byock, 1996; Derrikson, 1996; Dunbar, Mueller, & Medina, 1998; Reese, 1999; Smith, 1995) and spiritual assessment (Ellor et al, 1999), several have unfolded. Notice also how certain themes about his life re-merge: a family man, devoted to his wife, and not being a quitter. These qualities, in addition to the importance Joe attaches to his ability to think things through and then act, helps the practitioner understand the way Joe makes sense of his life. Finally, while difficult to grasp from a textual narrative, notice the way in which the practitioner suffers with Joe in re-telling painful experiences of past mistakes. Guilt over Chrissy's death and Joe's treatment of Kate are faced squarely without false assurances; Joe's attempts at making things right are affirmed. The interview continues:

SW: So you are at a 3 right now with knowing where you stand with God, and dying in peace. So Joe, what do you think needs to happen so that you can move up just one step on the scale, to a 4. What would it take to be a 4?

Joe: (long pause). I don't know… I have no idea.

SW: This is a very hard question. Dying in peace and being right with God seems very important to you. Take your time thinking about it. This is very hard.

Joe: This is bigger than I thought. I kind of forgot about how hard it was to take the first step with Kate. But I did, and now I can honestly say that there are no left-overs with any of my kids.

SW: Wow, really? That is amazing. You have a lot of kids, and to have no leftovers, that is something!

Joe: (laughing). It sure is… (long pause). Thinking out loud here, I am almost ready to say that to move to a four, I would read my Bible again, at least parts of it. But I'm not sure.

SW: If you were to decide that reading your Bible would be helpful to you, what will be different for you when you do that? What will you notice?

Joe: It's been a long time since I opened that book—maybe 20 years—except at Easter. I think there are some stories that would give me peace. I remember some of them sort of, or maybe I've just remembered them the way I want to remember them. A son who runs off and spends his father's inheritance and then comes home and the father loves him. Isn't that one? (SW nods). And one of those prophets, talking about how God can't let go of him, just like a husband loves a wife even though she is a prostitute. I think those would give me comfort. Maybe I would sleep better. . .

SW: So maybe you would sleep better if you read some of those stories? How is it that those stories would help you sleep better, do you think?

Joe: Well, if the stories are as I remember, they would give me peace that even though I have been gone from God for a long time, I can still come back. There would be room for me…

SW: So knowing that there is room for you—that brings peace? (Joe nods). On a scale from 1 to 10, Joe, where 1 means there is no way you will ever read the Bible, and 10 stands for I will do it as soon as you leave me alone (Joe laughs), how likely are you to decide that reading your Bible would be a good thing for you?

Joe: I am an 8.

SW: Oh my, an 8. That is very high—almost a 10. What tells you are an 8?

Joe: I don't know. Thinking about Chrissy dying and how I got through that guilt, and thinking about Kate and how we got things right after lots of ugly years. . . makes me think I can do this thing too. It doesn't seem so big right now, to pick up that Book and read it, or at least parts of it. But I need to think about it more. (Joe is getting tired. The nurse signals it would be best to stop.)

SW: Of course you do. You are a thinker, and from what you are telling me today, the decisions you make when you think them through carefully are wise and hard decisions. You don't take the easy way out. You thought hard about coming to this hospice. You thought hard about how to deal with your guilt when Chrissy died. You thought hard about getting right with Kate. And probably lots of other things in your life. And now you are thinking very hard about this big thing of getting right with God and dying in peace. So I would like for you keep thinking hard about this very big thing. (Joe nods). And if it is ok with you, I would like to talk with you again to hear about what you are thinking.

Joe: That's good. Come back.

SW: OK, when would you like me to stop by again?

Joe: Tomorrow?

SW: Tomorrow it is.

In this set of interactions, the practitioner and Joe begin to move toward figuring out what it would take for Joe to get right with God and die in peace. From a practice perspective, an interesting shift occurs when Joe thinks about this question. Earlier he stated that reading his Bible would be an indicator that he is dying in peace. Here he identifies reading his Bible as the necessary step to move from a three to a four; it now becomes a means to dying in peace. Notice too how earlier discussion of how he faced difficult decisions gives him encouragement to do something that he is very much afraid to do, and which in fact he has avoided for a number of years. The conversation with Joe ends with the practitioner giving Joe modified "end-of-session" feedback. The worker compliments previous difficult decisions that Joe has made, offers a bridging statement congruent with Joe's perception of himself as a thinker, and gives an assignment that Joe has already identified as being congruent with the thinker that he is. With respect to spiritual assessment, Joe is discussing concerns about "left-over" business with loved ones, and also his large fears about once again reading the Bible.

This interview in its entirety lasted about 40 minutes, ending because of Joe's fatigue. Clearly not all issues related to spirituality were addressed here. Several good things happened here, however. Joe had the opportunity to tell part of his story in a way that made sense to him. He moved easily between physical concerns (not sleeping), social and psychological concerns (guilt and relationship with Kate), and spiritual concerns (dying in peace and being right with God). His ability to figure out how best to deal with spiritual concerns was affirmed by remembering how he faced difficult decisions in the past, and was done in a way that respected his way of working and the way in which he defined himself (being a thinker).

Subsequent conversations with Joe using SBSF interviewing continued until his death. On difficult days, coping questions uncovered a number of interventions staff could use that would be helpful to Joe: sitting on the porch and watching the birds and squirrels; listening to music, including hymns he learned as a child; sharing a blueberry pie with Kate and Danny; looking forward to and being able to witness a great-grandchild's first communion (in tandem with going to Mass for the first time in more than 20 years); watching football on television; being outdoors in his wheelchair with the help of his children; and reading or having someone read his Bible to him.

Conclusion

A practice model drawing from narrative and SBSF practice, grounded in social constructionism, offers the Christian practitioner a way, first of all, to embody God's care and suffer with those who suffer. This model is sufficiently flexible and broad to bring together, rather than reduce, the complexities of human experience and emotion over the course of a life. Elders can tell their stories in a way fitting to them and in doing so, work toward maintaining both identity and integrity. Second, this model offers Christian practitioners a way to embody the notion of treasuring and preserving freedom. This model is persistent in its efforts to be respectful toward and affirming of clients' capacities to make decisions, or write the next chapter, in a manner that maintains integrity and preserves identities constructed over a life time. Yet is does not let just "anything go." SBSF interviewing, for instance, offers practitioners a way to affirm the importance of community in shaping who we are and become. The model, particularly through the use of relationship questions, is sufficiently inclusive to allow connections with significant others, who help shape, challenge, confront, and sustain our lives with meaning.

Notes

1 For ease of communication, I use the term "end-of-life" care in this paper. I mean for it to include the care one thinks of when someone is given a terminal diagnosis and also palliative care, that is, symptom relief or comfort care and psychosocial care earlier in the trajectory of expected death.

2 Attention to aging has received a boost from the Council on Social Work's Strengthening Aging and Gerontological Education for Social Work (SAGE-SW). The role of social work in end-of-life care is being re-defined as evidenced by the recent Social Work Summit on End-of-Life and Palliative Care in March 2002 (Stoesen, 2002) and various funding initiatives such as the Robert Wood Johnson State-Community Partnership grants and the Project on Death in America.

3 For expert-driven taxonomies, see Emmanuel and Emmanuel, 1998; Field and Cassell, 1997.

4 For examples, see Black 1999; Fallot, 1998; Kaufman, 1999/2000; Zlatin 1995.

5 For examples of other spiritual assessments compatible with narrative social work practice, see Boyd, 1998; Canda and Furman, 1999; Hodge, 2001a; Hodge 2001b.

6 For a helpful discussion of social constructionism, solution-focused interviewing, and the intersection between the two, see Berg and De Jong, 1996. To sum, social constructionism and solution-focused interviewing strategies both posit the social construction of reality and emphasize that change occurs through the discovery of new meanings perceptions of others.

7 Scaling questions assess persons' perceptions of many things, including "self-esteem, pre-session change, self-confidence, investment in change, willingness to work hard to bring about desired changes, prioritizing of problems to be solved, perception of hopefulness, and evaluation of progress" (Berg, 1994, pp. 102 –103; cited in DeJong and Berg, 2002, p. 108). Persons are asked to put their observations on a scale from one to ten, where one stands for the worst possible scenario and ten represents the best possible scenario.

References

Allen, J. (1993). The constructivist paradigm: values and ethics. In J. Laird, (Ed.) *Revisioning social work education: A social constructionist approach*. New York: Haworth Press.

Babler, J. E. (1997). A comparison of spiritual care provided by hospice social workers, nurses, and spiritual care professionals. *The Hospice Journal*, 12 (4), 15 – 27.

Berg, I. K. & De Jong, P. (1996). Solution-building conversations: Co-constructing a sense of competence with clients. *Families in Society*, 77, 376 – 391.

Black, H. K. (1999). Life as gift: Spiritual narratives of elderly African-American women living in poverty. *Journal of Aging Studies*, 13 (4), 441 – 455.

Bouma, H., Diekema, D., Langerak, E., Rottman, T., & Verhey, A. (1989). *Christian faith, health, and medical practice*. Grand Rapids, MI: William B. Eerdmans Publishing Company.

Boyd, T. A. (1998). Spiritually sensitive assessment tools for social work practice. In B. Hugen (Ed.) *Christianity and social work: Readings on faith and social work practice*. Botsford, CT: NACSW.

Byock, I. (1996). The nature of suffering and the nature of opportunity at the end of life. *Clinics in Geriatric Medicine*, 12 (2), 237 – 252.

Canda, E. R. & Furman, L. D. (1999). *Spiritual diversity in social work practice: The heart of helping*. New York: The Free Press.

De Jong, P. & Berg, I. K. (2002). *Interviewing for solutions*, 2/e. Pacific Grove, CA: Wadsworth Thomson Learning.

Derrikson, B. S. (1996). The spiritual work of the dying: A framework and case studies. *The Hospice Journal*, 11 (2), 11 – 30.

Dunbar, H. T., Mueller, C.W. & Medina, C. (1998). Psychological and spiritual growth in women living with HIV. *Social Work*, 43 (2), 144 – 154.

Ellor, J. W., Netting, F. E., & Thibault, J. (1999). *Religious and spiritual aspects of human service practice*. Columbia, South Carolina: University of South Carolina Press.

Emmanuel, E. J. & Emmanuel, L. L. (1998). The promise of a good death. *Lancet*, 351 (supplement II), 21 –29.

Engle, V. Care of the living, care of the dying: Reconceptualizing nursing home care. *Journal of the American Geriatric Society*, 46, 1172 – 1174.

Engle, V. F., Fox-Hill, E., & Graney, M. J. (1998). The experience of living-dying in a nursing home: Self-reports of black and white older adults. *Journal of the American Geriatric Society*, 46, 1091 – 1096.

Erikson, E. (1950). *Childhood and society*. New York: W. W. Norton.

Erikson, J. (1997). *The life-cycle completed: Extended version*. New York: W.W. Norton.

Fallot, R. D. (1998). Spiritual and religious dimensions of mental illness recovery narratives. *New directions for mental health services*, 80, 35 – 44.

Field, M. J. & Cassell, C. K. (1997). *Approaching death: Improving care at the end of life*. Institute of Medicine, Committee on Care at the End of Life. Washington, D.C: National Academy Press.

Hay, M. W. (1989, September/October). Principles in building spiritual assessment tools. *The American Journal of Hospice Care*, 25 – 31.

Hodge, D.R. (2001a). Spiritual assessment: A review of major qualitative methods and new framework for assessing spirituality. *Social Work*, 46 (3), 203 – 214.

Hodge, D. R. (2001b). Spiritual genograms: A generational approach to assessing spirituality. *Families in Society*, 82, 1, 35 – 48.

Ita, D. J. (1995). Testing of a causal model: acceptance of death in hospice patients. *Omega*, 32 (2), 81 – 92.

Kaufman, S. R. (1999/2000). The clash of meanings: medical narrative and biographical story at life's end. *Generations*, 23 (4), 77 – 82.

Knaus, W.A., Lynn, J., & Teno, J. (1995). A controlled trial to improve care for seriously ill hospitalized patients. *Journal of the American Medical Association*, 274 (20), 1591 – 1598.

Koenig, H. G. (1994). *Aging and God: Spiritual pathways to mental health in midlife and later years*. New York: Haworth Pastoral Press.

McGrath, P. (1997). Putting spirituality on the agenda: Hospice research findings on the 'ignored' dimension. *The Hospice Journal*, 12 (4), 1 – 12.

Measuring quality of care at the end of life: a statement of principles. (1997). *Journal of the American Geriatric Society*, 45, 526 – 527.

Millison, M. B. (1995). A review of the research on spiritual care and hospice. *The Hospice Journal*, 10 (4), 3 – 19.

Mohrman, M. E. (1995). *Medicine as ministry*. Cleveland, Ohio: The Pilgrim Press.

Neill, C. M. & Kahn, A. S. (1999). The role of personal spirituality and religious social activity on the life satisfaction of older widowed women. *Sex Roles*, 40 (3/4), 319 – 329.

O'Brien, P. J. (1992). Social work and spirituality: Clarifying the concept for practice. *Spirituality and Social Work Journal*, 3 (1), 2 – 5.

Piles, C. L. (1990). Providing spiritual care. *Nurse Educator*, 15 (1), 36 – 41.

Reese, D., J. (1999). Spirituality conceptualized as purpose in life and sense of connection: major issues and counseling approaches with terminal illness. *Healing Ministry*, 6 (3), 101 – 108.

Reese, D. J. & Brown, D. R. (1997). Psychosocial and spiritual care in Hospice: Differences between nursing, social work, and clergy. *The Hospice Journal*, 12 (1), 29 – 41.

Seale, C. (1998). *Constructing death: the sociology of dying and bereavement*. Cambridge: Cambridge University Press.

Singer, P. A., Martin, D. K., & Kelner, M. (1999). Quality end-of-life care: Patients' perspectives. *Journal of the American Medical Association*, 281 (2), 163 – 168.

Smith, E. (1995). Addressing the psychospiritual distress of death as a reality: A transpersonal approach. *Social Work*, 40 (3), 402 – 413.

Staton, J., Shuy, R., & Byock, I. (2001). *A few months to live: Different paths to life's end*. Washington, D.C: Georgetown University Press.

Stoesen, L. (2002). Role in end-of-life care examined. *NASW News*, 47 (5), 4.

Thayne, T. R. (1997). Opening space for clients' religious and spiritual values in therapy: A social constructionist perspective. *Journal of Family Social Work*, 2 (4), 13 –23.

Tornstam, L. (1999). Late-life transcendence: A new developmental perspective on aging. In Thomas, L. E. & Eisenhandler, S. A. (Eds.) *Religion, belief, and spirituality in later life*. New York: Springer Publishing Company.

Weick, A. (1993). Reconstructing social work education. In J. Laird, (Ed.) *Revisioning social work education: A social constructionist approach*. New York: Haworth Press.

Weick, A. (1999). Guilty knowledge. *Families in Society*, 80, 327 – 332.

Zinnbauer, B. J., Pargament, K. I., Cole, B., Rye, M. S., Butter, E. M., Belavich, T. G., Hipp, K. M., Scott, A. B., & Kadar, J. L. (1997). Religion and spirituality: Unfuzzying the fuzzy. *Journal for the Scientific Study of Religion*, 36 (4), 549 – 564.

Zlatin, D. M. (1995). Life themes: A method to understand terminal illness. *Omega*, 31 (3), 189 – 205.

Further Resources

Angell, G. B., Dennis, B. G., & Dumain, L. E. (1998). Spirituality, resilience, and narrative: Coping with parental death. *Families in Society*, 79 (6), 615 – 630.

Armer, J. M. & Conn, V. S. (2001). Exploration of spirituality and health among diverse rural elderly individuals. *Journal of Gerontological Nursing*, 27 (6), 28 –37.

Brooks, S. (1996). What's wrong with the MDS (Minimum Data Set)? *Contemporary Long Term Care*, 8, 18 – 25.

Bullis, R. K. (1996). *Spirituality in social work practice*. Philadelphia, PA: Taylor and Francis.

Cantwell, P., & Holmes, S. (1994). Social construction: A paradigm shift for systemic therapy and training. *The Australian and New Zealand Journal of Family Therapy*, 15, 17 – 26.

Carr, E. W. & Morris, T. (1996). Spirituality and patients with advanced cancer: A social work response. *Journal of Psychosocial Oncology*, 14 (1), 71 – 80.

Carrol, M. M. (1998). Social work's conceptualization of spirituality. In E. R. Canda, (Ed.) *Spirituality in social work: New directions*. Binghampton, NY: Haworth Pastoral Press.

Derezotes, D. S. (1995). Spirituality and religiosity: Neglected factors in social work practice. *Arete*, 20 (1), 1 – 15.

Derezotes, D. S. & Evans, K. E. (1995). Spirituality and religiosity and practice: In-depth interviews of social work practitioners. *Social Thought*, 18 (1), 39 – 56.

De Vries, P. (1984). *Slouching towards Kalamazoo*. New York: Penguin Books.

Erikson, E. (1982). *The life-cycle completed*. New York: W.W. Norton.

Fowler, J. W. (1981). *Stages of faith*. San Francisco: Harper and Row Publishers.

Franklin, C. & Jordan, C. (1995). Qualitative assessment: A methodological review. *Families in Society*, 76, 281 – 295.

Fry, P. S. (2000). Religious involvement, spirituality and personal meaning for life: existential predictors of psychological wellbeing in community-residing and institutional care elders. *Aging and Mental Health*, 4 (4), 375 – 387.

Graney, M. J. & Engle, V. F. (2000). Stability of performance of activities of daily living using the MDS. *The Gerontologist, 40*, 582 – 586.

Hanesbo, G. & Kihlgren, M. (2000). Patient life stories and current situation as told by carers in nursing home wards. *Clinical Nursing Research, 9*, 260 – 279.

Ingersoll, R. E. (1994). Spirituality, religion, and counseling: Dimensions and relationships. *Counseling and Values*, 38, 98 – 111.

Koenig, H. G. (1999). The healing power of faith. *Annals of Long-Term Care*, 7 (10), 381 – 384.

Koenig, H. G., George, L. K., & Siegler, I. C. (1988). The use of religion and other emotional-regulating coping strategies among older adults. *The Gerontologist*, 28 (3), 303 – 310.

Levin, J. S. (1994). *Religion in aging and health: Theoretical foundations and methodological frontiers*. Thousand Oaks, CA: Sage Publications, Inc.

Neill, C. M. & Kahn, A. S. (1999). The role of personal spirituality and religious social activity on the life satisfaction of older widowed women. *Sex Roles*, 40 (3/4), 319 – 329.

Ouslander, J. G. (1994). Maximizing the Minimum Data Set. *Journal of the American Geriatrics Society,* 42, 1212 – 1213.

Ouslander, J. G. (1997). The Resident Assessment Instrument (RAI): Promises and pitfalls. *Journal of the American Geriatrics Society, 45*, 975 – 976.

Ramsey, J. L. & Blieszner, R. (1999). *Spiritual resiliency in older women: Models of strength for challenges through the life span*. Thousand Oaks, CA: Sage.

Schoenbeck, Sue L. (September 1994). Called to care: Addressing the spiritual needs of patients. *The Journal of Practical Nursing*, 19 – 23.

Sheridan, M. J. & Bullis, R. K. (1991). Practitioners' views on religion and spirituality. *Spirituality and Social Work Journal*, 2 (2), 2 – 10.

Sherwood, D. (1998). Spiritual assessment as a normal part of social work practice: Power to heal and power to harm. *Social Work and Christianity*, 25 (2), 80 – 99.

Simmons, H. C. (1998). Spirituality and community in the last stage of life. *Journal of Gerontological Social Work*, 29 (2/3), 73 – 92.

Stuckey, J. C. (2001). Blessed assurance: The role of religion and spirituality in Alzheimer's disease caregiving and other significant life events. *Journal of Aging Studies*, 15 (1).

Teresi, J. A. & Holmes, D. (1992). Should MDS data be used for research? *The Gerontologist, 32*, 148 – 149.

Thomas, L. E. & Eisenhandler, S. A. (Eds.). *Religion, belief, and spirituality in later life*. New York: Springer Publishing Company.

Van Hook, M., Hugen, B., & Aguilar, M., (Eds.) (2001). *Spirituality within religious traditions in social work practice*. Pacific Grove, CA: Brooks/Cole Thomson Learning.

Wink, Paul. (1999). Addressing end-of-life issues: Spirituality and inner life. *Generations*, 23 (1), 75 – 80.

Wuthnow, Robert. (1998). *After heaven: Spirituality in America since the 1950s*. Los Angeles: University of California Press.

CHAPTER 14

SPIRITUALITY AND RELIGION IN CHILD WELFARE PRACTICE

Gary R. Anderson and Jill Mikula

Among the wide variety of fields of social work practice one of the most complex and challenging is child welfare. With the specter of abused and neglected children and the complications of working with multiple systems, this field of practice faces additional values questions and emotional dilemmas beyond the normal clinical and policy challenges for the social worker. Also, significantly for social workers, child welfare agencies are among the few places in which social work is the predominant profession. All social workers have a professional and legal responsibility to recognize and report suspected child maltreatment. Therefore all social workers, whether employed in child welfare or not, need to have some knowledge about child abuse and neglect and the systems designed to respond to it.

There is a strong, positive relationship between child welfare and religion. Compassion for children and a commitment to family life are common ground between the Christian community and professionals concerned about the well-being of children. But there is also a degree of tension. Some in child welfare might question the church's vigilance in protecting children from abuse or neglect, as demonstrated by the sexual abuse of children by clergy or other religious authority figures. Some might view various religious viewpoints as encouraging parents to be abusive and practice severe physical punishment in disciplining children. Conversely, religious people might be suspicious of the state's role and potential intrusiveness in parenting as it may seem to interfere with the autonomy and perhaps integrity of the family. Christian social workers in child welfare might find themselves in situations in which there is a shared concern for children and families but misunderstanding and, at times conflict, between the child welfare system and religion.

This chapter will begin with a brief history of child welfare practice, a description of the services currently in place, and an overview of the goals of the child welfare system. The congruence and tensions between Christianity and child welfare practice will then be explored. There will be a special focus on the role of religion in foster care practices.

History

A rudimentary system of child protection and child welfare began in the earliest days of the United States, as society responded to children who were orphaned or abandoned by their parents. Primarily, children were placed in congregate care facilities—orphanages—for at least part of their lives to be raised under adult protection and supervision. However, there were a number of other responses to caring for mistreated or abandoned children. For example, in the mid-1800s Charles Loring Brace developed Orphan Trains to transport and place young children and sibling groups from Eastern cities with potential adoptive parents in the Midwest and West (Cook, 1995).

In 1873, a child protection system was launched by the case of Mary Ellen in New York City. The young girl was repeatedly beaten by her stepmother, and a friendly visitor tried to intervene to protect the child. There was no agency charged with protecting children from intrafamily abuse, so the case was investigated by the Society for the Prevention of Cruelty to Animals. Soon after presenting this case in court, a private agency, the Society for the Prevention of Cruelty to Children was created. By the mid-1900s the function of child protection was accepted by public child welfare agencies (Costin, 1991).

Also in the early 1900s the use of orphanages began to be replaced by volunteer foster families recruited to take in mistreated children. By the 1950s, these foster homes had become the preferred placement, and they remain so today. The use of foster homes provided a family-like setting for vulnerable children. However, concern was expressed about the length of time children remained in temporary foster care, and the impact of separations and loss upon children. Research and practice experience pointed to the harmful effects of drifting in foster care with no permanent placement for the child. This drift could be compounded by multiple placements for the same child, and inattentiveness to the needs of the child once in the foster home.

After three decades of documenting the placement of children in foster care and the length of the time that children spent in out-of-home care, the federal permanency planning law was passed in 1980. This law (Public Law 96-272) established permanency planning as the prevailing philosophy, value and strategy for child welfare. In the early 1990s, a growing commitment to family preservation – a specific commitment to keeping families together – evolved through family support legislation and funding to prevent the unnecessary placement of children in out-of-home care. In 1997, the Adoption and Safe Families Act (ASFA) was passed by Congress. This law established some limitations on making reasonable efforts to reunite families, shortened time frames for permanency planning, and encouraged adoptions and kinship care.

Throughout the development of this system in the United States the church played a prominent role as sponsor and auspices for private child welfare services (Garland, 1994). Initially, many of the original orphanages and asylums were administered by various religious denominations. Over time, churches and their affiliate agencies have adjusted to the shifts in child welfare by providing required services, either by government contract or private practice. Currently, many of the foster care and adoptive placing agencies in the United States are affiliated with the religious sector, including such examples as Bethany Christian Services, Catholic Social Services, and Lutheran Social Services.

Range of Services in Child Welfare

The child welfare system in the United States has evolved to include a number of services in a continuum of care, which address a progression of severity, treatment need, service commitment and cost from one service level to the next. This continuum includes:

- **Family Support Services:** Counseling and other concrete services that provide supportive assistance to a family. Many cases involve a response to crisis or a lack of resources needed to reduce the risk of harm to the children.
- **Child Maltreatment Prevention Programs:** Counseling and other services designed purposely to address and reduce the risk of child abuse or neglect.
- **Family Preservation Services:** Short-term and oftentimes intense services targeted to families that are experiencing a crisis that can potentially result in serious harm to the child, resulting in out-of-home placement.
- **Crisis Nurseries/Respite Care:** Special projects to provide relief for overstressed parents who need to have some immediate and short-term assistance to provide some time away from their children/infant.
- **Emergency Shelters:** Homes or housing facilities with the capacity to provide care for children for a number of days or weeks who are in need of quick removal from a dangerous setting. These shelters could have a diagnostic capacity to determine the special needs of children awaiting placement in another setting. The shelter could be a transitional setting providing an interim place-

ment for a child while a proper setting is developed or identified. Children may be reunited with their families after assessment of the family and the introduction of needed services.

- **Foster Care:** Family homes providing temporary care for children who are unable to be with their parent(s). Foster homes are provided by volunteer families who are generally licensed and supervised by a licensing agency, and are provided a modest stipend to meet the expenses associated with the child in care. Children generally enter foster care by order of family or youth court in response to a petition from a protective services worker alleging child abuse or neglect.
  - Relative or kinship placement is often available when a relation or member of the family's fictive kin is able to provide a safe and suitable home for the child.
  - Specialized therapeutic foster homes are designed for children and youth with specific emotional and mental health challenges that require the special supervision and treatment resources that trained parents and professional staff can provide.
  - Voluntarily placement is also an option, through an agreement between the child's parents and the child welfare agency.
- **Group Homes:** Congregate care facilities that provide a home-like atmosphere for a small number of youth, supervised by live-in "house parents" or rotating staff members.
- **Residential Treatment Facilities:** Providing housing, education, and counseling for young people in a congregate care setting that may be organized around dormitories or cottages. Residential treatment facilities are often responsible for helping young people with complex challenges including emotional, mental health, and educational or developmental disabilities.
- **Adoption Services:** When it is determined that children cannot be reunited with their family, the legal system may terminate parental rights or parents may voluntarily relinquish their rights and the child welfare agency seeks to find an adoptive family for the child.

The child welfare system encompasses a number of varied services and settings that are designed to separately meet the child and family's needs or provide a continuum of care if the child's needs change or intensify over time. A number of relatively new strategies to work with children and families have been introduced in the past decade, including family group decision-making, mediation, and managed-care models of service delivery. Regardless of the setting or strategy, the American child welfare setting has a number of primary goals in service provision.

Goals

Child Welfare in America has three primary goals: (1) ensuring the **safety** of the child; (2) working to secure **permanency for children**; and (3) strengthening the child's **well being** while the child is under the agency's supervision (Williams, 1996).

The first goal of child welfare is the **physical safety** of the child. The Child Protective Service division of the public child welfare agency is charged with responding to reports from the public and professionals alleging or suspecting that a child is at some risk of harm under the care of the child's parent or guardian. Threats to safety include physical abuse of children or threats of personal harm, a number of types of child neglect (including physical, medical, educational, or supervisory neglect), and sexual abuse of children. By law, professionals are required to report suspected child abuse, and child protective service workers are empowered to investigate abuse and take steps to remove children from situations in which they are at serious risk or have been abused or neglected. In some states, this investigatory process includes using risk assessment guides, structured decision-making and other strategies to guide the level and intensity of intervention.

The second goal of **permanency** is defined as providing children with family connections with potential of remaining a safe, stable and lifetime family. The commitment to permanency was informed by the research in child development that documented the effect of separation and loss on children, the impact of a child's sense of time and its correlation with length of stay in out-of-home care, and concern about children drifting in foster care, particularly at the risk of experiencing several different foster care placements. The outcome of long and ill-defined stays in foster care and multiple placements could include detrimental effects on the child's mental health and social adjustment resulting in the need for more intense placements. In addition, overemphasizing foster care as a permanent solution to child maltreatment stood to damage the autonomy and integrity of family life, profoundly affecting both the child and the biological family regardless of whether out of home permanency (such as adoption) was achieved.

Based on this information, family reunification became the most desirable form of permanency, provided that the home situation had improved and the risk to the children greatly reduced. If the biological parents were unable or unwilling to provide a safe home for the child, another option for permanency, such as adoption, would be explored. For some older adolescents, a goal of establishing one's independence after age 18 or a guardianship arrangement might be considered in addition to reunification or adoption (Maluccio et al, 1986). The outcomes for young people who "age out" of group or foster care are coming under increasing scrutiny.

The third goal of child welfare is to address the **well being of children** served by agencies or in out-of-home care. This can include medical care, counseling, support services, and mental health issues, as well as appropriate education, recreation, and socialization.

These are worthy goals, but their implementation has often been incomplete, at best. With regard to safety, the child welfare system has been met by criticisms from two sides. Critics have charged that it has either responded too slowly, resulting in children being left in dangerous family situations. Conversely, some charge the child protection system with moving too quickly, without adequate evidence, and unnecessarily intruding into family life and at least temporarily traumatically separating parents and children. The overrepresentation of minority children in foster care could indicate that discriminatory practices have unfairly heightened this intrusiveness into families of color in the United States (Anderson, 1997).

With regard to permanency goals, the failure to implement permanency planning strategies or to internalize the necessity of permanency has allowed children to drift without their biological families and without the connection to parents that could become their psychological family.

The goals of the child welfare system are admirable. Their implementation is essential as they address the basic safety and mental health of the child. They provide a common focus for program planning, clinical practice and professional commitment.

Congruence with Christianity

A commitment to the safety of children, to their connection with loving adults and family members, and to the well being of children seems to be completely congruent with a Christian world and life view. For good reasons the churches provided early leadership in providing child welfare services. For a Christian social worker, working with vulnerable children and families would appear to be a natural expression of one's Christian beliefs and values.

The faith of the Jewish nation, its relationship with Jehovah, and its value on human life contrasted with the idolatry in Canaan where some worshipped Molech and required the human sacrifice of children. In Jesus' ministry (Matthew 19:13-15), Jesus welcomed young children who were being kept away by the disciples. He spoke of the need to become like little children with an innocence of faith and response to the gospel (Matthew 18:2-6).

The connection between children and parents in families was respected and valued. When Jesus saw the grieving widow at Nain following the casket of her son he understood her need for family and the importance of the parent and child relationship (Luke 7:11-17). This was also evidenced in other miraculous actions, including raising the daughter of Jairus (Luke 8:40-56). Among his final words on the cross, Jesus was concerned about his mother and proclaimed that John and Mary were to be as parent and child—preserving family ties and relationships (John 19:25-27). Throughout scripture there is the admonition to be sensitive to and assist the fatherless and the orphaned (for example, James 1:27). One of the most serious threats by Jesus in his teaching was the warning against causing the stumbling of a child (Matthew 18:4-6).

It is consistent with scripture and the example of Jesus to be concerned with the safety and well-being of children and to strengthen their connections to family. Efforts at family preservation,assisting orphans and the fatherless, serving the children most at risk, including reducing their chances of turning toward crime or substance abuse, are laudable tasks for child welfare agencies.

Tensions with Christianity

There may be significant challenges for Christians in integrating social work practice and their faith and belief systems. This is complicated by the potential negative contribution of distorted religious beliefs and practices to child and family well-being. Due to the recent revelations of harmful abuse of children perpetrated by religious leaders, the connection between religious faith, parenting, and maltreatment has become more complicated.

Genuine Christian compassion for the well being of children seems natural based on the compassionate example of Jesus, the Christian ethic of love, and specific scriptural admonitions to care for children without parents or basic necessities. However, historically there have been a number of areas in which there was tension between the professional child welfare community and religion. Several topics of tension include: (1) the *definition of child abuse and neglect*; (2) the *causes of child maltreatment*; and (3) *between worldviews.*

1. ***Definition***: In the United States there is no nationally accepted child abuse and neglect law or definition. Definitions of abuse and neglect vary from state to state, and are oftentimes general and vague, thus allowing multiple interpretations of conditions described as "harm" and "injury". This lack of clarity reflects a conflict of values, or at least dif-

fering viewpoints, with regard to parenting and discipline. The sanctity of the home and parents' rights to raise their children in the manner they choose may be in conflict with the value of protecting children from harm, and society's obligation to protect children and monitor parenting on behalf of children. For example, while for some parents it is considered traditional and quite normal to use physical discipline to correct a child, to Protective Services workers, any discipline which leaves a visible mark on a child might be considered child abuse.

Consequently, within a community it is possible to find those who define abuse as significant injury that is life threatening or results in wounds and broken bones; others might define any physical punishment as abusive. It is on this point that some criticize religion as allowing, if not promoting child abuse. The frequently cited "spare the rod and spoil the child" is viewed with concern by some child welfare professionals and yet viewed as the literal truth and interpreted as a directive to hit their children by some religious persons (Meier, 1985; Radbil, 1974). In the public sector, corporal punishment is sometimes viewed as child abuse. Although few, if any, Christians would argue that the Bible promotes excessive or injurious physical punishment, the child welfare professional might be concerned about the support of physical punishment and failure to sufficiently warn against excessive punishment (Dobson, 1970; Lovinger, 1990; Wiehe, 1990). Defining only extreme, life endangering physical harm as abuse (particularly combined with a belief that child abuse could not occur in a Christian family) could lead to the failure to recognize and respond to potentially harmful situations (Pagelow & Johnson, 1988).

Specific areas of concern involving religion and child maltreatment have also been identified. In the mid-1980's the American Humane Association began to collect information on child abuse and neglect in cults and religious sects (AHA, 1984). Issues of medical neglect by parents who failed to secure critical medical treatment due to the family's religious beliefs have also been identified (Anderson, 1983; Bullis, 1991).

Conversely, many supporters of Biblical teachings point to a range of perspectives on Biblical passages that provide instruction in the raising of children. They argue that the abuse of children (or women) is not condoned (Alsdurf & Alsdurf, 1989; Campbell, 1985; Tomczak, 1982). While acknowledging the authority of parents and the necessity to discipline children, there is also the admonition to love children and not provoke children to wrath due to one's parenting behavior.

Finally, attentiveness to the physical and psychological needs of children and families as well as the spiritual needs of parents and children does not have to be neglected or separated from its real life consequences.

For example:

> In a child abuse investigation, the worker discovered that a father had sexually mistreated his teenage son and daughter. The children were picked up at their Christian school and placed in emergency foster care. The worker immediately scheduled an appointment to meet with the parents.
>
> During this first interview, the father told the worker that the abuse had ended in recent months as he had a conversion experience and was now a genuine Christian. The worker expressed appreciation for this decision by the father but stated that the father's statement of belief needed to be demonstrated consistently by his actions. The father responded "Yes! Faith without works is dead!" With his wife's support and the worker's support, the father confessed his guilt in court, entered counseling, apologized to his children, and visited his children, who remained in foster care while he followed the court's order and case plan. Within six months, the family was successfully reunited as the father completed all required actions. Continued monitoring confirmed the father's change and the young peoples' safety.

2. ***Causes of maltreatment***: Broader than the issue of physical punishment, religion has been portrayed as providing the context or belief system that contributes to child abuse and neglect (Garbarino & Ebata, 1983; Garbarino & Gilliam, 1980). A number of theories of child abuse point to the role of an authoritarian or patriarchal family structure in creating an atmosphere in which children (and sometimes women) are viewed as subservient to fathers and husbands (Horton & Williamson, 1988; Peek, Lowe, & Williams, 1991). Equating patriarchy with authoritarian parenting styles, some express concern about physical abuse of children, emotional abuse or neglect, and a climate in which child maltreatment is justified or allowed. The child is expected to be obedient to the parent (Alwin, 1986). He or she is not allowed to display a "willful spirit" (Fugate, 1980; Hutson, 1983). The shaping of the child's will (sinful nature) and spirit, and discipline required for achieving maturity need to be firmly enforced by the parent (Hyles, 1974; Rice, 1982; Williams & Money, 1980). The implied relationship between patriarchal excess and child maltreatment is particularly noted in cases of child sexual abuse as the father or stepfather's actions are described as related to one's sense of power or powerlessness in the family and community (Pellauer, Chester, & Boyajian, 1987). Parental actions are justified as preserving a family hierarchy, breaking the child's willful spirit, or re-

sponding to the child who is born in sin and needs to learn submission to authority (Walters, 1975).

3. ***Worldviews***: The first two dynamics – supporting physical punishment and providing a belief system conducive to child maltreatment – sometimes portray religion as part of the child abuse problem. The "worldview" issue describes religion as irrelevant to the problem of child abuse and neglect. Some would say that the church's attention to the spiritual world, the inner world, and the afterworld dilutes or replaces attentiveness to the physical, material and present-day needs of children. Consequently, the church's knowledge of and support for public child protective and child welfare systems may not be present or strong.

Christian Perspectives on Child Welfare

In this challenging context of multiple viewpoints on child maltreatment, there are a number of Christian principles and perspectives that apply to Christians working in the field of child welfare. These perspectives include: (1) *spiritual resources*; (2) *social support*; and (3) *a sense of calling and purpose.*

1. ***Spiritual Resources:*** Spiritual resources for the Christian child welfare worker include the spiritual support for the individual worker that comes from the belief that one is placed in a certain position for a purpose and with certain safeguards. Spiritual safeguards include the Biblical teachings that God provides comfort, direction, and a meaningful personal relationship designed to guide and support the Christian worker. The Bible teaches that Jesus is intricately aware of each situation one faces, and is able to provide the worker with sufficient strength to fulfill the task at hand. This includes the guidance and support from one's colleagues, supervisor, and other consultants.

Other spiritual resources include prayer – communication with God about one's personal circumstances and challenges, requests for guidance and direction, and praying for the well being of children and families. One faith-based residential facility makes it common practice that after the team presents and discusses each individual case, they pause to pray for that youth and request God's intervention.

2. ***Social Supports:*** Participation in faith communities can provide social support for child welfare workers. The worker can gain encouragement from others; affirming the person's value, thereby increasing the worker's overall well-being. Participation in a faith community can

also provide a place for introspection, self-reflection, teaching, and expression that can potentially enhance the worker's ability to cope with the challenges experienced during social work practice.

Oftentimes faith communities also provide concrete support for families served by child welfare services by providing such things as food, clothes, furniture and meeting other concrete needs. One of the more significant contributions of the faith community is that of adoptive and foster parents. There are significant numbers of licensed foster parents and adoptive parents whose motives, coping ability, and compassion are inspired by their religious faith and convictions and supported by their involvement within and membership in faith communities. Churches and other faith communities comprise one of the most successful recruiting sources for agencies seeing new placements for children. One of the model programs that promotes a partnership between one's church and religious faith and the needs of children is the "One Child, One Church" adoption initiative that challenges each church to encourage at least one of its member families to adopt at least one child waiting for a permanent home. This initiative, which began in an African-American congregation in Chicago, has been promoted nationally by the federal government.

Another example of faith-based support are networks of resources for young mothers, volunteer aides from the church congregation that provide home help services to overworked mothers. In Grand Rapids, Michigan, a network of churches work yearly to organize a "Back to School" fair for low-income families, filling a local park and offering everything from haircuts to medical exams to school supplies to new shoes. These, along with any of a multitude of other community outreach efforts sponsored by local churches, stand as examples of the religious community's involvement in child welfare services.

Significantly in the field of child welfare, there is the formation of religiously based social service agencies that provide an ongoing service to the community with support from one or several religious constituencies. For example, in New York City there are federations of Catholic, Jewish and Protestant child welfare agencies. The religious community has made crucial contributions to services for children and families. Through its educational ministries, support services, and assistance to families, faith-based organizations and congregations provide a significant network and volume of family support services with a critical role in family preservation. The provision of formal child welfare services, such as foster care, group home care and residential treatment, and adoption services is frequently provided by private, faith-based organizations under contract to the state's public child welfare agencies. These service providers are essential to meeting the need for placements and homes for children and young people who are removed from their homes or need to be placed in specialized settings to meet the safety and mental health needs of the children and youth.

3. *A Sense of Calling and Purpose:* Christian workers may be able to draw upon a number of beliefs that could support their work with maltreated children and their families. As part of a larger worldview, a worker would recognize that family violence and neglect can be viewed in the larger context of a fallen world with sorrow and brokenness in primary relationships. The worker could affirm that he or she is in a professional position for a specific purpose—that there is some meaning and calling to their intervention with families. This meaning could be derived from the Scripture's reference to the well being of children and orphans as well as more general admonitions to love one's neighbors. Additionally, reference could be made to a Biblical commitment to individual and social justice. This commitment to justice could motivate one to work on behalf of maltreated children as well as address social systems or factors that fail to support or may actively oppress families. This desire to mend the brokenness of relationships in a fallen world, along with a Biblical commitment to individual and social justice, provides not only the motivation for many Christian social workers to enter the field, but also the means to sustain that sense of calling.

The Role of Religion in Foster Care Services

The child welfare worker and the child welfare agency have to balance a number of rights and responsibilities. In out-of-home placements, this balance includes weighing the rights and wishes of biological parents, respect for the rights and wishes of the foster parents, and respect for the foster child's cultural and family ties and self-determination.

These rights and perspectives raise a variety of complex dilemmas for child welfare agencies in responding to the needs and preferences of the biological parent, the foster child, and the foster parents and their family. If there are religious differences between any of these parties, the question of sensitivity to the religious choices of all becomes difficult to address. Particularly challenging issues are raised when one of the parties prefers that religion not be a part of the foster placement, or when the biological and foster families embrace two distinctly different religious views (Schatz & Horejsi, 1996b).

Cultural matching in out-of-home placement has, for the last twenty years, been one of the most controversial issues surrounding foster care.

Most often discussed is the practice of matching children to foster parents on the basis of race, a practice that has been legally forbidden in recent years. Experts on culture, racial issues, and child welfare differ sharply on the appropriate method for placing children, particularly minority children, with foster parents of a different race. The attention to culture for some time appeared to end here. Religion was less frequently noted as a significant factor in out-of-home placements (Schatz & Horejsi, 1996a). With increasing attention to religion in social work practice, religion is being examined as a significant cultural factor in foster care placement.

It is has been considered preferable to place a child in a home of matching religious values, based on the stated preference of the biological parent. However, in a significant number of cases, the biological parent does not indicate a preference of religion in the foster home, whether this is due to circumstances surrounding the removal of children from the home (including the failure to assess religious preferences and affiliations) or due to a lack of religious preference. In such situations, who is to make the decision of the appropriateness of a foster home in the context of religion?

There are a variety of concerns that foster parents, caseworkers, and biological parents have with regard to foster care placement and religion. Rarely is placement so convenient that Presbyterian children, for example, are automatically placed with Presbyterian foster parents at the biological parents' request. Instead, due to an ever-present need for available foster homes for children coming into placement, the closest possible fit is attempted. Oftentimes, locating a home—any foster home—is difficult. Also, other variables in placement decisions are prioritized, for example, finding a home that will accept a large sibling group. Foster care placing agencies are left with the delicate task of finding the most suitable home for children coming into care.

Some of the major dilemmas that arise, outlined in the Colorado *Fostering Families* training manual authored by Mona Schatz and Charles Horejsi (1992), include:

> 1. *The biological parent has no religious persuasion, and prefers that her child not be raised in a religious atmosphere.* In this circumstance, which is not uncommon, clearly it is preferable to place the child with a foster family that is not religiously affiliated. But given the high numbers of foster families who have some religious affiliation, there is a significant possibility that matching of this type could not happen without delaying the out-of-home placement of this child. The dilemma for the case-

worker and for the foster parents is finding an acceptable means of both respecting the biological parents' wishes while not forcing the foster family to alter their own private religious practices.

2. *The biological family has significantly different religious beliefs than the foster family.* Currently, the procedure for addressing this type of placement is for the foster placing agency to request that the foster family make every possible effort to allow their foster child to continue practicing his or her religious beliefs. In the Colorado Department of Social Services Staff Manual, this includes a foster child being encouraged and allowed to practice religious holidays, arranging attendance at the former church or religious institution of the foster child, and receiving written approval from the biological parents for any type of religious intervention used with the child.

However, when viewing religion as part of the culture of a family, it becomes clear that church service attendance and religious holidays are not the only ways in which religion can influence a child. If a child of a different religious affiliation is placed with a Christian family, for example, in what ways does this shape or affect the foster family's practice of their own religion? What are the implications for such traditions as mealtime prayers or family Bible study? What are the implications for the foster family's biological children practices? How does the foster child avoid feeling isolated in a family in which everyone else participates in faith-related expressions that the foster child does not? He or she can choose to participate, and enjoy accord with the family, or be excluded from several of the family's activities. This can hardly be helpful in a setting where a child is likely to feel some isolation already.

3. *The foster child chooses not to participate in the foster family's religious activities, or ridicules them.* In part this follows from the previous section, as an example of dilemmas that arise when placing a child of one religion (or no religion) with a family of another (or no religion). What is the appropriate response of the foster parent in this situation? By what means does the foster parent address these issues such that no religious views are imposed on the foster child?

4. *The biological parents object to or ridicule the foster parent's beliefs.* Assuming that this is a separate dilemma from the preceding issue, it could result that a foster child in placement is torn between two parental figures, one that practices and adheres to a certain religious belief and one that derides it. To which authority figure does the child listen?

5. *The foster child chooses to participate in or embrace the foster family's religious beliefs, against the biological parent's wishes.* Most states maintain that the biological parent retains the right to choose the religion of their minor child. Is the child then not allowed to choose his or her own religion? Even if that child is, for example, fifteen years old? How does an agency safeguard against foster parents consciously, or unconsciously, using their position to attempt to convert their foster children?

6. *The foster child undermines the religious beliefs of the foster family's birth children.* Whether the foster child practices a different religion, no religion at all, or simply does not agree with the religious teachings of his or her biological parent, the potential exists in the eyes of parents for their foster child to affect the religious beliefs of their own children. Matters become quite delicate when attempting to address issues such as this in a family unit without advocating for a specific religious belief.

Practically speaking, it is not difficult to find examples of value conflicts arising in the foster home. For instance, it may be the preference of a foster family to send all of their biological children to a Christian school. Once a foster child enters the home, several decisions must be made. Does the biological parent have a preference about the type of school attended? If that preference is for public schools, how does attending different schools affect the foster child's integration into the family? Even simpler decisions such as involvement in mealtime prayer on one hand, pose the risk of imposing values on a child unaccustomed to such rituals, and on the other, risk the child feeling a sense of alienation from the foster family.

Aside from their own personal experiences of faith, foster parents and caseworkers might be encouraged to view religion as another cultural aspect of a child or family, much as ethnic background or socioeconomic status plays a role in defining one as a person. As a cultural part of one's life, the impact of religion extends beyond formal religious practices and rituals. Values, decisions, moral codes, behavioral expectations—all can be influenced by a set of basic beliefs that are core to one's religious practices. Examining one's own values and being cognizant of areas in which there might be a conflict with those of a foster child or a biological parent is a useful tool for foster parents in gaining awareness of the cultural differences that might be present in the foster home.

Caseworkers, based on consultation with their supervisors and other agency personnel, are encouraged to address the issue of religious practices in the foster home. This may be difficult as workers sometimes think this crosses the boundary separating church and state, or fear that they may be perceived as promoting their own religious values. Religion is to be addressed with caution and neutrality by caseworkers; it is an important part of the personal cultures of foster children and their biological and foster parents.

A Role for Christians in Child Welfare Practice

The child welfare system is intended to provide comprehensive assistance to children who are abused and neglected. The mission is informed by permanency planning practices – the commitment that children need to be raised in families with the potential of lifelong relationships. The Christian commitment to love one's neighbor and care for the helpless is congruent with this mission. There are reasonable responses to concerns about religion and child welfare that affirm the role of Christians in social work and faith-based organizations and congregations in the community.

Why should a family care for its children? Why should a community care about the treatment of the children in its member families? The Christian response is simple and clear: affirming that children are God's creation and precious in His sight. Parents are responsible for the nurturing of their children, and that role is honored in Biblical teachings. Additionally, the community's obligation to provide for children, particularly those without parents, is affirmed in Scripture.

The child welfare system in the United States is a continuum of services designed to support families and protect children. When protection requires the removal of children from their parent's custody, the child welfare system's guiding philosophy of permanency planning informs plans and strategies to reunite children with their families. If this is not possible, then the child welfare worker should develop another option that provides the possibility of a home and lifetime family for the child. Child welfare includes a professional concern for the child's well-being, including the child's physical health, mental health, educational and social needs.

The role of religion and the church has at times been presented with some concern with regard to the impact on child abuse and neglect and responsiveness to at-risk children. However, the benefits of addressing child welfare practice from the perspective of a Christian social worker, and examining issues such as the role of religious preference in foster care placements, contribute to greater understanding of the implications of religion in the child welfare field as a whole. The troubling continuation of child abuse and neglect in our society, and the sometimes complicated system of services and strategies designed to respond to maltreated children, require the committed work of professionals in the child welfare system and the support and energy of the broader secular and faith-based community.

References

Alsdurf, J. & Alsdurf, P. (1989). *Battered into submission*. Downers Grove, Il: InterVarsity Press.

Alwin, D. (1986). Religion and parental child-rearing orientations. *American Journal of Sociology*, 92, 412-440.

American Humane Association. (1984). Child abuse and neglect in cults and religious sects. *Protecting Children*, 1, 17.

Anderson, G. (1997). Achieving permanency for all children in the child welfare system. In G. Anderson, A. Ryan, & B. Leashore (Eds.), *The challenge of permanency planning in a multicultural society*, New York: Haworth Press.

Anderson, G. (1983). Medicine vs. religion: The case of Jehovah's Witnesses. *Health and Social Work*, 8, 31-39.

Bullis, R. (1991). The spiritual healing defense in criminal prosecutions for crimes against children. *Child Welfare*, 70, 541-558.

Campbell, R. (1985). *How to really love your child*. Wheaton, Il: Victor.

Cook, J. F. (1995). A history of placing out: The orphan trains. *Child Welfare*, 74, 181-199.

Costin, L. (1991). Unraveling the Mary Ellen legend: Origins of the "cruelty" movement. *Social Service Review*, 65, 203-223.

Dobson, J. (1970). *Dare to discipline*. New York: Bantam Books.

Fugate, R. (1980). *What the Bible says about child training*. Tempe, AZ: Aletheia.

Garbarino, J. & Ebata, A. (1983). The significance of ethnic and cultural differences in child maltreatment. *Journal of Marriage and the Family*, 45, 773-783.

Garbarino, J. & Gilliam, G. (1980). *Understanding Abusive families*. Lexington, MA: Lexington Books.

Garland, D. (1994). *Church agencies: Caring for children and families in crisis*. Washington D.C.: Child Welfare League of America.

Horton, A. & Williamson, J. (1988). *Abuse and religion: When praying isn't enough*. Lexington, MA: Lexington.

Hutson, C. (1983). *The why and how of child discipline*. Murfreesboro, TN: Sword of the Lord.

Hyles, J. (1974). *How to rear children*. Hammond, IN: Hyles-Anderson.

Lovinger, R. (1990). *Religion and counseling: The psychological impact of religious belief*. New York: Continuum.

Maluccio, A., Fein, E., & Olmstead, K. (1986). *Permanency planning for children: Concepts and methods*. London and New York: Tavistock and Methuen.

Pagelow, M. & Johnson, P. (1988). Abuse in the American family: The role of religion. In *Abuse and religion: When praying is not enough*. Lexington, MA: Lexington.

Peek, C., Lowe, G. & Williams, L.S. (1991). Gender and God's word: Another look at religious fundamentalism and sexism. *Social Forces*, 69, 1205-1221.

Pellauer, M., Chester, B.,& Boyajian, J. (1987). *Sexual assault and sexual abuse: A handbook for clergy and religious professionals*. San Francisco: Harper and Row.

Rice, J. (1982). *God in your family*. Murfreesboro, TN: Sword of the Lord.

Schatz, M.S. & Horejsi, C. (1992). Religion and the foster home. *Fostering Families*. Department of Social Work Colorado State University, Fort Collins, Colorado. Designed in consultation with the Colorado Department of Social Services.

Schatz, M.S. & Horejsi, C. (1996a). From moral development to healthy relationships: The role of religion in out-of-home placement. ERIC Clearinghouse on Counseling and Guidance (ERIC-CASS) CG02. University of North Carolina at Greensboro, 1999. Presented at the 24th Annual Child Abuse and Neglect Symposium, Keystone, Colorado, May, 1996.

Schatz, M.S. & Horejsi, C. (1996b). The importance of religious tolerance: A model for educating foster parents. *Child Welfare*, 75, (January-February), 73-85.

Tomczak, L. (1982). *God, the rod, and your child's bod*. Old Tappan, NJ: Revell.

Walters, D.R. (1975). *Physical and sexual abuse of children: Causes and treatment*. Bloomington, Indiana: Indiana University Press.

Wiehe, V. (1990). Religious influence on parental attitudes toward the use of corporal punishment. *Journal of Family Violence*, 5, 173-186.

Williams, C. (1996). *Keynote speech: Mississippi permanency partnership, a vision*. Jackson, Mississippi.

Williams, G. & Money J. (1980). *Traumatic abuse and neglect of children at home*. Baltimore, MD: Johns Hopkins University Press.

CHAPTER 15

DOING THE RIGHT THING: A CHRISTIAN PERSPECTIVE ON ETHICAL DECISION-MAKING FOR CHRISTIANS IN SOCIAL WORK PRACTICE[1]

David A. Sherwood

You are on the staff of a Christian Counseling Center and in the course of a week you encounter the following clients:

1. A minister who became sexually involved with a teen-age girl at a previous church several years ago. His current church is not aware of this. He says he has "dealt with his problem."
2. A Christian woman whose husband is physically abusive and who has threatened worse to her and their young child if she tells anyone or leaves him. She comes to your office with cuts and bruises, afraid to go home and afraid not to go home. She doesn't know what she should do or can do.
3. A single mother who is severely depressed and who is not taking adequate care of her two young children, both under the age of four. She denies that her personal problems are affecting her ability to take care of her children.

The list could easily go on. Helping professionals, Christian or otherwise, are daily confronted with issues that are immensely complex and which call forth judgments and actions that confound any attempts to neatly separate "clinical knowledge and skill," our preferred professional roles and boundaries, and, fundamentally, our world-view, faith, moral judgment, and character. Much as we would like to keep it simple, real life is messy and all of a piece. All kinds of things interconnect and interact. How would you respond to clients like the ones I just mentioned?

Christian social workers need to know who they are and what resources they have to do the right thing as children of God—personally, socially, and professionally. What are our resources and limits in choosing and acting ethically as Christians who are placed in helping relationships with others? I will try to review briefly a Christian perspective on:

- When we have a moral problem.

- Conditions under which we choose and act.
- Faith and the hermeneutical spiral (understanding God's will).
- How the Bible teaches us regarding values and ethics.
- The Principle/Practice Pyramid.
- A decision-making model which integrates the deontological (ought) dimensions with the teleological (purpose and consequences) dimensions of a problem.
- The fundamental role of character formed through discipleship and the guidance of the Holy Spirit.

We cannot devise or forcibly wrench out of the scriptures a set of rules which will simply tell us what to do if we will only be willing to obey. It appears that God has something else in mind for us as He grows us up into the image of Christ. Ultimately, "doing the right thing" results from our making judgments which grow out of our character as we are "changed into his likeness from one degree of glory to another; for this comes from the Lord who is the Spirit" (II Corinthians 3:18).

When Do We Have a Moral Problem?

When do we have a moral "problem?" I would argue that value issues are so pervasive in life that there is virtually no question we face that does not have moral dimensions at some level. Even the choice regarding what brand of coffee to use (or whether to use coffee at all) is not a completely value-neutral question. However, for practical purposes I think it is helpful to realize that moral "problems" tend to be characterized by the following conditions:

1. **More than one value is at stake and they are in some degree of conflict.**
   This is more common than we would like to think. It need not be a conflict between good and bad. It is more usually differing goods or differing bads. A maxim that I drill into my students is "You can't maximize all values simultaneously." Which is to say life continually confronts us with choices and to choose one thing *always* means to give up or have less of something else. And that something else may be a very good thing, so serious choices are usually very costly ones. A familiar, lighthearted version of this is the adage "You can't have your cake and eat it too." This is one of life's truisms which is very easy to forget or tempting to ignore, but which is at the heart of all value and moral problems. No conflict, no problem.
2. **There is uncertainty about what values are, in fact, involved or what they mean.**

For example, what are all the relevant values involved in a decision regarding abortion? And what, exactly, is meant by choice, right to life, a person? Where do these values come from? What is their basis? How do they put us under obligation?

3. **There is uncertainty about what the actual facts are.**
   What is the true situation? What are the relevant facts? Are they known? Can they be known? How well can they be known under the circumstances?
4. **There is uncertainty about the actual consequences of alternative possible choices and courses of action.**
   Often we say that choices and actions should be guided by results. While it is true that their morality is at least in part influenced by their intended and actual consequences, Christians believe that God has built certain "oughts" like justice and love into the creation and that results always have to be measured by some standard or "good" which is beyond the naked results themselves. It is also crucial to remember that consequences can never be fully known at the time of decision and action. The best we can ever do at the time is to *predict*. We are obligated to make the best predictions we can, but we must be humbled by the limitations of our ability to anticipate actual results. However, unintended consequences turn out to be every bit as real and often more important than intended ones, especially if we haven't done our homework.

Under What Conditions Do We Have to Choose and Act?

Given this understanding of a moral "problem," it seems to me that real-life value choices and moral decisions are always made under these conditions:

1. **We have a problem.**
   An actual value conflict is present or at least perceived. For example, we want to tell the truth and respect our dying parent's personal rights and dignity by telling him the prognosis but we don't want to upset him, perhaps hasten his death, or create possible complications for ourselves and the hospital staff.
2. **We always have significant limitations in our facts, knowledge, understanding, and ability to predict the consequences of our actions.**
   What causes teen-age, unmarried pregnancy? What policies would lead to a decrease in teen-age pregnancy? What other unintended consequences might the policies have? Correct information and

knowledge are very hard (often impossible) to come by. As Christians we know that human beings are both finite (limited) and fallen (liable to distortion from selfishness and other forms of sin). The more we can do to overcome or reduce these limitations the better off we'll be. But the beginning of wisdom is to recognize our weakness and dependence.

3. **Ready or not, we have to decide and do *something*, at least for the time being, even if the decision is to ignore the problem.** Life won't permit us to stay on the fence until we thoroughly understand all the value issues, have all the relevant data, conduct a perfectly complete analysis, and develop a completely Christ-like character. So, we have to learn how to make the best choices we can under the circumstances. ("You can't maximize all values simultaneously" but you have to give it your best shot!)
4. **Whatever decision we make and action we take will be fundamentally influenced by our assumptions, world-view, faith—*whatever* that is.** "Facts," even when attainable, don't sustain moral judgments by themselves. They must be interpreted in the light of at least one faith-based value judgment. Where do my notions of good and bad, healthy and sick, functional and dysfunctional come from? Never from the "facts" alone (Lewis, 1947, 1943).
5. **We would like to have definitive, non-ambiguous, prescriptive direction so that we can be completely certain of the rightness of our choice, but we never can.** Not from Scripture, not from the law, not from our mother. We want to *know* without a doubt that we are right. This has always been part of the allure of legalism, unquestioning submission to authorities of various stripes, and simplistic reduction of complex situations. The only way (to seem) to be saved by the law is to chop it down to our own puny size.
6. **We may not have legalistic, prescriptive formulas, but we *do* have guidance and help.** Doing the right thing is not just a subjective, relativistic venture. God knows the kind of help we really need to grow up in Christ and God has provided it. We need to be open to the kind of guidance God actually gives instead of demanding the kind of guidance we think would be best. What God has actually given is Himself in Jesus Christ, the story of love, justice, grace, and redemption given witness in Scripture, the Holy Spirit, and the community of the church, historically, universally, and locally.

7. **Ultimately, doing the right thing is a matter of identity and character.**
   In the last analysis, our morality (or lack of it) depends much more on *who* we are (or are becoming) than what we know or the procedures we use. We must become persons who have taken on the mind and character of Christ as new creations. And it turns out that this is precisely what the Bible says God is up to—growing us up into the image of Christ, from one degree of glory to another. The "problem" of making and living out these moral decisions turns out to be part of the plot, part of God's strategy, suited to our nature as we were created. Instead of fighting and resenting the hardness of moral choice and action, maybe we should *embrace* it as part of God's dynamic for our growth.

Faith and the Hermeneutical Spiral

Walking By Faith Is Not Optional

Christian or not, consciously or not, intentionally or not, we all inevitably approach understanding the world and ourselves on the basis of assumptions or presuppositions about the nature of things. Walking by faith is not optional. All human beings do it. We do have some choice (and responsibility) for what we continue to put our faith in, however. That's where choice comes in.

Is love real or a rationalization? Does might make right? Do persons possess inherent dignity and value? Are persons capable of meaningful choice and responsibility? Are human beings so innately good that guilt and sin are meaningless or destructive terms? Is human life ultimately meaningless and absurd? Is the physical universe (and ourselves) a product of mindless chance? Is there a God (or are *we* God)? These are a few of the really important questions in life and there is no place to stand to try to answer them that does not include some sort of faith.

Interpreting the Facts

Like it or not, the world, life, and scripture are not simply experienced or known directly. Things are *always* interpreted on the basis of assumptions and beliefs we have about the nature of the world that are part of our faith position. Knowingly or not, we are continually engaged in hermeneutics, interpretation on the basis of principles.

My interpretation of the meaning of scripture, for example, is strongly affected by whether or not I believe the Bible is a strictly human product or divinely inspired. It is further affected by whether or not I assume the Bible was intended to and can, in fact, function as a legal codebook providing specific prescriptive answers to all questions. My beliefs about these things are never simply derived from the data of the scripture only, but they should never be independent of that data either. In fact, a good hermeneutical principle for understanding scripture is that our interpretations *must* do justice to the actual data of scripture (Osborne, 1991; Swartley, 1983).

The same is true regarding our understanding or interpretation of the "facts" of our experience. The same event will be seen and interpreted differently by persons who bring different assumptions and expectations to it. On the day of Pentecost, the Bible records that the disciples "were filled with the Holy Spirit and began to speak in other tongues as the Spirit enabled them" (Acts 2:4). Some in the crowd didn't know anything about the Holy Spirit, but were amazed by the fact that they heard their own native languages. "Are not all of these men who are speaking Galileans? Then how is it that each of us hears them in his native tongue" (Acts 2:7-8). Some, however, heard the speech as drunken nonsense and said, "They have had too much wine" (Acts 2:13). Different interpretive, hermeneutical frameworks were in place, guiding the understanding of the "facts."

As a child, I occasionally experienced corporal punishment in the form of spankings from my mother (on one memorable occasion administered with a willow switch). The fact that I was on rare occasions spanked is data. But what did those spankings "mean" to me? Did I experience abuse? Was I experiencing loving limits in a way that I could understand? The experience had to be interpreted within the framework of the rest of my experiences and beliefs (however formed) about myself, my mother, and the rest of the world. And those "facts" continue to be interpreted or re-interpreted today in my memory. In this case, I never doubted her love for me or (at least often) her justice.

The Hermeneutical Spiral

We come by our personal faith position in a variety of ways—adopted without question from our families, friends, and culture; deliberately and critically chosen; refined through experience; fallen into by chance or default. Or, more likely, it comes through some combination of all of these and more. However it happens, it is not a static, finished thing. Our interpretation and understanding of life proceeds in a kind of reciprocal hermeneutical spiral. Our faith position helps order and integrate (or filter and distort) the complex overload of reality that we confront. But at the same time reality has the capacity to challenge and at least partially modify or correct our assumptions and perceptions (Osborne, 1991; Sherwood 1989).

Once the great 18th century English dictionary-maker, writer, conversationalist, and sometime philosopher Samuel Johnson was asked by his biographer Boswell how he refuted Bishop Berkeley's philosophical theory of idealism (which asserted that the physical world has no real existence). Johnson replied, "I refute it *thus*." He thereupon vigorously kicked a large rock, causing himself considerable pain but gaining more than enough evidence (for himself, at least) to cast doubt on the sufficiency of idealist theory as a total explanation of reality.

This is a hermeneutical spiral. You come to interpret the world around you through the framework of your faith, wherever you got it, however good or bad it is, and however embryonic it may be. It strongly affects what you perceive (or even look for). But the world is not a totally passive or subjective thing. So you run the risk of coming away from the encounter with your faith somewhat altered, perhaps even corrected a bit, or perhaps more distorted. Then you use that altered faith in your next encounter (Osborne, 1991; Pinnock, 1984; Sire, 1980). Unfortunately, there is no guarantee that the alterations are corrections. But, *if* the Bible is true, and *if* we have eyes that want to see and ears that want to hear, we can have confidence that we are bumping along in the right general direction, guided by the Holy Spirit.

How Does the Bible Teach Us?

The Heresy of Legalism

For Christians, the desire for unambiguous direction has most often led to the theological error of legalism, and then, on the rebound, to relativism. Legalism takes many forms but essentially uses the legitimate zeal for faithfulness to justify an attempt to extract from the Bible or the traditions of the elders a system of rules to cover all contingencies and then to make our relationship to God depend on our understanding and living up to those rules (Sherwood, 1989).

It is theological error because it forces the Bible to be something that it is not—an exhaustive theological and moral codebook yielding prescriptive answers to all questions. It distorts the real nature and meaning of God's self-revelation in the incarnation of Jesus Christ, the Holy Spirit, the Scriptures, and even nature. Taken to its extreme, it effectively denies the gospel of justification by faith in Jesus Christ and substitutes a form of works righteousness. It can take the good news of redeeming, reconciling love and distort it into a source of separation, rejection, and condemnation.

The paradigm case in the New Testament involved some of the Pharisees. Jesus had some very strong words for them. When the Pharisees condemned the disciples for breaking the Sabbath by gathering grain to eat, Jesus cited the example of David feeding his men with the temple bread, also a violation of the law, and told them, in effect, that they were missing the point of the law. "The Sabbath was made for man, not man for the Sabbath" (Mark 2:23-28). In the parable of the Pharisee and the tax collector Jesus warned about those who "trusted in themselves that they were righteous and despised others" (Luke. 18:9-14). He talked of those who strain out gnats and swallow camels, careful to tithe down to every herb in their gardens but neglecting the "weightier matters of the law, justice and mercy and faith" (Mt. 23:23-24). When a group of Pharisees condemned the disciples because they didn't wash their hands according to the Pharisees' understanding of the requirements of purification, saying "Why do your disciples transgress the tradition of the elders?" Jesus answered "And why do you transgress the commandment of God for the sake of your tradition? . . . For the sake of your tradition you have made void the word of God. Hear and understand: not what goes into the mouth defiles a man, but what comes out of the mouth" (Matthew 15:1-11).

The Heresy of Subjective Relativism

If the Bible isn't a comprehensive lawbook out of which we can infallibly derive concrete, prescriptive directions for every dilemma, what good is it? Aren't we then left to be blown about by every wind of doctrine, led about by the spirit (or spirits) of the age we live in, guided only by our subjective, selfish desires? This is a good example of a false dichotomy, as though these were the only two alternatives. Either the Bible is a codebook or we land in total relativism. Yet this is the conclusion often drawn, which quite erroneously restricts the terms of the discussion. Once we cut loose from the deceptively certain rules of legalism it is very easy to become the disillusioned cynic—"I was tricked once, but I'm not going to be made a fool again." If the Bible can't give me all the answers directly then its all just a matter of human opinion. So the false dilemma is stated.

The Orthodoxy of Incarnation—What if God Had a Different Idea?

Such conclusions assume that, to be of any practical use, God's revelation of His will can only be of a certain kind, an assumption we are more likely to take *to* the Bible than to learn *from* it. It assumes that divine guidance must be exhaustively propositional, that what we need to be good Christians and to guide our moral lives is either specific rules for every occasion or at least principles from which specific rules can rationally be derived. What if such an assumption is wrong? What if it is not in keeping with the nature of God, the nature of human beings, the nature of the Bible, the nature of the Christian life?

What if the nature of Christian values and ethics cannot be adequately embodied or communicated in a book of rules, however complex and detailed? What if it can only be embodied in a life which is fully conformed to the will of God and communicated through the story of that life and its results?

What if God had to become a man, live a life of love and justice, be put to death innocently on the behalf of others, and raise triumphant over death to establish the kingdom of God? What if the Bible were book about that? A true story of how to become a real person?

The point I am trying to make is that if we go to the Bible for guidance on its *own* terms, not deciding in advance the nature that guidance has to take, what we find is neither legalism nor relativism but precisely the kind of guidance that suits the kind of reality God actually made, the kind of creatures we actually are, the kind of God with whom we have to do.

We learn that ethical practice has more to do with our identity, our growth in character and virtue than it does with airtight rules and that the Bible is just the kind of book to help us do this. It may not be as tidy as we would like. It may not be as easy as we would like to always tell the good guys from the bad guys. We may not always be able to act with the certain knowledge that we are doing just the right (or wrong) thing. But we will have the opportunity to get closer and closer to the truth of God, to grow up into the image of Christ. Growth is not always comfortable. But the Bible tells us *who* we are, *whose* we are, and *where* we're going.

God is Bigger Than Our Categories but the Bible is a Faithful Witness

The reality of God and biblical truth shatters our categories. At least, none of them, taken alone, can do the God of the Bible justice. Taken together, our categories have the potential to balance and correct each other. Human language can only carry so much divine freight in any particular car.

We are *all* susceptible to distorted use of Scripture. We need the recognition that we (*all* of us) always take preconditions to our Bible study that may seriously distort its message to us. In fact, we often have several *conflicting* desires and preconditions at work simultaneously. For example, we have the hunger for the security of clear-cut prescriptive answers ("Just tell me if divorce is always wrong or if I have a scriptural right to remarry") *and* a desire to be autonomous, to suit ourselves rather than submit to anyone or anything ("I don't want to hurt anyone, but my needs have to be met").

So, how do I think the Bible teaches us about morality? How does it guide us in making moral judgments in our professional lives? Struggling to rise above my own preconditions and to take the Bible on its own terms, to see how the Bible teaches and what the Bible teaches, I think I am beginning to learn a few things.

God's Project: Growing Us Up Into the Image of Christ

It seems to me that God is trying to reveal His nature and help us to develop His character. And it seems that the only way He could do that is in *personal* terms, creating persons with the dignity of choice, developing a relationship with a nation of them, becoming one of us Himself, revealing His love, grace, and forgiveness through a self-sacrificial act of redemption, and embarking on a process of growing persons up into His own image. The process requires us to be more than robots, even obedient ones. It requires us to make principled judgments based on virtuous character, to exercise wisdom based on the character of Christ. Neither legalism nor relativism produces this.

According to the Bible, growing us up to have the mind and character of Christ is an intrinsic part of God's redemptive project. We are not simply forgiven our sins that grace may abound but we are being rehabilitated, sanctified—being made saints, if you will. The theme is clear, as the following passages illustrate.

In Romans 6:1-2, 4 Paul says that, far from continuing in sin that grace may abound, we die to sin in Christ, are buried with him in baptism, and are raised that we too may live a new life. Romans 12:2 says that we do not conform to the pattern of this world but are to be transformed by the renewing of our minds which makes us able to test and approve what God's will is. II Corinthians 3:17-18 says that where the Spirit of the Lord is, there is freedom and that we are being transformed into His likeness with ever-increasing glory. Ephesians 4:7, 12-13 says that each one of us has been given grace from Christ to prepare us for service so that the body of Christ might be built up until we all reach unity in the faith and knowledge of the Son of God and become mature, attaining to the whole measure of the fullness of Christ. I John 3:1-3 marvels at the greatness of the love of the Father that we should be called children of God and goes on to affirm that, although what we shall be has not yet been made known, we do know that when Christ appears we shall be like him. In Philippians 2, Paul says that, being united with Christ, Christians should have the same servant attitude as Christ, looking out for the interests of others as well as ourselves. Then he makes this remarkable conjunction—"Continue to work out your own salvation with fear and trembling, for it is God who works in you to will and to act according to his good purpose."

And in I Corinthians 2 Paul says that we speak a message of wisdom among the mature, God's wisdom from the beginning, not the wisdom of this age, revealed to us by His Spirit. He explains that we have received the Spirit who is from God that we might understand what God has freely given us. He concludes, "Those who are unspiritual do not receive the gifts of God's Spirit for they are foolishness to them, and they are unable to understand them because they are spiritually discerned… But we have the mind of Christ."

A Key: Judgments Based on Wisdom Growing Out of the Character of Christ

It would seem that the key to integrating Christian values into professional practice (as in all of life) is making complex judgments based on wisdom growing out of the mind and character of God, incarnated in Jesus Christ.

In our personal and professional lives we face many complex situations and decisions, large and small. Real-life moral dilemmas confront us with having to make choices between (prioritize) values that are equally real (though not necessarily equally important—remember Jesus' comments on keeping the Sabbath versus helping a human being). Whatever we do, we cannot fully or equally maximize each value in the situation. (If the father embraces the prodigal son and gives him a party, there will be some who will see him as rewarding irresponsibility.) Whatever we do, we have to make our choices on the basis of limited understanding of both the issues involved and the consequences of our actions. Moreover, our decision is complicated by our fallen nature and selfish desires.

In situations like this, the answer is not legalism (religious or scientific) or relativism. The *mind* of Christ helps us to figure out *what* to do and the *character* of Christ helps us to have the capacity (i.e., character or virtue) to actually *do* it. It seems to me that in the very process of struggling through these difficult situations we are dealing with a principle of growth that God has deliberately built into the nature of things. The people of God are continually required to make decisions based on principles embodied in our very identity—the character of who we are, whose we are, and where we are going.

These virtues are not just abstract ones but rather they are incarnated in the history and *character* of Jesus Christ. Love and justice are the fundamental principles but we learn what they mean because Jesus embodies them. (Yes, keep the Sabbath but don't let that keep you from helping someone.)

How should a Christian social worker respond when a client says she wants an abortion? How should parents respond when an unmarried daughter tells them she is pregnant? How should a church respond to a stranger's request for financial aid? Should I be for or against our Middle Eastern policy? Should my wife Carol and I invite her mother to come and live with us? How much money can I spend on myself? It appears I have some complex judgments to make in order to live a life of love and justice.

So, one of God's primary dynamics of growth seems to be to place us in complex situations in which decisions based on judgment are required. These decisions require our knowledge of the character of Christ to make and they require that we be disciplined disciples at least beginning to take on the character of Christ ourselves to carry them out. It seems to me there is a deliberate plot here, daring and risky, but the only one that works, which fits the world as God made it.

Can the Preacher Have a Boat?

Permit me a personal example to illustrate the point. I remember a lively debate in the cafeteria as an undergraduate in a Christian college over whether or not a preacher (i.e. completely dedicated Christian) could have a boat. The issue, of course, was stewardship, our relationship and responsibility toward material wealth, our neighbors, and ourselves.

Being mostly lower middle class, we all easily agreed that a yacht was definitely an immoral use of money and that a row boat or canoe was probably o.k. But could it have a motor? How big? Could it possibly be an inboard motor? How many people could it carry? It was enough to cross a rabbi's eyes. Since we believed the Bible to contain a prescriptive answer to every question, we tried hard to formulate a scriptural answer. But we found no direct commands, approved apostolic examples, or necessary inferences that would nail it down.

What we found was much more challenging—things like:

The earth is the Lord's and the fullness thereof (Psalm 24:1).
Give as you have been prospered (I Corinthians 16:2).

What do you have that you did not receive (II Corinthians 4:7)?
Remember the fatherless and widows (Jas. 1:27).
Don't lay up treasures on earth (Mt. 6:19-20).
Follow Jesus in looking out for the interests of others, not just your own (Phil. 2:1-5).

Plenty of guidelines for exercising love and justice, lots of examples of Christ and the disciples in action—in other words, no selfish relativism. But no iron-clad formulas for what to spend or where—in other words, no legalism.

Instead, every time I turn around I am faced again with new financial choices, fresh opportunities to decide all over again what stewardship means—plenty of chances to grossly rationalize, distort, and abuse the gospel, to be sure. But also plenty of opportunities to get it right this time, or at least better. To grow up into the image of Christ.

Gaining the Mind and Character of Christ

So, only persons of character or virtue can make the kind of judgments and take the actions required of us. To do the right thing we need to be the right kinds of persons, embodying the mind and character of Christ (MacIntyre, 1984; Hauerwas, 1981).

The most direct route to moral practice is through realizing our identity as Christ-Ones. In Galatians 2:20 Paul said, "I have been crucified with Christ and I no longer live, but Christ lives in me. The life I live in the body, I live by faith in the Son of God, who loved me and gave himself for me" and in Galatians 5:13-14 he said "You were called to freedom, brothers and sisters; only do not use your freedom as an opportunity for self-indulgence, but through love become slaves to one another. For the whole law is summed up in a single commandment, 'You shall love your neighbor as yourself.'"

The mind and character of Christ is formed in us by the Holy Spirit as we submit to God's general revelation in creation (Romans 1-2), written revelation in Scripture (II Tim. 3:15-17), and, ultimately, incarnated revelation in Jesus Christ (John 1:1-18; Col. 1:15-20). We can only give appropriate meaning to the principles of love and justice by knowing the God of the Bible, the Jesus of incarnation, and the Holy Spirit of understanding and power. This happens best (perhaps only) in the give and take of two living communities—Christian families and the church, the body of Christ.

What we have when this happens is not an encyclopedic list of rules that gives us unambiguous answers to every practical or moral issue we may ever encounter. Neither are we left in an uncharted swamp of selfish relativity. And, it should be noted well, we are not given a substitute for the clear thinking and investigation necessary to provide the data. The Bible and Christ Himself are no substitute for reading, writing, and arithmetic (or practice wisdom, theory, and empirical research)—getting the best information we can and thinking honestly and clearly about it.

Instead, what we have then is the enhanced capacity to make and carry out complex judgment that is more in harmony with God's love and justice than we could make otherwise (Hauerwas & Willimon, 1989; Adams, 1987). We are still limited. We still know in part and "see but a poor reflection as in a mirror" (I Corinthians 13:12).

We may be disappointed that the Bible or Christ Himself don't give us the kind of advice, shortcuts, or easy black-and-white answers we would like, but what they give us is much better—the truth. Do you want to live a good life? Do you want to integrate your Christian values and your professional helping practice? Do you want to do what is right? The only way, ultimately, is to know God through being a disciple of Christ. This doesn't mean that only Christians can have good moral character—God's common grace is accessible to all. But it really is *true* that Jesus is the way, the truth, and the life (John 14:6). God is the one who gives *content* to the idea of "good." The mind of Christ is really quite remarkable, filling up and stretching to the limit our humanity with God.

Lord, help us to know
who we are,
whose we are, and
where we are going.

Applying Values in Practice: The Principle/Practice Pyramid

As I think about the relationship between basic faith (worldview assumptions and beliefs), core values or principles that grow out of our faith, the rules that we derive in order to guide our application of those principles to various areas of life, and the application of those values and rules to specific day-to-day ethical and practical decisions we must make, it helps me to use the image of a "Principle/Practice Pyramid." The shape of the pyramid gives a rough suggestion of the level of agreement and certainty we may have as we go from the abstract to the concrete. You can turn the pyramid whichever way works best for your imagination—sitting on its base or balanced on its top. I put it on its base (Sherwood, 2002).

Fundamental Worldview and Faith-Based Assumptions

The base or widest part of the pyramid represents our fundamental worldview and faith-based assumptions about the nature of the world, human beings, values, and God. All persons, not just "religious" people or Christians, have no choice but to make some sort of faith-based assumptions about the nature of the world and the meaning of life. These are the basic beliefs that help us to interpret our experience of life. This is part of the "hermeneutical spiral" we spoke of earlier. It is on this level that Christians are likely to have the broadest agreement (There is a God, God is creator, God has given human beings unique value, values derive from God).

Core Values or Principles

On top of and growing out of the faith-based foundation sits our core values or principles. What is "good"? What are our fundamental moral obligations? As a Christian I understand these to be the "exceptionless absolutes" of love and justice (Holmes, 1984). God is love. God is just. There is no situation where these values do not apply. And we must look to God to learn what love and justice mean. The social work analogy would be the core values expressed in the Code of Ethics: service, social justice, dignity and worth of the person, importance of human relationships, integrity, and competence (NASW, 1999).

Moral or Ethical Rules

On top of and growing out of the "principle" layer are the moral rules that guide the application of the principles to various domains of life. These are the "deontological" parameters that suggest what we ought to do. Biblical examples would be the Ten Commandments, the Sermon on the Mount, and other Biblical teachings that help us to understand what love and justice require in various spheres of life. Tell the truth. Keep promises. Don't steal. In the Social Work Code of Ethics, these would be the specific standards relating to responsibilities to clients, colleagues, practice settings, as professionals, the profession itself, and the broader society. Each of these categories in the Code has a set of fairly specific and prescriptive rules. Don't have sexual relationships with clients. Maintain confidentiality. Avoid conflicts of interest. These rules are very important in giving us guidance, but they can never provide us with absolute prescriptions for what we should always do on the case level (Sherwood, 1999, Reamer, 1990).

Cases Involving Ethical Dilemmas

At the top of the pyramid sit the specific cases involving ethical dilemmas in which we are required to use the principles and rules to make professional judgments in the messiness of real life and practice. It is at this very concrete level that we will find ourselves in the most likelihood of conscientious disagreement with each other, even when we start with the same values, principles, and rules. The short answer for why this is true is found in what we have discussed before. It is that we are fallen (subject to the distortions of our selfishness, fear, and pride) and finite (limited in what we can know and predict). And even more vexing, our principles and rules start coming into conflict with each other on this level. We must maintain confidentiality; we have a duty to warn. Our ability to know relevant facts and to predict the consequences of various courses of action is severely limited, yet some choice must be made and some action taken, now.

An Ethical Decision-Making Model

Given this understanding of the human situation, how God is working with us to grow us up into the image of Christ and the proper role that the Bible plays in giving us guidance, I would like to briefly introduce an ethical decision-making model for Christian helping professionals. It is a simple "problem-solving" model that assumes and is no substitute for developing the mind and character of Christ. It is simple only in concept, not in application. And it is what we need to do in all of our lives, not just in our work with clients.

Deontological and Consequentialist/Utilitarian Parameters

Ethical judgments and actions can generally be thought of as being based on two kinds of criteria or parameters—deontological and consequentialist/utilitarian. These are philosophical terms for describing two types of measuring sticks of whether or not something is good or bad in a moral sense and either ought or ought not to be done.

Deontological Parameters—The "Oughts"

Deontological parameters or criteria refer to moral obligation or duty. What are the moral imperatives or rules that relate to the situation? What are the "oughts?" For the Christian, it can be summed up by asking "What is the will of God in this situation?" Understanding the deontological parameters of an ethical dilemma we face is extremely important. But it is not as simple as it may first appear. Some think that ethics can be determined by deontological parameters only or that deontological parameters operate without consideration to consequences in any way. For example, the commandment "Thou shalt not lie" is taken to be an absolute, exceptionless rule that is to be obeyed in all circumstances and at all times, regardless of the consequences. By this principle, when Corrie Ten Boom was asked by the Nazis if she knew of any Jews, she should have led them to her family's hiding place.

Trying to answer all moral questions by attempting to invoke a particular deontological principle in isolation, even if it is biblical, may wind up leading us into actions which are contrary to God's will. That is the legalistic fallacy which we discussed before. Normally we have an ethical dilemma because we are in a situation in which more than one deontological principle applies and they are in conflict to some degree. Do we keep the Sabbath or do we heal? The Ten Commandments or the Sermon on the Mount, for example, contain deontological principles that are vitally important to helping us understand the mind of Christ and doing the will of God. But they cannot be handled mechanistically or legalistically or we will become Pharisees indeed. Does "turning the other cheek" require us to never resist evil in any way?

Most Christians properly understand that God's will is fully embodied only in God's character of love and justice, which was incarnated in the person of Jesus Christ. Love and justice are the only "exceptionless absolutes" in a deontological sense. The moral rules and principles of scripture provide important guidelines to help us to understand what love and justice act like in various circumstances, but they cannot stand alone as absolutes nor can they be forced into a legal system which eliminates the need for us to make judgments.

Consequentialist/Utilitarian Parameters—The "Results"

For God and for us, moral reality is always embodied. Part of what this means, then, is that the deontological "oughts" can never be completely separated from the consequentialist/utilitarian parameters. The consequentialist/utilitarian parameters refer to the results. Christian ethical decisions and actions always have to try to take into account their consequences. What happens as a result of this action or that, and what end is served?

Many people (quite erroneously) believe that moral judgments or actions can be judged exclusively on the basis of their results. Did it have a "good" or desired result? Then it was a good act. Many believe that if we value the end we implicitly accept the means to that end, no matter what they might be (say, terrorism to oppose unjust tyranny). This is just as much a fallacy as the single-minded deontological judgment. Pure utilitarianism is impossible since there must be some deontological basis for deciding what is a "good" result, and this can never be derived from the raw facts of a situation. And "goods" and "evils" must be prioritized and balanced against one another in means as well as the ends.

It is a fact that some adults engage in sexual activity with children. But so what? What is the moral and practical meaning of that fact? Is it something we should encourage or prevent? Without some standard of "good" or "health" it is impossible to give a coherent answer.

Another major limitation of consequentialist/utilitarian criteria in making moral judgments is that at best they can never be more than guesses or *predictions* based on what we *think* the results might be, never on the actual consequences themselves. If I encourage my client to separate from her abusive husband, I may think that he will not hurt her or the children, but I cannot be sure.

So, ethical and practical *judgments* are always required. They aren't simple. And they always involve identifying, prioritizing, and acting on *both* deontological and consequentialist/utilitarian parameters of a situation (Sherwood, 1986).

The Model: Judgment Formed By Character and Guided By Principle

1. **Identify and explore the problem:**
   What issues/values (usually plural) are at stake?
   What are the desired ends?
   What are the alternative possible means?
   What are the other possible unintended consequences?
2. **Identify the deontological parameters:**
   What moral imperatives are there?
   What is the will of God, the mind of Christ?
   What are the principles at stake, especially in regard to love and justice?
   Are there any rules or rule-governed exceptions, biblical injunctions, commands, or codes of ethics which apply?
3. **Identify the consequentialist/utilitarian parameters:**
   What (as nearly as can be determined or predicted) are the likely intended and unintended consequences?
   What are the costs and benefits? How are they distributed (who benefits, who pays)?

What must be given up in each particular possible course of action? What values will be slighted or maximized?

4. **Integrate and rank the deontological and consequentialist/utilitarian parameters:**
   What best approximates (maximizes) the exceptionless absolutes of love and justice?
5. **Make a judgment guided by character and act:**
   After gathering and analyzing the biblical, professional and other data, pray for wisdom and the guidance of the Holy Spirit.
   Make a judgment and act growing out of your character as informed by the character of Christ.
   Refusing choice and action *is* choice and action, so you must do the best you can at the time, even if, in retrospect it turns out you were "sinning bravely."
6. **Evaluate:**
   Grow through your experience. Rejoice or repent, go on or change.

Character Formed through Discipleship and the Guidance of the Holy Spirit

Ultimately, ethical Christian practice depends on one thing—developing the mind and character of Christ. It depends on our growing up into the image of Christ. This begins in the new birth as we become new creations in Christ. We are filled with the Holy Spirit and called to a life of discipleship in which we bring every thought and action in captivity to Christ (II Corinthians 10:5). We present our bodies "as a living sacrifice," not conformed to this world, but "transformed by the renewal of your mind" (Rom. 12:1-2). We hunger and thirst after righteousness. We seek to know God's will through scripture, the guidance of the Holy Spirit, and the community of the church. We identify with Jesus and the saints of God down through the ages. We daily choose to follow Christ as best we know and can. We repent and confess to our Lord when we fall. We thankfully receive his grace. We choose and act again.

Certainly piety is not a substitute for the discipline of professional training, careful research, and thoughtful analysis. Rather, the use of all of these is simply a complimentary part of our stewardship and discipleship. The most solid possible assurance that we will do the right thing in our personal lives and in our professional practice is our discipleship, growing to have more and more of the character of Jesus Christ, as we make judgments more in harmony with God's character and Spirit.

We become a "letter from Christ… Written not with ink but with the Spirit of the living God, not on tablets of stone but on tablets of human hearts.... ministers of a new covenant, not in a written code but in the Spirit; for the written code kills, but the Spirit gives life... Now the Lord is the Spirit, and where the Spirit of the Lord is, there is freedom. And we all, with unveiled face, beholding the glory of the Lord, are being changed into his likeness from one degree of glory to another; for this comes from the Lord who is the Spirit" (II Corinthians 3:3, 6, 17-18).

Note

A version of this chapter was previously published in *Social Work and Christianity*, 20(2), 1993.

References

Adams, R. M. (1987). *The virtue of faith*. New York: Oxford University Press.

Hauerwas, S. (1981). *A community of character: Toward a constructive Christian social ethic*. Notre Dame: University of Notre Dame Press.

Hauerwas, S. & Willimon, W. H. (1989). *Resident aliens: Life in the Christian colony*. Nashville: Abingdon Press.

Holmes, A. (1984). *Ethics: Approaching moral decisions*. Downers Grove, IL: InterVarsity Press.

Lewis, C. S. (1947). *The abolition of man*. New York: Macmillan.

Lewis, C. S. (1943). *Mere Christianity*. New York: Macmillan.

MacIntyre, A. (1984). *After virtue: A study in moral theory*. 2nd Ed. University of Notre Dame Press.

NASW. (1999). *Code of ethics*. Washington, DC: National Association of Social Workers.

Osborne, G. R. (1991). *The hermeneutical spiral: A comprehensive introduction to biblical interpretation*. Downers Grove, IL: InterVarsity Press.

Pinnock, C. (1984). *The scripture principle*. New York: Harper and Row.

Reamer, F. (1990). *Ethical dilemmas in social service*. 2nd Ed. New York: Columbia University Press.

Sire, J. W. (1980). *Scripture twisting*. Downers Grove, IL: InterVarsity Press.

Sherwood, D. A. (Spring 1989). How should we use the bible in ethical decision-making? Guidance without legalism or relativism. *Social Work & Christianity*, *16*, 29-42

Sherwood, D. A. (Fall 1986). Notes toward applying Christian ethics to practice: Growing up into the image of Christ. *Social Work & Christianity, 13*, 82-93.

Sherwood, D. A. (1999). Integrating Christian faith and social work: Reflections of a social work educator. *Social Work & Christianity, 26*(1), 1-8.

Sherwood, D. A. (2002). Ethical integration of faith and social work practice: Evangelism. *Social Work & Christianity, 29*(1), 1-12.

Smedes, L. (1983). *Mere morality*. Grand Rapids: Eerdmans.

Swartley, W. M. (1983). *Slavery, sabbath, war, and women: Case issues in biblical interpretation*. Scottsdale, PA: Herald Press.

Resources

Keith-Lucas, A. (1994). *Giving and taking help*. Botsford, CT: North American Association of Christians in Social Work.

Keith-Lucas, A. (1985). *So you want to be a social worker: A primer for the Christian student*. Botsford, CT: North American Association of Christians in Social Work.

Mott, S. C. (1982). *Biblical ethics and social change*. New York: Oxford University Press.

O'Donovan, O. (1986). *Resurrection and the moral order: An outline for evangelical ethics*. Grand Rapids: Eerdmans.

Sherwood, D. A. (Spring-Fall 1981). Add to your faith virtue: The integration of Christian values and social work practice. *Social Work & Christianity, 8*, 41-54.

Sherwood, D. A. (2000). Pluralism, tolerance, and respect for diversity: Engaging our deepest differences within the bond of civility. *Social Work & Christianity, 27*(1), 1-7.

Verhay, A. (1984). *The great reversal: Ethics and the new testament*. Grand Rapids: Eerdmans.

CHAPTER 16

GETTING DOWN TO BUSINESS: MODELS AND FIRST STEPS FOR CHRISTIAN SOCIAL WORKERS

Amy L. Sherman

Over the last eight years of helping churches think through their community outreach ministries, I've heard one question more often than others: "How can we really make a difference in the lives of the poor, and not just offer Band-Aids?" Many congregations that have offered traditional benevolence programs (e.g., food pantries, clothing closets, and emergency cash assistance) want to know how their efforts can be remodeled to engage persons in longer-term relationships through which positive, permanent transformation can occur. Staff and volunteers from faith-based nonprofit agencies are also exploring new ministry ventures in the era of welfare reform. They are eager to know "what works" and where they can connect to others who have already implemented creative innovations. No one wants to reinvent the wheel, and everyone asks for "best practices." All want, in short, exposure to real-life ministry *models* that they can imitate or learn from.

This "felt need" is positive, since much of the battle for increasing the scope, scale, and effectiveness of Christian social ministry around the country rests simply on plausibility. People need to be shown that it really *is* possible for them to make a difference in their communities: it is possible, because real Christians in real places are running real programs with real results! Social workers armed with knowledge about a diverse range of ministry models will be well-positioned to work with pastors and lay people who have the desire to help, but lack "how-to" skills. This chapter offers brief summaries of ministry models being employed in a variety of settings by small, medium, and large-sized churches and nonprofit agencies. It also lists suggested first steps for social workers in leading the charge to implement such community ministries.

The possibilities for creative ministry are, of course, endless. This chapter can hardly address them all; instead, we'll focus on a handful of projects representing effective models of ministry for children, youth, and families. Many more models are available in a variety of resources—

books, magazine articles, websites, and training conferences (see Resource listing at the end of this chapter).

Models: Children and Youth Ministries

Through **Kid's Hope USA**, congregations "adopt" a local elementary school and provide tutoring in reading skills for at-risk children in first through fourth grades. Founded in Michigan by Virgil Gulker, author of *Helping You is Helping Me* and the visionary behind the Love, INC ministry model, Kids Hope programs currently involve 179 congregations in 27 states. The programs are based on solid research findings indicating that children who learn to read by the fourth grade are much less likely than those who do not read to drop out of school, get pregnant as teenagers, or use drugs.

Gulker has long been an advocate of face-to-face relational ministry, recognizing that a genuine friendship between a church volunteer and a person in need can radically transform both individuals. Through Kids Hope, participating children are growing in their self-esteem as they watch adults give them their most precious commodity—their time. Stories abound of kids with better grades, more positive attitudes toward school, and improved behavior. Meanwhile, the volunteer tutors have their eyes opened to needs in their community. That can be sobering for the volunteers—for example, when they learn that "their" child's father is in prison. But Gulker reports that these experiences are also driving the volunteers into a deeper prayer life, as they intercede for the kids and families that become dear to them.

Here's how the ministry works. A Kids Hope team composed of the pastor, lay people, and parents develops the ministry. This involves identifying a partner school– usually an elementary school located near the church building. Team representatives meet with school personnel to describe the program and solicit buy-in. Typically, the church identifies a program coordinator from the congregation and this person works part-time (paid or volunteer) to oversee the initiative. In some cases, existing staff, such as the Outreach Pastor or Missions Pastor may assume the coordinator responsibilities as part of his or her job. This individual coordinates the mobilizing and training of volunteer tutors. For a fee, which is pro-rated based on the size of the congregation, the national Kids Hope office provides start-up tools and consulting help. Tutors receive training in child development and educational "tips" for serving their kids. Prayer partners are also mobilized to undergird each tutor-child pair. School personnel identify kids in need of extra help, and invite parents to consider enrolling their children in the Kids Hope program. Once matched, tutors meet on school grounds one hour per week with an individual student. They work with the child on assignments prepared by the teacher.

On school grounds, the focus is on the friendship between the adult and child and on the child's academic development. Tutors are also free to join the student in the lunchroom or volunteer in other ways at the school. Off school grounds, church members can also connect with their students' families through various recreational and social events sponsored by the Kids Hope program. These events, such as church picnics, fellowship dinners, and other activities, occur at the church where there is freedom for spiritual ministry, such as Bible stories, preaching, or free Christian counseling. These activities also permit interaction between the tutors and the children's parents. Church leaders can inform the Kids Hope families of additional services available to them, strengthening the bridge being built between the congregation and the families.

City of Refuge Church in Houston, a racially and economically mixed congregation of about 100 members, has pioneered an innovative **Vocation Bible School** program (note the "o" in vocation) for kids ages 10 to 14. Pastor Rufus Smith was tired of the traditional Vacation Bible School programs ubiquitous in the city. These provided good ministry to kids for a single week, but, in his experience, rarely led to much contact with parents or to a long-term relationship with children. Consequently, Smith developed a summer-long program targeted to a particularly vulnerable group in his inner-city context: middle school kids. Smith found that struggling single moms of children these ages often cannot afford daycare for them, but the children are not old enough to work summer jobs. Left unsupervised, these children can fall into trouble—hence the need for an-ongoing outreach to engage them in positive, constructive activities.

Through the Vocation Bible School initiative, the middle school youths come daily for a several hour program. The church has launched two micro-enterprises–a mobile car washing service and a mobile deck/driveway cleaning business–that engages the kids in work each morning. Church leaders have garnered support from local businessmen for the program. One, for example, donated the high-volume deck spraying/cleansing equipment and other businesses match the dollars earned on particular days by the students.

The church youth pastor oversees the program. He and Pastor Smith have identified large office complexes, located not far from the church, that house multiple businesses and nonprofit agencies. They meet with the heads of these organizations, suggesting that employees sign up to have their cars washed by the kids in the parking lot throughout the morning. Employees then make a donation. Staff members also secure the permission of the building management company for the enterprise. Having the youth work in one location all morning cuts down on the number of supervisors needed and simplifies transportation arrangements.

In the afternoon, the students gather back at the church for lunch and spend time going through a Biblically based youth entrepreneurship curriculum. The course, called YES!, was developed by Christian businessman Duane Moyer. Pastor Smith reports that he has not had to alter the lessons; the materials are already age-appropriate and "accessible" to the urban students.

City of Refuge leaders consider the program a triple win—for the kids, their parents, and the church. Kids end the summer with new life skills, their own hard-earned cash in their pockets and savings accounts, and a vibrant relationship with church staff and volunteers. Parents are delighted. Their sons and daughters are responsibly supervised throughout the day and are earning their own spending money (which helps single parents on tight budgets). Church leaders are excited about the developing ties with these neighborhood families. Many of the kids who participated in the first summer Vocation Bible School have since joined City of Refuge Church—some with their moms or dads. That affords opportunity for a year-round relationship. Encouraged by all he has seen happen among his own flock, Pastor Smith is now championing the program among other inner-city ministers.

Models: Adult and Family Ministries

Through the **New Focus** ministry, 65 churches in 18 states are learning how to move from short-term benevolence that only involves distributing food, to effective, relational, holistic ministry among low-income families. Individuals with financial needs who solicit help from congregations are invited to become New Focus members. Membership involves attending weekly life skills and personal budgeting classes at New Focus churches. Members bring their children, who take part in a church-run program that meets simultaneously during the New Focus classes. Members also receive a personal budget counselor and are rewarded with various practical helps (financial aid, groceries, and laundry supplies) as they make progress in advancing through their self-designed personal action plans. Members are also enfolded into a "Compassion Circle," a group of church volunteers willing to encourage and support the New Focus member as he or she takes small steps to change.

Others in the congregation have opportunity to be involved through the ministry's "Giving Tree." New Focus members write down requests on pieces of paper shaped as apples. These requests can range from "a winter coat for my son" to "a used car for transportation to work." The requests are hung on the Giving Tree display, located in a central gathering area at the church such as the fellowship hall or the front lobby. Church members read the "apples" and supply the requested items as they are able. Both giver and receiver are kept anonymous.

Participating churches rave about the success of the program. Earlier benevolence approaches, they admit, often helped people simply to manage their poverty rather than to escape it, and rarely afforded the opportunity of developing a real friendship with the family in need. Previous "commodified charity" might involve only a one-time exchange of money or food. Through New Focus, church volunteers develop genuine relationships with struggling families in the community, through which mutual encouragement and learning are occurring. Additionally, the New Focus approach creates a variety of roles for church members, allowing them to find a position suited to their particular skills and spiritual gifts. Some can serve as budget counselors, others as teachers in the life skills classes, some as mentors on the Compassion Circles, and others as child care volunteers.

Establishing a New Focus ministry may require cultivating a new mindset about outreach ministry at the church. The deeper level of engagement means the congregation typically assists fewer families overall than was the case under previous benevolence programs that focused on a one-time distribution of food or other goods. The "bigger is better" mentality does not lead to effective ministry. The New Focus approach, though promising a more meaningful impact, also demands more of volunteers. No longer is contact with the poor limited to church members on one side of a soup kitchen line and low-income recipients on the other. That model permits an involvement that is "clinical" and takes place at arms-length—less rewarding, too, but easier and less emotionally costly than the relational, holistic, New Focus model. Thus, casting vision for a greater investment in the lives of struggling families and equipping members for an on-going, rather than sporadic, outreach are critical preparatory steps.

In Orlando, the **Jobs Partnership of Florida** engages churches and businesses in partnerships to serve unemployed and underemployed Floridians. Jobs Partnership, unlike New Focus, is a multi-church model. It is usually developed in a community when pastors from a variety of churches and Christian business professionals unite around a vision for prayer, racial reconciliation, and life transforming ministry among neighbors struggling to makes ends meet. Typically, for the first year, participants in the program are recruited from the inner-city congregations involved in the Jobs Partnership leadership team. As pastors see the program work for their own members, their excitement multiplies and they take the model "to the streets," inviting unemployed community members to join.

The 12-week program involves classes twice per week. One class uses a Biblically based life skills curriculum called "KEYS to Personal and Professional Success." The other class focuses on practical job searching and job readiness issues and uses a curriculum called "STEPS to Personal and Professional Success". Each student is matched with a personal mentor who attends the KEYS classes with them, providing transportation if necessary. The National Jobs Partnership office provides the curriculum and training for pastors from the participating Jobs Partnership congregations who take turns teaching the KEYS classes. Ideally, job coaches are also recruited for each participant; these individuals attend the STEPS classes and walk alongside the participants as they design resumes, prepare for job interviews, and tackle the logistical issues of daycare and transportation. Participating business professionals help to teach the STEPS classes and bring information to class members regarding specific job opportunities. Job openings are also listed in a Jobs Partnership Clearinghouse, posted for students in a notebook, on a bulletin board, or on a website. Program graduates are introduced to affiliated businesses and guided into new jobs suited to their interests and skills. When possible, the business provides the new hires with "job buddies," fellow employees who have worked at the firm for a few years and know the ropes. These individuals help acclimate the graduates to their new jobs, trouble-shooting problems and answering questions.

Jobs Partnership programs have now been developed in over 20 cities in the U.S. Nationally, the Jobs Partnership boasts a job retention rate of 83 percent, an astonishingly impressive record when compared to other job training programs that typically claim retention rates in the 50 to 60 percent range. In Orlando, graduates are not only doing better at keeping their jobs, they are also earning higher wages than are individuals graduating from government-sponsored programs. They are also mobile. The Jobs Partnership of Florida has partnered with Charity Cars, a nonprofit agency that provides donated vehicles to the working poor. Charity Cars gives vehicles to Jobs Partnership graduates with transportation needs. The agency pays the down payment on car insurance and fees for titles and tags, and offers classes in car maintenance.

Models: Collaborating with the Local Department of Social Services

In many communities across the nation, churches are partnering with their local government social welfare agencies to provide supportive services to low-income families:

In San Diego, a consortium of churches called All Congregations Together (ACT) has partnered to staff **ACT Help Desks** in the lobbies of local "One Stop Centers." Clients visit One Stop Centers to meet with caseworkers, learn about California's welfare reform programs and rules, apply for assistance, or use the job bank or computer lab services. The Help Desks are an "oasis" for clients who may feel overwhelmed by the process of applying for aid or effectively utilizing the employment-related services offered by the One Stops. Volunteers help clients to navigate the One Stop, and can refer them to services provided by the faith community if they have needs that the government agency cannot meet.

In Montgomery, Alabama, several congregations are collaborating with their local department of human services through the **Adopt-a-Social Worker** program. As the name suggests, the program matches individual congregations with specific caseworkers. With clients' permission, caseworkers inform their sponsoring church of needs that their clients have. These are wide-ranging: perhaps a math tutor for a daughter struggling in school, or kitchen supplies to furnish a new apartment, or short-term transportation assistance while a client's car is in the shop, or help with tax preparation, or respite care for low-income parents raising a disabled child.

In Ottawa County, Michigan, **Good Samaritan Ministries** has mobilized over fifty congregations to provide mentor teams that are matched with TANF families referred by the Michigan Family Independence Agency. Good Samaritan trains the church volunteers and coordinates the match-making process. Mentor teams work for several months with the clients, offering emotional and practical support.

Implementation: First Steps

The models just summarized above are diverse, but the processes of implementing these new ministries involve a number of common elements. Specifically, some of the first steps involve *activities within the church* (or nonprofit agency). These include assessing strengths and weaknesses; casting vision for outreach; defining a mission and designing an initiative; establishing basic organizational and operational policies; raising resources; mobilizing and training volunteers; and, most importantly, praying often and vigorously. Then there are a variety of *activities to be undertaken in the community* to be served, such as assessing assets and needs, learning what others are already doing, and building relationships with potential ministry partners. In their enormously useful "Good News, Good Works Holistic Ministry Resource Kit,"Heidi Unruh, Ron Sider, and Phil Olson(2002) have identified seven key components of a ministry launch that cover the spectrum of such internal and external preparatory steps. Each of these components involves a variety of activities and decisions. Some of the steps can be taken sequentially, but others, such as the church assessment and neighborhood assessment, can be conducted simultaneously if there are enough volunteers and other workers.

Social workers can help to lead congregations and nonprofit agencies through the various components, but they cannot do everything alone. Rather, the social worker may serve as Project Coordinator on a ministry team. Unruh, Sider and Olson (2002) suggest that a ministry team be composed of at least 13 members, including the congregation's senior pastor.

The ministry team will guide the development of a new ministry launch through the initial stage of getting approval for the project and planning the format and timeline for it. Social workers will need to be acquainted with the leadership structures and decision-making apparatus of their particular context, since congregations "do business" in different ways. Conversations that lead to a verbal decision in a staff meeting may be enough to get the ball rolling in one church, whereas another congregation may have a leadership group that needs to review and vote on a formal, written proposal.

Seven Steps for Launching Outreach Ministries

Step 1 involves *learning about holistic ministry*—that is, reading about the Biblical and practical principles of holistic ministry and "seeing" ministry models through readings, interviews or, preferably, on-site visits. As mentioned earlier, engaging in a relational holistic ministry like a New Focus program or a Jobs Partnership model is more time-consuming and emotionally costly than are traditional one-time benevolence approaches. Given that church members are busy people who are fallible human beings, inspiring, motivating, and equipping congregants for this deeper service is vital. And where better to find that inspiration than in the pages of scripture, the model of Jesus, and the real-life testimony of fellow Christians from other churches who are living out effective, relational ministry?

Mercy ministry is not all action and no talk; rather, contemplation and study lay the foundation for a successful outreach. In my own church, which is a large, predominantly white, suburban congregation, the senior pastor preached for several weeks on the characteristics of the Kingdom of God prior to our launch of a new, ambitious urban ministry. A considerable portion of the congregation had also completed a 13-week adult Sunday School course on evangelism and social action that had cycled through the various teaching fellowships over the past year. And the Urban Ministry Team, which led the charge for the new ministry, had read together John Perkins' compelling book, *Beyond Charity*. All of this meant that by the time the church stepped out into the new urban ministry venture, many leaders and lay people had been challenged by the clear, Biblical message of God's heart for the poor and were educated and inspired by what they had heard and read about others who were making that heavenly compassion visible in distressed communities.

Step 2 involves *assessing the church's ministry context*—that is, undertaking a congregational self-study and conducting a community assessment. Church leaders can tackle this internal and external work simultaneously, assigning some volunteers to assess the strengths, weaknesses, assets, history, and vision of the congregation while others seek to learn about the needs and assets of the community.

Unruh, Sider and Olson (2002) suggest that the internal review team engage congregants who have been at the church long enough to know it fairly well but who can offer an objective, detached, honest assessment of it. These individuals should investigate the outreach ministry history of the church to determine whether God has given the congregation particular passion for a certain kind of ministry or for a certain population, such as the homeless, single parents, or persons who are physically or mentally challenged. An inventory of current ministries can also be helpful, especially to identify gaps that should be filled or floundering programs that may need to be terminated so that something fresh can arise. The team should also seek to understand the congregation's demographics and what those may imply for ministry. A church with many retired persons may be well-suited to launch a "Senior Corps" outreach to provide pro-bono consulting help to nonprofit agencies or start-up inner-city entrepreneurs. A congregation with many skilled trade workers may wish to launch a single mom's car repair program or a widow's home maintenance ministry. A church located in a university town, with many educators and college students in the congregation, may wish to start an after-school tutoring program for at-risk kids.

While the internal team assesses the church context, the community assessment team educates itself (and eventually, the whole congregation) about the needs of the community beyond the church walls. Much can be learned through meetings with the city's community development staff, census data research, and discussions with leaders of secular and faith-based nonprofit social service agencies. The community assessment team can also visit other ministries on-site; take guided tours through distressed neighborhoods, or interview social workers to gain a better understanding of the issues faced by lower-income families in the community. Importantly, the team should seek to understand the neighborhood's assets. Participation in a training seminar on asset-based community development would well-equip the members for this research. Moreover, they should be eager to discern where in the city God is already at work, and whether the congregation is being called to join as partners with existing ministries or to start a new program that meets an identified service gap.

Step 3 involves *cultivating the ministry vision*—that is, praying, discussing, and discerning God's plan for the church's mission and vision and beginning to outline specific plans for "putting feet" to that vision. Having gained a sense of what the church's strengths, gifts, and resources are, and where those might be most fruitfully invested, the team now needs to articulate a specific vision and action steps. Unruh, Sider and Olson (2002) label this stage, "unleashing the vision." It involves discerning what Christ's plans may be for *this* specific expression of His Body, given this church's unique history, demographics, passions, and context for ministry.

The unleashing the vision phase involves some exciting and "heady" work as well as mundane, down-to-earth tasks. First, leaders should articulate vision, mission, and philosophy of ministry statements. The vision statement outlines the long-term picture of what the future might look like if the ministry accomplished its goals. The mission statement is a shorter, more specific explanation of the "what" of ministry; what concrete purposes the ministry is pursuing in order to achieve the future vision. The "philosophy of mission" statement lists the core values or the "how" of ministry.

For the urban ministry our church launched several years ago, the vision was to see our target neighborhood—a place of beauty, but also of crime, poverty, and violence—increasingly reflect the values and attributes of God's Kingdom. Our mission statement elaborated on how we sought to equip neighborhood residents to flourish in the home, school, workplace, church, and community through Christ-centered educational, vocational, and recreational programs. Our philosophy of ministry statement made clear our commitment to conducting these programs in a way that emphasizes our core values of relationship, reconciliation, personal responsibility, prayer, and indigenous leadership development.

In addition to setting vision, the team must begin grappling with a variety of practical administrative issues. For example, the church may need to address the question of whether the ministry will be launched as a program of the church or under a separately incorporated nonprofit agency. Leaders may also need to review liability and insurance questions, exploring whether the church's current insurance policy will be adequate to cover incidents that could arise in conjunction with the operation of the new ministry's program(s). Staffing concerns should also be discussed. Will the envisioned ministry be supervised by a current staff member or by a new director? Will that individual be paid? Does that individual need to be a member of the congregation? Will volunteers be used in the ministry, and if so, will only Christian volunteers be allowed to participate? The congregation will also need to wrestle with questions about fund-raising. Will the church supply all the required resources or is money needed from outside sources? If outside money is needed, will the ministry apply for funding only from private sources (individuals and foundations) or also from public sources (for example, competing for government grants)? Practical-minded folk in the congregation may be enthused to hear of a grandiose new ministry vision, but will have hard questions about how the church is actually going to do it. The team should be prepared and have some answers ready.

Step 4 involves *strengthening the congregational foundation for ministry*—that is, equipping the congregation for outreach through Bible study on holistic ministry and through specific training to for engagement in community outreach programs. This phase might involve encouraging the church's home Bible study groups to use, for a season, devotional materials that highlight God's heart for the poor. Or it could involve a special missions conference focused on community ministry. Or a team of core volunteers for the new ministry might travel together to a training conference, such as those offered each fall by the Christian Community Development Association or by the national office of the ministry model the church is adopting (such as New Focus or Kids Hope training seminars). It may mean establishing a course through which congregants learn to discern their own spiritual gifts and calling. Or it might involve a preaching series from the pulpit on servanthood.

Step 5 involves *pursuing spiritual power for mission*—that is, mobilizing a strong prayer team to undergird the effort and support the frontline leaders and encouraging all the holistic ministry team members to engage in personal devotions that nourish them and shape their thinking about outreach. Prayer should permeate every phase of the ministry launch. 1 Peter 4: 11 states, "if anyone serves, he should do it with the strength God provides, so that in all things God may be praised through Jesus Christ." This kind of God-dependent service gets fleshed out through prayer. Prayer is a posture of dependence, an explicit admission of our weakness and our need for God's equipping. Continual prayer also works to cultivate humility, which helps restrain a paternalistic or condescending attitude that can sometimes begin to arise in our fallen hearts as we serve among people whose needs are more obvious than ours.

Step 6 involves *offering special events to renew and rejoice*—that is, keeping the ministry vision and process alive by celebrating successes along the way. It can mean getting key leaders away on retreats that rejuvenate and refresh them and allow uninterrupted time for reflection and any necessary changes in course. These events can also widen the participation of the whole congregation in the visioning process. The leadership team must necessarily be limited in size in order to function effectively, but the goal is for the congregation at large to embrace the vision of invigorated, holistic outreach. Special worship services, congregational dinners at which the leadership team presents information, answers questions, and casts vision, or community events that expose congregants to the places where ministry is planned, can all serve to create "buy-in" and enthusiasm by church members.

Finally, **Step 7** involves *planning next steps*—that is, developing a strategic plan to guide the implementation and successful continuation of the ministry, as well as designing an evaluation process that can be used to keep the ministry on track. Think of it this way: the vision, mission, and philosophy of ministry documents serve to identify a destination, create a general roadmap, and articulate what kind of vehicle will be driven. The strategic plan tackles such practical issues as how to raise funds for the car, how to mobilize and train the drivers, and what items should be packed in the trunk.

Much thought and planning needs to go into the initial ministry launch. Some may prefer a "big splash" approach where the launch does not move forward until all the ministry components are in place, volunteers are mobilized and trained, and program participants recruited. Others may want to begin quietly in a pilot project, testing the waters and making adjustments as needed before widening the circle of participation in the new venture.

Commitment Over the Long Haul

How long will it take to go through all seven steps of a ministry launch? Unfortunately, the answer is not easy. It depends. Unruh, Sider, and Olson (2002) estimate that a holistic ministry team within a congregation needs nine to twelve months to prepare for a ministry launch. They acknowledge, nonetheless, that some churches may be able to do things more quickly, perhaps within six months. My own experience in launching our church's urban ministry suggests that, however long one thinks it is going to take, it will probably take longer! While the steps we needed to take within the congregation could have been accomplished within six months, the task of acquainting ourselves with the community, building relationships, and establishing credibility took over a year. Going slowly, and gaining the ear and trust of community residents, was crucial for us. Without this trust, we could have been accused of simply barging into the neighborhood and imposing a program on it, rather than working in partnership with community residents to design and inaugurate the ministry.

Six to twelve months or more may sound annoyingly slow to congregants with much vision, energy, and a Nike "just do it" spirit. But while it may be very possible to build a new ministry program much faster, the question is: What kind of foundation will a hastily constructed model stand upon? Probably, one that is not deep and strong and that may not be able to support the new initiative over the long run. All talk and no action is, of course, a problem to be avoided. But the launching process should involve a good balance of action and reflection. The congregations could couple Bible studies on holistic ministry with on-site visits to real models. Develop a timeline of steps and at various points along the way, celebrate with specific events–especially those that afford opportunities to connect with the community or individuals that the ministry will eventually serve. Or, get potential volunteers involved in a short-term training program to promote the feeling that their active service has already begun, even though they have not actually started the more tangible ministry tasks.

Conclusion

Launching a new ministry is exciting, if strenuous, work. Social workers desiring to lead new efforts should beware, though, of some potential obstacles. One of the biggest concerns is to determine how a new ministry venture will affect the current programs of the congregation or nonprofit agency. Leaders of existing programs may feel threatened by the new venture, if they are not invited into the discussions or never are helped to understand how the new programs will relate to the old ones. Another potential challenge relates to timing. Ministry leaders may have wonderful, God-inspired visions for new outreach, but lack a good sense of when to initiate such plans. Congregations or nonprofit agencies that are in the midst of transitions, such as hiring new leadership or embarking on a major capital campaign, or that have recently gone through a crisis (like a church split or scandal), may be ill-prepared to launch new ministries. Some time is needed, instead, for disciplined focus on current challenges or on reconciliation and healing. A season of "in-reach" may need to precede the expansion of outreach. In short, wisdom is required not only about the "what" and "how" questions of ministry, but also the "when."

Finally, social workers should capitalize on their unique strengths when offering assistance to churches and nonprofit agencies seeking new ministry endeavors. Some Christian leaders may be unaware of the challenges faced by lower income families in the community. Others may know little about the public assistance system. Others may be ignorant of existing community resources—both private and public. Still others may have little experience interacting with secular social service agencies. And others may have a sincere heart to help the poor, but no real relationships with poor people and little personal familiarity with distressed neighborhoods. Social workers bring knowledge and experience in all of these areas. They can help to educate and equip ministry leaders and volunteers about everything from potential partners in the community, to navigating the welfare system, to preparing for both the joys and challenges of outreach. Social workers may be especially well-equipped to shape leaders' understandings in ways that protect against the church or nonprofit operating out of stereotypes, unrealistic expectations, or unwittingly patronizing attitudes. In these and other ways, social workers can help ministry leaders build a solid foundation on which to construct initiatives that are holistic, relevant, and effective in fostering positive transformation.

References

Unruh, H.R. Sider, R.J., & Olson, P. N. (2002). *Good news, good works holistic ministry resource kit: User's guide*. Wynnewood, PA: Evangelicals for Social Action.

Resources for Models of Ministry

BOOKS

Carlson, D. (1999). *The welfare of my neighbor*. Washington, DC: Family Research Council.

Dudley, C. S. (2002).*Community ministry: New challenges, proven steps to faith-based initiatives*. Bethesda, MD: The Alban Institute.

Sherman, A. L. (1997). *Restorers of hope: Reaching the poor in your community with church-based ministries that work*. Wheaton, IL: Crossway Books.

NATIONAL TRAINING CONFERENCES

Christian Community Development Association (www.ccda.org)

North American Association of Christians in Social Work (www.nacsw.org)

WEBSITES

www.churchesatwork.org

www.network935.org

www.hudsonfaithincommunities.org

CHAPTER 17

EVANGELISM AND SOCIAL SERVICES

Heidi Rolland Unruh and Ronald J. Sider

Social workers are commonly taught that evangelism is not a valid activity in their profession. Why then include a chapter on evangelism in a book about social work? One reason is that "a dynamic relationship exists between the Christian life and social work practice," as noted by the NACSW Statement of Faith and Practice. Christian social workers are professionals pledged to uphold a code of ethics. But they are also followers of Christ, confronted with his command, "Go therefore and make disciples of all nations..." (Matt. 28:19). This creates a tension which social workers should be equipped to negotiate.

Another reason is that not all those who are trained in social work enter the profession as social workers in secular settings. Many provide care in faith-based settings where spiritual nurture may be not only allowed but an intentional aspect of the program, such as Teen Challenge or the Salvation Army. Others become administrators of social service programs and must make decisions regarding the program's spiritual character. Some may enter the public policy arena and help craft guidelines for faith-based initiatives. Others, working in the field of training, will be called on to direct social service staff and volunteers in how they may express their faith on the job. Understanding the principles of appropriate evangelism will enable persons to function in these positions more effectively and responsibly.

A third reason is that changes in the relationship between church and state have created more opportunities—and ambiguity—for social services that incorporate a religious dimension. Charitable Choice, the provision enacted into law with the 1996 welfare reform bill, assures faith-based programs more control over their religious practices. The law prohibits proselytizing with public funds, but leaves the door open for privately-funded religious activities or more indirect faith-sharing. Increasing numbers of religious organizations collaborate with government, and many report doing so without compromising their religious character and commitments (Monsma, 2002). In this climate, persons trained in social work must be prepared to encounter issues pertaining to evangelism. Even those who serve in positions that do not allow direct evangelism may work for or alongside programs that include a faith-based dimension.

Neither author of this chapter is trained in social work, and so our ability to interact with the standards of the profession is limited. However, in our experience of studying church-based social services, engaging with faith-based initiatives, networking and consulting with faith-based providers, and developing materials to empower Christian social action, we have gained a perspective on evangelism in the context of social services that can be helpful to social workers. We believe Christians in the field of social services would benefit from education about the appropriate contexts and methods for evangelism.

What is Evangelism?

We begin with our definition of evangelism:

> *Sharing Jesus' gospel by word and deed with non-Christians with the intention and hope that they will embrace the message and repent, accept and follow Christ, and join a Christian church community for ongoing discipleship.*

Note that the definition goes beyond the aim of leading people to a profession of faith. The goal of evangelism, according to the Great Commission (Matt. 28:19), is not only to win converts but to make disciples. By discipleship, Jesus meant a life of total, unconditional submission to him as Lord. Conversion is an ongoing process, "a once-in-a-lifetime choice that takes a lifetime to do" (Schaper, 1992, p. 36). Discipleship-oriented evangelism thus attends not only to those who do not call themselves Christians, but also to disaffiliated Christians in need of spiritual renewal. Effective evangelism helps people take the next step in their relationship with God. This approach is especially critical with marginalized persons, such as homeless persons, who have been "over-evangelized." Often people who depend on faith-based aid have heard the basic gospel message presented so many times, with so little practical effect, that it has lost its meaning. What they need is not just an altar call but to be connected with opportunities for ongoing discipleship.

Our definition thus concludes with the words *and join a Christian church community.* The radical life of obedience preached by Christ is impossible without the teaching, accountability and *koinonia* (fellowship) of a loving church community. After studying religious beliefs and behavior in the United States, sociologist Robert Wuthnow concluded that "religious inclinations make very little difference unless a person becomes involved in some kind of organized religious community" (Wuthnow, 1991, p. 13). If we fail to help root new converts in a supportive, discipling congregation, we have not completed the evangelistic mandate.

Evangelism and Social Work

We will first consider the relationship between evangelism and the profession of social work, and then look at the place of evangelism in social services more generally.

Evangelism is seen by many to violate the principles and values of social work practice, for several reasons (see Cnaan, 1999, chapter 4). First, social work is based on client-defined needs, as the NASW (1996) *Code of Ethics* makes clear: "Social workers respect and promote the right of clients to self-determination and assist clients in their efforts to identify and clarify their goals" (p. 7). From this perspective, if a client is not aware of or interested in a spiritual dimension to their need, it is not the social worker's role to introduce religious ideas. The social worker is to remain focused on the problem as the client defines it, and to respect the client's right "to chart their own spiritual journey according to their felt needs" (Sherman, 1997, p. 58). Evangelism, however, encourages clients to acknowledge their spiritual need and to make a particular religious response.

Moreover, professional norms require social workers to adopt an objective stance toward clients, refraining from moral judgments. "Social work does not blame the person in need or see a moral pathology in the situation that led to the need" (Cnaan, 1999, p. 82). Evangelism, in contrast, is predicated on the understanding that all persons are sinners in need of salvation. The process of discipleship includes moral teachings that censure certain lifestyles and personal choices. It does not appear that a social worker can promote Christian faith and maintain objective neutrality.

Social work ethics also teach professionals to confine their relations with clients to the social work contract. Anything outside that is considered a dual relationship, which carries "a risk of exploitation or potential harm to the client" (NASW *Code of Ethics*). This principle would disallow relational evangelism that creates an informal space for dialogues about spiritual matters beyond the boundaries of the social work relationship. Social workers may also perceive that addressing a client's spiritual needs puts them in the position of a spiritual counselor, creating role confusion.

Finally, professional social work emphasizes treatment modes that have been documented through scientific methods and that achieve quantifiable results (Hugen, 1994). The claim that persons have spiritual needs alongside social needs which can be met through evangelism and spiritual nurture cannot be verified empirically: "Spirituality is troublesome to define and difficult to document" (Cnaan, 1999, p. 74). Thus conventional social work practice rejects religious approaches to social problems.

The first response to these concerns is to demonstrate the ways that evangelism is consistent with professional social work principles. The NASW (1996) *Code of Ethics* asserts: "Social workers' primary responsibility is to promote the well-being of clients" (p. 7). Christians believe that the well-being of clients is served by a relationship with the God who created, redeemed, and loves them. In fact, recent research increasingly documents that a strong faith and ties to a church community helps a person's chances of developing a better quality of life. In study after study, people with religious commitments enjoy better mental and physical health, stay married longer, and avoid socially destructive behaviors like alcohol abuse (e.g. Fagan, 1996; Larson & Johnson, 1998; Johnson, 2002). The connection between physical, emotional, relational and spiritual health means that social workers are acting in a client's best interest by exploring the spiritual dimensions of a client's felt need (Canda, 1998). With clients' informed consent, this can take place from an explicitly Christian perspective.

Similarly, there is no real clash of values in the social work principles of "respect for the client and the client's freedom of choice and self-determination" (Cnaan, 1999, p. 76). The difference lies in how one interprets "respect" and "freedom of choice." Often this is interpreted as "the right to religion-free service" (Cnaan, 1999, p. 79). Ironically, however, these principles have religious roots. They are grounded in the Judeo-Christian teachings that the creation of humanity in the image of God endows persons with inestimable dignity and worth, and that each person has both freedom and responsibility to make their own moral choices. We believe it is acceptable for Christian social workers to inform clients of the religiously based perspective grounding their professional values. A social worker need not pretend to be religiously neutral in order to respect their client's autonomy.

In other areas, however, the conflict between professional social work norms and evangelistic faith is real. Christian social workers must resist the "postmodern credo that 'Individuals are free to chart their own spiritual journey according to their felt needs' and that 'all spiritual journeys are equally valid.'" Social work guided by this credo "does not challenge people to conform their behavior to an objective standard of morality; it encourages them to do whatever they *feel* helps them" (Sherman, 1997, pp. 58-60). Such neutrality lacks spiritual credibility and transformational power, we believe, particularly in addressing deep-seated negative patterns. The gospel confronts people with the ways they have fallen short of God's standards, and presents salvation by faith in Christ and discipleship guided by the Scriptures as a uniquely valid path to a new life. Social workers should emphasize clients' freedom of religious conscience in choosing this path, and should help clients learn about other spiritual options (or none at all) if so requested, but they can do so without endorsing the notion that clients can create and validate their own spiritual reality.

Professional social work ethics have been shaped by secularization theory, which addresses social needs solely in terms of material, socio-economic forces (Hugen, 1994). Many social workers accept that spirituality may have a place in a person's private life, but view religious beliefs as irrelevant to effective practice, or even detrimental to a client's progress toward secular goals (Derzotes & Evans, 1995; Cnaan, 1999). Our understanding of evangelistic faith, in contrast, presupposes an understanding of persons as body-soul unities created in God's image and invited to live forever in God's presence. Psychological, physical, social and economic problems have spiritual ramifications, and spiritual well-being has a profound effect on other dimensions of a person's life as well. Evangelism invites persons into a process of total life transformation, looking beyond the presenting need to the "new thing" that God desires to do in each person's life (Isa. 43:1). An evangelistic approach works toward both "the temporal and eternal well-being" of persons (NACSW Statement of Faith and Practice).

Is it ever appropriate for social workers to evangelize? While many in the profession would answer an unqualified "No," we suggest that Christian social workers be open to the response, "It depends." First, it depends on the social worker-client relationship. When a significant power differential exists, as with a caseworker who controls the flow of benefits to a client, overt evangelism is potentially exploitative. However, in some situations we suggest that a social worker may offer spiritual guidance without being perceived as being coercive. Social workers must be sensitive to the unique dynamics of each relationship.

Moreover, some evangelistic approaches are more appropriate to the social work profession than others. Mandating participation in religious activities is not valid social work practice. Making religious content optional - such as offering times of prayer preceding or following appointments - is more acceptable. Many contexts will allow a social worker to adopt an invitational strategy, informing clients about religious resources or activities relevant to their situation, such as a Christian video on parenting or a church-based singles group. Social workers can also be prepared to suggest references for ministers or spiritual counselors.

Another form of evangelism that is often acceptable is sharing first-person insights on faith from one's own experiences that connect with a client's situation, without pressuring the client for a response. While social workers must avoid dual relationships, they can relate to clients within appropriate boundaries in a way that communicates a sense of caring for the whole person - body, soul, and spirit.

Finally, opportunities for evangelism depend on the felt needs of the client. Social workers may never impose religious teachings against a client's will. However, when a person conveys spiritual concerns ("God must hate me!"), acknowledges potential spiritual needs ("I wish I didn't feel so guilty"), or expresses a connection with Christianity ("my mother taught me how to pray"), we believe it can be consistent with good social work practice to offer to address these issues from a Christian framework. This is particularly the case when the social worker serves with a faith-based agency. Spiritual assessment tools such as that proposed by Sherwood (1998) can help discern a person's spiritual background and needs, and relevant religious interventions.

Every Christian is called to share the gospel. Christian social workers implicitly model the message by serving people faithfully with the love of Christ; at times their situation may allow them to witness more explicitly to the Good News of Christ. Each social worker has to wrestle with the ambiguities of this calling for themselves, given the particulars of their clientele and work environment. The NACSW Statement of Faith and Practice urges Christians in social work "to examine and evaluate all human ideologies and social work theories and methods as to their consistency with the Bible, their consciences, social laws, and professional codes of ethics." It is our hope that social workers will not accept uncritically the premise that explicit evangelism has no place in ethical social work practice. Social workers may find some guidance for incorporating evangelism into their practice in the discussion below.

Evangelism in the Context of Social Services

We now turn to the question of the role of evangelism in the provision of social services in general. Evangelism in the context of social services can take many forms: religious teachings and discussions, sharing of personal testimonies, spiritual counseling, sermons and worship services, use of the Bible or other religious literature, use of evangelistic videos, music or other media, invitations to special evangelistic activities, and prayer. These activities can be integrated into the social service program or stand alone as separate components; they can be mandatory or optional; they can take place with a group of people or one-on-one; and they can be planned, formal elements of the program or have a more spontaneous, relational quality. Evangelism can also be expressed implicitly in the modeling of a Christlike attitude and lifestyle. For the purposes of this chapter, however, we are primarily referring to verbal, overt evangelism.

Our research on church-based outreach ministry identified five overarching strategies for integrating evangelistic elements into a social service program (Sider & Unruh, 2001).

1. *Passive*: A spiritual message is largely modeled, rather than expressed verbally. The program may be located in a religious environment (such as a church), but has no religious content; evangelistic materials or spiritual counseling may be available but only if clients seek them out.
2. *Invitational*: No evangelistic content is involved in social service delivery, but clients are invited to attend optional events of a religious nature. These might be regular church activities (like worship services or youth group meetings), special church activities designed particularly for clients (like a Bible study on family relationships), or religious activities offered on-site in conjunction with the social service (such as a devotional service following a meal).
3. *Relational*: In the context of relationships formed with clients beyond the structured programmatic activities, program staff or volunteers share their faith and address clients' spiritual concerns informally, one-on-one.
4. *Integrated-optional*: The program clearly has a religious character. Religious content is woven into the delivery of social services, and staff or volunteers may verbally share their faith. However, the program is structured so that clients may opt out of participating in religious rituals or explicitly religious teachings.
5. *Integrated-mandatory*: The program has a religious and overtly evangelistic character. Religious content is woven into the delivery of social services, and staff or volunteers verbally share their faith. Spiritual transformation is at the heart of the program.

Challenges in Evangelism and Social Services

When and how is it appropriate for service providers to integrate a religious component? Many Christian service providers prefer a passive approach, letting their actions stand alone as their witness. The view that explicit verbal evangelism is superfluous echoes a saying attributed to St. Francis: "Preach the gospel at all times; if necessary, use words." A volunteer in one faith-based program put it this way: "We show our faith in God through our kindness to others." If a ministry does good deeds without ever pointing explicitly to Christ, however, many will miss the connection between human aid and God's love. Returning to our definition of evangelism, we affirm that evangelism consists of both word *and* deed. Modeling the gospel through acts of compassion and the pursuit of justice can draw people to Christ - *if* they learn the spiritual source of your actions. Social service by itself is not evangelism. Ultimately, we believe, loving acts need the complement of the verbal presentation of Christ's life, death, and resurrection.

Others raise the concern that evangelism in the context of social service is inherently unethical. The word "proselytizing" has, in some circles, become synonymous with aggressive, insensitive tactics that force religion on unwilling targets. In a culture that tends toward a "vaguely privatized and weakly integrated faith" (Roozen, 1995), affirmations of absolute truths are often labeled intolerant. Explicitly religious activities such as worship and religious instruction involving persons outside the church are viewed as distasteful, even offensive. These concerns are magnified for those in the vulnerable position of needing aid from a service agency. One writer, for example, critiques Charitable Choice for allowing religious organizations to conduct privately-funded, voluntary religious activities, saying, "Such practices and a heavy presence of religious symbolism could become tantamount to religious coercion" (Eisenberg, 2001).

We must distinguish, however, between appropriate persuasion and inappropriate coercion. Evangelism exposes persons to religious ideas or images in a manner designed to influence their beliefs. Providers of care must take care to present evangelistic claims in a manner that respects persons' dignity and freedom of religious conscience. But religious expression does not *inherently* constitute religious coercion. There is nothing intrinsically unethical about an honest, respectful attempt at persuading someone to accept a different system of belief, particularly when the dialogue is motivated by genuine concern for the person's current and eternal well-being. Whether such persuasion is appropriate in a given situation, however, depends on contextual factors, as will be addressed below.

Potential Benefits of Evangelism and Social Services

First, however, we look at the ways that evangelism complements social services. Evangelism and social services can have a mutually reinforcing relationship. Evangelism that considers spiritual needs in the total context of a person's life circumstances and felt needs can empower clients as whole persons. While the efficacy of faith-based methodologies in social service provision has not been proven, anecdotal evidence as well as Christian theology point to the potential benefits of nurturing religious commitments (Johnson, 2002). Briefly, spiritual transformation can enhance the impact of social services by:

Giving people new hope, motivation, dignity and self-esteem.

Healing scars from past negative experiences and relationships.

Freeing people from spiritual bondage to evil forces and self-destructive patterns.

Teaching new moral principles and guidelines for healthy living.

Introducing people to the power of the Holy Spirit that enables Christians to live differently, to overcome obstacles, and to persevere.

Imparting a new vision of social justice and the boldness to work for change and wholeness in one's social context.

Addressing the personal sinful choices as well as the structural injustices that contribute to poverty and social need.

Bringing people into a community of faith that provides emotional, physical and spiritual support, in a context of mutual accountability.

Further, evangelism builds the capacity of the Christian community for social ministry by:

Transforming "clients" into "servants," able and willing to give back to the community as part of the solution.

Expanding and energizing the community of dedicated Christian ministry workers.

Revitalizing the church's commitment to social outreach with the testimonies of new people coming to Christ through social service ministries.

Breaking social barriers when a congregation receives those served as brothers and sisters in Christ.

Spiritual care and social services, when woven together, can thus yield a stronger fabric than either strand alone (Sider, Olson & Unruh, 2002).

Ethical Considerations in Evangelism and Social Services

While we affirm that overt evangelism is not inherently inappropriate—and in fact can be beneficial to clients—this does not mean that it is always appropriate in every situation, or that all evangelism methods are valid. We turn now to examine five ethical issues arising from the integration of evangelism and social services.

1. *Evangelism versus "recruitment"*

As Ram Cnaan writes, one reason many are skeptical of faith-based social ministries is the perception that they are "more interested in saving the souls of the needy than solving their problems. ... It is argued that some congregations use welfare activities to attract new members" (Cnaan, 1999, p. 80). Ethical issues arise when a religious organization appears to offer a social service mainly in order to gain converts or to enlarge its membership rolls. No one wants to feel like the "catch of the day." Programs associated with a church or denomination must take care that their motivation is to provide genuine care for clients, rather than inducements for people to join their faith group. Clients must not be pressured to feel a sense of loyalty to a sponsoring congregation that prevents them from connecting with another church that is better suited to their needs.

On the other hand, it is also unethical to discourage clients, either overtly or subtly, from attending the sponsoring church. Evangelizing clients without inviting them into the church's fellowship sends the message: "You are welcome in God's family but not in our congregation." If Christian clients never return after visiting a sponsoring church's worship services, this may indicate obstacles that prevent clients from feeling at home as church members.

It is important to help clients with new or renewed faith connect with a supportive church, whether or not it ends up being your own. For church-based social services, the goal should be to love clients enough to offer the embrace of the sponsoring congregation, while empowering them to select the church family best equipped to support their journey of faith.

2. *Mandatory versus voluntary evangelistic elements*

Faith itself can never be forced. It is never appropriate to make a service conditional on conversion, or to penalize a client for having different beliefs. However, may faith-based programs require exposure to religious ideas or participation in religious activities? When is it appropriate to make evangelistic components of a service program mandatory, and when should they be optional?

We see mandatory religious elements as potentially appropriate in several contexts:

> *Ministries to spiritual seekers or self-professing Christians.* Clients who are seeking to develop their spiritual life may prefer an approach to their social need which structures in religious elements. They may view required participation in spiritual activities as an asset.
>
> *Ministries that address deep-seated negative patterns,* such as drug dependency or chronic homelessness. Many of these ministries place spiritual nurture at the heart of the program. Religious teachings and activities are designed to address the spiritual dimensions of the need, in combination with other therapeutic methods. If spiritual components are not mandatory, clients will not reap the full benefit of the program.
>
> *Ministries that offer a one-time or minor benefit in conjunction with an evangelistic activity.* For example, a program might offer a free meal or food basket to people who attend a worship service. In such ministries the focus is the evangelism, and the social benefit is an accompanying "perk" that tangibly represents the message of God's love.
>
> *Ministries to children.* In some children's ministries, such as day care and after-school programs, part of the purpose of the program is to teach children Bible lessons and Christian values. Children may be expected to sing Christian songs, memorize Scriptures, participate in times of prayer, and listen to Bible stories. However, caution should be taken in exposing younger children to overtly evangelistic invitations, such as "altar calls," which can pressure them prematurely to make a decision for Christ.

Social service programs that incorporate mandatory evangelistic elements should adhere to several ethical guidelines. First, programs should distinguish between *active* and *passive* participation in activities of a spiritual nature. Passive participation entails being present during a prayer, worship service, or evangelistic presentation. Active participation that mandates a personal spiritual response (such as repeating a prayer) may cross the line into inappropriate coercion. Second, the program must be careful that the benefit is offered as a blessing and not a bribe. Staff must communicate that they will care about clients and seek to meet their needs regardless of whether they choose to accept the faith teachings. Another ethical key is to inform prospective beneficiaries in advance about the program's religious nature, and not to force people to enter the program against their will. People must have advance notice of the evangelistic activity so they do not feel tricked into hearing a "sales pitch."

Mandatory evangelistic elements are not appropriate when they abuse the relationship or erode the trust between client, program, and donors. Contexts that warrant caution against mandatory evangelistic elements include the following:

> *Ministries that serve a population that largely belongs to another religion*, such as Muslim immigrants. Even passive participation in the activities of another religion can violate the edicts of some faiths; joining in foreign religious activities may also be seen as disloyalty to one's culture. Adherents to other religions may face pressure from their family and community not to convert. Clients must not be placed in the position of choosing between their religious conscience or cultural allegiances, and the receipt of aid.

> *Ministries to emotionally and socially vulnerable clients.* It is unethical to use religion as an instrument of power over desperate persons (indeed, over any person!). Mandatory religious elements may seem threatening to clients who feel powerless or have been abused by authority figures in the past, such as mothers on welfare or victims of domestic violence. Vulnerable clients may not be aware, or may not believe, that they have the right to reject the beliefs of the host agency. They may go along with religious activities and mouth faith statements out of fear or guilt without experiencing real inner transformation. This demoralizing experience can lead to resentment against Christianity and create further obstacles to evangelism.

> *Ministries that work in partnership with secular or interfaith agencies.* The conditions set by ministry partners may limit the options for required (or even optional) evangelistic presentations. Community organizing coalitions often have an inter-faith or even a non-faith-based membership, making it inappropriate for one partner to impose religious elements that contradict the beliefs of other partners.

> *Ministries that receive government funds, or private funds with restrictions on evangelism.* While public policy has been changing to allow greater freedom of religious expression in faith-based social services, for most programs funded directly by government, religious elements must be optional (this is discussed in

more detail below). Some private foundations also have strictures against required (or any) evangelistic elements.

We note that some form of *optional* evangelistic elements may be appropriate in each of these cases. Programs that refrain from mandatory religious activities may be intentional about fostering relational evangelism, for example. Just because clients should not be required to participate in religious activities does not mean that they must be deprived of voluntary opportunities to receive spiritual nurture.

3. *Manipulative versus appropriate evangelism methods*

As discussed above, evangelism is not inherently manipulative. Claims about religious truth do not, in themselves, pose a threat to clients. Rather, providers of social care are to empower clients to make informed life decisions based on their assessment of those claims. This means that the evangelistic component must be presented in a loving, sensitive, respectful and relevant way. Clients must be allowed freedom to make their own decisions on matters of faith. High-pressure tactics, guilt manipulation, degrading harangues, and forced conversions can create lasting wounds and close people's minds to the gospel. Inappropriate evangelism methods discourage people from coming to faith, as well as impeding the social service goals.

Manipulation entails trying to bribe, threaten, or shame clients into a religious response. Manipulation may be overt, as in giving preferential treatment to those who convert or penalizing those who reject the invitation to faith; or it may be understated, as in conveying a general sense of disapproval for non-believers. One woman's testimony, posted on a secular welfare-to-work website, provides a lamentable example of religious manipulation:

> The job I work on is run by a Christian organization. Some of the people who work there belong to the owner's church. I am not a Christian but I do have respect for all religions. These people do not.... Some of the names I have been called [by Christian co-workers] are devil spirit, nonbeliever, and welfare recipient. My job is always threatened by the management. Each week I go to work wondering whether I'll be fired.... I have never stated my religion to any of my co-workers; however, I have declined requests to come to their church.... This job is over for me, I know.

Manipulative tactics also include "stealth" evangelism, or sneaking in religious elements, particularly mandatory elements, without clients' prior knowledge or consent. Manipulation can also take the form of promising that conversion will bring an immediate change in one's socioeconomic status. It is disingenuous to present faith as a quick-fix or feel-good answer to all of someone's problems. Evangelistic efforts should stress not only the relevance of Christian faith to personal well-being, but also the long road of discipleship that true Christian faith entails.

The attitude of staff and volunteers towards clients is another key factor in ethical evangelism. How are clients treated - with condescension or respect, condemnation or loving kindness? Are staff considerate of people with different beliefs? Do staff make the attempt to get to know clients as unique and valued individuals? Is the evangelistic message presented in a way that is relevant to clients' felt needs and issues? Is the presentation sensitive to their cultural and socioeconomic context? Program evaluations can seek clients' feedback on the religious and relational aspects of the program in order to assess these questions. Clients can discern whether staff share the gospel because they authentically care for them, or out of a sense of obligation or condescension. "Evangelism takes place best when the target community is treated not as a project, but as a people who have dignity and deserve respect" (Tiersma, 1994, p. 18).

4. *"Faith-specific" versus "faith-neutral" evangelism*

Faith-based programs may be either "faith-specific" or "faith-neutral." They may convey a specific set of religious beliefs rooted in a particular religious tradition, or they can affirm "faith" in a more general sense. The Transitional Journey welfare-to-work program sponsored by Cookman United Methodist Church includes examples of both approaches. The material in the "Sisters of Faith" spirituality class, which is optional, is explicitly Christian. The teacher lays out the basics of Christian faith and invites students to experience spiritual renewal through conversion. The mandatory self-esteem class, in contrast, is faith-neutral. It draws on religiously-rooted concepts such as humanity's God-endowed dignity, but the texts and teachings are not specific to Christianity. The class encourages clients to develop their spiritual side, but leaves open how they define spirituality.

Whether a program should be faith-neutral or faith-specific depends in part on context. Some government-funded programs must avoid "sectarian" expressions in order to comply with church-state restrictions. (This is true for some funding streams not covered by Charitable Choice, which permits faith-based programs to maintain their specific religious identity.) Interfaith programs present another context, which may call for a faith-neutral approach. For example, the Interfaith Hospitality

Network, which houses homeless families at area congregations for week-long spells, has a clear spiritual ethos. They do not, however, teach guests explicitly about any particular religion during their stay. As a church volunteer in this program explains: "It is appropriate to say, 'When I am stressed I light candles and meditate, or I pray and give my burden to God.' But it is not appropriate to say, 'Let me tell you about Jesus.'"

In many contexts, however, we believe faith-specific evangelism is not only ethically justified but theologically proper. Faith-neutral programs that talk about God's love only in a generic sense stop short of the whole truth about God's plan for humanity. They can imply endorsement of a deistic religion that substitutes faith in "faith" for faith in Christ, spirituality for salvation, and self-realization for conversion. This message finds popular acceptance in social service programs such as Alcoholics Anonymous, and in our broader culture through shows like *Touched by an Angel*. This approach can be helpful in introducing people to faith, but if people are never encouraged to take the next step of trusting in Jesus, their relationship with God will remain shallow. The Christian message centers on Christ. Evangelism should ultimately point to the Jesus who proclaimed, "I am the way, the truth and the life," and "Come, follow me!" Faith-neutral programs deprive clients of an opportunity to encounter the Christ who died for their sins, who rose to bring them salvation, and lives to intercede for their needs (Romans 8:34).

Faith-specific does not, however, mean faith-exclusive. While Christians should not be neutral about what we believe, we must be neutral in accepting all people regardless of what they believe. We must be honest with people in presenting truth-claims about our faith, without rejecting or condemning people who believe otherwise. We may tell clients, "This is what I believe, and according to my understanding of biblical faith this is the only way to know God"—but not, "You are a bad person if you believe otherwise." We may say, "I do not share your beliefs, but my faith leads me to respect and serve you no matter what"—but not, "I do not share your beliefs, and if you don't agree with me it is a waste of time to help you." We must model civic dialogue by respecting persons of other religions or no religion, even if we disagree with their beliefs.

We must also convey our trust in clients' capacity to make reasonable choices concerning their spiritual journey. This means assuring clients that we support their right and responsibility to reach their own conclusions regarding their beliefs, without conceding that all beliefs are equally valid. At times—for example, if the client has made it clear that he or she is not interested in Christianity but still wishes to explore matters of faith—the client's best interest requires our listening and asking guiding questions while reserving our personal convictions.

5. *Evangelism in the context of secular programs.*

Most of the above discussion has centered on faith-based programs. But what of service providers of social care in secular programs, whether private or public? What does appropriate evangelism mean for them?

Many secular programs prohibit employees from bringing up religion with clients or engaging them in spiritual activities. Christians must adhere to workplace regulations (see Col. 3:22). Illicit evangelism is not a credit to the gospel. Even when policies do not permit overt evangelism, however, staff members have several options open to them:

> In many cases it is appropriate to let clients know that you are a Christian - either verbally or through ornamental symbols such as a cross - and that you are available to address spiritual issues, if they choose to initiate it.
>
> It is always appropriate for staff to respond honestly and explicitly to spiritual questions raised by clients, particularly in speaking autobiographically about your faith (rather than telling others what to believe).
>
> When a client expresses a desire to explore spiritual topics like salvation or Scripture interpretation, arrange a time to do so outside the context of the program, if such a meeting would be appropriate to the nature of your relationship with the client.
>
> Be prepared to give references to churches, ministers or spiritual counselors who are competent to address spiritual felt needs in a loving and culturally appropriate way.
>
> There is no law against praying for clients on your own time! Seek out another Christian staff worker to join you in interceding for clients. (Be sure to respect rules of confidentiality in sharing prayer requests.)

Talk to your supervisors to clarify the guidelines. The boundaries may not be as strict as you have assumed. While verbal faith-sharing might be prohibited, for example, some employers may not object to offering clients printed religious material such as a devotional book, particularly when the material is relevant to the need at hand. Raising the question with supervisors can also heighten their awareness of the connection between spiritual and social well-being.

Evangelism in the Context of Government-funded Social Services

Because of the First Amendment, programs that receive government funding pose a special case. The laws concerning government-funded religious social service programs are still in transition, and different kinds of government funding (depending on the level of government and the type of program) are covered by different laws. However, we believe the following general guidelines for faith-based programs are consistent with the letter and spirit of Charitable Choice statutes.

1. *No government funds may be expended on direct evangelism.* The 1996 legislation known as Charitable Choice includes this provision: "No funds provided directly to institutions or organizations to provide services and administer programs under [this provision] shall be expended for sectarian worship, instruction, or proselytization." Faith-based programs may spend their own money on evangelistic elements (such as Bibles or religious tracts), but spending direct government funds on religion violates the First Amendment. (It currently appears that indirect funds, such as vouchers, may be expended for religious activities.)

2. *Evangelistic elements must be voluntary.* Clients must be allowed to opt out of participation in religious activities. For this right to be meaningful, programs must be able to compartmentalize the overtly evangelistic activities from the social service, so that clients can receive the social benefit without participating in religious exercises if they so choose. (This does not mean that the social service must be sanitized from religious influence altogether.) Clients cannot be penalized for their religious beliefs (or non-belief).

3. *Clients have the right to request an alternative provider if they object to the religious setting.* No one should be forced to receive services from a faith-based provider. Clients must be able to choose freely between programs.

4. *Programs must disclose their religious nature.* Agencies must be up-front with clients about their religious affiliation and activities, so that clients can make an informed choice about their program selection.

If your program is funded by government, become knowledgeable about Charitable Choice and relevant case law. Clarify any gray areas with appropriate officials - but do not assume that officials correctly understand the law themselves! You may need to advocate for your position if local government officials are not properly implementing Charitable Choice, for example by prohibiting even voluntary, privately funded religious activity in your program.

Conclusion: A Model of Appropriate Evangelism in the Context of Social Services

The type and amount of evangelism involved in a faith-based social service program ultimately depends on the specifics of the program context and the needs of individual clients. The following seven guidelines can help providers of social care discern and develop "a gentle and winsome public witness" (Sherman, 2001, p. 34) that is appropriate in any setting.

1. *Appropriate evangelism is based in love and respect for the client.* Christ-like love—not guilt, rote obligation, or moral censure—is the cornerstone of genuine evangelism. We love clients because Christ first loved us (1 John 4:19), and we want to share the goodness of God's grace. We long to see clients experience a healing, transforming encounter with Jesus. At the same time, respect for clients' God-given dignity ensures that evangelism does not become condescending or overbearing. Evangelism rooted in love means listening to clients rather than doing all the talking, gently persuading rather than pushing, demonstrating God's love through our lives and actions as well as words, and allowing people to explore Christianity at their own pace.

2. *Appropriate evangelism is not manipulative.* The theological doctrine of freedom of conscience cherished in the Judeo-Christian tradition insists that we should not—indeed cannot—force faith on others. While required participation in religious activities is sometimes appropriate, aid must never be conditioned on receptiveness to the evangelistic message. We must serve people whether or not they accept the gospel, care about their whole being whether or not they recognize the spiritual dimension of their needs, and love them whether or not they understand that God loves them through us. This is the standard set by the grace of God, who freely "sends rain on the righteous and on the unrighteous" (Matt. 5:45).

3. *Appropriate evangelism is intentional and invitational.* A prevalent myth is that if you simply give non-Christians a chance to rub shoulders

with Christians, they will catch a dose of the gospel. But if people do not ask, and we never tell, how will those we serve learn the good news about Christ? Many contexts allow evangelism to be more than simply an open-door policy for clients to inquire about faith. Staff should be trained in how to discern spiritual needs and to share their beliefs in sensitive ways. Be intentional about creating opportunities for spiritual nurture and inviting people to take the next step in their faith journey. Be patient but persistent in looking for ways to help people connect with the gospel.

4. *Appropriate evangelism is founded on relationships.* Formulaic, impersonal evangelism methods rarely connect with people in a meaningful way. While corporate evangelistic events, such as worship services or group Bible studies, have an important place, they should be complemented whenever possible by the cultivation of personal relationships which foster openness and trust and add credibility to the message. Social service providers, however, must be aware of how power dynamics shape their relationships with clients. They must be careful not to take advantage of persons, reinforce dysfunctional relational patterns, or reduce relationships to a evangelistic tool.

5. *Appropriate evangelism is context-sensitive and creative.* There is no such thing as "one size fits all" evangelism. As Moody Memorial Church pastor Michael Allen writes, "Although the very essence of the message, namely, who Jesus is and what He did, cannot change, the presentation of the message must" (p. 224). Developing an appropriate evangelism strategy requires familiarity with the program's constituency, cultural context, organizational dynamics, and external restrictions, as well as the needs and attributes of individual clients. Effective evangelism also entails sensitivity to the leading of God's Spirit, and creativity in devising fresh ways to communicate God's grace.

6. *Appropriate evangelism is transparent and honest.* Whether by choice or in response to external pressures, many Christian programs do not include explicit references to Christianity in their mission statement or other descriptive documents. If a program does integrate religious elements, however, it ought to be clear about its spiritual character. The Faith-based Ministries' Code of Conduct declares:

   > We commit ourselves to open, straightforward, clear, consistent communication about our religious identity to our volunteers,

> service beneficiaries, donors, and government. ...Our desire is to allow potential staff, volunteers, participants, and government contacts to make choices about involvement with our organization on the basis of full and accurate information... (Sherman, 2001, p. 34).

In other words: Say who you are, and be who you say you are.

7. *Appropriate evangelism complies with rules and regulations.* Abide by guidelines for religious activity set by your employers and by the program's partners and funders. If these regulations unduly constrain your commitment to caring for persons' spiritual needs, you may wish to consider other employment or funding options.

What does this model look like in action? One example comes from Transitional Journey Ministries (TJM), the church-based welfare-to-work program mentioned above. Students are taught job skills (computer, GED, and work readiness classes) and matched with employment opportunities. They are also provided with optional spiritual resources: weekly worship services, prayer, and a spiritual development class. Upon entering the program, students sign a waiver confirming their awareness of the program's religious nature and of their right to opt out of religious activities. TJM staff also address spiritual and emotional needs informally, one-on-one as students share their personal struggles. Students are invited but not pressured to attend the sponsoring church. Student evaluations note that TJM seems different than other programs where they have encountered demoralizing, condescending attitudes. One student, Shawna (not her real name), came to the program with ten children, an eighteen-year history of substance abuse, and a fourth grade education. Her life was in turmoil, and the five-year limit on her welfare clock was ticking. The program's therapist helped her set goals and develop an action plan, but Shawna was simply unable to cope. She became suicidal. The therapist asked Shawna if she wanted to meet with the pastor of the church for spiritual counseling. In the pastor's office, Shawna reaffirmed her faith in Christ. She was welcomed by the congregation at Cookman United Methodist Church and was baptized there. Eventually she graduated from the program with a job. While she still faces many obstacles, she has started making progress toward her life goals.

Conclusion

If you believe that Christian faith offers hope and strength to people in desperate circumstances, then why not cultivate opportunities for those in need to embrace or deepen their faith in Christ? If you believe that salvation gives people a new identity as children of God†and empowers them to pursue paths of justice and peace, then why not share this message in sensitive ways with those who struggle with low self-esteem or oppressive surroundings? If you believe that the Holy Spirit endows a divine power to heal emotional wounds and break destructive habits, why not offer to pray with people to invite God to do this work of supernatural transformation? If you believe that a loving, supportive Christian community helps to provide the social networks and constructive moral paradigms needed for social stability, why not seek to establish people in a strong Christian church?

Resistance to the idea of evangelism in the context of social services warrants an honest appraisal of its source. Does reluctance arise from a principled objection to addressing spiritual issues in the context of service provision? Or does it reflect a more personal discomfort with the notion of talking about one's beliefs and spiritual experiences? Professional norms should not be used to justify distancing oneself from the spiritual dimensions of clients' needs.

The Good News of the gospel is the best treasure we have to share with the people we serve. Christians who provide social care can enhance clients' total well being by offering spiritual nurture in sensitive, respectful, creative and appropriate ways.

References

Allen, M. N. (1999). New wineskin-same vintage wine. In J. Fuder (Ed.) *A heart for the city.* Chicago: Moody Press.

Canda, E. R. (1998). Afterword: Linking spirituality and social work: Five themes for innovation. *Social Thought*, 18 (2), 97-106.

Cnaan, R. A. with Wineburg, R. J. & Boddie S.C. (1999). *The newer deal: Social work and religion in partnership.* New York: Columbia University Press.

Derezotes, D. S. & Evans K. E. (1995). Spirituality and religiosity in practice: In-depth interviews of social work practitioners. *Social Thought*, 18 (1), 39-56.

Eisenberg, P. (2001, August 23). Senate should start fresh on crafting faith measure. *The Chronicle of Philanthropy.*

Fagan, P. F. (1996). Why religion matters: The impact of religious practice on social stability. *Backgrounder no. 1064*. Washington, D.C.: The Heritage Foundation.

Hugen, B. (1994). The secularization of social work. *Social Work and Christianity*, 21 (1), 83-101.

Johnson, B. R. (2002). Objective hope: Assessing the effectiveness of faith-based organizations: A review of the literature. *CRRUCS Report*. Philadelphia: Center for Research on Religion and Urban Civil Society, University of Pennsylvania.

Larson, D. B. & Johnson B. R. (1998). Religion: The forgotten factor in cutting youth crime and saving at-risk urban youth. *Report 98-2*. New York: The Manhattan Institute.

Monsma, S. V. with Mounts C. M. (2002). Working faith: How religious organizations provide welfare-to-work services. *CRRUCS Report*. Philadelphia: Center for Research on Religion and Urban Civil Society, University of Pennsylvania.

NACSW. (1993). *Statement of Faith and Practice*.

NASW. (1996). *Code of ethics*.

Roozen, D., McKinney, W., & Roof, W. C. (1995). Fifty years of religious change in the United States. In W. C, Roof et al. (Eds.) *The post-war generation and establishment religion*. Boulder, Colo.: Westview.

Schaper, D. (1992). Bricks without straw: Ministry in the city. In E. S. Meyers (Ed.) *Envisioning the new city: A reader on urban ministry.* Louisville: Westminster/John Knox Press.

Sherman, A. L. (1997). *Restorers of hope*. Wheaton, IL: Crossway Books.

Sherman, A. L. (2001). *The Charitable Choice handbook for ministry leaders*. Annapolis, MD: Center for Public Justice.

Sherwood, D. (1998). Spiritual assessment as a normal part of social work practice: Power to help and power to harm. *Social Work and Christianity*, 25 (2), 80-99.

Sider, R. J. & Unruh H. R. (Spring 2001). Evangelism and church-state partnerships. *Journal of Church and State*, 43 (2), 267-295.

Sider, R. J., Olson P., & Unruh H. R. (2002). *Churches that make a difference: Reaching your community with good news and good works.* Grand Rapids, MI: Baker Books.

Tiersma, J. (1994). What does it mean to be incarnational when we are not the Messiah? In C. Van Engen & J. Tiersma (Eds.) *God so loves the city.* Monrovia, Calif.: MARC.

Wuthnow, R. (May 1991). Evangelicals, liberals and the perils of individualism. *Perspectives: A Journal of Reformed Thought*, 6, 10-13.

CHAPTER 18

ETHICAL INTEGRATION OF FAITH AND SOCIAL WORK PRACTICE: EVANGELISM[1]

David A. Sherwood

As I sat down to write this, I couldn't help but think of the old adage, "Fools rush in where angels fear to tread." Probably right. However, it seemed like it might be useful, at least as a conversation starter, to take a stab at trying to apply Christian and social work values, ethics, and practice principles to some of the controversial issues that seem to raise questions for most of us. This time the focus is the relationship between professional social work practice and evangelism.

I need to warn you from the beginning, on the other hand (my naturally cautious side coming out), that I do not propose to state the definitive Christian position on anything. What I do propose to do is to try to think through the application of Christian and social work values and practice principles to working with clients regarding evangelism in ways which maintain integrity for both our clients and ourselves.

Not Just an Issue for Christians

The first point I want to make is that this matter of trying to figure out how to have integrity and competence in the handling of our own beliefs and values as we work respectfully and ethically with clients is not just an issue for Christians. Every single one of us comes our work profoundly influenced by assumptions, beliefs, values, and commitments which we hold in part on faith. That is part of what it means to be a human being. Our reason and our science can only take us so far, but they can never take us to the bottom line of values and meaning. "Facts," to the degree that we can ever really discern them, never answer the "so what" question. Values are never derivable from facts alone.

The first level of self-disclosure and informed consent that every social worker owes is critical personal self-awareness. This can be spiritual, religious, ideological, or theoretical—any "meta-narrative" that we use to make sense out of our experience of life. "Hello, my name is David and I'm a Christian." Or, "I'm a Buddhist," "I'm an agnostic," "I'm an atheist," "I'm a logical positivist," "I'm a behaviorist," "I'm a postmodernist." Or a Punk or a Goth or a Democrat or a Republican, for that matter. I'm not saying that we should greet our clients this way, but I am saying that we need to be aware of our beliefs and be self-critical in regard to how they affect our work.

What are my fundamental assumptions, beliefs, and values? How do they affect my practice? The way I interact with my clients? My selection of theories and interpretation of facts? It is not simply a matter of what I believe, but how I believe it, how I handle my beliefs, which in itself comes back around to the nature of my value commitments.

Lawrence Ressler frequently tells the story of his MSW class at Temple University with Jeffrey Galper, who announced at the beginning of the semester, "I am a Marxist, and I teach from a Marxist perspective." I hope this meant that he had achieved this critical personal self-awareness and that his self-disclosure was in the service of facilitating informed consent on the part of his students. The proof of the social work practice pudding, of course, would be in his conscientiousness in not imposing this view on his students, his willingness to permit or even facilitate disagreement. Of course, the more deeply held the beliefs and the greater the disagreement, the more difficult it is to support self-determination. This is true even when self-determination is one of the core values believed in.

So—integrating faith and practice is not just a Christian thing. It is a human thing. Those who don't understand this basic truth are the ones who may pose the greatest risk of all of "imposing their beliefs on others," precisely because they may think that they are not susceptible to the problem (Sherwood, 2000). However, the rest of my comments are going to be addressed primarily to Christians in social work, even though I think the basic principles will apply to those who are not Christians. Many of us may feel tempted to "evangelize" in more way than one.

Addressing Spiritual and Religious Issues with Clients is Not (Necessarily or Normally) Evangelism

"Talking about God" with clients is not necessarily or normally evangelism. This is an important distinction. For too long social workers (secular and otherwise) have tended to "solve" the problem of evangelism by avoiding spirituality and religion and offering a blanket condemnation—"Thou shalt not discuss spiritual and religious issues with clients." If you do, it is automatically presumed that you are "imposing your own values on clients." This happens in spite of overwhelming evidence that issues of meaning and purpose are central in the lives of clients, that spirituality and religion have great importance to many people, and that religiously-based groups, congregations, and organizations are vital sources of support for people (as well as barriers, at times).

Well, sometimes social workers do impose their values (religious, political, or otherwise) on clients and it is an ethical violation when they do. I would stress that it is a violation of Christian ethics as well as social work ethics. But deliberately avoiding spiritual and religious issues is professional incompetence. The presumption has often been that spiritual and religious issues should simply be referred to chaplains or other clergy. In what other important area of life would social workers condone such a policy of withdrawal and referral? How can we say we deal with the whole person-in-environment while ignoring one of the most important dimensions of people's lives (for good or ill)? Or how can we claim competence in dealing with diversity while ignoring or misunderstanding such a fundamental kind of diversity (Sherwood, 1998)?

The short answer is that we can't and shouldn't ignore spiritual and religious issues. The key is that we must do it from a client-focused and client-led perspective. This normally means that we may not ethically engage in evangelism with our clients. Exceptions would typically be when we are practicing in a faith-based context with a clearly identified Christian identity and with clients who clearly express informed consent. Even then, it is not transparently obvious that evangelism would be appropriate. I hope I can make it clear why I say this.

Proclamation versus Demonstration of the Gospel

A perhaps simplistic but none-the-less useful distinction is this: It is always ethical and appropriate to demonstrate the gospel to our clients, but it is seldom ethical to proclaim the gospel to them in our professional role as social workers.

The Bible describes evangelism in the sense of demonstrating or living out the gospel as the calling of every Christian. "Therefore be imitators of God, as beloved children, and live in love, as Christ loved us and gave himself up for us" (Ephesians 5:1-2). "We know love by this, that he laid down his life for us—and we ought to lay down our lives for one another. How does God's love abide in anyone who has the world's goods and sees a brother or sister in need and yet refuses help" (I John 3:16-17).

The profession of social work provides us all with unique opportunities to demonstrate the gospel of Christ—to give to our clients the grace-filled gift of knowing what it feels like to be treated with love and justice, what it feels like to experience caring, grace, forgiveness, trustworthiness, honesty, and fairness, what it feels like to be treated with respect and dignity as a person with God-given value. Often our clients have few opportunities in their lives to be in a respectful, non-exploitive relationship. The power of this experience can be transforming. It can be a form of "pre-evangelism," preparing the soil for the good seed of the gospel proclaimed.

We do not all have the same part to play in God's work in a person's life. The New Testament frequently talks about varieties of gifts among the various parts of the body, and evangelism is one of them (Romans 12:3-8, I Corinthians 12:4-31, Ephesians 4:11-16). "What then is Apollos? What is Paul? Servants through whom you came to believe, as the Lord assigned to each. I planted, Apollos watered, but God gave the growth" (I Corinthians 3:5-6). As Alan Keith-Lucas has said (1985, p. 28):

> Paul said that faith was the gift of the Spirit, which is true, but what we can do as social workers—and we do have a wonderful opportunity to do so—is to show such love and forgivingness that a confused and desperate person can understand the Spirit's message when it comes.
>
> A consideration of the Parable of the Sower may be helpful here. The seed only grows to maturity when there is good ground to receive it. But stony or even shallow ground can be converted to good ground by the addition of nutrients (love) or ploughing (facing reality) or breaking up of clots (getting rid of blocks) and perhaps what social workers can do for the most part is to be tillers of the ground, rather than the Sower, who must in the long run be God Himself. It is true that certain men and women, powerful preachers or prophets, may act, as it were, for God as sowers, but even they have for the most part audiences that have some readiness to listen.

On the other hand, explicit evangelism of clients (proclamation) in professional social work is almost always unethical. Why? What are the values and ethical principles involved?

Values and Practice: The Principle/Practice Pyramid

Christian and social work values largely agree at the level of principles. However, we may disagree on both the foundational assumptions/worldviews which support the principles, the rules/strategies for prioritizing the values principles when they conflict, and the practice implications of the value principles.

It helps me to conceptualize these relationships in the form of a "Principle/Practice Pyramid." The base of the pyramid is formed by our fundamental worldview and faith-based assumptions (religious or not) about the nature of the world, what it means to be a person, the nature of values, and the nature of knowledge.

On top of and growing out of this foundation sits our core values or principles. As a Christian I understand these to be the "exceptionless absolutes" of love and justice. The social work Code of Ethics might say (and Christians would agree) that this includes service, social justice, dignity and worth of the person, importance of human relationships, integrity, and competence.

On top of and growing out of this "principle" layer are the moral rules which guide the application of the principles to various domains of life. These are "deontological" parameters which suggest what we ought to do. Biblical examples would be the Ten Commandments, the Sermon on the Mount, and other Biblical teachings which help us to understand what love and justice require in various spheres of life. In the social work Code of Ethics, these would be the specific standards relating to responsibilities to clients, colleagues, practice settings, as professionals, the profession, and the broader society. These rules can guide us, but they can never provide us with absolute prescriptions for what we should do on the case level.

At the top of the pyramid sit the specific cases in which we are required to use the principles and rules to make professional judgments in the messiness of real life and practice. It is here that we will find ourselves in the most likelihood of conscientious disagreement with each other, even when we start with the same values, principles, and rules. The short answer for why this is true is that we are fallen (subject to the distortions of our selfishness, fear, and pride) and finite (limited in what we can know and predict). And even more vexing, our principles and rules start coming into conflict with each other on this level. It is here that we have to resolve ethical dilemmas in which any actual action we can take is going to advance some of our values (and the rules that go with them) at the expense of some of our other values (and the rules that go with them).

The Use and Limits of the Code of Ethics (and the Bible): Ethical Judgments Are Required Because Legitimate Values Come into Conflict

Ethical analysis and decision making is required when we encounter an ethical problem and at the case level we cannot maximize all values simultaneously. In my paradigm, the definition of an ethical problem or dilemma is that we have more than one legitimate moral obligation that have come into some degree of tension in the case that we find ourselves dealing with.

For example, I believe in client self-determination (one legitimate moral obligation) and I believe in the protection of human life (another legitimate moral obligation). Most of the time these values do not come into conflict. However, now I have a client who is threatening to kill his wife. I now have an ethical problem in which any action I take will compromise one or more of my moral obligations. Values and ethical principles can and do come into conflict on the case level.

It is important to realize from the beginning what the Bible and Code of Ethics can do for us and what they cannot. They can give us critical guidance and direction, but they can never give us prescriptive formulas which will tell us exactly what to do in every case, precisely because in the particular instance not all of the values can be fully achieved and not all of the rules can be completely followed. The Code of Ethics (1999, pp. 1, 2-3) says it very well:

> Core values, and the principles that flow from them, must be balanced within the context and complexity of the human experience… The Code offers a set of values, principles, and standards to guide decision making and conduct when ethical issues arise. It does not provide a set of rules that prescribe how social workers should act in all situations. Specific applications of the Code must take into account the context in which it is being considered and the possibility of conflicts among the Code's values, principles, and standards.

Sometimes one of these biblical rules or Code of Ethics standards may have to give way to another in order for us to come as close to love and justice as the situation allows. At the case level, we are always going to have to take responsibility for making judgments that prioritize our values and approximate the good we seek as closely as we can.

Ethics and Evangelism

So, what are some of the core values and ethical principles from the Bible and the Code of Ethics that relate to evangelism with clients? I'll try to list a few and give some comments, although several of them overlap and interact with each other. And I would say that they all fall under the Biblical absolutes of love and justice.

1. The Great Commission:

Well, what Christians call the "Great Commission" is certainly one of these core values, the reason we are exploring this issue in the first place. While the imperative "Go therefore and make disciples of all nations" (Matthew 28:19) was given to Jesus' original disciples, the New Testament makes it quite clear that bearing testimony to the good news about Jesus' healing and saving work on behalf of humankind is in some sense the responsibility of all of us who are disciples of Jesus Christ. And if the gospel of Christ is true, what could be more important for people to hear? This value is real for us and explains why we struggle with the question of evangelism in our professional roles.

2. *My Calling and Role:*

Remember our discussion above about demonstration and proclamation? While it is true that not only evangelists bear witness to the gospel, it is also true that our particular calling and role in a given situation has a great impact on what it is appropriate for us to do. If you are convinced that your calling from God is evangelism in the sense of direct proclamation, then you should be an evangelist and not a social worker (or a nurse, or a car salesman, or a loan officer). Under what auspice are you working? What are the functions associated with your role? My father-in-law for many years demonstrated the grace and love of Christ in his role as a bank teller at the Potter's Bank and Trust in East Liverpool, Ohio, including taking money out of his own pocket to make sure that certain poor customers were able to get at least a little cash at the end of the month. But he could not, and did not, use his position to hand them tracts with the cash. As a social worker you may at times find it appropriate to share your faith directly, but most of the time you won't.

3. *Self-Determination:*

From the first chapter of Genesis on, the Bible presents a picture of human beings endowed with the gift and responsibility of choice with consequences. We are presented with the paradox and mystery (on our level of understanding) of God's sovereignty and our freedom. God is depicted as calling us, but not coercing us, warning us, but not protecting us. Conscience and commitment cannot be compelled, even though external behavior might be. Self-determination is also a standard of the Code of Ethics (1999, p. 7), growing out of the principle of the inherent dignity and worth of the person. If ever a social work value stood on a theological foundation it is belief in the inherent dignity and worth of every person. While I may have my perceptions of what might be best for my clients, I have no right to compel or manipulate them to that end. I do have a responsibility to help facilitate their ability to exercise their self-determination, including the exploration of available alternatives and their possible consequences, so that their choices are as informed as possible. God grants us the fearful dignity of self-determination; we can hardly try to deny it to our clients, explicitly or implicitly.

4. Informed Consent:

A fundamental component of informed choice is informed consent, another standard of the Code of Ethics (1999, pp. 7-8). Informed consent essentially means that people should know what they are getting into and agree to it. This principle interacts intimately with the next one—integrity. Informed consent is one of the key determinants of whether or not evangelism with clients is ethical. Related concepts are agency auspice and client expectations. Why are clients coming to your agency or to you? What expectations do they have? Is there anything upfront that would lead them to understand that the sharing of your religious beliefs or evangelism would be a likely part of their experience with your agency or you? I have found that even in explicitly faith-based agencies there surprisingly few times when direct evangelism is the appropriate focus or outcome of interaction with clients. Christian clients struggle with the same kinds of issues as other clients. Sometimes we can help them sort through how their beliefs are resources or barriers for them. But sometimes religious clients want to use "religious talk" to avoid coming to grips with their issues. There would be almost no cases in a public or secular private agency when direct evangelism an appropriate focus or outcome of interaction with clients.

5. Integrity:

Honesty and integrity are core Biblical and social work values. A number of "rules" derive from this value, such as truth-telling, trustworthiness, and keeping agreements. Some of the standards in the Code of Ethics deriving from this principle come under the general heading of "Conflicts of Interest' (1999, pp. 9-10). These rules are particularly relevant to the question of engaging in evangelism with clients. These rules say that "Social workers should be alert to and avoid conflicts of interest that interfere with the exercise of professional discretion and impartial judgment" (1999, p. 9). They speak to the importance of setting clear, appropriate, and culturally sensitive boundaries and being careful of dual or multiple relationships with clients. Of particular relevance to the issue of evangelism is the standard that says "Social workers should not take unfair advantage of any professional relationship or exploit others to further their personal, religious, political, or business interests" (1999, p. 9).

So, What about Evangelism?

The main reason that evangelism in the context of a professional social work relationship is normally unethical is that it almost always involves the risk of exploitation of a vulnerable relationship. It usually involves taking advantage of our professional role and relationship with our clients. It lacks the integrity of informed consent. And even when there seems to be a certain consent or even request from the client to go through the evangelistic door, it is the social worker's responsibility to be the boundary keeper. I am not saying that there can never be a legitimate open door under any circumstance, but I am saying that the social worker, acting in the professional capacity, bears a heavy weight of responsibility to avoid taking advantage of the client's vulnerability.

I think most Christians have little difficulty understanding the analogous rule in the Code of Ethics which says that "Social workers should under no circumstances engage in sexual activities or sexual contact with current clients, whether such contact is consensual or forced" (1999, p. 13). We also understand that it is the social worker's responsibility, not the client's, to maintain these boundaries. I hope no one is offended by my comparison of sexual exploitation to evangelism. Clearly there are significant differences. I believe in evangelism and I do not believe in sexual exploitation. However, we also need to understand the way in which evangelism in the context of a professional relationship does have some significant likeness to sexual exploitation, or any other taking advantage of the professional role.

For example, evangelizing a client coming to a public Rape Crisis Center would be unethical and, I would say, un-Christian. She is in a physically and emotionally vulnerable situation, there is nothing about the sign on the door that would lead you to believe that her coming is even giving implied consent to evangelism, and she is trusting you for specific kinds of help. The nature of your role and relationship means that you have a special responsibility not to exploit that role. What you can most certainly do with her is to give her the opportunity to experience what it is like to receive "grace," love and justice; what it is like to experience respect, caring, support, trustworthiness, honesty; what it is like to not be taken advantage of.

It would also probably be going much to far to ask her, "Are you a Christian?" Even if she said no, and you quietly moved on, the question would hang in the air, coming from a representative of the Rape Crisis Center to a person in a state of vulnerability who had a very particular reason for coming to this agency. How would she read that? How would it affect her response?

However, it might be quite competent and ethical professional practice to use a more appropriate probe which could be stated in "non-religious" terms—"This must be hard. Is there anything in your life that helps you get through things like this?" Then if she mentions something about her spiritual or religious beliefs, you are in a position to make a better judgment about how you might help her, even perhaps including engaging spiritual and religious resources. That could be good "spiritually-sensitive" social work practice (Sherwood, 1998).

Even then, you would be faced with the necessity of using good assessment skills, discernment, and judgment. For example, you would think that praying with clients in Christian agencies would be obviously the right thing to do. However, some clients are "religious" manipulators, and consciously or unconsciously use the appearance of spirituality to avoid dealing with hard issues. When a client says, "Let's just pray about that," or "I think we just have to trust the Lord," you have to try to discern whether doing that is helpful or their way of avoiding dealing with their anger, fear, abusive behavior, or whatever else they may need to face.

No Prescriptions, but Guidance

You will have probably noticed that I have avoided words such as "never" or "always" in what I have said. This is quite deliberate, and goes back to my earlier comments about what ethical principles and rules can do for us and what they can't. They can give us meaningful guidance but they can't give us simple formulas to prescribe our response to every situation. Although I might have come close to it, I have not argued that evangelism is never compatible with our professional role as social workers. I have tried to suggest ethical considerations as we try to make our best judgments about how we relate to our clients.

Morally and practically, a sense of certainty is highly attractive. Who doesn't want to be sure that they are "right" and that they are doing the right thing? But that level of certainty is often not available to us as human beings. And yet we do have to decide and act. These judgments always require prioritizing our values based on the best understanding we can achieve at the time regarding the relevant values involved and the potential consequences of the choices available to us.

Ultimately, how we respond in these hard cases has more to do with the moral virtue or character that we have developed, by God's grace and through God's Spirit, than it does with the specific facts and theories we have learned. Lord, help us to be people who hunger and thirst for your "more excellent way" (I Corinthians 12:31).

Note

1 This chapter was first published in 2002 in *Social Work & Christianity*, 29 (1), 1-12. North American Association of Christians in Social Work.

References

Keith-Lucas, A. (1985). *So you want to be a social worker: A primer for the Christian student*. Botsford, CT: North American Association of Christians in Social Work.

NACSW. (1999). *Code of ethics*. Washington, DC: National Association of Social Workers.

Sherwood, D. A. (2000). Pluralism, tolerance, and respect for diversity: Engaging our deepest differences within the bond of civility. *Social Work & Christianity*, 26 (2), 101-111.

Sherwood, D. A. (1998). Spiritual assessment as a normal part of social work practice: Power to help and power to harm. *Social Work & Christianity*, 24 (2), 80-89.

CHAPTER 19

FAITH-BASED INITIATIVES: AN ESSAY ON THE POLITICS OF SOCIAL SERVICE CHANGE

Douglas L. Koopman

The current debate about faith-based delivery of social services is complex. It has a self-identified jargon that touches upon a unique mix of questions about constitutional law, government program evaluation, and political calculation. In this essay I will attempt to provide some clarity and order to these and other issues in the unfolding debate on faith-based initiatives by focusing on the development of the initiatives in the first eighteen months of the George W. Bush Administration.

Introduction

President George W. Bush's faith-based initiative is not one single idea with a narrow objective. It is, in fact, a lengthy list of ideas with one far-reaching goal: to expand the variety of religiously affiliated social services that receive financial help from the federal government (Bush, 2001). There are two major barriers to doing so. First, traditional constitutional interpretations of the First Amendment religion clauses severely restrict permissible financial interactions between government and religious entities (Brownstein, 1999). While traditional interpretations are being loosened by the latest Supreme Court decisions, there is no new agreed-upon principle (Stern, 2001).

The legal uncertainty contributes to the second difficulty in expanding the relationship between government and faith-based groups, that is, current administrative practices of most federal agencies. The federal government's contracting process is largely closed to intensely religious service providers, especially those not in the traditional form of a non-profit organization with tax-exempt status. Sometimes intensely religious groups are directly and intentionally prohibited, and sometimes indirectly and unintentionally (White House, 2001). One major goal of the Bush Administration, through its White House Office of Faith-Based and Community Initiatives (WHOFBCI) and satellite offices in key agencies, was to identify and loosen these barriers (Tenpas, 2002). In the first year and one-half, however, the Administration was constrained in these efforts by administrative inertia and public controversy.

Elements of the President's faith-based initiative address each of these two difficulties. One group of ideas within the initiative aims to bring religion more fully into the public square, with a legislative proposal called "Charitable Choice" as its main feature. As described by its proponents, this first set of faith-based initiatives is dedicated to ending government discrimination against certain types of faith-based social service providers while simultaneously protecting the religious integrity of these institutions. Passing a comprehensive Charitable Choice provision would, in this view, restore the proper but long abandoned constitutional reading of the First Amendment's free exercise and establishment clauses (Esbeck, 1999; 2001).

The second portion of the faith-based initiative seeks, in the eyes of its supporters, to elevate all types of faith-based social service providers to competitive equality with established providers in securing government funding for social services. This second set of faith-based initiatives would provide government money for technical advice to faith-based providers, and offer tax incentives, liability reform, and administrative relief to smaller, newer, and volunteer-intensive groups—provider categories full of faith-based entities. Its advocates claim that this set of initiatives would level the playing field between current federal contractors, and those who are not, but ought to be, "players" in the government's social services network (White House, 2001).

President Bush has described these two combined sets of proposals as his faith-based initiative, offering them as a package in the very first days of his Administration. Yet he and his congressional supporters experienced great difficulty controlling the legislative process, and moving these proposals through it.

Faith-based initiative supporters have been frustrated by two assumptions opponents have made about their efforts, and the power of these assumptions in today's policy making environment. The first assumption is that robust religion is dangerous in the public square. According to this view, to the extent that the President's faith-based initiative gives greater government respect to and support for religion, it ought to be opposed. From this perspective, religion is by nature, or at least nearly always in practice, intolerant, coercive, and imperialistic. Religion, from this view, operates as an exclusivist ideology that has no place in America's secular and tolerant public arena. Whether such charges are true or not, thinking about faith-based initiatives as a question of government's official relationship to religiously motivated expression helps clarify a number of issues relevant to the present social welfare policy debate.

The second assumption that supporters have discovered they must counter is the view that social services mixed with strong doses of religion are inferior to secular social services. According to this portion of the faith-based opposition, intensely faith-based social services are likely to be unscientific, ineffective, and unprofessional. To preserve the quality of social services generally and especially those funded by government, this argument also urges against the President's initiative. Again, whether such charges are true or not, examining the effectiveness question illuminates another set of important issues in the faith-based debate.

Each of the two separate controversies is about legitimacy—religion's legitimacy in the public square and faith-based social services' legitimacy in meeting human needs. Each brings its own jargon, lines of argument, and political questions. The two controversies together provide a reasonably full picture of what is at issue in the debate about faith-based initiatives.

The legislative path of the faith-based initiative in 2001 and early 2002 was influenced by these two questions. Interestingly, the January to August 2001 debate in the U.S. House of Representatives on its faith-based bill was dominated by "public square concerns" (Nather, 2001; Nitschke, 2001; Cummings & VandeHei, 2001). For partisan and institutional reasons, the House's consideration of the faith-based bill left that question largely unresolved. Senate actions, formally commencing only after the House finished its work, centered on the second issue of efficacy. In general terms, the Senate made slow but steady progress on faith-based matters, but in quite a different direction than the House (Bumiller, 2002).

This chapter on the social policy aspects of the faith-based initiative has four parts. Part one presents a brief summary of how the federal government's social welfare policy has developed in recent decades, with faith-based initiatives as the most recent part of an ongoing story of continuous change. Part two analyzes the faith-based initiative debate from the perspective of increasing the role of religion in the public square. Part three analyzes the issue from the questions of efficacy and efficiency in social service provision. The final portion of this chapter comments on the faith-based initiative in a broader political context.

How We Got Here: The Politics of Recent Social Service Delivery Reform

The federal government provides funds and many other incentives for social service delivery. Many of the services it supports are targeted toward people with low incomes—means tested programs in which eligibility is determined on an economic basis. The federal government also encourages additional social services such as mental health, drug treatment, crime prevention, and education, for wider populations beyond the poor. Many of these social services in practice are provided to predominately poor populations, where socially corrosive behaviors occur with greater incidence. Acknowledging the risk of oversimplified labeling, this paper uses the terms "human services," "social services," and "social service programs," to refer to programs that are either means-tested or predominately serve lower income populations.

A Brief Historical Sketch[1]

Religious organizations have operated human service programs throughout U.S. history. Caring for one's neighbor has been seen as a religious act and obligation, and churches or religiously inspired voluntary organizations responded. As problems of industrialization, mass immigration, and racial tension became more complex in the late nineteenth century and throughout the twentieth century, religious groups responded with more complex and durable organizations to address these needs. But fighting alone, or nearly alone, was a losing battle. In the early and mid-twentieth century industrialization and economic depression increased the frequency and intensity of requests from religious organizations that government assist them in human service tasks deemed too large and complex to be addressed solely by private efforts.

Some local and state governments moved earlier, but the federal government did not formally get involved in welfare programs until the Great Depression. The 1935 Social Security Act established the federal Aid to Dependent Children program, which gave states matching federal funds to "assist, broaden and supervise existing mothers' aid programs." The middle decades of this century saw a marked expansion of government-funded social welfare programs, with thousands of workers and billions of dollars devoted to the cause. As government assistance grew, religious efforts were by no means reduced. Old problems were never solved, and new issues were always emerging.

The late 1950s brought the civil rights movement and growing national awareness of poverty in the South, Appalachia, and industrial cities across the United States. Pressure built to bring government social services to a broader and higher level. In response, President Johnson in his 1964 State of the Union address declared an "unconditional war on poverty." New federal social service programs such as Job Corps, Head Start, and Medicaid followed. A constantly improving economic climate and growing spending by these and other federal programs reduced the poverty rate significantly throughout the remainder of the 1960s, and kept it fairly level through the mid-1970s. Much was accomplished beyond reducing the incidence of poverty; social problems among some target populations, especially the elderly, declined. Religious groups and government were often partners, formally and informally, in these Great Society efforts. But because the focus was on the new and growing federal role, the longstanding role of churches and other religious organizations was largely overlooked in the literature and in public debates.

The religious element of social service delivery was still large, and differences among religious groups were becoming more apparent. Those religious organizations that did partner with government were of a particular stripe; those that did not were of another. The politics of most of the religious partners tended to be liberal and their theology ecumenical and humanitarian. The political perspective had the effect of making such groups more willing to be junior partners to the government in providing services supported by government dollars. The theological perspective made these private partners more willing to downplay the religious content of their programs to meet concerns of government administrators about sectarianism and coercion. They established non-sectarian and even non-religious governing boards, applied for and received 501c3 tax exempt status, partnered with secular non-profits and all levels of government, and became more sophisticated organizationally and more directly involved politically. Many such groups are long established and have years of experience dealing with government programs.

More theologically conservative and evangelical groups continued to provide services that mixed social services with religious messages. Many of them became joint church efforts or parachurch organizations, but generally did not seek government funds nor arrange their management and staff to meet the expectations of such funders. These groups tended to be smaller, more recently established, more independent from each other, and often existed only informally, rather than formally, separate from a sponsoring church. In some cases intensely and overtly religious groups may have received direct support from government, which may have ignored religious content or affiliations of programs as long as social services were provided to targeted groups.

Just as Great Society programs became established in the early 1970s, large changes in the political environment came to threaten them. The energy crisis and the dual wars on poverty and in Vietnam stalled the post-WWII economic boom, sharply limiting the natural rise in federal revenues that were partially spent on anti-poverty programs. Good manufacturing jobs became scarce as competition from the rebuilt economies of Japan and Western Europe increased. As the peak events of the civil rights movement faded into history, there was a growing indifference to the rights and social situation of minorities. Stories of waste in government social service programs accumulated, eroding public support. The progress against poverty and other negative social indicators had stalled, if not reversed, by the late 1970s.

In this new environment, there arose three distinct but related criticisms of federally supported social services. First, critics charged that the federally directed War on Poverty was excessively detailed and restrictive. National control, they said, stifled the creativity, knowledge, adaptability, and participation that locally run programs provided. They argued that the federal government should pull back to release the energies of others. Second, some claimed that federal spending on social services was simply too high, given tight federal revenues and the unique obligations of the central government for national defense and international affairs. They argued that the federal government could simply not afford to fund social services; state and local governments and the nongovernmental sector would have to carry a larger burden. Third, it became common to argue that the stalled improvement of social indicators implied that the root cause of poverty was more moral than economic. Spending more money, at least in the same places with the same programs, simply would not do any good; permanent and self-directed behavioral change on the part of the poor and needy was required.

Waves of Change

These criticisms have had their effects on federal social service policy in the intervening twenty-five years. Social service spending as a share of the federal budget has declined and federal policy has called for increased responsibility by other actors—state and local governments, nonprofit organizations, and program recipients themselves—to do more to address social needs.

Changes have come in three successive waves, each with a slightly different emphasis. The major impact of the Reagan Administration in the early 1980s, the first wave of policy change, was to simply reduce the federal share of social service spending. A few policy makers generated some public discussion about increasing state and local flexibility in managing federally supported programs as an alternative or supplement to cuts, but at least in the first few years little flexibility was provided. And no additional aid to specifically religious service providers was urged. However, faith-based social service organizations were often touted as effective service providers that could take up any slack in services due to government cuts.

The next wave of federal social service reform emphasized increased state and local flexibility in social services. In the mid-1980s and beyond the federal government began to solicit from states and grant to them waivers of administrative rules and client eligibility guidelines so that they and their subdivisions could experiment with innovative economic and behavioral incentives. This federal deregulation of social services greatly increased the incidence of state and local governments contracting with and/or purchasing services from private, mostly non-profit, agencies. This devolution has meant that state and local governments have taken increased management responsibility for social welfare, and private organizations have increasingly delivered social services under government contracts and other arrangements, as a sort of government-by-proxy.

The Republican-led debate over faith-based social services is one clear indicator that we are now in a third wave of reform, which began rather inauspiciously with the passage of the 1996 welfare reform law. Since 1996, the federal government has stopped trying to cut federal welfare funds, a modest but real change in the dynamics of social welfare policy. This is the first important characteristic of this third wave of change. In addition, a little noticed "Charitable Choice" provision was attached to the 1996 law, prohibiting discrimination against religious providers in making contracting arrangements for the welfare programs reauthorized under this particular law (Segal, 1999). Generally, Charitable Choice language clarified that it is constitutional to provide direct government support to at least the non-religious elements of social service programs provided by even quite intensely and vocally religious providers, including individual churches with service programs. This openly declared policy to be more welcoming to a diversity of religious groups that represent a wide range organizationally and confessionally, is the other key characteristic of today's reform wave.

Bush's faith-based initiative exemplifies both key elements of the third wave of reform. His major push is to expand the marketplace of providers that bid for government-funded social service contracts, and to eventually expand the pool of covered programs to nearly every federally funded social program. The Bush Administration, partly after the example and partly at the urging of innovative states, wants this market to be less dominated by large government-directed, secular, and nominally religious providers, and more open to smaller, community-based, and more intensely and overtly religious providers. Supporters claim that what is needed is a level playing field on which all providers compete. Opponents attack the potential disruption and dangerous competition these changes would bring. While the Bush Administration has promised no additional program funds in a more competitive market, one of its central arguments is that a better provider marketplace will lead to more effective and efficient social services, thus serving more people in need at any given spending level (Bush, 2001).

There are many complex political dynamics surrounding these waves of change. In its efforts on behalf of the faith-based initiative, the Bush Administration was frustrated by many of these complexities, which slowed its progress in seeking reforms. For interested observers, seeing clearly the importance of the faith-based initiative requires one to independently think through its implications about religion in the public square and the religious dimensions of social service delivery.

Religion in the Public Square: Unconstitutional and Dangerous?

The public square debate about the faith-based initiative involves two related but separate questions. The first question is whether the additional government support to religion that has been proposed by the faith-based initiative is constitutional, conforming to First Amendment establishment clause interpretation.[2] A second question, related but distinct, is whether religion is too dangerous to be more openly expressed in political debates.

No Establishment of Religion[3]

The First Amendment's establishment clause is essential to the understanding of religious freedom in the United States. Many people came to the New World to escape religious persecution because they practiced a minority religion at odds with the officially supported religion of their native land. The Framers placed the establishment clause in the Constitution to protect similar religious minorities that might develop in the United States. At the very least, the establishment clause intends to prevent the federal government from supporting a particular religion through its laws and subsidies. The establishment clause later was interpreted to prohibit state and local governments from advancing particular religions.

Over the past fifty years the establishment clause has taken on new and even more expansive meaning. In the 1947 *Everson v. Walls* decision, the Supreme Court decided that the establishment clause had built a high "wall of separation" between church and state, borrowing a phrase from a letter by Thomas Jefferson expressing his personal opinion about the proper relationship. "No establishment" after *Everson* meant more than not supporting a particular religion; it now barred any action that established, or even touched upon, religion generically. In the past few years the Supreme Court has lowered somewhat *Everson*'s high wall, but that extra-constitutional and increasingly anachronistic phrase still guides many legal and political discussions.

After *Everson*, the Supreme Court gradually created two different meanings of the term separation, each of which it applies in different contexts and sometimes in ways that appear inconsistent. One meaning is *strict separation*—that law and government should not touch religion in any way. This definition is prevalent in cases that prohibited organized prayer in public schools, prayer led by public school teachers or other public officials, and on-campus released-time or after-school programs for religious activities. At other times, the Court has advanced another definition of separation, which it terms *neutrality*. Neutrality means that it might be possible under some situations for religion generally to benefit from a law or government action. Some examples of neutrality rulings include allowing property tax exemptions for churches, or allowing the Bible to be read in public schools as long as it is taught as literature.

The neutrality definition has been employed more frequently and over a broader range of programs, especially in recent years. However, this does not mean the Court has made it easier to predict its rulings. The so-called *Lemon* test, derived from the 1971 *Lemon v. Kurtzman* decision, provides a means to look at the Court's decisions. In *Lemon*, a majority of the Court held that government involvement in religion might be acceptable provided the program in question met three tests. First, the government must have a *secular purpose*, not a religious one, in whatever program or policy is challenged. Second, the program must *neither advance nor inhibit religion*, either a specific religion or religion in general. Third, the operation of the program must not create an *excessive entanglement* between government and religion. If the challenged government program or policy met all three criteria, it was constitutional. If it failed even one prong of the test, the Court would strike it down as unconstitutionally establishing religion.

The *Lemon* test is relatively clear on paper, yet devising rules from later applications of the test is not. Courts rule on particular cases that have unique sets of facts and circumstances. While courts articulate broader principles into which these unique cases supposedly fit, it is sometimes difficult to discern a consistent logic to court decisions in complex areas. Church-state cases are one such area. The Supreme Court has said that Congress can hire chaplains who open with prayer each day it is in session, yet public school teachers cannot begin their classes with prayers or with even a moment of silence if prayer is listed as one of the options for students to spend that quiet time. Public school professionals can come to church-related schools to administer diagnostic hearing and eyesight tests to such students, but if they find a problem they must provide therapy off private school grounds. Children in church-related schools can ride a public school bus to and from their school, but not the same bus on a field trip. A public school district can lend a religious school its textbooks on U.S. history with a picture of Abraham Lincoln on its cover. It cannot, however, lend the same picture, by itself, to the same school.

It is not too misleading to give some order to the Court's post-*Lemon* decisions by dividing the rulings into three categories: one, those that are about government support to individuals who then use the funds on their own; two, those that are about direct government support for religions institutions; and, three, those that are about supporting clearly religious activities.

In the first category, the court has been willing to allow many things that support religion, if such support flows first to individuals who then choose to use those funds for services offered by religious providers. For example, federally supported childcare in the form of vouchers to parents can be used at intensely religious day care centers in churches run by church employees. The Court believes that these vouchers are grants to parents and children, not to churches. Similar logic allows tuition tax credits and federal educational grants and loans for parents who send their children to religious colleges.

The second category, direct support for programs operated by religious institutions, is less clear. Sometimes the Court allows government to directly support religious institutions such as hospitals and religious liberal arts colleges. Other times it does not; for example it rarely permits the direct support of religious elementary schools. In general, the younger the beneficiary of a questioned program and the more educational (as opposed to material) the assistance, the less likely the court is to allow it. For example, direct support to a Christian elementary school is at this time clearly unconstitutional, but direct support for church-sponsored housing for the elderly may well be considered constitutional. There is, apparently, two "sliding scales," which are used to examine programs based on beneficiary age and program content. Younger recipients are more likely to be influenced by religious messages that older persons can filter out, so programs for the young are treated more skeptically. Intangible benefits such as education or counseling are more likely to carry religious content than more tangible benefits such as housing, health care, and clothing, so schools are treated more skeptically than food banks.

The third prong of the `*Lemon* test, the "excessive entanglement" clause has until recently been an automatic disqualifier for direct aid to what the Court has called "pervasively sectarian" institutions. Until recently, a Court majority would automatically disqualify these pervasively sectarian institutions—a term the justices often used but never clearly defined—because, even if such intensely and vocally religious organizations *could* run a government-funded program in a sufficiently secular manner, the administering government agency would have to monitor the program and organization so closely that such oversight would amount to excessive entanglement.

In the third category of directly supporting religious expression, the Court is almost never willing to permit government support for clearly and directly religious activities such as posting the Ten Commandments in government buildings, allowing devotional Bible reading in public schools, or printing prayers at government expense. The rare exceptions are when the Court determines that the religious content of the activity in question has been so diluted that it is merely a cultural habit or public convenience.

Faith-based social services are thrust in the thick of establishment controversies because the faith element of these services comes in such great variety. First, "faith-based" can refer to the location of the social service, such as a church, a religious school, or an office building owned by a religious organization. A religious location in itself has no effect on program content, but such services are sometimes prohibited by federal regulation from receiving government funds (White House, 2001).

Second, the faith element can be tied to employees or managers of a social agency. Services may be provided by members of a religious order, for example, or by the hired clergy or staff of a local church. The management or governing board of a service agency may include members of a particular faith tradition, while the professional staff with direct contact with clients may be chosen entirely independent of religious affiliation. Such providers may also be categorically prohibited by regulation from receiving government funds, without regard to the content of the program.

Third, volunteers assisting a government-funded agency may come chiefly or exclusively from religious groups. Nuns may volunteer at a government-funded hospice; church members may tutor in an after-school program for public school students. No government funds may go to these volunteers, avoiding one major criterion the court usually looks at in determining the constitutionality of such arrangements, but the program may be deemed ineligible for government support.

Finally, religion may become an integral part of a treatment program. Clients may be encouraged to make religious commitments as part of their recovery from drug or alcohol addiction. Prayer before meals may be required to receive food at a soup kitchen. Memorization of Bible passages about the use of money may be part of a financial management seminar. Only this set of situations, the direct mixing of religious messages with programs, is of doubtful constitutionality to today's Supreme Court. And for some of the Court's members, even many of these programs might be eligible for direct government funds under certain circumstances.

A universally applied "Charitable Choice" provision would allow all types of faith-based organizations to operate all types of programs with federal funds. Some organizations might find compliance with a particular program very easy; other organizations and programs might be more problematic. In all contracts, however, the government would tend to assume funding guidelines were followed, rather than assuming they cannot be, as is often the case today.

Additional Complications

There are at least three more complicating judicial factors related to faith-based initiatives. First, in the Court rulings there are many apparent inconsistencies. While a general rule for what is and is not constitutional can be devised, there are exceptions. For example, Head Start, a federally supported educational program for pre-school age children, may be housed in churches.

Second, actual practice does not always follow constitutional guidelines. There appear to be many longstanding practices at variance with explicit court decisions and operating rules. Some government administrators unnecessarily prohibit certain organizational arrangements, while others probably knowingly allow religious practices in funded programs (White House, 2001; Monsma, 1996). Complex partnerships among all types of providers also exist, and the line between government and private funds may not be clear, even to the staff and managers of the groups involved.

Third, the Supreme Court changes its views on these issues, as current members revise their thinking and, especially, as replacements to the Court are named. While the Charitable Choice portion of President Bush's faith-based initiative would probably be supported by a majority of the Supreme Court as of this writing, in a different place and time it could face a less favorable fate.

Religion as Dangerous

The constitutional questions about advancing religion are only one part of the public square controversy. Proponents of faith-based initiatives still have to deal with politically powerful impressions about how religion tends to operate in politics.

An effective democracy requires that participants in political debates abide by certain rules of engagement. Civility toward opponents is essential. Disagreement in democracy is appropriate and inevitable, but one should fairly describe the positions of opponents, and debate issues in thoughtful engagement rather than attacking personalities in ad hominem rhetoric. Another requirement for democratic deliberation is that all contestants in the public square be fundamentally committed to pluralistic viewpoints. That is, one should argue for many voices in the debate not only while one is in the minority and without power, but also when one is in the majority, alone or in a coalition, and able to stifle opposition.

Some religious elements in the United States have been accused of lacking civility, pluralistic commitment, or both, and thus unfit to enter public debates. Favorite whipping posts, rightly or wrongly, have been politically conservative evangelical Protestant leaders such as Pat Robertson and Jerry Falwell, and other politically active evangelical Protestant Christian leaders generally. Because members of such groups have been increasingly loyal to the Republican Party, it has become common to equate the motives, positions, and policies of Republican politicians with politically conservative evangelical Protestants.

Because President George W. Bush is Republican and a highly religious Protestant , many commentators assumed that his faith-based initiative was targeted to help, and was fully supported by, such religious leaders. This assumption continued despite these leaders' early ambivalence about the proposal. Falwell, Robertson, and other politically conservative evangelical leaders such as commentator Marvin Olasky and Richard Land of the Southern Baptist Convention expressed strong reservations over elements of the President's plan (Goodstein, 2001; Edsall, 2001; BeliefNet, 2001). And research suggests that the strongest interest in the faith-based initiative is not coming from white conservative churches in the suburbs. Rather, African-American and theologically liberal churches express the most interest, and they are far more closely tied to the Democratic Party and liberal politics (Chaves, 1999; Pew Research Center, 2001).

These nuances between the faith-based initiative and politically relevant religious constituencies were largely lost in public debates. Comments by the traditionally Republican-linked religious leaders that seemed uncivil and intolerant impeded the faith-based initiative. Such comments also advanced the opponents' more fundamental proposition that religious leaders and religiously based arguments do not belong in the public square. These public square issues dominated discussion of the president's faith-based initiative during its development and eventual passage in the House of Representatives. But, while these issues were central in those critical early months of the Bush Administration, their airing did not lead to their resolution. The tactical mistakes of politically conservative evangelical leaders, both supporters and opponents of President's initiative, tarnished their image and hurt the proposal. But the short-term goal to move the bill through the House still was achieved. The Republican majority there could push through the legislation without compromising or waiting for broader support. It controlled the procedures and the content of the bill, and President Bush could call on party and personal loyalty to convince Republican doubters to at least move the bill along.

Are Faith-based Social Services Second Rate?

The unresolved public square argument became a secondary issue almost as soon as the bill passed the House. The Senate is usually less partisan than the House, and party loyalty is much harder to enforce among Senators. A close party division in the Senate demanded a bipartisan approach for any significant bill to become law. The two Senate faith-based initiative leaders, Republican Rick Santorum of Pennsylvania and Democrat Joseph Lieberman of Connecticut, were suitable choices to push legislation through such a Senate. While a proponent of strong and broad Charitable Choice language, Senator Santorum was flexible on the content of a faith-based bill as long as one would become law. While a strong Democrat, Senator Lieberman appreciated the constructive role that religion usually plays in individual lives and public debates. These two senators were willing to work together and with others inside and outside the Senate to produce legislation that had broad support, more favorably treated intensely and vocally religious social service providers compared to previous law, and addressed some systemic problems in how the federal government managed and delivered social services.

The issue of effectiveness also appealed to both proponents and opponents of the faith-based initiative. Proponents were assured that faith-based programs were more effective; although they resisted the delays implied by gathering more research results, they were confident of the final outcome of the effectiveness debate. Opponents hoped to fight the widespread but incompletely documented impression that faith-based services were more effective. They hoped that existing research already showed, or new research would show, clear advantages of secular services. For all these reasons, the Senate focused on the effectiveness and "level playing field" questions.

Grant-Making Realities

On first impression the effectiveness debate leads to more objective questions and less contestable answers than the public square debate. How effective are federally funded social service programs? Would effectiveness improve with increased competition among providers? Would more people be served? Are the new providers that would be allowed to bid for service provision if a faith-based bill becomes law as good as the current providers? If so, let them in; if not, keep them out.

But the reality of federally funded social services is not that simple. In an ideal world, federal government agencies would fund the most effective social service providers in each program, in a simple and straightforward process. The government would identify an area of need or inadequacy on which it desires to spend money, and then specify the desired outcome to be purchased for the government funds that are spent. In a logical and consistent manner, government agencies would solicit bids from all eligible organizations, and then distribute funds for a few years to those that promised to most efficiently achieve desired outcomes. Under initial contracts the government would evaluate performance, would gather sufficient information to make sound judgments, and then would grant or deny additional contracts in a new competitive round.

This ideal process is not, of course, how government works. Although the federal government has mechanisms to ensure that awarded funds are used for the designated purposes and without fraudulent diversion, it has accumulated little evidence that the grants it provides make a significant positive difference in outcomes. In fact, the federal government has little idea of the actual effect of the billions of social service dollars it spends directly or sends to state and local governments (White House, 2001). A small number of organizations perennially win large federal grants, with the same few providers in each program listed year after year as major grant recipients. Many of these grants are routinely re-granted to the same organization time and again.

Rules are modified by Congress and administrators, often with the help of interest groups involved in operating the programs. As they help Congress to rewrite laws and help administrators revise procedures, these interest groups naturally are working to ensure that their organizations will continue receiving funds. So they typically ask for revisions that qualify their agencies but exclude others. One would naturally expect legislative and administrative revisions to become increasingly non-competitive and based on experience, not effectiveness.

Measuring Effectiveness

Some critics of opening federal contracting to faith-based organizations complain that there is little proof that these organizations are effective or have the capacity to manage large-scale social service programs. There is some truth to that charge, but it is also true that the federal government routinely awards contracts to organizations whose own efficacy and cost-effectiveness have not been validated. In fact, effectiveness measurement, or "outcomes measurement" as it is more frequently labeled, is relatively new even in the most current social service fields. Private foundations, umbrella service networks, and some usually larger free-standing social service providers have worked to make reliable outcomes measurement a part of program delivery and evaluation (Independent Sector, 2001; United Way of America, 1998). Many of these same groups have undertaken significant outreach initiatives to expand the development and use of outcomes measurement by providers, and to help private foundations and other funders and evaluators use these more reliable and relevant measures in program evaluations.

But the growth of outcomes measurement in the non-governmental sector has almost entirely failed to influence the federal government. Government oversight, evaluation, or funding decisions rarely use measurements of effectiveness, despite laws like the 1993 Government Performance and Results Act that demand such action. Most government agencies use indirect measures—such as organizational licensing, professional credentialing and education, professional peer review, and extensive record keeping of inputs and outputs (data such as persons contacted, contact hours per person, meetings held, dollars spent). Critics contend that the widespread use of these indirect measures is not because of their validity, but rather because they serve to reinforce current funding arrangements and traditional treatment regimens, regardless of their effectiveness and sometimes in the face of increasing evidence of their ineffectiveness.

The growing awareness that little is known about the effectiveness of federally supported social services influenced the Senate debate. The Senate has already passed, and the pending faith-based bill also includes, "compassionate capital" funds, aimed at developing better evaluation measures in relevant social service programs by leveling the playing field and targeting more aid and attention to small and faith-based programs.

Another measurement issue is correctly categorizing the players under the faith-based initiative. The Charitable Choice language in welfare reform has been in effect more than five years, and data is being gathered about the numbers and characteristics of new entrants (Sherman, 2000; 2002). But many social service providers that called themselves "faith-based" had previously been eligible for direct government contracts for welfare programs, and many similar organizations run other programs with federal help. Even if one wanted to compare faith-based programs generally with secular programs, it is no easy task to conceptualize and then develop measurable indicators of faith. It is all the more difficult to identify and study the appropriate range of groups that are being discussed in the debates over President Bush's proposals.

Recent Consideration

Interested parties working on the faith-based issue since the Senate started its process have made some progress in addressing these controversies and understanding their complexity. A large working group representing the range of interests working for and against the faith-based initiative devised a five-fold typology of faith-based groups, ranging from "faith-saturated" to "secular," illustrating the ambiguity of the faith-based term itself. They also noted that the "faith factor" is actually many factors—it can refer to location of the program in a religious setting, the personnel, such as a board of directors, management, staff, or clients, its history or founding by a religious group, its source of financial support, and its program content. A particular agency may have none, one, few, or all of these "faith factors." Program content is the key relevant factor affecting eligibility for government aid. Most types of groups should already be eligible for direct federal funds. Others, except for most of those with faith-saturated content, would be helped by many elements of the faith-based initiative. Charitable Choice language directly helps the most intensely and vocally religious providers, which this categorization called "faith-saturated" and "faith-centered" (Search for Common Ground, 2002).

Some points of agreement about faith-based groups, however they might be defined, are starting to develop (Search for Common Ground, 2002; Johnson, 2002). Faith-based groups have historically provided aid in areas of need not covered (at least at the time) by government programs, and this is commendable. Faith-based providers actively addressed the homelessness of the late 1970s and early 1980s. In the early years of the AIDS epidemic, faith-based providers sometimes seemed to be the only willing agents to provide support services. Faith-based groups frequently are involved in services where recovery is not expected. In such instances, such as hospice care or custodial care of the mentally impaired, traditional evaluation measures such as cost effectiveness may be inappropriate. Outcomes such as extended life span or life quality for a client are desirable outcomes, but they may come with higher financial costs. And many local congregations have historically helped to meet immediate short-term needs to congregants and community members by providing services for which there are no government programs. Other frequently cited faith-based advantages are that they may have broader access than other providers to financial and volunteer support networks, and deeper commitments by professional and volunteer staff. (Search for Common Ground, 2002).

There is a developing consensus among professionals that high levels of religious involvement in individuals are associated with positive physical and emotional health factors. And religious involvement is also positively correlated with helpful social behaviors. There is also basic, preliminary, but almost uniformly positive evidence supporting the notion that faith-based organizations are more effective in providing various social services, especially to "niche" populations identified by race, infirmity, or religious belief (Johnson, 2002). At this stage, the evidence on faith-based effectiveness is a question of whether the early positive correlations are valid, not whether the correlation is positive or negative.

The Broader Political Context

The public square and effectiveness debates dominate the policy discussion of faith-based initiatives. The future direction of legislation encouraging faith-based social services depends in part on how these debates proceed. While the above discussion addressed the most important questions involved in this debate, a few other matters are worth noting.

One important issue raised by some faith-based supporters is whether the effectiveness question is even a fair one at this point. Few federally supported social service programs or organizations have to meet effectiveness criteria now, much less before they were first allowed to apply. Why should prospective grant recipients have to meet criteria that do not apply to current recipients, just to become eligible to compete with them? Abstractly, this is a good argument. Evaluation should come after a relationship with government is established. But in the actual policy making world, advocates for intensely and vocally religious organizations must make a strong case for their view if they expect policy makers to take the time and risk to change current arrangements.

Another interesting issue in this debate is the lack of clarity and agreed upon definitions of key terms. "Charitable Choice" officially refers to the "choice" that a beneficiary of a federal program should have to choose either secular or faith-based groups to address his or her relevant need. For a time, some supporters tried to substitute the more accurate term "beneficiary choice" for Charitable Choice. By that time, however, the debate had been ongoing among elites for so long that the original term was established in the jargon. Interestingly, the free choice of beneficiaries has had very little political clout in a debate dominated by politicians and service provider elites. And the central term "faith-based" has ballooned in usage, both within this debate and more commonly in the public arena, with probably less precision attached to it than ever.

Third, the religious community is divided on the initiative. Not all deeply religious faith traditions or social service organizations support it. Many intensely and vocally religious opponents argue that the robust nature of religion in the United States is because of, not in spite of, government's official distance from and indifference to it. Our nation has, as it were, a "free market" in religion which government neither promotes nor inhibits. That free market has allowed different religious traditions, and religion in general, to appeal directly to deeply felt human needs. Religion and religions rise or fall based at least in part upon their ability to meet human needs, not on their political connections. The fear of its religious opponents is that the faith-based initiative's more direct government support for religion generally and its close oversight of programs would sap faith of its power. Others on the other side of the issue assert that all persons and systems reflect worldviews that operate as religions. To them, the government now has effectively established secularism as a faith with a preferred power position over all traditional faiths. In their view, enactment of the full range of faith-based initiatives will "disestablish" secularism and achieve true non-discrimination between it and the full range of traditional faiths.

The faith-based initiatives debate is also one with fairly cold and calculated political dimensions. Neither major political party is the obvious majority party today. The major parties are looking to keep old constituencies that may be slipping, and attracting new constituencies to expand their electoral base. Republicans see the faith-based initiative as helping to shore up their base and attract new constituencies. Some, but not many, Democrats believe the faith-based issue is helping their party, too, by bringing the party closer to the cultural mainstream.

Policymaking is a complex process. It often combines fairly straightforward analysis of predominantly empirical questions, profound and controversial views about bedrock issues such as constitutional interpretation and the meaning of religion, cold calculations about political power, and the impact of uncontrolled and uncontrollable events. The faith-based initiative debate reflects all of these factors. Ironically, the Senate debate, through its attention to the prosaic concerns of outcomes and effectiveness, did more than the House debate to advance the legitimacy of religion in the public square.

Religious social service professionals and political observers should find the faith-based debate interesting. Most would probably appreciate a greater role for religion in the public square, and believe in the intellectual respectability and clinical effectiveness of faith-based approaches. But the political dynamics are complex. There are good grounds for persons of deep faith to support faith-based initiatives, and some reasonable grounds to oppose it. Deeper issues of public debate are also raised. Our individualistic society does not have a language of group rights that addresses religious identity and is not captured by political extremes. No matter one's particular views or political position, the issues surrounding faith-based initiatives raise interesting and important controversies for those who seek to combine deep religious commitment with contemporary politics and effective social welfare policy.

Notes

1 This portion of the paper is my own interpretation and summary of a variety of sources, including Cnaan, 1999; Koch, 2000; Monsma, 1996; Nather, 2001a; Olasky, 1992; Schaefer, 1999; Skocpol, 2000; & Wineburg, 2001.

2 The First Amendment states, in part, that "Congress shall make no law respecting an establishment of religion, nor prohibiting the free exercise thereof." As such, much constitutional debate about religion has been about "free exercise" and "establishment," and whether the two phrases are complementary, in conflict, or even directly contradictory. Questions of government support for faith-based groups have generally focused on whether it might violate the establishment clause.

3 This portion of the paper is my own interpretation and summary of Esbeck, 2001a; Guliuzza, 2001; Laycock, 2001; & Stern, 2001.

References

BeliefNet. (2001). Leading religious conservatives criticize President Bush's faith-based initiative. <http//:www.*BeliefNet.com*> Retrieved from Yahoo News Service, March 7, 2001.

Brownstein, A. (1999). Constitutional questions about charitable choice. In D. Davis & B. Hankins (Eds.) *Welfare reform and faith-based organizations* (219-265). Waco, TX: Baylor University Press.

Bummiler, E. (2001). Accord reached on charity aid bill after Bush gives in on hiring. *New York Times*, February 8. A19.

Bush, G. W. (2001) *Rallying the armies of compassion.* White House Office of Faith-Based and Community Initiatives. Washington, D.C.

Chaves, M. (1999). Religious congregations and welfare reform: Who will take advantage of 'charitable choice'? *American Sociological Review*, 64(6), 836-846.

Cnaan, R. (1999). The challenge of devolution and the promise of religious-based social services: An introduction. In R. Cnaan, S. Boddie, & B. Wineburg (Eds.) *The newer deal*. New York: Columbia University Press.

Cummings, J. & VandeHei, J. (2001). Faith-based charity initiative takes worldly, rocky path. *Wall Street Journal*, August 16. A16.

Edsall, T. B. (2001). Robertson joins liberals in faulting Bush's 'faith-based' plan. *Washington Post*, February 22. A5.

Esbeck, C. H. (1999). The neutral treatment of religion and faith-based social service providers: Charitable choice and its critics. In D. Davis & B. Hankins (Eds.) *Welfare reform and faith-based organizations*. Waco, TX: Baylor University Press.

Esbeck, C. H. (2001). Concerning Sec. 701 (Charitable Choice) of S. 304, Drug Abuse Education, Prevention, and Treatment Act of 2001. Statement before the Committee on the Judiciary of the United States Senate. June 6, 2001, Washington D.C. U.S. Department of Justice.

Esbeck, C. H. (2001a). Religion and the first amendment: Some causes of the recent confusion. *William and Mary Law Review*, 42(3), 883-918.

Goodstein, L. (2001). For religious right, Bush's charity plan is raising concerns. *New York Times*, March 3. A1.

Guliuzza, F. (2001). Religion and the judiciary. In Corwin Smidt (Ed.) *In God we trust? Religion and American political life*. Grand Rapids: Baker Academic.

Johnson, B. (2002). *Objective hope: Assessing the effectiveness of faith-based organizations: A review of the literature*. Philadelphia, Pennsylvania: Center for Research on Religion and Urban Civil Life. http://www.manhattan-institute.org/crrucs_objective_hope.pdf.

Koch, K. (2000). Child poverty. In *CQ Researcher* (283-303). Washington, D.C.: Congressional Quarterly, Inc.

Laycock, D. (2001). Faith based solutions: What are the legal issues? Statement before the Committee on the Judiciary of the United States Senate. June 6, 2001. Washington, D.C.

Monsma, S. V. (1996). *When sacred and secular mix: Religious nonprofit organizations and public money*. Lanham, Maryland: Rowman & Littlefield Publishers.

Nather, D. (2001). Bush's house win on 'faith-based' charity clouded by bias concerns in senate. *Congressional Quarterly Weekly Report*, 59, 1774-1775.

Nather, D. (2001a). Welfare overhaul's next wave. Welfare overhaul's next wave. *Congressional Quarterly Weekly Report*, 59, 585-590.

Nitschke, L. (2001). Faith-based charity bill advances in house with little democratic support. *Congressional Quarterly Weekly Report*, 59, 1586-1587.

Olasky, M. (1992). *The tragedy of American compassion*. Lanham, Maryland: Regnery Gateway.

Pew Research Center. (2001). *American views on religion, politics, and public policy*. Washington, D.C.

Schaefer, K. C. (1999). The privatizing of compassion: A critical engagement with Marvin Olaksy. In D. Gushee (Ed.) *Toward a just and caring society: Christian responses to poverty in America*. Grand Rapids, Michigan: Baker Books.

Search for Common Ground. (2002). Finding common ground: 29 recommendations of the working group on human needs and faith-based and community initiatives. Washington, D.C.: Search for Common Ground - USA.

Segal, J. (1999). A 'holy mistaken zeal:' The legislative history and future of charitable choice. In D. Davis & B. Hankins (Eds.) *Welfare reform and faith-based organizations*. Waco, TX: Baylor University Press.

Sherman, A. (2000). A survey of church-government anti-poverty partnerships. Washington, D.C. American Enterprise Institute. http://www.aei.org/e%20drive/web/public/tae/taejune00i.htm.

Sherman, A. (2002). Collaborations catalog: A report on charitable choice implementation in 15 states. Indianapolis, Indiana: Hudson Institute.

Skocpol, T. (2000). Religion, civil society, and the social provision in the U.S. In M. J. Bane, B. Coffin, & R. Thiemann (Eds.) *Who will provide: The changing role of religion in American welfare*. Boulder, Colorado: Westview Press.

Stern, M. D. (2001). Charitable choice: The law as it is and may be. In A. Walsh (Ed.) *Can charitable choice work?* Hartford, Connecticut: The Leonard E. Greenberg Center for the Study of Religion in Public Life.

Tenpas, K. D. (2002). *Can an office change a country? The White House Office of Faith-Based and Community Initiatives. A year in review.* Washington, D.C. Brookings Institution. http://pewforum.org/events/022002/tenpas.pdf.

United Way of America. (1998). Outcome measurement activities of national human service organizations. Washington, D.C.

White House Office of Faith-Based and Community Initiatives. (2001). Unlevel playing field: Barriers to participation by faith-based and community organizations in federal social service programs. Washington, D.C.

Wineburg, R. J. (2001). *A limited partnership: The politics of religion, welfare, and social service*. New York: Columbia University Press.

CHAPTER 20

THE FAITH CONNECTIONS APPROACH: INCLUDING PEOPLE WITH DEVELOPMENTAL DISABILITIES IN THE LIFE AND WORSHIP OF CONGREGATIONS

Rick Chamiec-Case

Several years ago, Anne, a prominent attorney and a pillar of Grace Church in Ohio gave birth to a beautiful baby girl named Melinda, who was born with Down Syndrome. Anne's pregnancy had been uneventful, and so the news of Melinda's disability was quite unexpected. Because Anne was well-liked within the congregation, many had been waiting expectantly for her first child to be born, and had eagerly planned to visit her in the hospital or send gifts to mark the big day. However, when they heard that Melinda had been born with Down Syndrome, most shied away from their plans to visit or send gifts – primarily because they weren't sure whether to offer congratulations or condolences. Anne's husband, who did not attend church regularly, wondered aloud about the absence of Anne's "church friends" during this important event in her life.

Following Melinda's birth, Anne continued to attend Grace Church, although she was not able to be as active as she had been in the past. Between her fulltime work as an attorney, and the extra time she devoted to meeting Melinda's special needs, Anne had much less time to play a leadership role at Grace. Still, she attended worship services each Sunday, always accompanied by Melinda.

Melinda was an adorable child, full of life and energy. Although characteristic Down Syndrome facial features and delays in meeting early developmental milestones made it evident that she had a disability, in many ways she was much like the other small children in the congregation. Still, the women in charge of the church nursery were clearly quite uncomfortable when Anne asked if she could occasionally leave Melinda there, so Anne decided it would just be best to keep Melinda with her during worship services and other church activities.

As Melinda grew, several families in the congregation who also had a family member with a disability went out of their way to befriend Anne, and to let her know that they understood the challenges – and joys – of raising or living with someone with a disability. Interestingly, though, in most cases Anne could not recall seeing their disabled family member at church activities, except perhaps during a Christmas or Easter service, and then usually sitting in the very back of the church.

As she got to know these families, Anne asked why their disabled family member did not attend worship services or other church activities more often. In some cases, the explanation was that their family member lived out of the area (in a group home or institution). In other cases, however, these families indicated that they wished their family member could participate more fully in the congregation, but that there just didn't seem to be a place for them. When Anne asked why this was the case, the families suggested a number of reasons:

- The worship services usually required that participants be quiet and still for extended periods of time. If (or when) their disabled family members became fidgety or loud, others in the congregation would complain that their worship was disrupted.
- The Sunday school program assumed that once participants reached a certain age, they could read, write and think abstractly. This usually left out their disabled family member.
- The pastor of the church had concerns about giving communion to individuals with developmental disabilities. He felt that even if they completed a confirmation class, they probably couldn't *really* understand what communion represented. As a result, the pastor decided it would not be appropriate to offer communion to persons with developmental disabilities.

Anne felt terribly for these families and their family members with disabilities. She also felt more than a little guilty that although she had been a leader within Grace Church for many years, she had been almost totally unaware of the frustrating challenges these families had been facing. At the same time, Anne began to wonder (and worry about) what would happen as Melinda continued to grow: in view of her disability, would Melinda be able to fully participate in the life and worship of Grace Church? Of any church?

Introduction

Many individuals from various walks of life attach significant value and meaning to membership and participation in a congregation or community of faith. There are a number of reasons for this. First of all, by participating in the life and worship of a congregation, persons have the opportunity to join with others in learning about, loving, serving, honoring, and enjoying God, whom they believe to be worthy of their ultimate commitment and devotion. Second, within a congregation, a person feels that she "belongs." A congregation provides a community with which a person can identify and form a sense of identity (Riordan & Vasa, 1991). Third, through participation in a congregation, persons have increased opportunities for serving others, enabling them to live out their shared beliefs and values by "giving back" to meet the needs of others. And last, a congregation offers persons the benefit of being integrated into a social network, providing access to valuable information and resources that are often not available to persons who are not a part of that network (McNair & Smith, 1998).

At the same time, including individuals with developmental disabilities in its life and worship benefits the congregation in a number of important ways as well. First, many people with developmental disabilities provide for the congregation a tangible model of the "child-like" faith that Jesus held in such high regard (cf. Luke 18:17), as demonstrated by their uninhibited, unwavering trust in God and those around them. Second, inclusion of people with disabilities often helps sensitize non-disabled members of a congregation to a more immediate level of human need and dependency, bringing home in a new and powerful way the need and dependency all persons have with respect to God.[1] Third, people with developmental disabilities are often steady and dependable workers and volunteers, making them a valuable asset in congregational service ministries. Fourth, inclusion of people with developmental disabilities expands the diversity of a congregation, making it a more accurate reflection of (and thereby potentially more responsive to, and viewed in a more positive way by) the larger community around it. And last, including people with developmental disabilities is one way that a congregation can reach out to those many in our society perceive as among "the least of these," and by doing so, discover at the same time that people with developmental disabilities are much more like non-disabled persons – fully able to serve as well as to be served – than they are different.

Unfortunately, people with disabilities are notably under-represented in most congregations (ANCOR, p.29),[2] as many congregations have not made including people with disabilities a high priority (McNair & Swartz, 1997). As a result, people with developmental disabilities often miss out on a rich opportunity to participate in a community group that could add significant value and meaning to their lives – in spite of the fact that many indicate a desire to participate in a faith community (Kregel, J. et al., 1986).

The under-representation of people with developmental disabilities in many congregations is caused by a number of factors. First of all, during the lifetime of many of the readers of this chapter, the majority of people with disabilities were placed in self-contained institutional settings outside the mainstream of society. People in institutions often lived their entire lives within the walls of that institution, far beyond the reach of most congregations. Yet even progress in assisting individuals with developmental disabilities to return to community settings in recent years has not done enough to reverse this trend of under-representation. Partially due to many decades of institutionalization, there is a limited history of successful interactions, experiences, and relationships shared between people with disabilities and members of local communities of faith from which to learn. Often people with disabilities and members of congregations are just not sure how to relate in a healthy, reciprocal way.

Second, many of the activities and events that occur in congregations presuppose that participants have a level of skill or knowledge that people with developmental disabilities may not have, including the ability to read, communicate articulately, and reason abstractly:

> ...in most churches, religious education still means reading, writing, and rote memorization of Bible stories along with group discussion where participation requires a certain level of verbal fluency (Webb-Mitchell, p. 32).

Imagine attempting to sing without having access to the music or words, to participate in a liturgical service or Bible study without being able to read, or to sit in on discussions where the conversation is consistently over one's head. Many forums and activities that congregations offer are just not accessible to a person with developmental disabilities.

Third, there are often logistical barriers that block the participation of individuals with disabilities in the life and worship of a congregation. For example, since many people with developmental disabilities don't drive (and alternate forms of public transportation often don't run regularly on weekends), getting to and from congregational events can prove to be a significant challenge. In addition, many worship services and congregational activities are held in rooms that cannot be reached without climbing up or down a set of stairs. For individuals who have limited mobility (the prevalence of physical disabilities in persons with developmental disabilities is significantly higher than in the general population), this can create an almost insurmountable barrier. Compared to many businesses and community organizations, congregations have often been slow to overcome a wide range of barriers that prevent full participation of people with disabilities:

> If supermarkets and bars are more accessible than altars, then we must all bear the shame.... Justice and love will triumph only when segregating walls are knocked down and the barriers of architecture, communication and attitudes are removed. Only then will people with disabilities become full participants in the celebrations and obligations of their faith. (Anderson, p. 44)

The resulting widespread exclusion of people with developmental disabilities from full participation in the life and worship of congregations represents a tragic loss, both for persons with disabilities, as well as for communities of faith. This chapter outlines an approach, the Faith Connections Approach that has been developed to foster the participation of people with developmental disabilities in congregational life and worship. The Faith Connections Approach is based on the results of a recent survey[3] and an adaptation of techniques central to the person-centered planning process that has enjoyed widespread acceptance in the field of developmental disabilities for a number of years (Mount, pp. 12-17). This approach employs a method designed to match the strengths, preferences, and interests of persons with developmental disabilities with the strengths, needs, and opportunities for participation within a congregation. The Faith Connections Approach has been developed from a strengths and competence perspective, and calls upon a variety of social work roles in its implementation, including the roles of case manager/service broker, advocate, teacher /trainer, and consultant/ facilitator.

Natural Supports

The field of mental retardation over the past several decades has placed a growing emphasis on the role of *natural supports* in the provision of services for people with developmental disabilities (McNair & Smith, 1998). But just what are natural supports? In the early 1970s, Wolf Wolfensberger wrote an influential book developing a concept he called the *normalization principle*, which advocated that people with disabilities should be treated as normally as possible (that is, as similar as possible to the way people without disabilities are treated in our society), with a goal to help them live lives that are as normal as possible (Wolfensberger, 1972). Even though persons with developmental disabilities often need varying levels of support to meet the demands of everyday life, advocates for people with developmental disabilities maintain that these supports should be provided "with a light touch" and only when the existing resources of the community experienced by most people are insufficient (McNair, 2000).

Following from this line of thought, natural supports help people with disabilities to meet their needs and achieve goals that are important to them, by means that:

- Are as similar as possible to the types of supports accessed by a majority of people in a given social group or community.
- Draw as much as possible from already-existing resources within established social groups and networks.
- Encourage the development of social relationships and participation in activities and events that are as similar as possible to those experienced by people without disabilities.
- Are effective in helping a person meet his or her needs, but no "heavier" than needed to achieve desired outcomes.

It is important at this point to make a distinction between two ways in which the connection between natural supports and congregations will be discussed within this chapter. On the one hand, in a narrower sense, the Faith Connections Approach provides a practical strategy for drawing on natural supports within a given congregation in order to help a person with developmental disabilities participate more fully within that particular congregation. On the other hand, in a broader sense, one of the most important benefits that people with developmental disabilities can derive from becoming active members of congregations is to gain access to natural supports that can help them to more effectively meet the demands of everyday life, achieve important life goals, and become more fully connected with the life and resources of the larger community.

Social Capital

As a social network within the community, congregations are optimal sources of natural supports for people with developmental disabilities in this broader sense because of the surplus of *social capital* they generate. Social capital can be thought of as the embedded resources and assets found in a given social network (Lin, N. et al., 2001). Individuals with disabilities who become members of congregations potentially benefit from the social capital generated by those congregations in at least four ways:

1. They obtain information about and access to valued activities, events, and opportunities otherwise not known or available to them.

2. The persons within the congregation with whom they form social relationships potentially exert a positive influence on members of the wider community, thereby influencing decisions that could have a desired impact on them (for example, a member of the congregation might put in a "good word" for them with a prospective employer, thereby helping them obtain a desired job).
3. They potentially acquire "social credentials" (they are perceived by the community as having access to the congregation's shared resources, and as a result, are able to more easily access additional community resources).
4. Their worth as an individual and as a member of that congregation is reinforced in the eyes of the community (Lin, N. et al., 2001).

As pervasive social networks (McNair & Smith, 2000), congregations generate a wealth of social capital, which can be translated into a wide range of natural supports for people with disabilities. Importantly, these supports tend to be especially effective because they help people with disabilities gain access to information and resources they might not be able to obtain on their own. In addition, these supports tend to be especially natural because they are similar, if not identical, to the supports offered to all members of the congregation.

The Faith Connections Approach

However, in order to tap the social capital of a given congregation, a person with developmental disabilities must first become a recognized, participating member of that community of faith. The Faith Connections Approach describes an approach for developing a congregational ministry (or enriching an existing ministry) that intentionally draws on the natural supports (in the narrower sense) of that community of faith to more fully include people with developmental disabilities in its life and worship.

In keeping a focus on natural supports, the Faith Connections Approach seeks to draw on one of its own members with professional skills in social work or a related discipline (and ideally with some prior experience with persons with developmental disabilities) to provide leadership for the development of this ministry. One of the most important advantages of calling on a member to provide ministry leadership is that he or she has an insider's understanding of the culture, life, mission and rhythm of that community of faith. At the same time, while the skills and experience volunteers bring to the ministry are an invaluable asset, it is critical to communicate that general participation in this ministry does *not* require prior professional training or experience with persons with developmental disabilities. To fail to bring this message across serves to perpetuate the myth that only "professionals" or people with prior experience can successfully support and interact with people with disabilities, which undercuts the ministry goal of full acceptance and inclusion of people with developmental disabilities, and the use of natural supports to help achieve that goal.

Therefore, in the description of the Faith Connections Approach that follows, it is suggested that the leader of this congregational ministry be a social worker (or related professional) with some prior experience in the field of developmental disabilities who is already a member of that congregation—we'll call this leader the Faith Connections Approach (FCA) Coordinator. However, while the FCA Coordinator plays a key role in leading, facilitating, and guiding the work of this ministry, it will be maintained that the hands-on delivery of supports should be provided by any and all members of the congregation drawn to this ministry, regardless of their prior knowledge of or experience with persons with disabilities.

To keep a focus on the practical application of the Faith Connections Approach, as we explore each successive stage of this approach, we will attempt to apply it to the situation described in the case scenario presented at the beginning of this chapter. As you recall, this scenario described Anne, a long-standing member of Grace Church, and her daughter Melinda, who was born with Down Syndrome. Let's fill out this scenario a bit, picking up where we left off, with Anne beginning to wonder: in light of Melinda's disability, would Melinda be able to fully participate in the life and worship of Grace Church?

Anne decided that, based on the experience of the other families within the congregation who had a disabled family member, she needed to express her concerns openly to the leadership of the church. She set up a time for herself and several of these families to meet with the pastor and staff at Grace to share their dream of seeing their family members richly integrated in the life and worship of Grace Church—along with their concerns about the many barriers currently preventing them from seeing this dream fulfilled.

Several of the families thought this was an excellent idea and were quite enthused about meeting with the pastor and staff. A few others, however, declined Anne's invitation to participate, either because they did not think any real change was possible, or because they didn't want to "rock the boat" and draw additional attention to themselves. Two of the individuals with developmental disabilities were young adults, and so Anne invited them to be a part of this meeting as well to represent their perspective.

They met early one evening at the church. Anne began the meeting by summarizing some of her hopes for Melinda there at Grace, as well as some of her fears and concerns. After she was done, she invited the other family members and persons with developmental disabilities to share with the group as well. At first, the group was fairly quiet. But then, one by one, family members and individuals began sharing their own personal stories, frustrations, fears, and hopes. It was a very moving experience, perhaps most of all for the pastor and staff, who were largely unaware of how excluded individuals with developmental disabilities felt from the life and worship of the congregation.

To their credit, the pastor and staff really listened to what Anne and the others had to say, and by the end of the meeting, were genuinely persuaded that they needed to do something to respond to the issues they had heard. What was not as clear to them, or to families and persons with developmental disabilities who had come to the meeting, was how or what the congregation could do to address to these concerns.

After floundering a while on this question, someone in the group mentioned that one of the members of the congregation, Wilma, was a social worker who worked for a local ARC (Association for Retarded Citizens), and so she might also be a good resource person to bring into this discussion. Relieved that there might be help to figure out what the congregation could do to address the concerns raised during this meeting, the group asked the pastor to contact Wilma to see if she would be willing to be a part of a follow-up discussion.

Wilma was more than willing. She jumped at the invitation to talk with the group about ways that the congregation might encourage fuller participation of persons with developmental disabilities in its community life and worship. Three weeks later, the group met again, this time with Wilma in attendance. After carefully listening to the group's hopes and concerns, Wilma agreed to help them form an FCA (Faith Connections Approach) ministry at Grace Church to support people with developmental disabilities.

Stages of the Faith Connections Approach

The key stages of the Faith Connections Approach are as follows:

1. Congregational Assessment
2. Individual Assessment - Exploring the Spiritual Dimension
3. Matching Strengths, Needs, Interests, and Opportunities for Participation
4. Developing a Support Plan
5. Congregational Coaching and Support

Stage One: Congregational Assessment

Prior to forming a ministry committed to promoting the fuller participation of people with developmental disabilities, it is important to explore the congregation's understanding of and support for this type of ministry. This exploration can take several forms. First of all, it is helpful to provide the congregation with background information about individuals with developmental disabilities, a description of what the ministry might look like when formed, and snapshots of similar ministries in other congregations.

Second, it is useful to help the congregation make a connection between forming this ministry, and the congregation's mission as driven by the beliefs and values of its religious tradition.

Third, it is important to explore the level of the congregation's support of the proposed ministry. This exploration often provides valuable information for ministry leaders such as the number of people likely to contribute their time to the ministry, the likelihood regarding whether the congregation would be willing to funnel significant resources into this ministry, and whether this ministry would be perceived as important compared to the congregation's other ministries.

There are a number of ways to explore congregational support for this type of ministry. Possible strategies could include discussion and study groups, forums or presentations to the congregation, written or telephone surveys, and targeted focus groups. Key questions that might be covered in this exploration process include:

- What is the fit between the congregation's mission and this ministry?
- In what sense does the congregation feel "called" to this type of ministry?
- How stable is the congregation financially? In terms of its volunteer and leadership bases? What impact would its stability in these areas have in terms of the amount of time, resources, and energy the congregation would have to devote to this ministry?
- What is the fit between the culture of the congregation and the provision of supports for people who might be perceived as "different?"
- Is the congregation open to the possibility that including people with disabilities will make a valued contribution to the life and worship of the congregation?
- Is the congregation aware of ways the life and worship of the congregation may contribute to the lives of people with disabilities?

Application to the Case Scenario

Wilma explained that before taking any significant steps or proposing major changes, it would be important to explore and cultivate the congregation's support of this new ministry. The FCA planning group started by educating the congregation at large and talking in depth with two targeted focus groups.

The FCA planning group agreed that a good first step would be to expose the congregation to some basic information about developmental disabilities – such as what developmental disabilities are (and are not), how they impact both individuals and families at a variety of levels, and in particular, how they potentially affect the ability of individuals and families to participate fully in the life and worship of a community of faith. The FCA planning group worked with the congregation's education programs to set up a number of forums for presenting this information to members of the congregation. Some of the strategies they put into place included naming a specific Sunday as Developmental Disabilities Awareness Sunday. On the appointed Sunday, each Sunday School teacher was asked to present age-appropriate information about developmental disabilities gathered by the FCA planning group. To prepare for the "Developmental Disabilities Awareness Sunday" the FCA planning group conducted a training for all Sunday School teachers. Wilma offered a 6-week adult education class focusing on congregations in the US who had developed effective ministries for people with developmental disabilities. The pastor made room on the agenda for the FCA planning group to provide a 45-minute presentation summarizing their dreams and concerns at an upcoming meeting of the congregation's Board of Elders (the leadership group within Grace Church).

Following these educational forums, the pastor helped the FCA group recruit two focus groups, each with four to five representatives from various age groups and backgrounds. Facilitated by Wilma, these focus groups grappled with questions about the potential fit between the congregation's understanding of its mission and the forming of this ministry, their perception about the ministry's relative importance, and the number of members who they thought might be willing to devote time and resources to this ministry. The work of the focus groups generated the following findings:

- The congregation felt strongly that both its mission and its religious beliefs and values strongly supported the position that every individual who wanted to be a member of Grace Church should be able to fully participate in its community life and worship, including people with developmental disabilities.

- The congregation noted that some of its members were finding it difficult to keep up with the expanding number of activities and ministries at Grace Church, and that this could present a challenge in terms of recruiting people and resources for this new area of ministry.
- The congregation confessed that for many years it had been unaware and inattentive to the needs of individuals and families with developmental disabilities within its community, and that the congregation should be committed to giving this new area of ministry top priority in terms of staff time and resources due to its direct relevance to Grace's mission.

Assessing the Congregation[4]

Once a concerted effort has been made to educate the congregation and explore support for a ministry to promote inclusion of people with developmental disabilities, the next step is to take an inventory of congregational strengths, needs, and opportunities for participation. The goal of this step will be to get a clearer picture about the key strengths and current or potential opportunities for participation that exist within the congregation, as well as those areas of congregational need that individuals with developmental disabilities might be able to help meet.

To conduct such an inventory, the FCA Coordinator would work with others interested in this ministry to explore some of the questions that follow below. It is important to note that the focus of these questions should be sufficiently broad to generate general information about the congregation that might or might not appear relevant to this ministry at first glance in a conscious attempt to help participants think "outside the box."

Strengths

- What does the congregation see itself as doing particularly well?
- What current services, programs, and ministries are most effective or most popular, and why?
- What networks (both within and outside the congregation) are the members of the congregation particularly well connected?
- What specific areas of background or expertise are well represented by individuals in the congregation that might be relevant to this ministry?
- What resources and facilities does the congregation have in ample supply?

Needs

- What are some areas in which the congregation wants to grow or is currently struggling?

- What aspects of the congregation's mission are not currently being fulfilled (at least to the satisfaction of the members of the congregation)?
- What are some opportunities for ministry currently being missed because of lack of time, resources, or volunteer support?
- What needs of current members are going unmet, or are not being adequately met?

Opportunities for Participation

- What ministries, programs, and service opportunities does the congregation currently have in place?
- What ministries, programs, or service opportunities would the congregation like to develop?

The information from this inventory will be instrumental in helping match individual and congregational strengths and needs.

Application to the Case Scenario

Encouraged by the positive response of the focus groups, and with the full support of the pastor and staff, the FCA planning group under Wilma's leadership eagerly moved to the next step – working with members of the congregation to define what the congregation was already doing well, what its most significant needs were, and what types of opportunities for participation it already had to offer. Wilma convened the two focus groups one more time, and led them through a series of exercises designed to assess the congregation's strengths, needs, and existing opportunities for participation. A sampling of the information generated during this assessment process included the following:

Congregational Strengths

- A strong commitment to families in the congregation, with many programs and ministries recently developed to serve them.
- A large constituency that had been members of Grace Church for many years, giving the congregation a strong sense of roots and continuity.
- A surplus of members within the congregation who worked in various professional and community leadership positions, giving the congregation ready access to many facets of the surrounding community.

Congregational Needs

- Additional volunteers to support the many new programs and ministries the congregation had started over the past few years,

especially those serving families.
- More effective strategies to welcome and follow up with the large number of visitors who came to Grace each week.
- Additional ushers, lay readers, and liturgists to support a recently-established additional service each weekend.

Opportunities for Participation
- Large variety of service ministries and programs requiring many volunteers with varied backgrounds and abilities.
- Thriving Sunday School program for children and adults of all ages.
- Longstanding music program offering several choices of choirs and musical groups.

Stage Two: Individual Assessment - Exploring the Spiritual Dimension

It has long been recognized in the field of developmental disabilities that providing individuals with a range of supports can play a key role in helping them integrate more fully into their communities. Without appropriate supports, the options for individuals with developmental disabilities to be included in community life can be severely limited.

In recent years, the identification of needed supports for people with developmental disabilities has been driven primarily by an individualized assessment of each person's strengths, needs, and interests. Particularly for individuals who are receiving funding and services from the state in which they live, this assessment is driven by an interdisciplinary team planning process. This interdisciplinary team (IDT) is generally made up of the person receiving services, key family members or guardians, an advocate or close friends, representatives of service providers (if applicable), and a team leader, often with ties to the state department that oversees and funds the individuals' services.

As the first step toward identifying supports that the person might need to meet his or her needs and goals, the IDT gathers to identify the individual's most significant strengths, gifts, interests, preferences, dreams, and capacities in all areas of life (Mount, pp. 12-17). Unfortunately, while invariably looking at the physical, cognitive, emotional, and social domains of the person's life, in most cases, individual assessments do not include an exploration of the person's spiritual or religious strengths, needs, gifts, interests, preferences, and dreams. One of the distinctive elements of the Faith Connections Approach is its inclusion of a rich spiritual component in the individual assessment process. This emphasis is driven by the Judeo-Christian belief that all persons are made in the image of God (Genesis 1), and as a result are spiritual and religious, as well as physical, cognitive, emotional and social beings.

It is important to note that the Faith Connections Approach optimally does not attempt to introduce this spiritual and religious component as separate from the overall assessment process. Rather, it advocates for the spiritual and religious domain to be integrated into the overall assessment of the individual. However, including spiritual and religious components in the assessment process often proves to be no small challenge. Because spirituality and religion have not traditionally been a part of the assessment process, many - including seasoned social workers - have little to no experience in conducting a spiritual assessment, even if they are relatively comfortable discussing spiritual or religious issues (which many are not). The FCA Coordinator can often play a key role in this process. The Coordinator might offer to help the team develop questions to guide their discussion with the person with developmental disabilities. Or the Coordinator might help the team explore creative assessment approaches such as role playing exercises or observations of the person in selected spiritual activities.

Key areas the FCA Coordinator could help the team explore include (but are not limited to):

a. Spiritual and religious practices, rituals, and traditions.
b. Beliefs about God and the person's relation to God.
c. Exploration of religious experiences, both individually, as well as within a community of faith.
d. Values inventory.
e. Evaluation of spiritual mentors or "heroes."
f. History of experiences (positive and not-as-positive) with current/prior congregations, if applicable.

For a sample spiritual assessment tool that can be used to assist in this process, see Figure 1.

In summary, the FCA Coordinator must be committed to working with the person's IDT to help identify the individual's spiritual strengths, gifts, interests, preferences, dreams, and capacities that can be drawn upon to help discover the best fit with existing congregational strengths, needs, and opportunities for participation.[7]

Application to the Case Scenario

The FCA planning group at Grace Church decided to begin facilitating individual assessments for the individuals with developmental disabilities who had experience with a team planning process. One of these individuals, Bob, was a 22 year-old man who lived in a privately-operated group home with four other men in a nearby town. Because the group home was funded and licensed by the state, Bob had been supported by an IDT assessment and planning process for a number of years. The leader of Bob's team worked for the state's Department of Mental Retardation. In addition to Bob, the interdisciplinary team included Bob's parents, the manager of his group home, his day program instructor, and the part-time nurse employed by the agency that operated the group home.

Wilma contacted Bob's team leader, Donna, and filled her in regarding Bob's active interest in participating more actively at Grace Church. Wilma further explained that Grace Church was working to develop a ministry that would provide individualized supports for Bob and others to meet their goal of fuller inclusion within Grace's congregation, and that the ministry's FCA planning group was working with teams to expand individuals' assessments to explore spiritual strengths, needs, and interests.

Although Donna openly admitted that she did not have any prior experience with spiritual assessments, she recognized and respected that it was Bob's "right" to practice a faith of his choosing, and that she would encourage Bob's team to work with Wilma and support Bob's interest in this area.

Wilma and Donna set up a meeting at Bob's house to bring together his interdisciplinary team to add this spiritual component to the overall assessment. A couple of weeks before the scheduled meeting, Wilma met with Bob to get to know him better, gather some background information, and to let him know some of the topics they would be talking about at the meeting. Wilma also spoke on the phone with several members of Bob's family to gather additional information, and asked if they would take him to church the week before the meeting so that she could observe him there.

The scheduled meeting at Bob's house went well. Bob seemed very comfortable talking about his faith and interest in spirituality. Bob's parents explained at the meeting that he used to go with them to Grace Church every week when he was much younger, but starting in his early teenage years, they began dropping him off at a neighbor's house instead of bringing him along to church. Apparently, some of the members of Grace had begun complaining that Bob was too noisy and distracting during the worship service, and that he made some of the teenage girls nervous because he would "stare" at their legs. Since that time, Bob only went to church with his family on Christmas and Easter; however, he usually began talking excitedly about "going back to church" weeks in advance of the holidays. He expressed to the group that he missed going to Grace Church a great deal, and wanted very much to start attending again each Sunday.

During the meeting, a number of important themes emerged. Some of the themes included the following:

- What Bob seemed to remember most vividly about attending church when he was younger was singing in the young children's choir. He often played cassette tapes with hymns and spirituals that he had collected through the years.
- Bob was an exceptionally friendly person who especially enjoyed spending time with children. As Bob remarked, "Jesus never got so busy that he didn't have time to play with the kids."
- Bob loved to sing, and had a strong, pleasant voice; however, he was sometimes reluctant to sing in front of others because he had a difficult time with the words of most songs and keeping up with a group.
- Bob sometimes stared at the legs of girls or young women that he found especially attractive. He believed that as long as he didn't go up to them or touch them, he was "being good" and "keeping the rules."
- Bob liked doing things for other people, especially those who needed his help.
- Bob felt closest to God when singing and praying at church.
- Bob did not enjoy long worship services, and found it difficult to keep quiet, especially during the "boring sermon."

Stage Three: Matching Strengths, Needs, Interests, and Opportunities for Participation

Up until this point, most of the focus has been on gathering information about the congregation and the individual(s) with developmental disabilities. The goal in gathering this considerable amount of information comes into focus in stage 3 of the Faith Connections Approach. In this stage, this information is used to match the individual strengths, needs, and interests of the person with developmental disabilities with the congregational strengths, needs, and opportunities for participation.

Matching at the Individual Level

At the individual level (focusing on one person with developmental disabilities at a time), the key to stage 3 is for the FCA Coordinator to lay out the information gathered during the spiritual and religious component of the assessment process, and to encourage the FCA planning group to think creatively about ways to tap the resources of the congregation to build on the strengths, support the needs, and connect with the interests of the person with developmental disabilities. Equally important, however, the FCA planning group is charged to explore ways that the person with developmental disabilities can make a tangible, valued contribution to the congregation. The best possible matches are those in which the individual and the congregation both give and receive.

Matching at the Group Level

At the group level (focusing on activities that are responsive to larger numbers of individuals with developmental disabilities), the FCA Coordinator must work with ministry leaders to discover trends and patterns of strengths, needs, and interests uncovered in the assessments of individuals so that the ministry begins to develop supports that effectively meet the needs of the many. For example, the kind of support that might be offered (at the individual level) to assist one person with developmental disabilities who needs transportation to attend services might be significantly different than the kind of support that would be offered (at the group level) to assist 15 individuals who have similar transportation needs.

As the ministry grows and develops, the FCA Coordinator and other ministry leaders must continue to stay attuned to information uncovered at both the individual and group levels so that the supports the congregation develops are both highly individualized to persons seeking services, as well as strategically tailored to make the best possible use of valuable volunteer time and congregational resources to serve the individuals who participate in this ministry.

Application to the Case Scenario

Wilma brought together the FCA planning group to brainstorm about potential matches between Bob's strengths, needs, and interests, and the congregation's strengths, needs, and opportunities for participation. The team generated the following potential matches:

1. Support Bob to join Grace's old-time gospel music choir, which sang every other week during the church service, and several times a year in other local congregations, often combining with other gospel music choirs. Participation in the gospel music choir had fallen off in recent years, so Bob's strong voice would be particularly welcome there.
2. Support Bob to volunteer with Grace Church's "children's chapel"

program, which met each week during the second half of the worship service (during the sermon). Designed to create a fun space and place for children ages 4 through second grade who found it too difficult to sit through an entire worship service, the children's chapel program had rapidly expanded over the past year, and its coordinator was having a difficult time recruiting a sufficient number of adults to supervise the growing number of children that attended each week.

3. Support Bob's attendance at an informal Sunday evening "hymn sing" and pot luck supper held once each month.
4. Encourage Bob to sign up for the "Circles" program sponsored by the social worker at the agency that operated Bob's group home. "Circles" is a sexual education program designed to help participants distinguish different types of relationships (such as acquaintances, friends, family, close friends, boy or girlfriends), and the socially accepted rules that guide behavior associated with each of these relationships.
5. Support Bob to sign up to become a Sunday morning greeter, whose main responsibility was to welcome guests and newcomers who visited Grace.

It was also noted by the FCA planning group that the large number of professionals and community leaders who attended Grace Church could be a potentially useful resource in the future for Bob in terms of job and career mobility, and obtaining quality health care (which is often a challenge for individuals with Medicaid insurance coverage).

Stage Four: Developing a Support Plan

Of course, simply identifying potential matches between the strengths, needs, and interests of persons with developmental disabilities, and strengths, needs, and opportunities for participation within a congregation is not enough in and of itself. What is still needed is the development of a support plan spelling out the specific, concrete action steps that will enable the match to take root and have the best chance of succeeding. The specific steps can range from relatively minimal, informal supports to much more intensive, formal ones.

For clarity's sake, a support plan should include a listing of the specific supports that will be extended to the individual, the persons who are responsible for providing each of the identified supports, and the approximate time frames for implementation. It is important to develop a support plan that neither over estimates nor underestimates the supports the person might need for the match to be a success. In addition, the FCA planning group should from the outset begin thinking about how and when it might be able to fade at least some of these supports, so that as much as is possible, supports are seen as time-limited and transitional.

Application to the Case Scenario

Encouraged by the exciting potential they saw in the potential matches they had generated, the FCA planning group at Grace Church worked together to develop the following support plan for Bob:

Action Task	Person Responsible
a. Recruit a longtime member of the old-time gospel choir to mentor Bob (work with him individually to learn the music and words of each song) and ensure that he had transportation to and from rehearsals	Jan (FCA Ministry Volunteer)
b. Ask the coordinator of the children's chapel program to meet with Bob and orient him to the children's chapel program. It was suggested that the coordinator could assign Bob specific responsibilities each week, including spending time with some of the young boys who could be difficult to manage if they were not engaged in a supervised activity. Also, ask the coordinator to assign one of the other adult volunteers to keep an eye out for Bob and be available to field any questions (at least for Bob's first few weeks).	Jim (Grace staff person)
c. Recruit a family that regularly attends the monthly Sunday evening gospel sing and pot luck supper to provide transportation to and from this event each month.	Mary (Bob's mom)
d. Speak with the social worker that runs the Circles program at Bob's group home about signing Bob up for an upcoming Circles class. Also ask if the social worker could work with the family to be able to coach Bob when he is in particular social situations in the church (such as when Bob is in the presence of girls or young women that he found attractive).	Wilma (FCA Coordinator)
e. Ask the coordinator of the "greeters" program to meet with Bob and provide him with an orientation to the roles and responsibilities of "greeting" at Grace Church. In addition, ask the coordinator to assign an experienced greeter to keep an eye out for Bob, help Bob read the schedule to know which Sundays he would be on duty, and be available to field any questions Bob might have.	Ralph (FCA Ministry Volunteer)

Stage Five: Congregational Coaching and Support

Once the team has developed a support plan, the most critical part of the process still remains: implementing and sustaining the plan over time. The key to the plan's long-term effectiveness is the selection and training of a Congregational Coach who will provide direction to the various persons identified in the individual's support plan, and encourage them to maintain their commitment to the individual with disabilities on an on-going basis. The Congregational Coach is also the "eyes and the ears" of the FCA planning group, and is responsible to communicate regularly with the FCA Coordinator to let him or her know how the support plan is working, and if it appears that the plan needs to be adjusted.

To underscore a point made earlier, it is *not* necessary that the Congregational Coach be a professional social worker or have experience working with persons with disabilities. On the contrary, one of the keys to developing an effective ministry for persons with developmental disabilities is eliminating the perception that only "experts" can provide needed support. Only in the absence of this perception can the FCA ministry, and the people it is supporting, grow and thrive.[8]

Application to the Case Scenario

The FCA planning group at Grace Church felt confident that the support plan they had developed, if implemented consistently, could play an important role in helping Bob become more fully included in the life and worship of Grace Church. However, the congregation also recognized that because it was already scheduled to begin developing support plans for the next individuals interested in participating in this ministry, it would need to rely on a Congregational Coach to directly oversee the implementation and monitoring of Bob's support plan.

So the last task of the FCA planning group at this point in the process was to think about who they might ask to take become Bob's congregational coach. After discussion, they decided to approach a longstanding member of Grace Church, Ralph, to consider this role. Ralph was their first choice for a number of reasons. First of all, Ralph had known Bob and his family for a number of years (Ralph worked at the same small office as Bob's father). In addition, Ralph sang in the adult choir, and so was familiar with Grace's choir programs. Lastly, Ralph was well-respected within the congregation, and through his participation in one of the FCA focus groups, had become known as a strong advocate for the FCA ministry. The FCA planning group was delighted when Ralph enthusiastically agreed to take on the role as congregational coach for Bob.

The implementation of Bob's support plan was relatively smooth, with only a few small glitches that were quickly addressed by the FCA planning team. Over the next six months, the FCA planning team developed detailed support plans for three more individuals with developmental disabilities. Although in one case the support plan did not work well (and had to be redone from scratch), in the other cases, the individuals began to be much more active, contributing members of the congregation.

However, the amount of time needed to facilitate the development of multiple support plans was far greater than what the congregation had originally envisioned. In addition, as the reputation of the ministry grew, the number of individuals with developmental disabilities who were interested in participating grew as well. After six months, it became evident to the staff and ministry leaders at Grace Church that the role of FCA Coordinator was becoming too time-intensive to remain a volunteer role.

As a result, the church's leadership decided to create a part-time staff position to provide the time and focus needed to support the growing FCA ministry, and to expand the focus of the ministry to include people with other disabilities as well. It was agreed at the outset, however, that even as the FCA Coordinator role became a paid staff position, it would remain focused on facilitating the planning process described above, and not on the hands on delivery of supports, which would continue to be more "naturally" provided by volunteer members of the congregation.

Social Work Perspectives and Roles Inherent in the Faith Connections Approach

The development of the Faith Connections Approach has been strongly influenced by the social work profession's strengths perspective. It also requires that the FCA Coordinator assume a variety of traditional social work roles. This section of the chapter will describe the reliance of the Faith Connections Approach on the strengths perspective, and outline four traditional social work roles that are inherent in this approach.

Strengths Perspective

The strengths perspective, which has become increasingly prominent in the field of social work in recent years (Miley, p. 61), maintains that the best way to serve clients (taken as either individuals or as a larger system) is to help them discover and build on their strengths, as opposed to identifying and trying to "fix" their weaknesses:

> Adopting a strengths perspective influences the way that social workers view client systems and involve them in the change process. Focusing on clients' strengths leads to an empowering approach that promotes clients' competence rather than working to erase their deficits... Strengths-oriented social workers believe that the strengths of all client systems - individual, interpersonal, familial, organizational, and societal - are resources to initiate, energize, and sustain change processes (Miley, pp. 62-63).

This strengths perspective is a central emphasis of the Faith Connections Approach. In both stages 1 and 2 of our case study scenario, the foci of the assessment processes led by the FCA Coordinator were on identifying Grace Church's as well as Bob's most significant strengths and assets.

Then, in Stage Three, the FCA planning team took the results of these assessment processes and used this information to seek matches that intentionally built on Bob's strengths and interests. In fact, one of the priorities in seeking these matches was to identify needs within Grace Church that Bob was able to help meet. This created a situation in which Bob was not only receiving help, but was at the same time making a positive, valued contribution within Grace Church, an important indicator of success for Bob's long-term participation in the life and worship of that congregation.

Key Social Work Roles

The effectiveness of the Faith Connections Approach depends to a large extent on the skills and abilities of the FCA Coordinator, who is called upon to assume a variety of traditional social work roles when facilitating the implementation of the five stages of this approach. These traditional social work roles (Haynes, pp. 285-291; Miley, pp. 16-26) include:

- services broker/case manager
- consultant/facilitator
- teacher/trainer
- client advocate

The Role of Service Broker/ Case Manager

One of the most important traditional roles of the social worker is to function as a broker of services or overall case manager. This means that the worker must know enough about available services to help clients connect with the supports they might need or benefit from, but might not otherwise know about or know how to access. It also means that the worker tracks a client's progress over time, and acts to adjust clients' service plans if needs change or if plans are not successfully helping clients meet their treatment goals. In summary, a case manager is responsible to see that:

> ...the client is (1) connected to the appropriate service provider(s) and that (2) appropriate services are actually being received.... (T)heir primary roles and functions are to (1) identify the appropriate service providers, (2) link clients with those providers, (3) continue to coordinate services as needs change, and (4) continually monitor progress (Haynes, p. 287).

In our case scenario, the Faith Connections Approach relied upon Wilma to assume the role of service broker/ case manager in at least two ways. First, Wilma worked with the FCA planning group to help connect Bob to various types of support within Grace Church, as well as a supplementary service (the Circles sexual education program) outside Grace. Second, once a support plan had been developed, Wilma worked with Ralph as the congregational coach to monitor the effectiveness of the plan, and stood ready to reconvene the FCA planning group if it appeared that the support plan was in need of change or revision.

The Role of Consultant/Facilitator

Another important traditional role of the social worker is that of a consultant or facilitator. As consultants/facilitators, social workers are responsible to work with their clients (as well as significant people within their clients' lives) to gather critical information and develop plans for change to help clients (at various levels) meet their identified service goals:

> As a function of social work, consultancy refers to social workers and clients conferring and deliberating together to develop plans for change.... Consultancy acknowledges that both social workers and clients systems bring information and resources, actual and potential, which are vital for resolving the issue at hand. Through consultancy, social workers seek to find solutions for challenges in social functioning with clients systems at all levels including individuals, families, groups, organizations, and communities (Miley, pp. 16-17).

In our case scenario, Faith Connections Approach relied upon Wilma to assume the traditional social work role of consultant or facilitator in a number of ways. In stages 1 and 2, Wilma facilitated a process involving selected representatives from the Grace Church as well as Bob's IDT to gather information and identify potential resources. It is important to note the way in which Wilma reinforced the centrality of Bob's role as the driving force in the individual assessment and goal selection processes. Then in Stages Three and Four, Wilma facilitated a discussion that enabled the FCA planning group to draw on the information gathered in Stages One an Two to identify potential matches and develop a support plan designed to help Bob participate more fully in the life and worship of Grace.

The Role of Teacher/Trainer

A third traditional role of the social worker is that of a teacher and trainer. A teacher/trainer develops an array of strategies to communicate vital information and promote the acquisition of critical skills to their clients as well as those individuals and groups that support their clients:

> As teachers, social workers use learning strategies to promote skill development and enhance the information base of client systems.... Trainers provide instruction to... formal groups and organizations (Miley, pp. 23-24).

In our case scenario, the Faith Connections Approach relied upon Wilma to assume the role of a teacher and trainer in a number of ways. First of all, in Stage One, Wilma provided leadership in supporting the FCA planning group's efforts to teach the members of Grace about developmental disabilities and the challenges faced by disabled individuals within their congregation. Then in Stages Two, Three, and Four, Wilma helped train other members of the FCA planning group how to do congregational assessments, how to identify the most significant strengths, needs, and interests of persons with developmental disabilities, how to match these with the strengths, needs, and opportunities for participation within the congregation, and last how to develop support plans. In addition, in Stage Five, Wilma was instrumental in providing training and support related to Ralph's efforts as congregational coach.

The Role of Advocate

One more important traditional role of the social worker is that of being a staunch advocate for clients. An advocate is one who acts to bring about change on behalf of or for the benefit of another:

> ...(t)he advocate is committed to ensuring that service delivery systems are responsive to clients' needs, and that clients receive all the benefits and services to which they are rightfully entitled. ...(c)ase managers can and do engage in advocacy on behalf of specific clients who are not being served appropriately (Haynes, pp. 289-90).

In our case scenario, Wilma led the FCA planning group in advocating on behalf of persons with developmental disabilities to remind members at Grace Church of their faith-driven responsibility to welcome and support individuals with disabilities in the life and worship of their community. Importantly, this advocacy included pointing out that Grace Church itself would be strengthened when it took such inclusion efforts seriously. This case for congregational responsibility as well as congregational benefit is powerfully stated in a passage from the Christian Scriptures that employs the metaphor of the Body of Christ to represent the congregation:

> The body is a unit, though it is made up of many parts; and though all its parts are many, they form one body.... Now the body is not made up of one part but of many.... And if the ear should say, "Because I am not a eye, I do not belong to the body," it would not for that reason cease to be part of the body.... If the whole body were an eye, where would the sense of hearing be?... But in fact God has arranged the parts in the body, every one of them, just as he wanted them to be.... As it is, there are many parts, but one body.
>
> The eye cannot say to the hand, "I don't need you!" And the head cannot say to the feet, "I don't need you!" On the contrary, those parts of the body that seem to be weaker are indispensable, and the parts that we think are less honorable we treat with special honor.... But God has combined the members of the body and has given greater honor to the parts that lacked it, so that there should be no division in the body, but that its parts should have equal concern for each other (Selected verses from I Corinthians 12: 12-25, New International Version).

In conclusion, the Faith Connections Approach represents an approach to congregational ministry that demonstrates the value of applying social work skills and perspectives within the setting of a faith community. It provides a tangible example in which the integration of Christian belief and professional social work practice is alive and well!

Notes

1 *This insight is from Amy Sherman's* Establishing a Church-based Welfare-to-Work Mentoring Ministry: A Practical "How-To" Manual *(1998), The Center for Civic Innovation at the Manhattan Institute, New York, p. 3. Although this manual refers primarily to working with individuals who are economically disadvantaged, this insight can also be applied to a congregation's work with other groups or persons that are struggle more than most in our society for their "daily bread."*

2 It would be misleading not to mention that some recent surveys indicate a more positive representation of people with disabilities in congregations. For example, a survey in Southern California (McNair & Swartz, 1997) found that approximately 82% of the surveyed churches had at least some members with developmental disabilities. However, in a personal interview, the author communicated that the survey was not designed to determine how many people with developmental disabilities were members of any given congregation, and that it was possible that the number of people with disabilities in any given congregation was very small in comparison to the overall size of the congregation. This survey also only measured the presence of individuals with developmental disabilities on membership rolls, but not their actual level of participation within the congregations surveyed.

3 To gather information for the writing of this chapter, the author conducted a series of telephone interviews with 5 congregations in various locations around the United States recommended by the National Organization for Disabilities in Washington, DC as examples of congregations committed to providing supports and services for people with developmental disabilities. The congregations that participated in these interviews included:

Name of Congregation/ Denominational Affiliation	**Location of Congregation**
Holy Comforter Church; Episcopal	Atlanta, Georgia
McLean Bible Church;Non-Denominational	Vienna, Virginia
Open Door Christian Church; Non-Denominational	Navato, California
St. Jude the Apostolic Catholic Church; Roman Catholic	Atlanta, Georgia
Trinity Evangelical Free Church; Evangelical Free	Redlands, California

4 Some of the ideas for questions related to congregational assessment were found in The Drucker Foundation, 2001; *Meeting the Collaborative Challenge: Developing Strategic Alliances Between Nonprofit Organizations and Businesses*; New York: Jossey-Bass.

5 It is important to note the need for a delicate balance here. On the one hand, conducting thorough assessments that under gird a careful matching process and the eventual development of strong support plans provides valuable information and direction to help the FCA planning group help individuals with developmental disabilities meet their inclusion goals. On the other hand, the more complicated and time-intensive the process seems to the members of the congregation, the more attention it draws to the differences between people with and without disabilities, and the more "un-natural" it begins to feel to members of the congregation. Achieving an appropriate balance here is no small challenge.

6 The important distinction here is between an acknowledgment of the value of having an FCA Coordinator who has training, expertise, and experience in social work or a related profession, while at the same time giving a clear message that the majority

of members of the FCA planning group, as well as the persons serving as congregational coaches and/or providing the hands-on supports, do not need to be "professionals," nor have prior experience working with people with disabilities.

7 It should be acknowledged here that recommending a fairly extended process of identifying the spiritual strengths, needs, and preferences of individuals with a disabilities does tend set them apart from other members of the congregation, and so is in tension with the emphasis on providing "natural" supports. A long-term goal for a congregation might be to become so sensitive and responsive to the strengths, needs, and preferences of *all* of its members – as an intentional strategy for supporting the fuller inclusion of *all* its members - that this more formal spiritual assessment for individuals with disabilities would become superfluous.

8 Most of these questions were gleaned from an article written on conducting a strengths assessment written by C. Tice and K. Perkins (1996).

I would like to express my appreciation for the collaborative support provided by Dr. Jeff McNair, professor of special education at Cal University. Perhaps partly because we come to this topic with varying perspectives, Jeff's critique of successive drafts of this chapter provided invaluable insight for this work. In addition, Jeff was instrumental in assisting with the implementation of the congregational survey and supplying bibliographic references.

References

ANCHOR - American Network of Community Options and Resources. (1995). *LINKS*, Volume XX (1), 29.

Anderson, R. C. (1994). A comprehensive look at disability laws and the religious community. *Exceptional Parent*, December, 43-44.

Haynes, K. & Holmes, K. (1994). *Invitation to Social Work*. New York: Longman.

Kregel, J., Wehman, P., Seyfarth, J., & Marshall, K. (1986). Community integration of young adults with mental retardation: Transition from school to adulthood. *Education and Training of the Mentally Retarded*, 21(1), 35-42.

Lin,N., Cook, K., & Burt, Ronald. (2001). *Social capital: theory and research*. New York: Walter de Gruyter, Inc.

McNair, J. & Swartz, S.L. (1997). Local church support to individuals with developmental disabilities. *Education and Training in Mental Retardation and Developmental Disabilities*, 32(4), 304-312.

McNair, J & Smith, H.K. (June, 1998). Community-based support through local churches. *Mental Retardation*,. 237-241.

McNair, J. (2000). The local church as a network supporting adults with disabilities in the community: One perspective. *Journal of Religion, Disability, and Health* Vol. 4(1), 33-56.

McNair, J. (July, 2000). A discussion of networks supporting adults with disabilities in the community. Website posting at <http://www.geocities.com/Athens/2926/4networks_article1.html>.

Miley, K.K., O'Melia, M. & DuBois, B.L. (1995). *Generalist social work practice: An empowering approach* Boston: Allyn and Bacon

Mount, B. (1995). *Capacity works: Finding windows for change using personal futures planning* New York: Graphic Futures.

Riordan, J. & Vasa, S.F. (Winter, 1991). Accommodations for and participation of ersons with disabilities in religious practice. *Education and Training in Mental Retardation*, 24, 653-655.

Tice, C. & Perkins, K. (1996). *Mental health issues and aging: Building on the strengths of older adults*. California: Brooks/Cole.

Webb-Mitchell, B. (1994). Toward a more inclusive protestant Sunday school: Making religious education accessible to all. *Exceptional Parent*, December, 31-33.

Wolfensberger, W. (1972). *The principle of normalization in human services*. Toronto: National Institute on Mental Retardation.

Select Bibliography for Additional Reading

Bradley, V.J., Ashbaugh, J.W. & Blaney, B.C. (1994). *Creating individual supports for people with developmental disabilities*. Baltimore, MD: Brookes Publishing.

Clegg, J. & Standen, P. (1991). Friendship among adults who have developmental disabilities. *American Journal on Mental Retardation*, 95 (6) 663-671

Ducharme, G., Beeman, P., DeMarasse, R., & Ludlam, C. (1994). Building community one person at a time. In Bradley, V., Ashbauch, J. & Blaney, B. (Eds.) *Creating individual supports for people with developmental disabilities*. Baltimore: Brookes Publishing.

Faith Group Resources. (1994). *Exceptional Parent*, December, 38-39.

Fewell, R. R. (1986). Supports from religious organizations and personal beliefs In R.R. Fewell & P.F. Vadasay (Eds.), *Families of handicapped children: Needs and supports across the life span* Austin, Texas: Pro-Ed, 297-316.

Forest, M. & Pearpoint, J. (1992). Families, friends and circles. In J. Nisbet (Ed.), *Natural Supports in School, at Work, and in the Community for People with Severe Disabilities* Baltimore: Brookes Publishing.

Gaventa, Bill. (1994). Religious participation for all. *Exceptional Parent*, December, 22-25.

Hoeksema, T.B. (1995). Supporting the free exercise of religion in the group home context. *Mental Retardation*, 33(5), 289-294.

Hoeksema, T.B., & Stimson, R.O. (1993a, January). Normalization pro and con. *Networks*, 1-5.

Hoeksema, T.B., & Stimson, R.O. (1993b, January). Reactions to normalization. *Networks*, 3-5.

Lin, N/, Cook, K., & Burt, R. (2001). *Social capital: theory and research*. New York: Walter de Gruyter, Inc..

Hollane, P. & Leinhardt, S. (Eds.) (1979). Perspectives on social networks. New York: Academic Press.

Hornstein, B. (1997). How the religious community can support the transition to adulthood: A parents perspective. *Mental Retardation*, 485-487.

McNair, J. & Smith, H. (June, 1998). Community based natural support through local churches. *Mental Retardation*, June, 237-241.

McNair, J. & Smith, H. (2000). Church attendance of adults with mental retardation. *Education and Training in Mental Retardation and Developmental Disabilities*, 35(2) 222-225.

McNair, J. & Swartz, S.L. (1997). Local church support to individuals with developmental disabilities. *Education and Training in Mental Retardation and Developmental Disabilities*, 32, 4, 304-312.

McNair, J. (2000). The local church as a network supporting adults with disabilities in the community: One perspective. *Journal of Religion, Disability and Health*, 4,1, 33-56.

Moore, J., Hamerlynck, L., Barsh, E., Spieker, S., & Jones, R. (1982). *Extending family resources*. Seattle WA: Children's Clinic and Preschool.

Newbigin, L. (1979). Not whole without the handicapped. In G. Muller-Fahrenholz (Ed.), *Partners in Life*: Faith and Order Paper No. 89. Geneva: World Council of Churches.

Perske, R. (1980, Fall). Some new policies and practices in churches and synagogues. *Journal of the National Apostolate with Mentally Retarded Persons*, 19.

Peters, R.K. (1991). Accomodations for and participation of persons with disabilities in religious practice. *Education and Training in Mental Retardation*, 26, 151-155.

Riordan, J. & Vasa, S.F. (1991). Accomodations for and participation of persons with disabiities in religious practice. *Education and Training of the Mentally Retarded*, June, 151-155.

Webb-Mitchell, Brett (1994). Toward a more inclusive protestant sunday school: Making religious education accessible to all. *Exceptional Parent*, December, 31-33.

Westerhoff, J. (1976). *Will our children have faith*? New York: The Seabury Press.

Wolfensberger, W. (1972). *The principle of normalization in human services*. Toronto: National Institute on Mental Retardation.

Figure 1: Sample Spiritual Assessment Tool

The following assessment/survey tool has been developed to facilitate an informal interview process that should include the individual with developmental disabilities as well as family members, friends, and other key members of the interdisciplinary team. Many of the concepts that appear here will need to be reframed in more concrete terms or adapted by the interviewer as appropriate to the comprehension level of the person being interviewed. As such, the effectiveness of this tool might be somewhat limited with individuals with more significant disabilities.

A. Spirituality Inventory[8]

1. When you think about your life, what gives you the most hope?
2. What are some of the most meaningful (important, valued) aspects of your life?
3. Do you believe there is some real purpose for your life? If so, what?
4. What in your life gives you a sense of safety and security, especially when facing great difficulty or danger?
5. What gives you the most confidence in your life?
6. How would you describe yourself to another person? How would you describe your worth as a person?
7. What do you like about yourself? What do you not like about yourself and would want to change if you could?

B. Religious Practices and Traditions

1. What personal religious practices, activities, or traditions do you participate in and/or find meaningful?

___ individual prayer
___ fasting
___ meditation
___ confession
___ taking communion
___ use of a rosary
___ personal sacrifices
___ group prayer
___ Bible study
___ solitude
___ acts of service
___ singing hymns, etc.
___ making offerings

2. How often do you attend religious services? How often would you like to? What types of services?

3. How often do you pray? How much satisfaction do you find in private prayer?
___ none at all ___ a little ___ some ___ a moderate amount ___ a great deal

C. Beliefs about God

1. Do you (does the individual) believe in God or a Higher Power?

<To Be Completed by Individuals Who Believe in God or the Concept of God>

2. How would you describe God? What words or images best describe God to you?

3. Do you believe that God loves you and cares about you as an individual? Do you believe that God is interested in your individual problems and daily life situation?

4. Do you believe that is God in control of all that goes on in the world today? How about in your daily life?
5. How do you believe that God communicates to people? Do you feel that God communicates with you?
6. Do you recall a favorite Bible story or character that has special meaning for you? What makes it special?
7. Why do you think many people – even good people – sometimes suffer and have difficult lives?
8. Do you believe in life after death? What do you think will happen to you after you die?

D. Feelings Inventory

1. How much of the time in your life do you feel:

   __% happy, satisfied, fulfilled
   __% unhappy, depressed, sad, discouraged
   __% angry, upset, frustrated
   __% anxious, scared, intimidated
   ____
   100%

2. What types of experiences or situations cause you to be happy, satisfied, or fulfilled? Unhappy, depressed, sad, or discouraged? Angry, upset, or frustrated?
3. On a scale of 1 - 10, do you feel your life is empty (1) or full (10)?

E. Religious Experience/Relationship with God

1. When do you/have you felt closest to God?
2. When you want to feel close to God, is there anything you can do to help bring about the experience of feeling close to God?
3. Do you consider that you have a personal, meaningful relationship with God or a Higher Power?

<To Be Completed by Individuals Who Consider Themselves to Have a Relationship with God>

4. What words or images would you use to describe your present relationship with God?
5. What kinds of things can/do you do that contribute to your relationship with God?
6. Has your relationship with God been helpful to you in the past when you have gone through difficult times? When you have celebrated special times?

F. Values Inventory

1. Rate (VP = very important, I – important, S = somewhat important, N = not important) some of the things which you value:

___ family	___ friendship	___ self-respect
___ excitement	___ good health	___ happiness
___ freedom	___ sense of pride	___ social status
___ world peace	___ faith community	___ salvation
___ inner harmony	___ relationship with God	

2. Of those things you rated a very important in the above question, which 2-3 would you say are the most important to you of all?

G. Spiritual Heroes/Mentors and Your Faith Community

1. What people in your life would you describe as some of your heroes? Why were these people heroes to you?

2. Do you identify with a particular congregation or faith (for example, a particular denomination, faith tradition, church, synagogue, fellowship group, etc.)? If so, which one(s)?

<To Be Completed by Individuals Who Identify Themselves with a Particular Faith Community>

3. Do you feel that you are an important part of your faith community? Why or why not?

4. What activities or practices have you found to be especially meaningful in your faith community(s)?
   ___ worship services ___ educational classes ___ Bible studies
   ___ discussion groups ___ seminars/conferences __ group singing
   ___ group prayer

5. You can rely on the support and help of the other members of your faith community when you need it most:
   ___ not at all ___ a little ___ a moderate amount ___ a great deal

6. What do you feel is your most important contribution to your faith community? What else would you like to contribute to your faith community?

ABOUT THE EDITORS

Beryl Hugen received a BA from Calvin College, a MSW from Western Michigan University, and a PhD from the University of Kansas. He is professor of social work and practicum coordinator in the Department of Social Work and Sociology at Calvin College in Grand Rapids, Michigan. He has served as a board member and publications editor for the North American Association of Christians in Social Work. He has published papers on mental health, the integration of Christian faith and social work practice, and social work history. He is co-editor of *Spirituality Within Religious Traditions in Social Work Practice* (Brooks Cole, 2001) and *Spirituality and Religion in Social Work Practice: Decision Cases with Teaching Notes* (Council on Social Work Education, 2002). Currently he is a research associate for the project *Service and Faith: The Impact on Christian Faith and Congregational Life of Organized Community Caring* (Lilly Endowment, Inc., 2000).

T. Laine Scales earned her BA at University of North Carolina, MSW at Carver School of Church Social Work, and PhD at University of Kentucky. She is Assistant Professor of Social Work at Baylor University, Waco, Texas. Dr. Scales has published in the areas of social welfare history, spirituality and religion in social work, and rural social work. She is author of *All That Fits a Woman: Training Southern Baptist Women for Charity and Mission, 1907-1926* (Mercer University Press, 2000). She is co-editor of *Spirituality and Religion in Social Work Practice: Decision Cases with Teaching Notes* (Council on Social Work Education, 2002) and of *Asset-Building to Sustain Rural Communities* (Brooks Cole, forthcoming 2003). She is co-leading a research team studying the role of Latina women in congregations in the USA and Mexico. Dr. Scales is a member of the Publications Consortium of the North American Association of Christians in Social Work and has held leadership positions in the National Association of Social Workers, Texas Chapter.

ABOUT THE CONTRIBUTORS

Katherine Amato-von Hemert received a BA in History/Women Studies/Drama from Lake Forest College, a MA in General Studies in the Humanities, and a MA and PhD from the School of Social Services Administration, University of Chicago. She served on the faculty of the College of Social Work, University of Kentucky, and as an adjunct Professor at Lexington Theological Seminary. Presently, Dr. Amato-von Hemert is living in Denver, Colorado. Her professional interests are researching the intersection of Christian congregation life and social service policy and program, the Medieval and Reformation history of poverty and social responses to it, along with the variety of religious influences in the history of the social work profession.

Gary R. Anderson received a BRE from Cornerstone University (Grand Rapids, Michigan), a MSW from the University of Michigan, and PhD from the School of Social Service Administration at the University of Chicago. Presently, he is a Professor and the Director of the School of Social Work at Michigan State University. He has social work practice experience as a child protective service worker. He has published extensively in the areas of child welfare, ethics, and health care. He is the Editor of the journal Child Welfare.

Cheryl K. Brandsen earned a BA from Calvin College, a MSW from the University of Michigan, and PhD from Michigan State University. Presently she is Professor of Sociology and Social Work at Calvin College and director of the Social Work program. Her research and practice interests are in gerontology, and specifically, end-of-life care. She is co-chair of the Social Work Research Group of the Michigan Partnership for the Advancement of End-of-Life care, a Robert Wood Johnson-funded initiative, and project director for the Hartford Geriatric Enrichment in Social Work Education at Calvin College.

Rick Chamiec-Case earned a BA in Philosophy from Wheaton College, a MAR in Religion from Yale Divinity School, and a MSW from the School of Social Work at the University of Connecticut. He worked for a number of years as Senior Vice President at ARI of Connecticut, whose mission it is to provide homes, jobs, and opportunities for people with disabilities and their families. He has several previous practice experiences in administering clinical, case management, quality assurance, family support, staff training, and management information services for people with disabilities like mental retardation. He has written and presented at conferences on various topics addressing the integration of faith with various management and disability issues. He has been the Executive Director of the North American Association of Christians in Social Work since 1997.

Roger D. Fallot received a BA (in Culture and Behavior), MS, and PhD (both in clinical psychology) from Yale University. His MDiv is from the Iliff School of Theology. He is currently Co-Director of Community Connections, a comprehensive human services agency in Washington, D.C. An ordained minister in the United Church of Christ, Dr. Fallot is also a member of the adjunct faculty in pastoral counseling at Loyola College in Maryland. Professional areas of interest include the role of spirituality in recovery—from trauma, mental illness, and substance abuse—and the development and evaluation of services for trauma survivors.

Diana R. Garland received her BA, MSSW, and PhD degrees all from the University of Louisville. She currently is Chair of the School of Social Work at Baylor University in Waco, Texas. Her interests include church social work, family ministry, and child welfare. She serves as Editor of the *Journal of Family Ministry*. She has authored, co-authored, or edited fifteen books, including Sacred *Stories of Ordinary Families; Family Ministry: A Comprehensive Guide; Church Social Work; Precious in His Sight: A Guide to Child Advocacy* and *Church Agencies: Serving Children and Families in Crisis*. In 1996, Dr. Garland received the Jack Otis Whistleblower Award from the National Association of Social Workers to honor her public stance against unethical practices of the administration of The Southern Baptist Theological Seminary.

David R. Hodge, is a Rene Sand doctoral fellow at Washington University in St. Louis and a retired member AFL-CIO. With an extensive multicultural practice background in the area of spirituality, Mr. Hodge has presented at national conferences, conducted in-service trainings, and is widely published. His scholarly work has appeared in Social Work, Social Work Research, the Journal of Martial and Family Therapy, Families in Society, and forthcoming chapters will appear in the Encyclopedia of Social Measurement and the 10th edition of Social Work: A Profession of Many Faces. To draw attention to his scholarly work in the area of spirituality, the National Association of Social Workers (NASW) and Washington University have issued national press releases featuring his work.

Crystal Holtrop, obtained her BSW from Dordt College and her MSW from the University of Iowa. Currently, she is a Clinical Supervisor and Marriage and Family Therapist at Catholic Charities, a community-based child welfare agency. As a clinical member of the American Association of Marriage and Family Therapy, Ms. Holtrop has 14 years of experience specializing in marriage and family therapy. She has conducted in-service trainings, facilitated workshops, and participated in the redesign of a two-county social service delivery system.

Douglas L. Koopman earned an AB in mathematics from Hope College (Michigan), a Masters of Theological Studies from Wesley Seminary (Washington, D.C.) and an MA and PhD in Politics from the Catholic University of America (Washington, D.C.). Presently he is Professor of Political Science and Interim Director of the Center for Social Research at Calvin College in Grand Rapids, Michigan. Previously, Professor Koopman was the Program Director of the Paul B. Henry Institute for the Study of Christianity and Politics at Calvin College from 1997 to 2002. His research interests are in Congress, American politics generally, and the intersection of religion and American politics. Prior to his academic career, he served on Capitol Hill in several committee, leadership, and personal office staff posts in the U.S. House of Representatives for fifteen years between 1980 and 1995.

Sarah S. Kreutziger earned a BA from Columbia College (South Carolina), a MSSW from the University of Tennessee, and a PhD from Tulane University. Presently, she is Associate Professor and Director of the Division of Extended and Lifelong Learning at Tulane School of Social Work. Previously she served as Director of Communications for the Louisiana Conference of the United Methodist Church and as a medical and psychiatric social worker in several health care organizations. Her research and practice interests are women's spirituality and religious beliefs; community planning; policy development; and social work administration. She was recognized as social worker of the year in Florida and has received several volunteer service awards. Currently, she serves on the Board of Directors of the Council on Social Work Education, the Board of Visitors of Duke University's School of Divinity and on the Foundation for Evangelism Board of the United Methodist Church.

Jill Mikula received a BSW from Calvin College. She is currently a Families First In-Home Therapist for Catholic Social Services in Grand Rapids, Michigan. Her professional experience includes direct practice in family preservation and crisis intervention. Other social work involvement includes instruction and practice with social work interviewing skills at Calvin College. Her professional interests include child welfare, adoption issues, international social work, and the integration of social work and the Christian faith.

Mary Anne Poe earned a BA from Vanderbilt University, a MDiv from The Southern Baptist Theological Seminary in Louisville, Kentucky, and a MSSW from the University of Louisville. Presently she is Associate Professor and Director of the Social Work Program at Union University in Jackson, Tennessee. She has served previously as a social worker on church staffs in Minnesota and Kentucky. Her research and practice interests are how to engage congregations in effective and culturally sensitive ministry in the community, what is the role of the church as an advocate for social and economic justice, and what are appropriate relationships among faith-based organizations, congregations, and other social service providers.

Jason Pittman earned a BA and MSW from Baylor University in Waco, Texas, as well as a MDiv from George W. Truett Seminary. He is presently the Coordinator of Urban Ministry in Detroit, Michigan, for the Cooperative Baptist Fellowship. He has social work experience in a variety of areas related to urban ministry and community development and was instrumental in establishing an alcohol and drug treatment center in Waco. Jason's practice and research interests include faith-based drug and alcohol treatment programs, urban Christian ministries, community development, and congregational social work. Baylor's School of Social Work recognized Jason as 2002 Social Work Graduate Student of the Year.

Lawrence E. Ressler received a BSW from Eastern Mennonite College, a MSW from Temple University, and a PhD from Case Western Reserve University. He is currently Academic Dean and Professor of Social Work at Roberts Wesleyan College, Rochester, New York. His social work practice experience has been in individual, family, and organizational counseling, and mediation. Professional areas of interest include conflict management, research, church/state relationship, and family counseling. He has held leadership roles in the National Association of Social Workers and in social work education at the state level, and as a National Delegate. He served as President of the North American Association of Christians in Social Work for seven years.

Amy L. Sherman earned her PhD at University of Virginia and is currently Senior Fellow at the Welfare Policy Center of the Hudson Institute, where she directs the Faith in Communities Initiative. She also serves as Urban Ministries Advisor at Trinity Presbyterian Church in Charlottesville, Virginia. She is the author of four books, most recently, *Reinvigorating Faith in Communities* [Hudson Institute, 2002], and nearly 70 published essays. Her work has appeared in a variety of religious and secular publications, including *The Public Interest*, *First Things*, *Books & Culture*, *The American Enterprise*, *Philanthropy*, *Christianity Today*, and *The Chronicle of Philanthropy*. She has written numerous "how-to" manuals for Christian ministry practitioners and is a frequent speaker at training conferences. In 1996, Dr. Sherman was named by *Christianity Today* as one of the "Top 50 Evangelical Leaders Under Forty."

David A. Sherwood received his BA from Lipscomb University (Nashville, Tennessee), a MSW from Bryn Mawr, and a PhD in Social Work from the University of Texas. He is currently Professor of Social Work at Baylor University. His professional interests include the integration of Christian faith and social work practice, ethics, spirituality and religion, practice with individuals and families, and social work in health care and with the elderly. He has written several articles on ethics and topics related to the integration of Christian faith and social work practice. Dr. Sherwood is a co-editor of *Spirituality and religion in social work practice: Decision cases with teaching notes.* He is a member of the Commission on Accreditation of the Council on Social Work Education and consults with social work programs in Christian colleges and universities. Dr. Sherwood has served on the Board and as President of the North American Association of Christians in Social Work and is Editor of the journal *Social Work & Christianity*.

Ronald J. Sider earned his BA from Waterloo Lutheran University, and his MA, BD and PhD from Yale University. He is Professor of Theology and Culture at Eastern University and the founding president of Evangelicals for Social Action. A widely known evangelical speaker and writer, Sider's publications include twenty-three books (including the influential *Rich Christians in an Age of Hunger*) and scores of articles. Sider is the publisher of *PRISM* and a contributing editor of *Christianity Today* and *Sojourners*. Recent books include *Just Generosity* (Baker, 1999) and *Churches That Make a Difference,* co-authored with Phil Olson and Heidi Rolland Unruh (Baker, 2002). He and Heidi Unruh are currently working on a book on faith-based social services to be published by Oxford University Press.

Hope Haslam Straughan earned a BA from Samford University (Alabama), a MSW and Certificate in Theology from The Southern Baptist

Theological Seminar (Kentucky), and a PhD in social work from Barry University (Florida). Presently she is the Coordinator of Field Education and Assistant Professor of Social Work at Wheelock College (Massachusetts). Previous social work experience has been as consultant to APERFOSA (Spain) around the establishment of an AIDS hospice, and collaboration with services to persons escaping prostitution, and to indigent persons with HIV/AIDS. Her research interests include graduate education for social workers around the issue of HIV/AIDS, spiritual development across the lifespan, and community and organizational collaboration. She is currently serving on the board of the North American Association of Christians in Social Work.

Scott W. Taylor holds a BS from Indiana State University and will receive a MSW from Baylor University, as well as a MDiv from George W. Truett Theological Seminary in May 2003. His work experience includes six months in India, establishing a program of Clinical Pastoral Education in a hospital setting. His professional and career interests are in international social work, with special emphases on global sustainable development, social justice, and environmental issues. He is currently a Graduate Assistant in the Baylor School of Social Work.

Heidi Rolland Unruh received a BA from Wheaton College, and a MA in Theology and Public Policy from Eastern Baptist Seminary. She is the Associate Director of the Congregations, Communities and Leadership Development Project at Eastern University, and a policy analyst with Evangelicals for Social Action. Her work includes analysis of church-state collaborations, research on faith-based social services†and evangelism, and the development of resources for congregational outreach. Publications include various articles, book chapters, and *Churches That Make a Difference: Reaching Your Community with Good News and Good Works*, co-authored with Ronald Sider and Phil Olson (Baker, 2002). She and Ronald Sider are currently working on a book on faith-based social services to be published by Oxford University Press.